SURVIVE! INSIDE THE HUMAN BODY

VOL. 2: THE CIRCULATORY SYSTEM

SURVIVE! INSIDE THE HUMAN BODY

VOL. 2: THE CIRCULATORY SYSTEM

GOMDORI CO. AND HYUN-DONG HAN

no starch press

SAN FRANCISCO

SURVIVE! INSIDE THE HUMAN BODY, VOL. 2: THE CIRCULATORY SYSTEM.
English translation copyright © 2013 by No Starch Press.

Survive! Inside the Human Body, Vol. 2: The Circulatory System is a translation of the Korean original, *Comic Survival Science Series 26 - Survival in the Human Body 2* (서바이벌 만화 과학상식 26 – 인체에서 살아남기 2), published by Mirae N Co., Ltd. of Seoul, South Korea, text copyright © 2010 by Gomdori co. and illustration copyright © 2009 by Hyun-dong Han. This English translation is arranged with Mirae N Co., Ltd. (I-seum).

Printed in China
First printing

17 16 15 14 13   1 2 3 4 5 6 7 8 9

ISBN-10: 1-59327-472-6
ISBN-13: 978-1-59327-472-6

Publisher: William Pollock
Author: Gomdori co.
Illustrator: Hyun-dong Han
Coloring: Jae-woong Lee
Technical Assistance: Byung-sup Lee (Assistant Professor at Seoul Asan Medical Center)
Images: Shutterstock, TIMESPACE, Wikimedia Commons, Yonhap News
Production Editor: Alison Law
Developmental Editor: Tyler Ortman
Technical Reviewers: Wei Cheng Chen and Dan-Vinh Nguyen
Compositors: Riley Hoffman and Lynn L'Heureux
Copyeditors: Katie Grim and Pam Schroeder
Proofreader: Kate Blackham
Indexer: BIM Indexing and Proofreading Services

For information on bulk sales, please contact No Starch Press, Inc. directly:

No Starch Press, Inc.
38 Ringold Street, San Francisco, CA 94103
phone: 415.863.9900; fax: 415.863.9950; info@nostarch.com; www.nostarch.com

Library of Congress Cataloging-in-Publication Data

Inside the human body / by Gomdori Co. and Hyun-dong Han.
       p. cm. -- (Survive!)
   ISBN 978-1-59327-471-9 (v. 1) -- ISBN 978-1-59327-472-6 (v. 2) -- ISBN 978-1-59327-473-3 (v. 3)
  1. Human physiology--Juvenile literature. 2. Human physiology--Comic books, strips, etc. 3. Graphic novels. I. Han, Hyun-dong, ill. II. Gomdori Co.
  QP37.I563 2013
  612--dc23
                               2013002904

Production Date: 5/24/2013
Plant & Location: Printed by Everbest Printing (Guangzhou, China), Co. Ltd
Job / Batch #: 110474.2

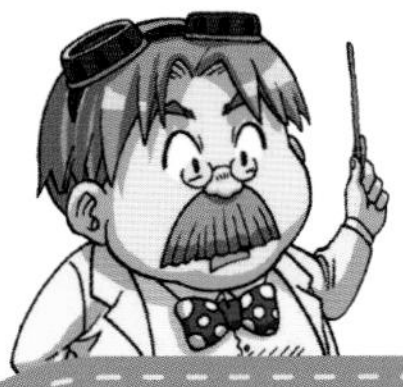

PREFACE

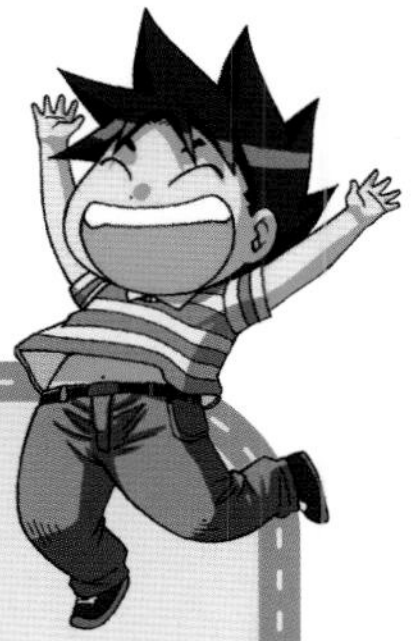

Every morning, we open our eyes and get out of bed to start the day. We eat breakfast, wash our faces, and pack our bags to go to school. But what's really happening inside our bodies all this time? It's quite easy to take our amazing bodies for granted.

Even when we are not conscious of it, our bodies are doing a *lot* of work. Each and every day, you blink 10,000 times and your heart beats *100,000 times*. And you never even think about it! Our bodies also digest food, fight germs and bacteria, and do all sorts of incredible things.

Aren't you curious about the body and all the work it does to keep you alive? Knowing more about your body can help keep you happy and healthy.

And the more you learn, the more you'll discover that our bodies have many wonderful surprises. I hope that Geo's exciting adventures inside the human body will show you just how complex our bodies are, how each part cooperates with the others, and what really gets our bodies moving.

Our adventure features Geo, a troublemaker with endless curiosity; the eccentric Dr. Brain, who claims to have invented the world's first human-piloted, artificial virus; his assistant, the high-strung Kay; and their friend, the kind-hearted Phoebe. What kind of adventure awaits them? Let's take a journey into the human body!

Hyun-dong Han

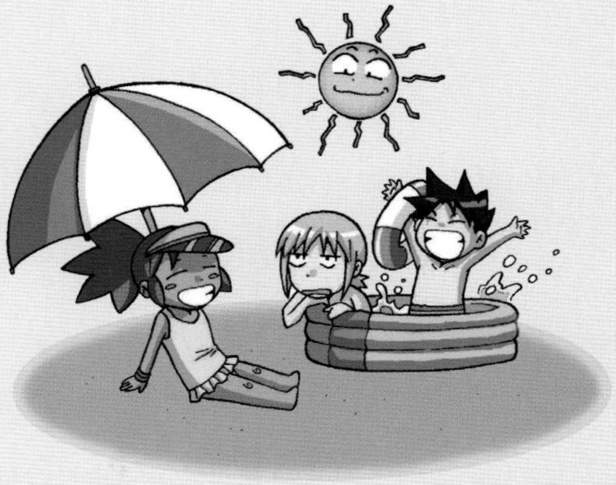

CONTENTS

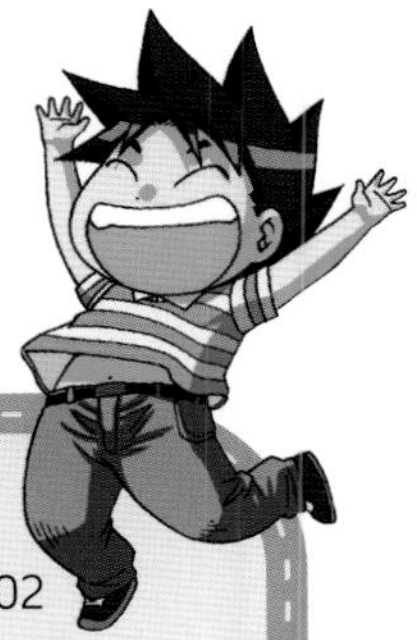

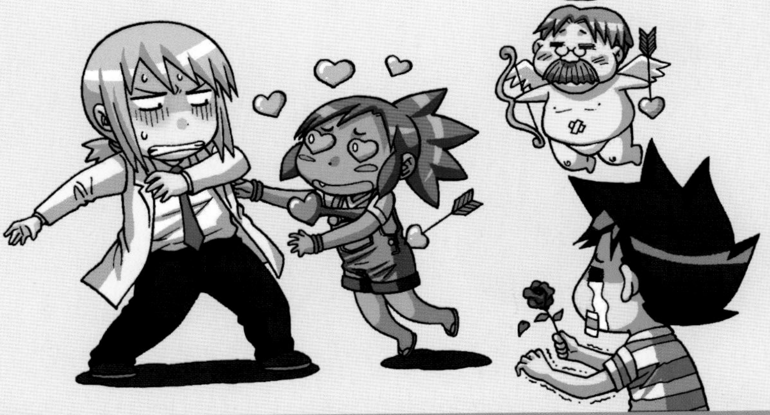

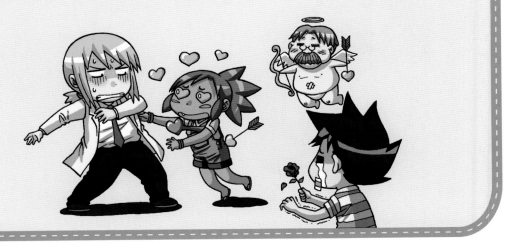

MEET THE CAST!

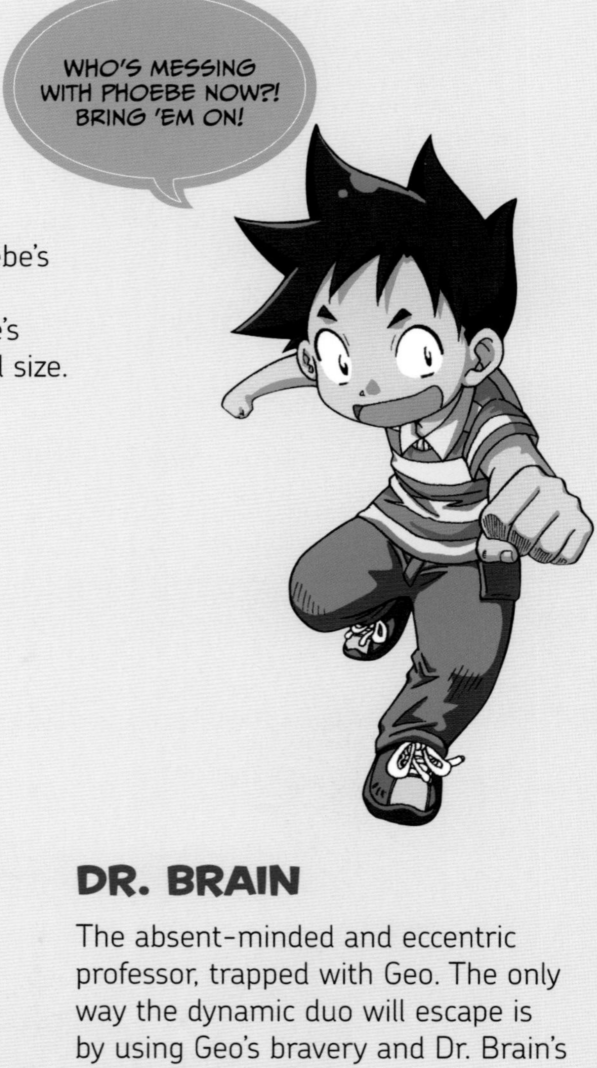
WHO'S MESSING WITH PHOEBE NOW?! BRING 'EM ON!

GEO

Our hero trapped inside Phoebe's body. This might be his most exciting adventure yet, but he's anxious to get back to normal size.

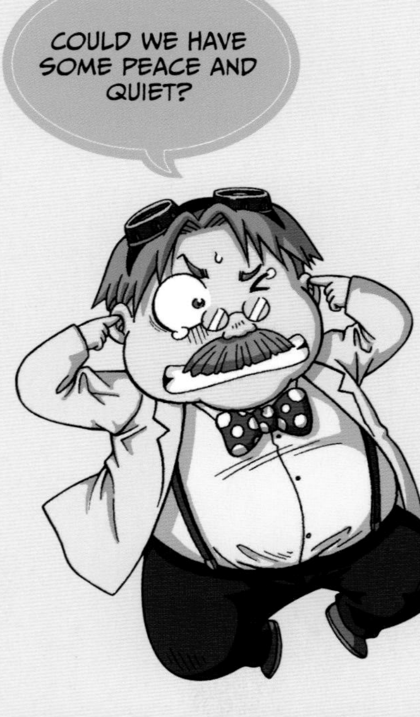
COULD WE HAVE SOME PEACE AND QUIET?

DR. BRAIN

The absent-minded and eccentric professor, trapped with Geo. The only way the dynamic duo will escape is by using Geo's bravery and Dr. Brain's medical know-how.

KAY

The high-strung medical student. He'll go to any lengths to rescue the missing SS *Hippocrates*, but he's also got his hands full entertaining Phoebe.

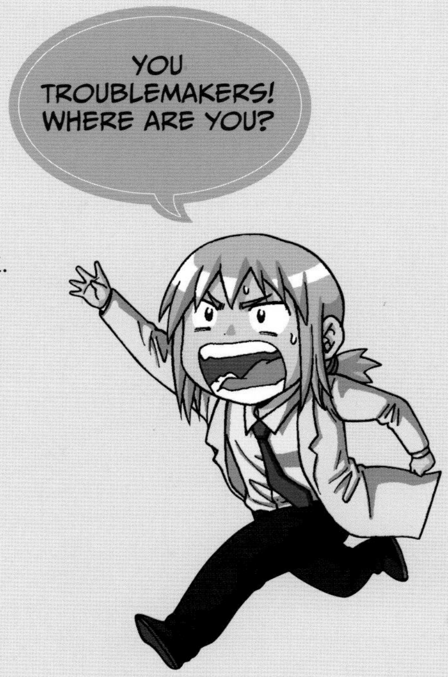
YOU TROUBLEMAKERS! WHERE ARE YOU?

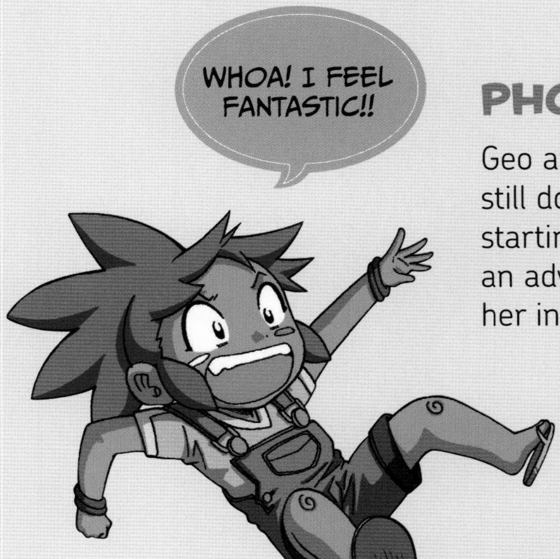
WHOA! I FEEL FANTASTIC!!

PHOEBE

Geo and Kay's energetic friend. Phoebe still doesn't know where Geo is, and she's starting to get restless. She's come to have an adventure, and she won't let Kay trap her in some boring research lab all day.

WHERE IN THE WORLD IS GEO?

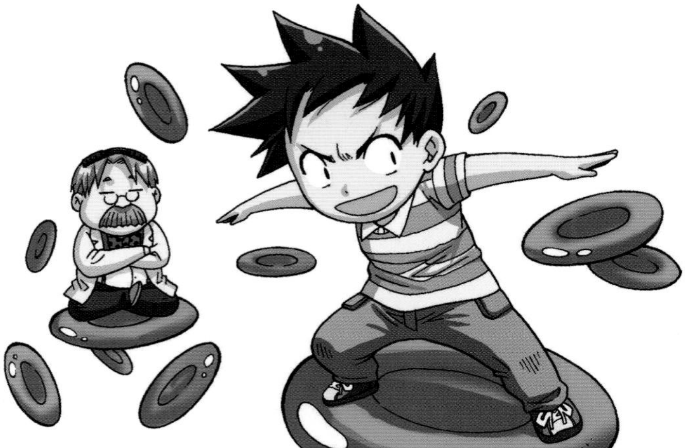

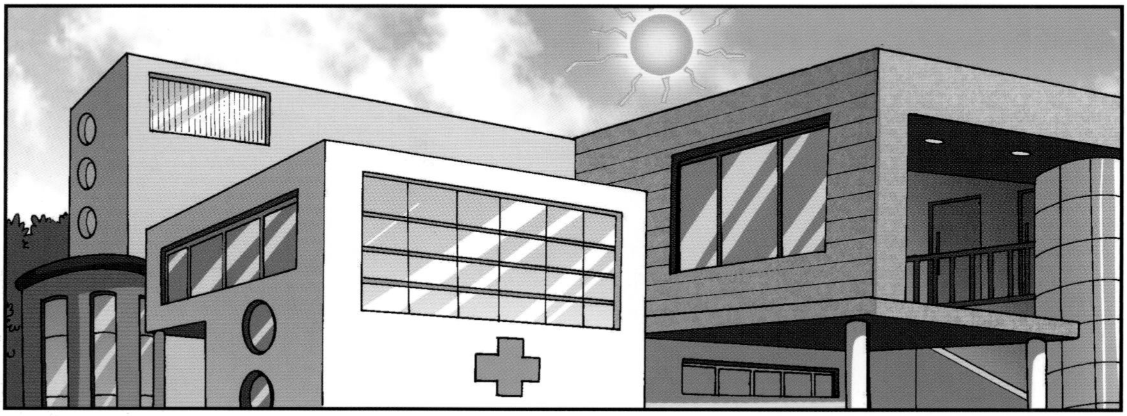

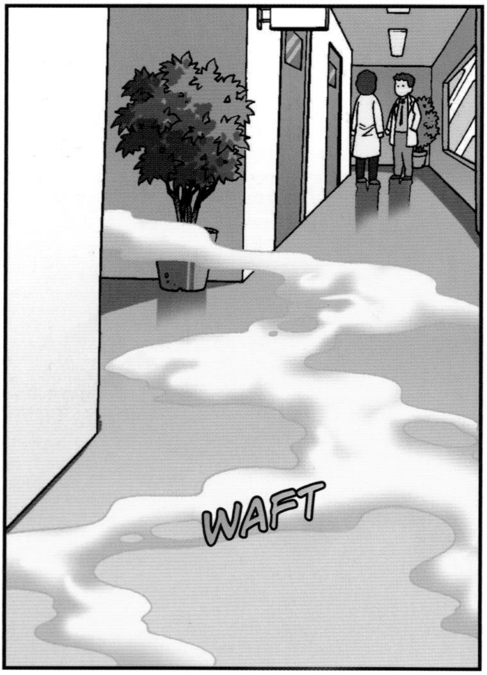
WAFT

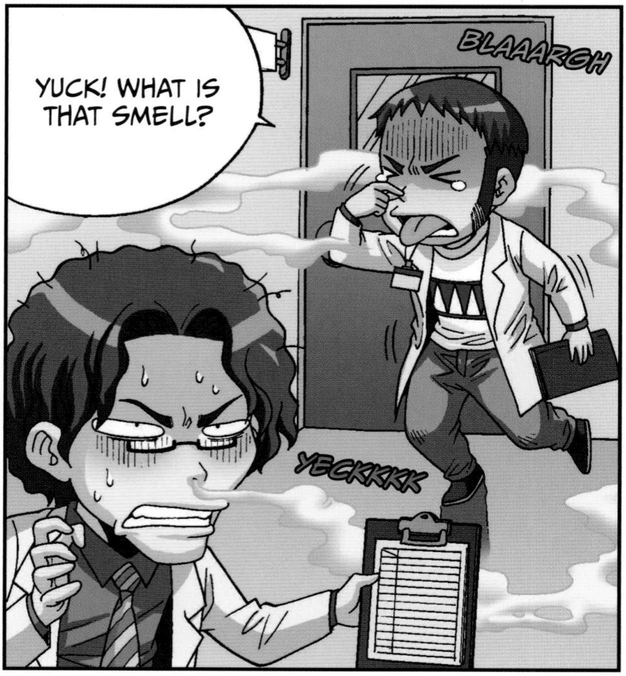
BLAAARGH
YUCK! WHAT IS THAT SMELL?
YECKKKK

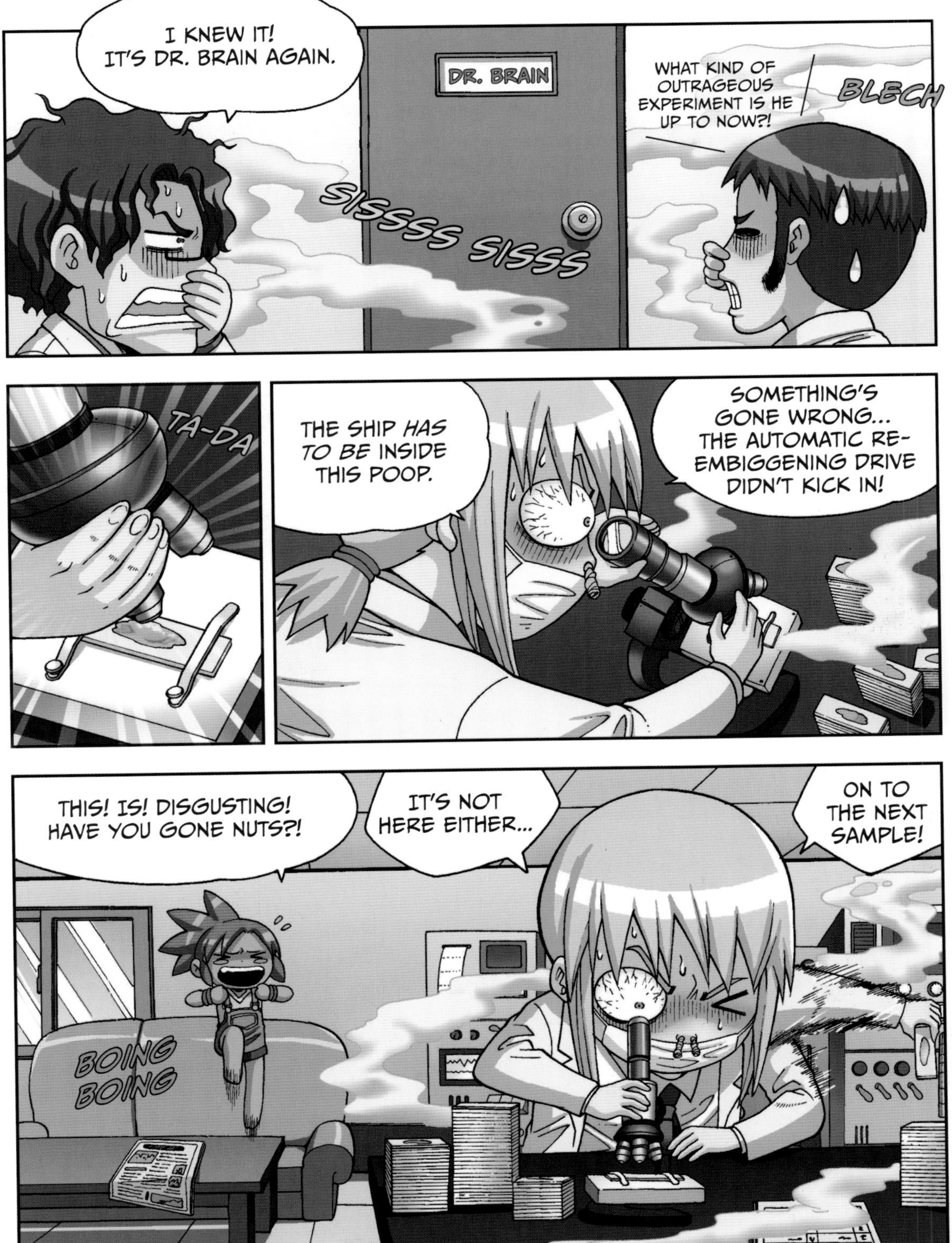
I KNEW IT! IT'S DR. BRAIN AGAIN.
DR. BRAIN
SISSSS SISSS
WHAT KIND OF OUTRAGEOUS EXPERIMENT IS HE UP TO NOW?!
BLECH
TA-DA
THE SHIP *HAS TO BE* INSIDE THIS POOP.
SOMETHING'S GONE WRONG... THE AUTOMATIC RE-EMBIGGENING DRIVE DIDN'T KICK IN!
THIS! IS! DISGUSTING! HAVE YOU GONE NUTS?!
IT'S NOT HERE EITHER...
ON TO THE NEXT SAMPLE!
BOING BOING

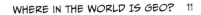

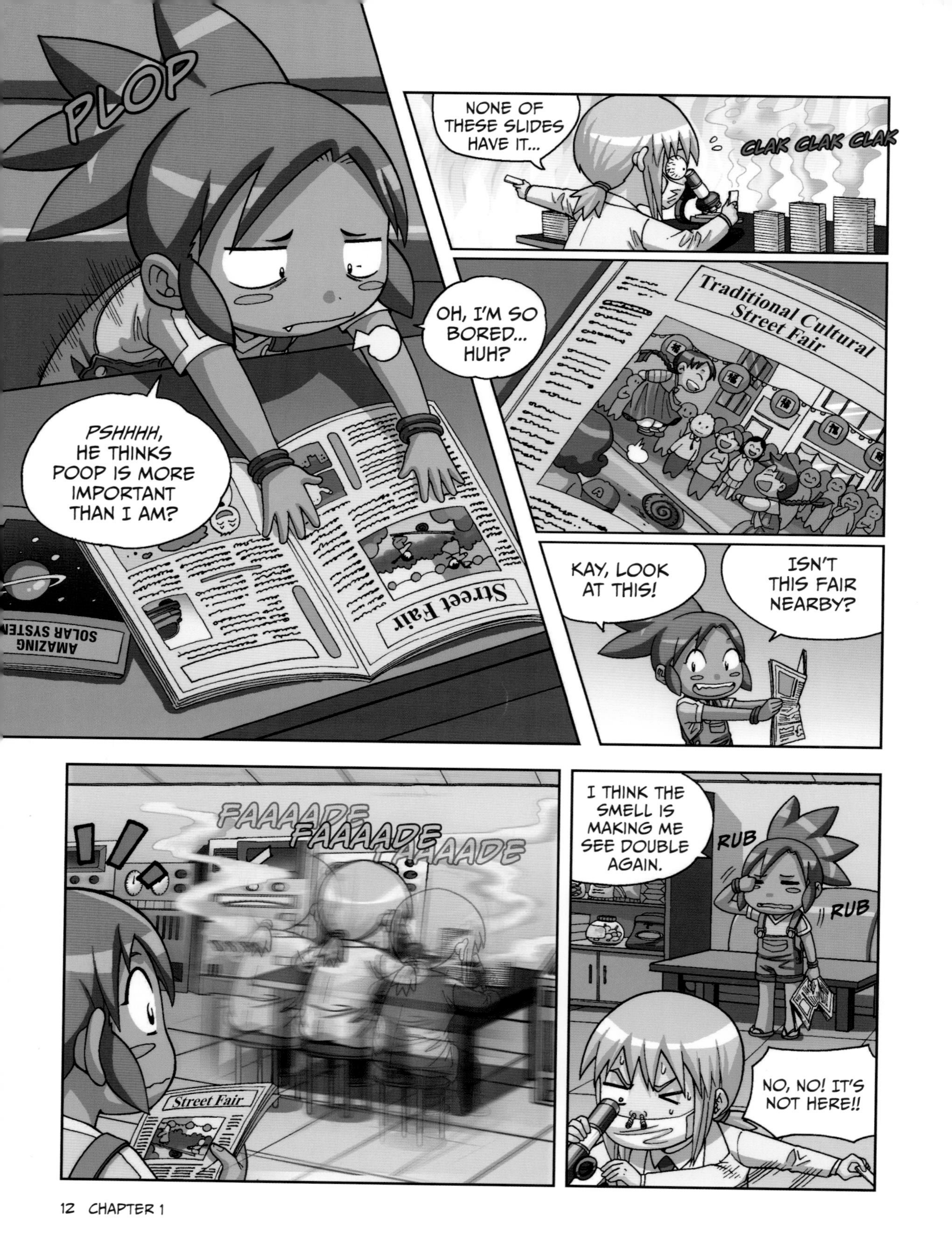
PLOP
NONE OF THESE SLIDES HAVE IT...
CLAK CLAK CLAK
OH, I'M SO BORED... HUH?
PSHHHH, HE THINKS POOP IS MORE IMPORTANT THAN I AM?
Street Fair
AMAZING SOLAR SYSTEM
Traditional Cultural Street Fair
KAY, LOOK AT THIS!
ISN'T THIS FAIR NEARBY?
FAAAADE FAAAADE FAAAADE
Street Fair
I THINK THE SMELL IS MAKING ME SEE DOUBLE AGAIN.
RUB
RUB
NO, NO! IT'S NOT HERE!!

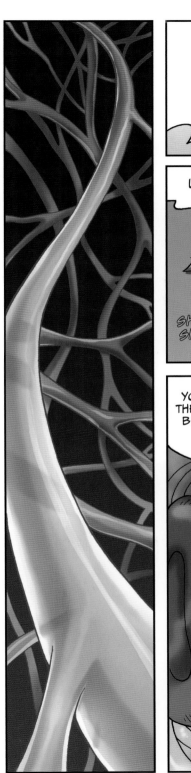

DR. BRAIN! WAKE UP! PLEASE WAKE UP!

WE'RE IN A REALLY WEIRD PLACE! PLEASE GET UP!

UGH...

SHAKE SHAKE

YOU SAID WE'D GO INSIDE THE BLOOD VESSELS AFTER BEING ABSORBED BY THE LARGE INTESTINE!

WAHHHH.

SOMETHING IS REALLY WRONG.

OH, PLEASE BE QUIET. WE WERE ABSORBED BY THE LARGE INTESTINE WITH THE WATER, SO...

MY GUESS IS WE'RE IN THE CAPILLARIES.

I KNOW! BUT BLOOD IS SUPPOSED TO BE RED!

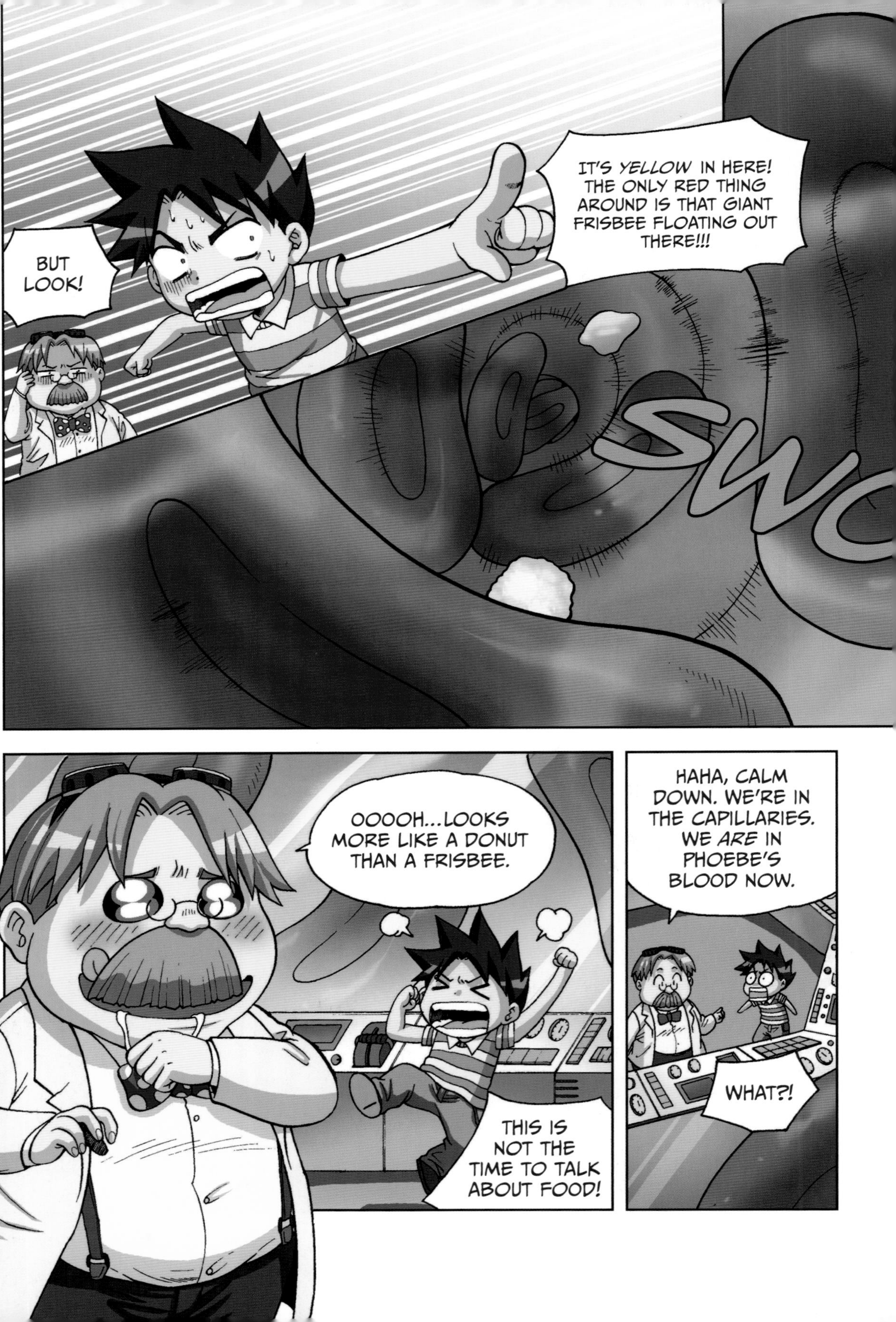
BUT LOOK!
IT'S *YELLOW* IN HERE! THE ONLY RED THING AROUND IS THAT GIANT FRISBEE FLOATING OUT THERE!!!
SWO
OOOOH...LOOKS MORE LIKE A DONUT THAN A FRISBEE.
THIS IS NOT THE TIME TO TALK ABOUT FOOD!
HAHA, CALM DOWN. WE'RE IN THE CAPILLARIES. WE *ARE* IN PHOEBE'S BLOOD NOW.
WHAT?!

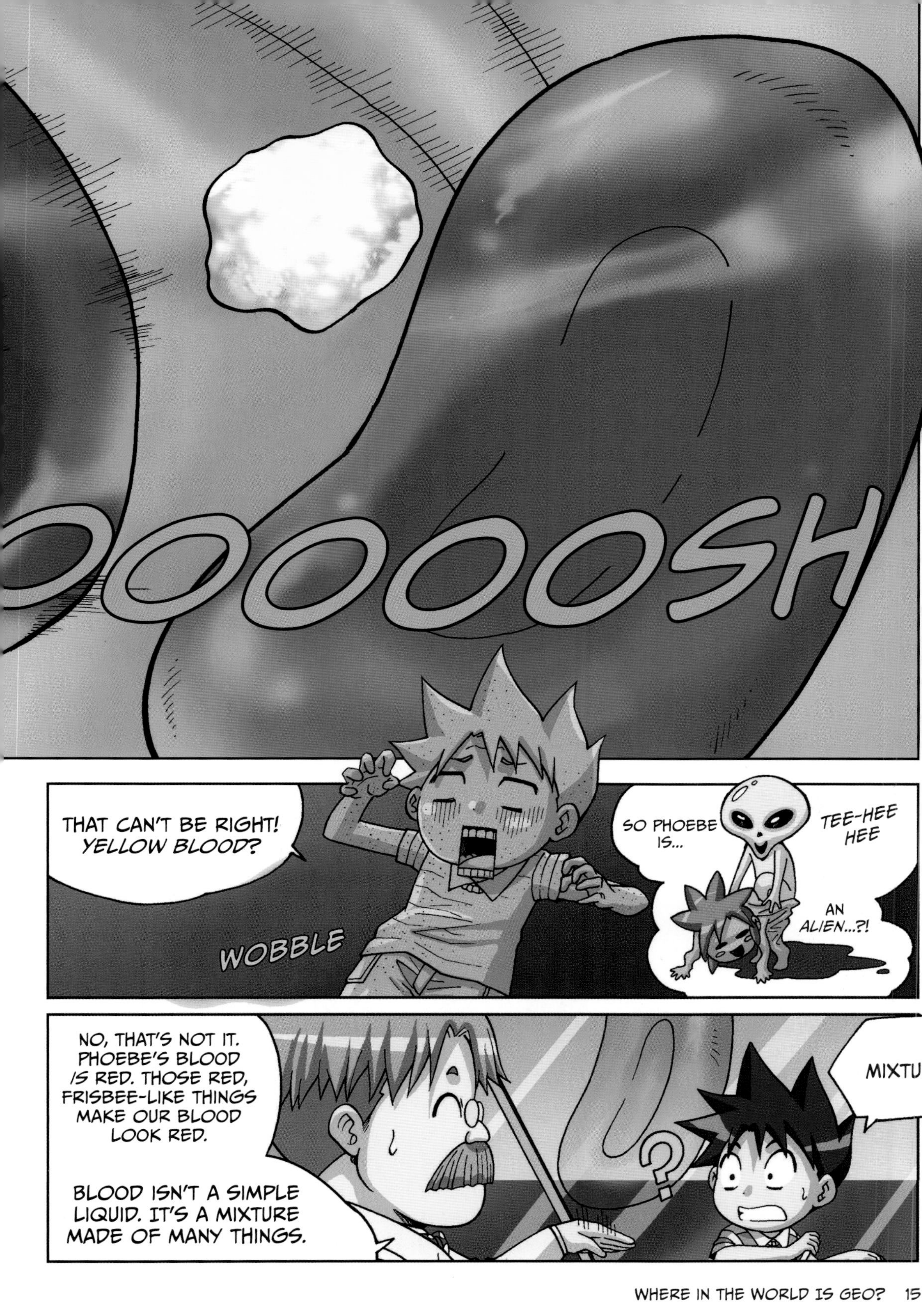
WHOOOOOOSH
THAT CAN'T BE RIGHT! *YELLOW BLOOD?*
WOBBLE
SO PHOEBE IS...
TEE-HEE HEE
AN ALIEN...?!
NO, THAT'S NOT IT. PHOEBE'S BLOOD *IS* RED. THOSE RED, FRISBEE-LIKE THINGS MAKE OUR BLOOD LOOK RED.
BLOOD ISN'T A SIMPLE LIQUID. IT'S A MIXTURE MADE OF MANY THINGS.
MIXTURE?

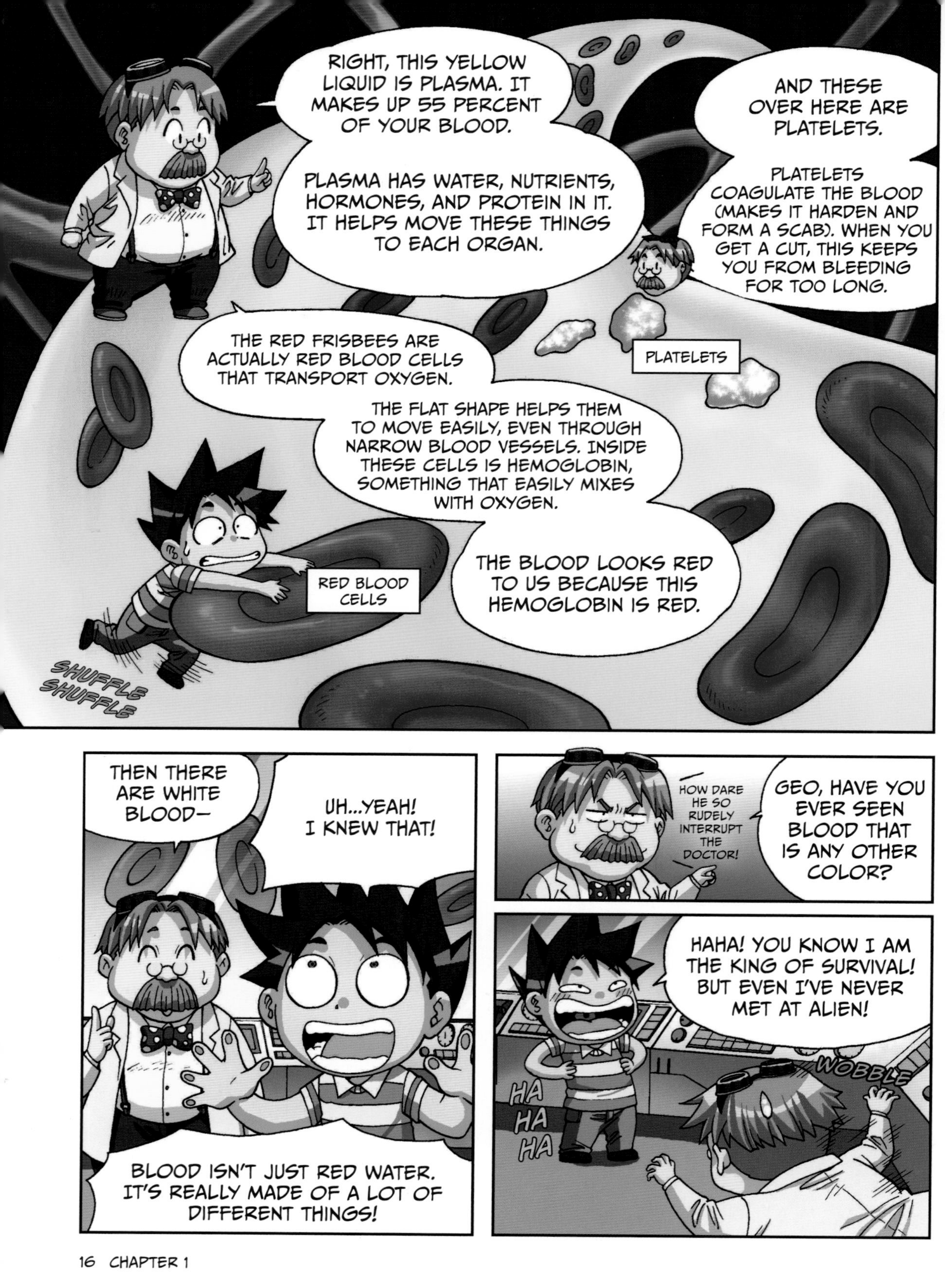

RIGHT, THIS YELLOW LIQUID IS PLASMA. IT MAKES UP 55 PERCENT OF YOUR BLOOD.
PLASMA HAS WATER, NUTRIENTS, HORMONES, AND PROTEIN IN IT. IT HELPS MOVE THESE THINGS TO EACH ORGAN.
AND THESE OVER HERE ARE PLATELETS.
PLATELETS COAGULATE THE BLOOD (MAKES IT HARDEN AND FORM A SCAB). WHEN YOU GET A CUT, THIS KEEPS YOU FROM BLEEDING FOR TOO LONG.
THE RED FRISBEES ARE ACTUALLY RED BLOOD CELLS THAT TRANSPORT OXYGEN.
PLATELETS
THE FLAT SHAPE HELPS THEM TO MOVE EASILY, EVEN THROUGH NARROW BLOOD VESSELS. INSIDE THESE CELLS IS HEMOGLOBIN, SOMETHING THAT EASILY MIXES WITH OXYGEN.
THE BLOOD LOOKS RED TO US BECAUSE THIS HEMOGLOBIN IS RED.
RED BLOOD CELLS
SHUFFLE SHUFFLE
THEN THERE ARE WHITE BLOOD—
UH...YEAH! I KNEW THAT!
BLOOD ISN'T JUST RED WATER. IT'S REALLY MADE OF A LOT OF DIFFERENT THINGS!
HOW DARE HE SO RUDELY INTERRUPT THE DOCTOR!
GEO, HAVE YOU EVER SEEN BLOOD THAT IS ANY OTHER COLOR?
HAHA! YOU KNOW I AM THE KING OF SURVIVAL! BUT EVEN I'VE NEVER MET AT ALIEN!
HA HA HA
WOBBLE

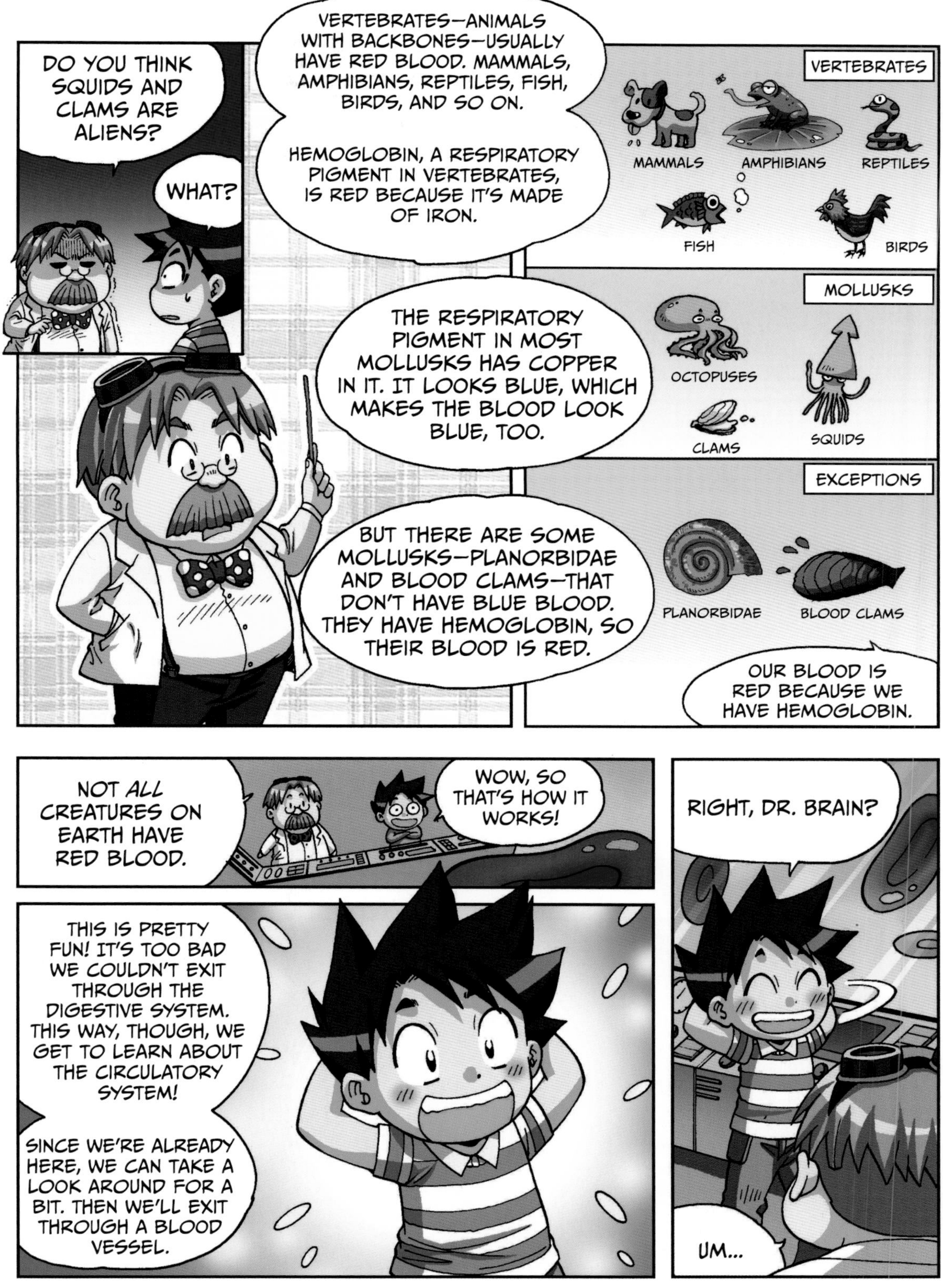
DO YOU THINK SQUIDS AND CLAMS ARE ALIENS?
WHAT?
VERTEBRATES—ANIMALS WITH BACKBONES—USUALLY HAVE RED BLOOD. MAMMALS, AMPHIBIANS, REPTILES, FISH, BIRDS, AND SO ON.
HEMOGLOBIN, A RESPIRATORY PIGMENT IN VERTEBRATES, IS RED BECAUSE IT'S MADE OF IRON.
VERTEBRATES
MAMMALS
AMPHIBIANS
REPTILES
FISH
BIRDS
THE RESPIRATORY PIGMENT IN MOST MOLLUSKS HAS COPPER IN IT. IT LOOKS BLUE, WHICH MAKES THE BLOOD LOOK BLUE, TOO.
MOLLUSKS
OCTOPUSES
CLAMS
SQUIDS
BUT THERE ARE SOME MOLLUSKS—PLANORBIDAE AND BLOOD CLAMS—THAT DON'T HAVE BLUE BLOOD. THEY HAVE HEMOGLOBIN, SO THEIR BLOOD IS RED.
EXCEPTIONS
PLANORBIDAE
BLOOD CLAMS
OUR BLOOD IS RED BECAUSE WE HAVE HEMOGLOBIN.
NOT ALL CREATURES ON EARTH HAVE RED BLOOD.
WOW, SO THAT'S HOW IT WORKS!
RIGHT, DR. BRAIN?
THIS IS PRETTY FUN! IT'S TOO BAD WE COULDN'T EXIT THROUGH THE DIGESTIVE SYSTEM. THIS WAY, THOUGH, WE GET TO LEARN ABOUT THE CIRCULATORY SYSTEM!
SINCE WE'RE ALREADY HERE, WE CAN TAKE A LOOK AROUND FOR A BIT. THEN WE'LL EXIT THROUGH A BLOOD VESSEL.
UM...

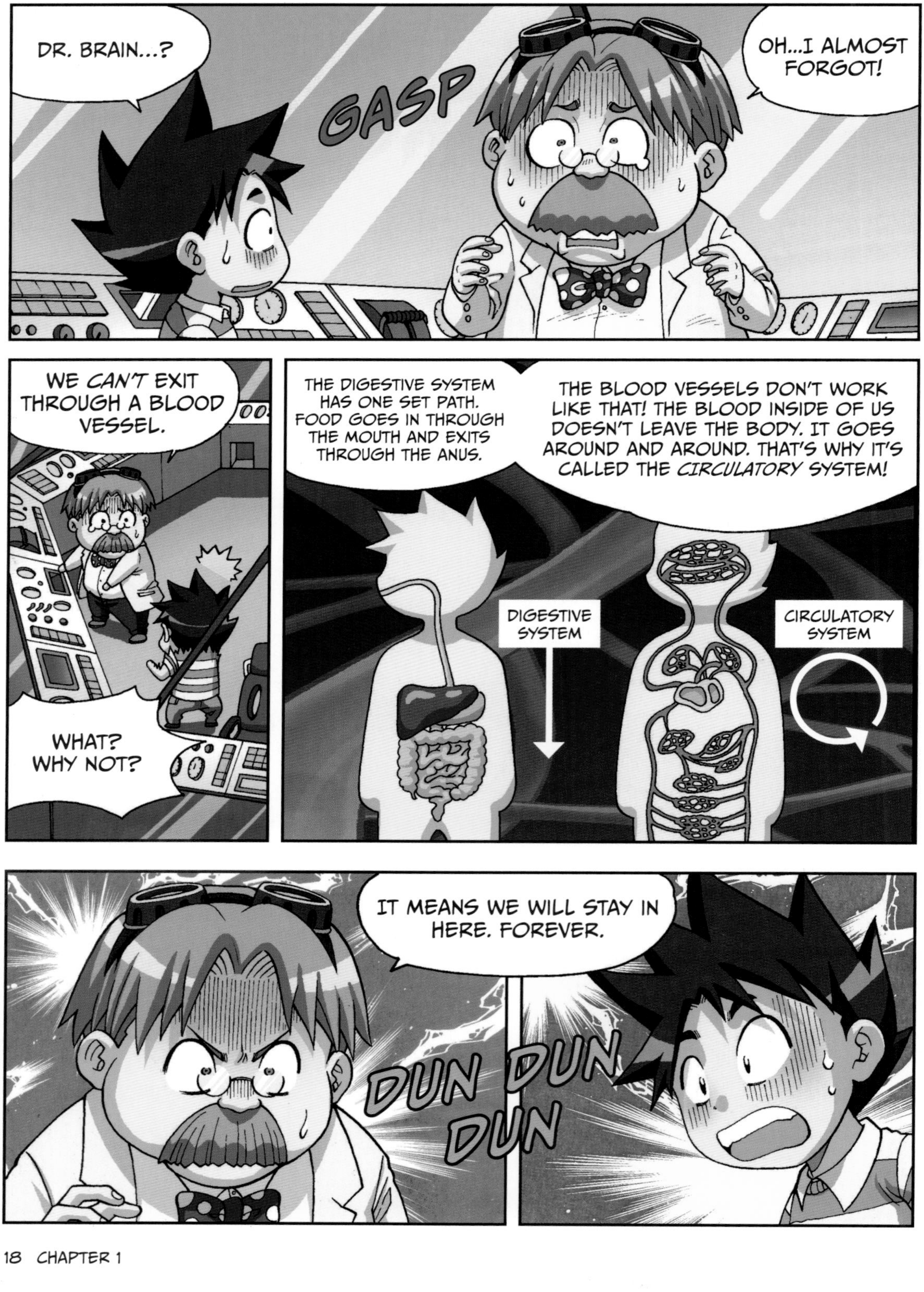
DR. BRAIN...?
GASP
OH...I ALMOST FORGOT!
WE CAN'T EXIT THROUGH A BLOOD VESSEL.
WHAT? WHY NOT?
THE DIGESTIVE SYSTEM HAS ONE SET PATH. FOOD GOES IN THROUGH THE MOUTH AND EXITS THROUGH THE ANUS.
THE BLOOD VESSELS DON'T WORK LIKE THAT! THE BLOOD INSIDE OF US DOESN'T LEAVE THE BODY. IT GOES AROUND AND AROUND. THAT'S WHY IT'S CALLED THE CIRCULATORY SYSTEM!
DIGESTIVE SYSTEM
CIRCULATORY SYSTEM
IT MEANS WE WILL STAY IN HERE. FOREVER.
DUN DUN DUN

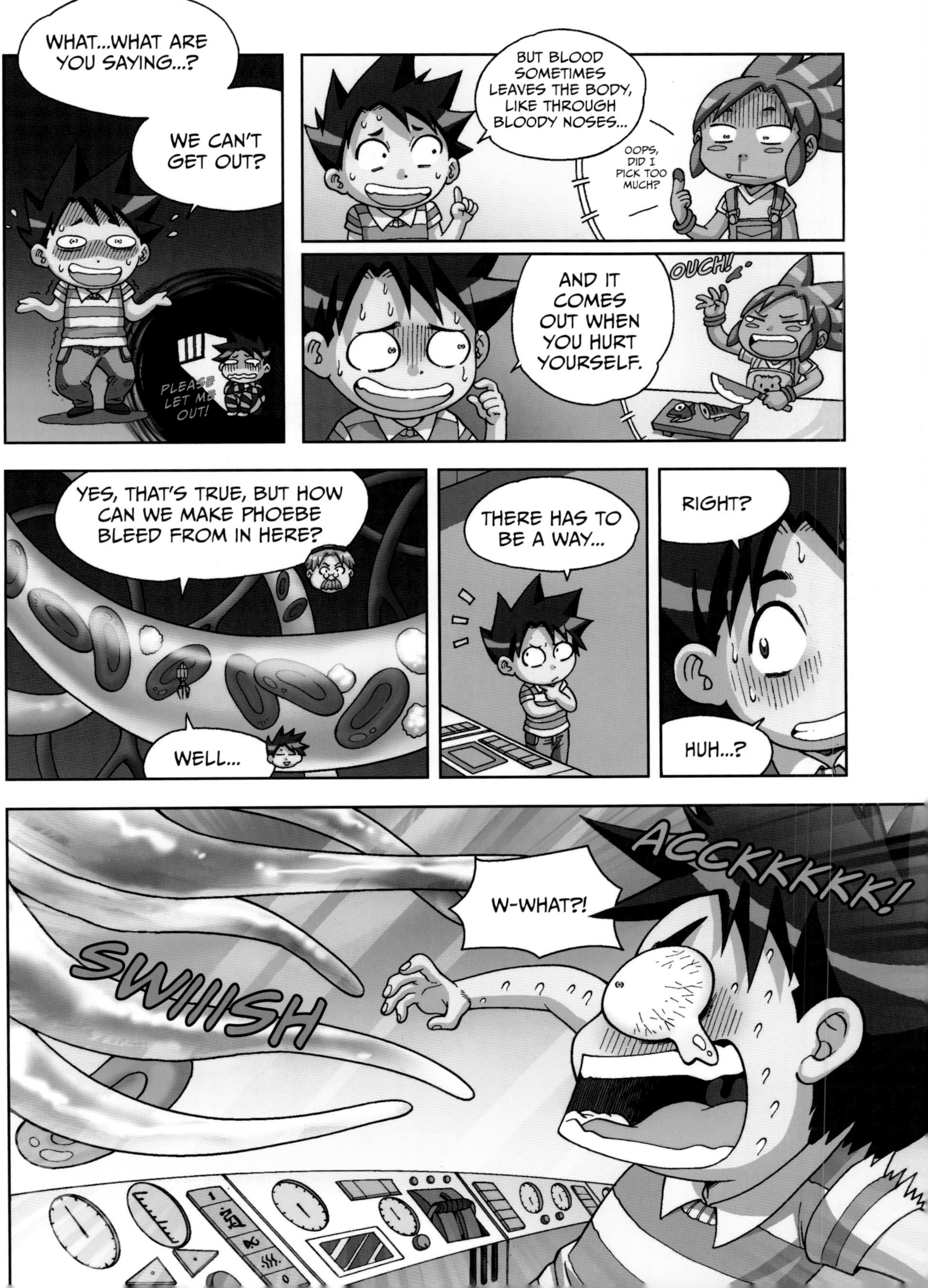

WHAT...WHAT ARE YOU SAYING...?
WE CAN'T GET OUT?
PLEASE LET ME OUT!
BUT BLOOD SOMETIMES LEAVES THE BODY, LIKE THROUGH BLOODY NOSES...
OOPS, DID I PICK TOO MUCH?
AND IT COMES OUT WHEN YOU HURT YOURSELF.
OUCH!
YES, THAT'S TRUE, BUT HOW CAN WE MAKE PHOEBE BLEED FROM IN HERE?
WELL...
THERE HAS TO BE A WAY...
RIGHT?
HUH...?
ACCKKKKK!
W-WHAT?!
SWIIISH

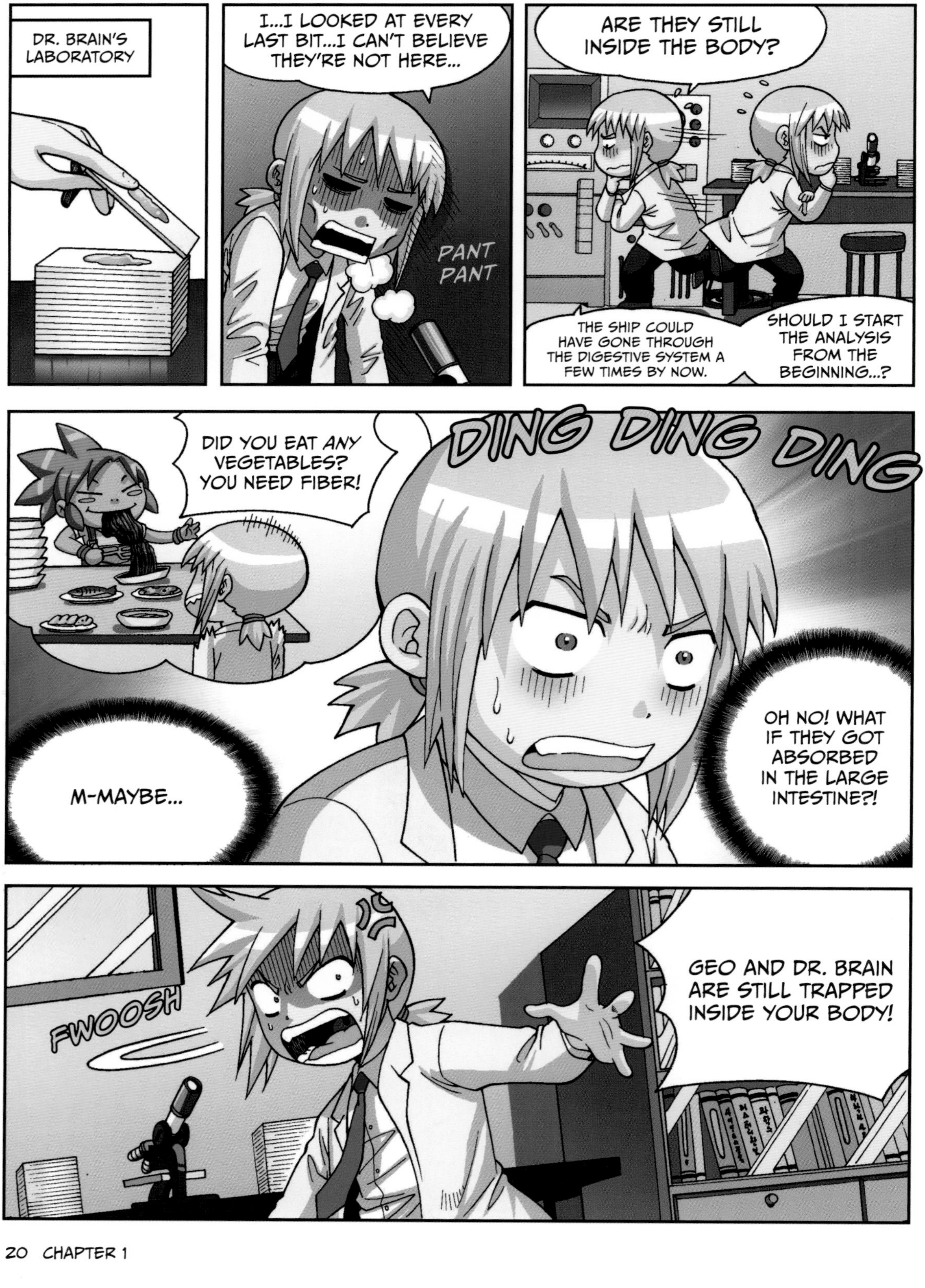
DR. BRAIN'S LABORATORY
I...I LOOKED AT EVERY LAST BIT...I CAN'T BELIEVE THEY'RE NOT HERE...
PANT PANT
ARE THEY STILL INSIDE THE BODY?
THE SHIP COULD HAVE GONE THROUGH THE DIGESTIVE SYSTEM A FEW TIMES BY NOW.
SHOULD I START THE ANALYSIS FROM THE BEGINNING...?
DID YOU EAT ANY VEGETABLES? YOU NEED FIBER!
DING DING DING
M-MAYBE...
OH NO! WHAT IF THEY GOT ABSORBED IN THE LARGE INTESTINE?!
FWOOSH
GEO AND DR. BRAIN ARE STILL TRAPPED INSIDE YOUR BODY!

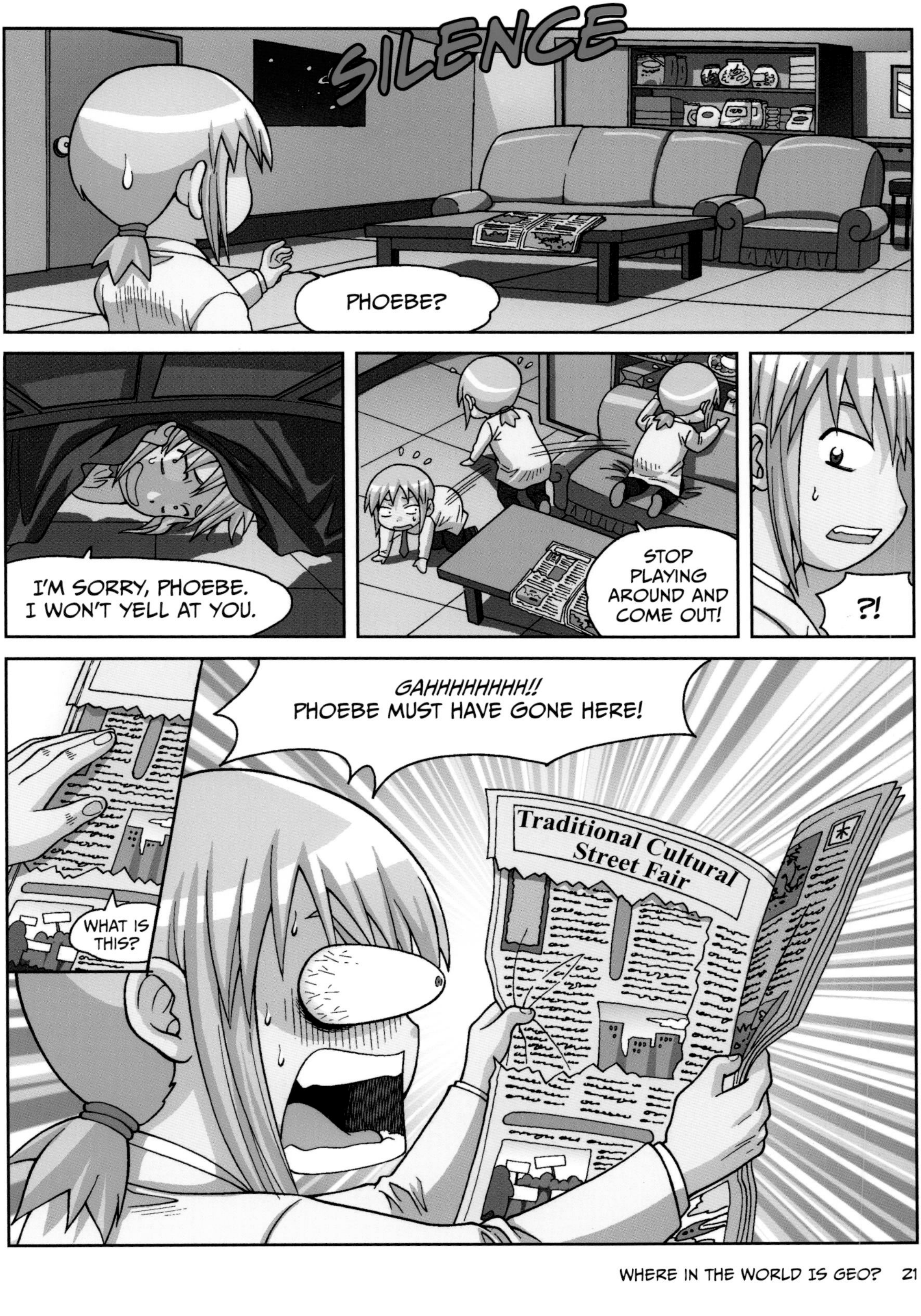
SILENCE
PHOEBE?
I'M SORRY, PHOEBE.
I WON'T YELL AT YOU.
STOP PLAYING AROUND AND COME OUT!
?!
WHAT IS THIS?
GAHHHHHHHH!!
PHOEBE MUST HAVE GONE HERE!
Traditional Cultural Street Fair

ARTERIES, CAPILLARIES, AND VEINS

Blood doesn't stay in one place. The heart constantly pumps blood throughout the entire body. Blood goes through arteries, capillaries, and veins before coming back to the heart. The tubes that make up this route are called *blood vessels*. If you connected all the blood vessels in your body, they would be more than 60,000 miles long. That's like walking across the United States 20 times!

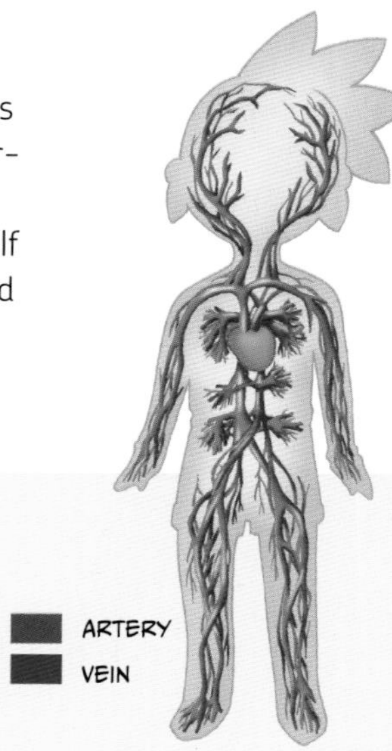

TYPES OF BLOOD VESSELS

ARTERY
These tubes send the oxygen-rich blood from the heart to every organ of the body. Arteries are thick enough to withstand the strong pressure from the heart. They also have a layer of stretchy muscle. Blood that flows through the arteries has a lot of oxygen and nutrients.

ARTERY
VEIN

BLOOD VESSELS OF THE BODY

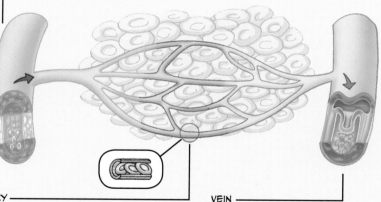

CAPILLARY
Capillaries are tiny blood vessels spread out like a net. They help blood from the arteries to reach every part of the body. Oxygen, carbon dioxide, nutrients, and waste travel through the capillaries' thin walls, which are only a single layer of cells thick.

VEIN
These tubes return blood to the heart after it exits the capillaries. They carry blood with carbon dioxide and waste. Far away from the heart, blood flow is weak, so many veins have valves to keep the blood moving toward the heart, not backward.

WHAT'S THE DEAL WITH BLOOD?

Blood makes up about 8 percent of our body weight. It is made of 55 percent plasma and 45 percent blood cells. Plasma is a yellow liquid, a mixture of water, nutrients, and hormones. Blood has red and white blood cells floating in the plasma. Blood does a bunch of important jobs in the body.

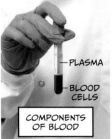

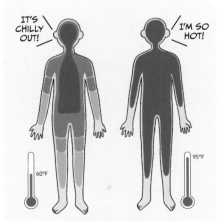

© TIMESPACE

—PLASMA

—BLOOD CELLS

COMPONENTS OF BLOOD

When doctors separate blood using a centrifuge (a fast-spinning machine), we can see the difference between plasma and blood cells.

TRANSPORTING THE ESSENTIALS

Blood moves materials that are essential to survival—like oxygen, proteins, and vitamins—throughout the entire body. Blood also takes carbon dioxide from the cells and brings it to the lungs, so we can breathe it out. Other wastes are taken to the liver to be broken down. Or they are sent to the kidneys and exit the body in urine.

DEFENDERS OF THE BODY

When invaders like bacteria or viruses enter the blood, white blood cells work to destroy them.

White blood cells kill bacteria using a process called *phagocytosis*. The invaders are swallowed and "eaten" by white blood cells! White blood cells also make antibodies when bacteria invade for the first time. Antibodies help to prevent the body from getting the same sickness again.

KEEPING BODY TEMPERATURE STEADY

Organs in our bodies create heat when they do their jobs. Blood circulates throughout our bodies to move this heat around so that one area doesn't get too hot or too cold. Our blood can warm or cool the overall temperature of our bodies depending on what's happening outside. When the air temperature goes up, our blood flows near the skin and releases our bodies' heat to the air. When the temperature goes down, blood gathers inside the body to keep us warm.

IT'S CHILLY OUT!

I'M SO HOT!

60°F

95°F

BLOOD DISTRIBUTION ACCORDING TO TEMPERATURE

ATTACK OF THE WHITE BLOOD CELLS

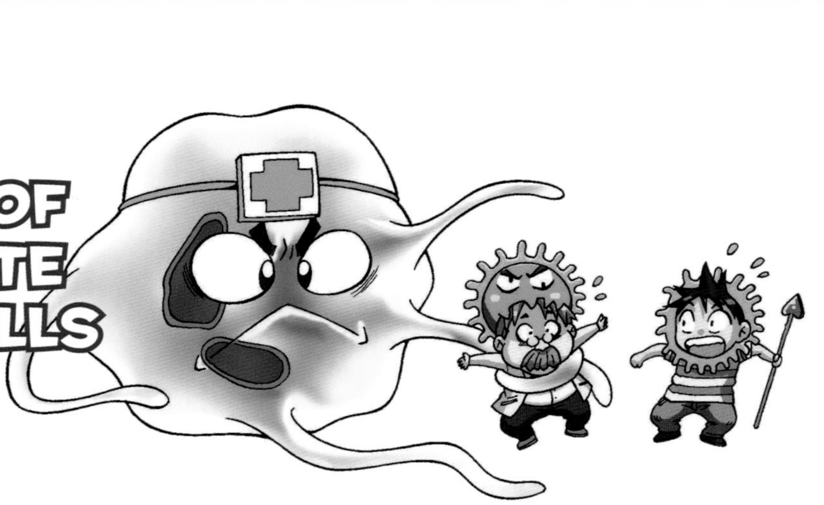

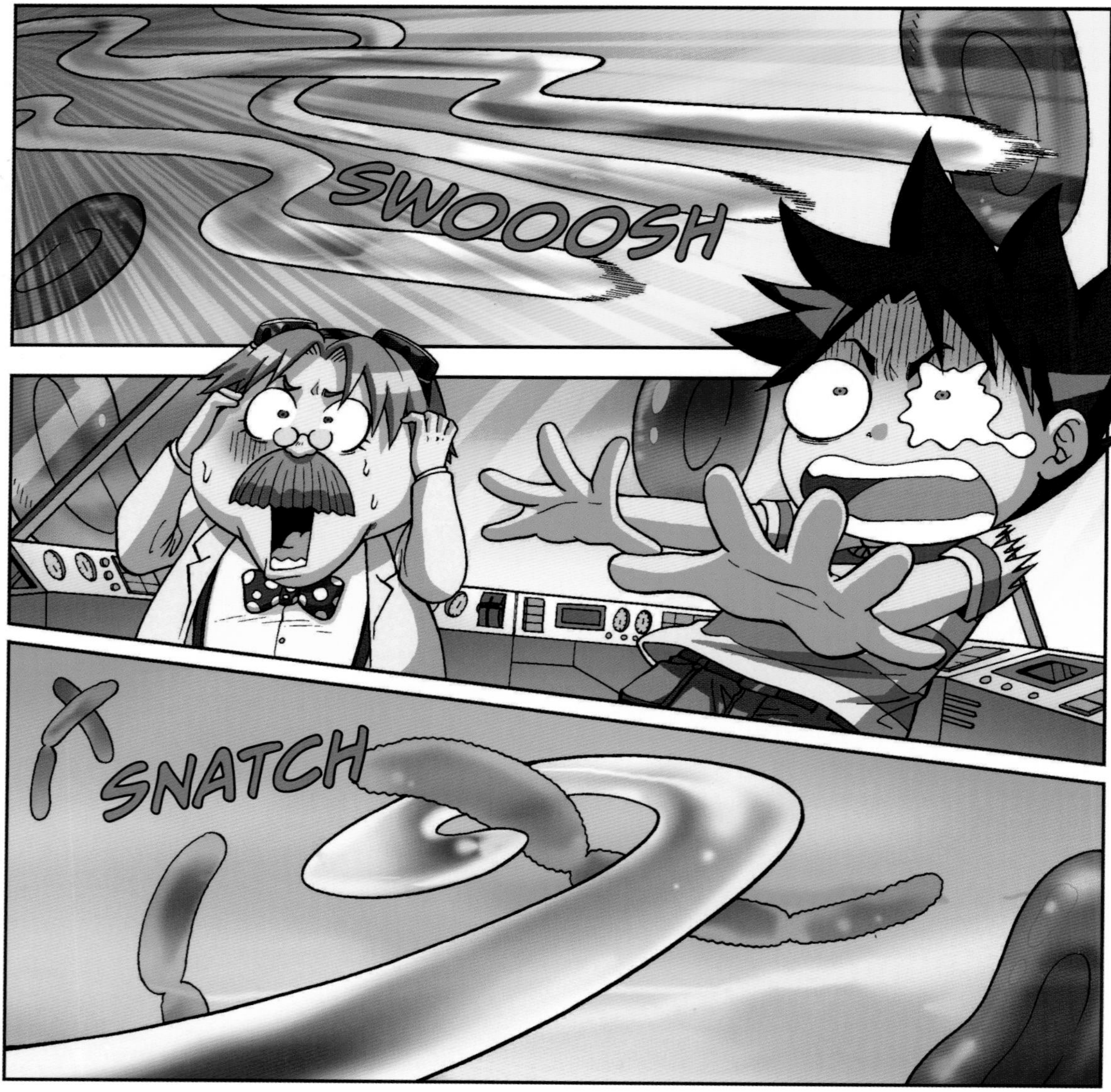
SWOOOSH
SNATCH

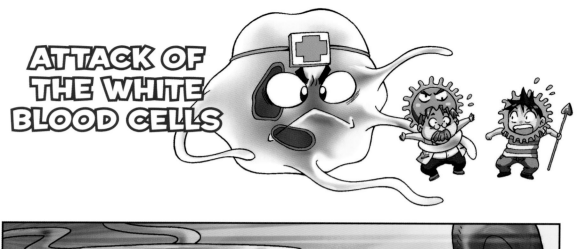

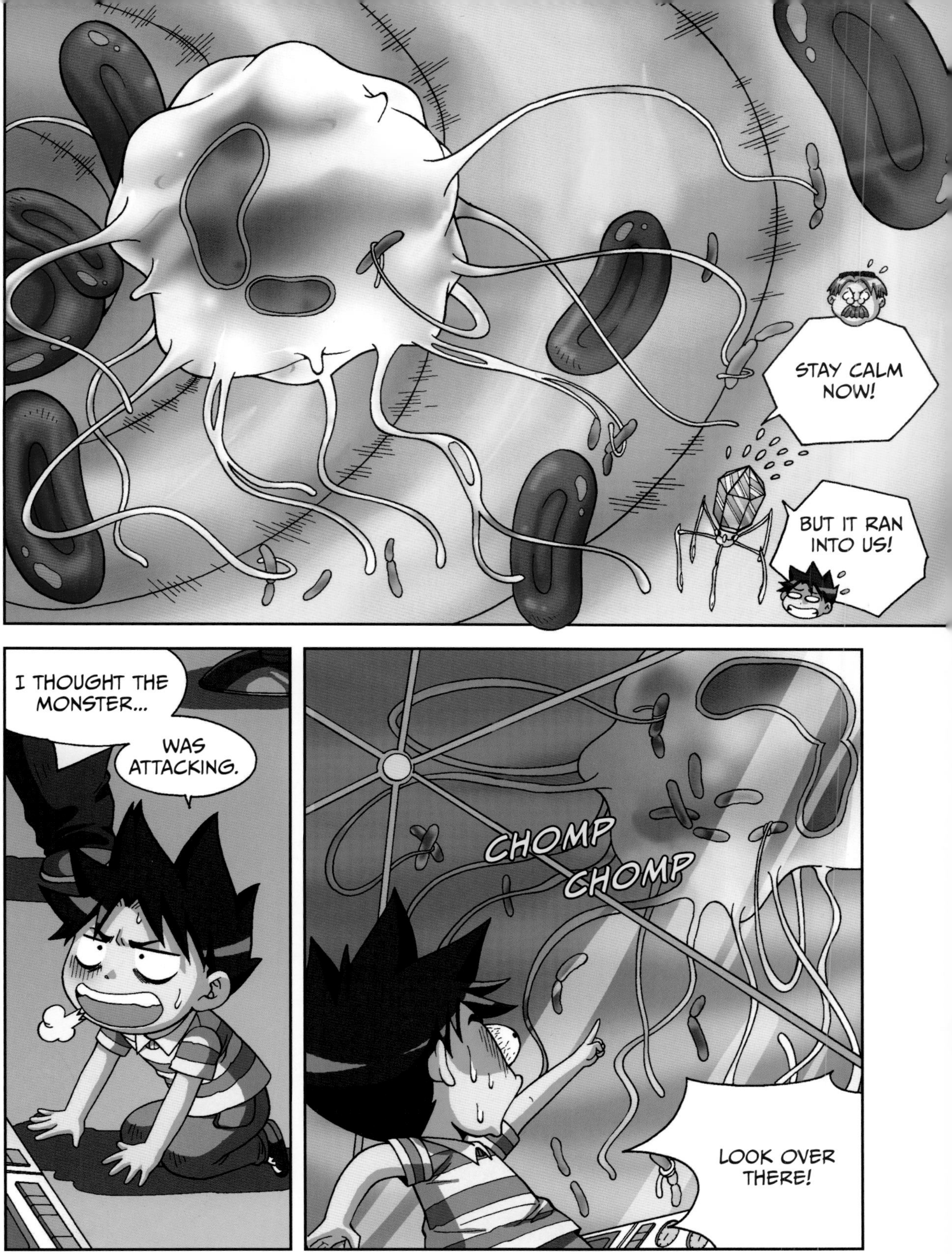
STAY CALM NOW!
BUT IT RAN INTO US!
I THOUGHT THE MONSTER...
WAS ATTACKING.
CHOMP
CHOMP
LOOK OVER THERE!

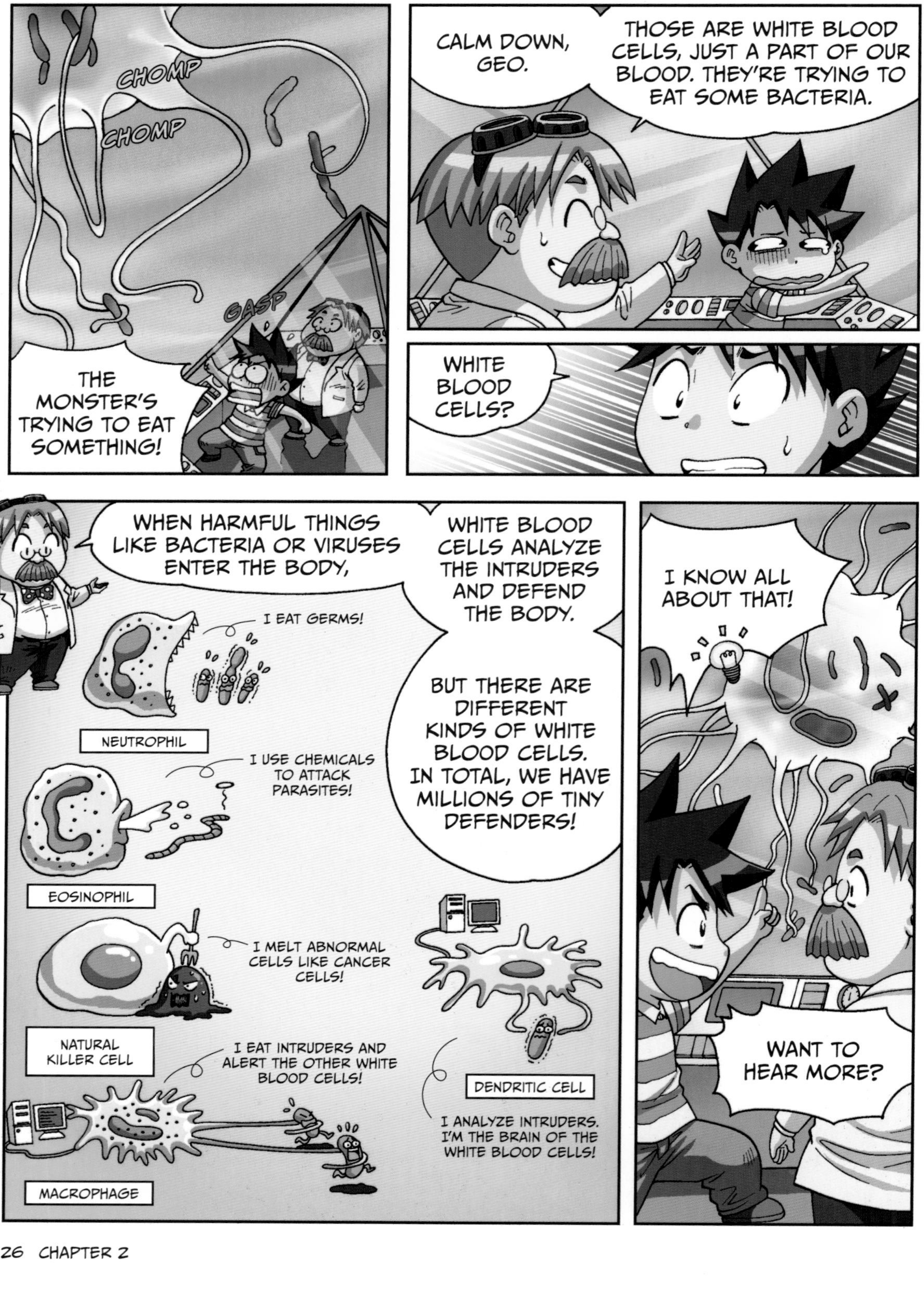
CHOMP
CHOMP
GASP
THE MONSTER'S TRYING TO EAT SOMETHING!
CALM DOWN, GEO.
THOSE ARE WHITE BLOOD CELLS, JUST A PART OF OUR BLOOD. THEY'RE TRYING TO EAT SOME BACTERIA.
WHITE BLOOD CELLS?
WHEN HARMFUL THINGS LIKE BACTERIA OR VIRUSES ENTER THE BODY,
WHITE BLOOD CELLS ANALYZE THE INTRUDERS AND DEFEND THE BODY.
BUT THERE ARE DIFFERENT KINDS OF WHITE BLOOD CELLS. IN TOTAL, WE HAVE MILLIONS OF TINY DEFENDERS!
I EAT GERMS!
NEUTROPHIL
I USE CHEMICALS TO ATTACK PARASITES!
EOSINOPHIL
I MELT ABNORMAL CELLS LIKE CANCER CELLS!
NATURAL KILLER CELL
I EAT INTRUDERS AND ALERT THE OTHER WHITE BLOOD CELLS!
MACROPHAGE
DENDRITIC CELL
I ANALYZE INTRUDERS. I'M THE BRAIN OF THE WHITE BLOOD CELLS!
I KNOW ALL ABOUT THAT!
WANT TO HEAR MORE?

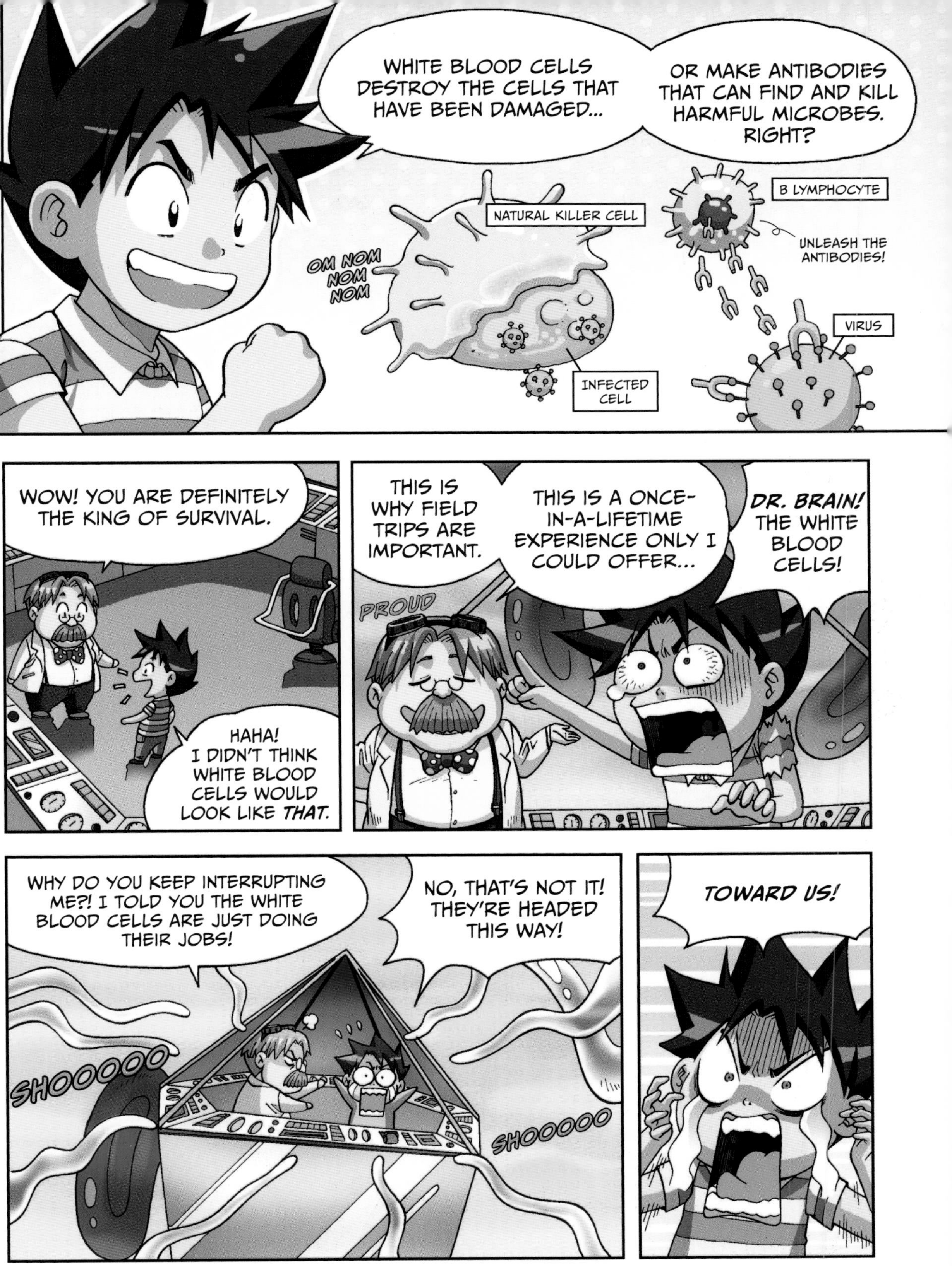
WHITE BLOOD CELLS DESTROY THE CELLS THAT HAVE BEEN DAMAGED...
OR MAKE ANTIBODIES THAT CAN FIND AND KILL HARMFUL MICROBES. RIGHT?
NATURAL KILLER CELL
B LYMPHOCYTE
UNLEASH THE ANTIBODIES!
OM NOM NOM NOM
VIRUS
INFECTED CELL
WOW! YOU ARE DEFINITELY THE KING OF SURVIVAL.
HAHA! I DIDN'T THINK WHITE BLOOD CELLS WOULD LOOK LIKE THAT.
THIS IS WHY FIELD TRIPS ARE IMPORTANT.
THIS IS A ONCE-IN-A-LIFETIME EXPERIENCE ONLY I COULD OFFER...
PROUD
DR. BRAIN! THE WHITE BLOOD CELLS!
WHY DO YOU KEEP INTERRUPTING ME?! I TOLD YOU THE WHITE BLOOD CELLS ARE JUST DOING THEIR JOBS!
NO, THAT'S NOT IT! THEY'RE HEADED THIS WAY!
SHOOOOO
SHOOOOO
TOWARD US!

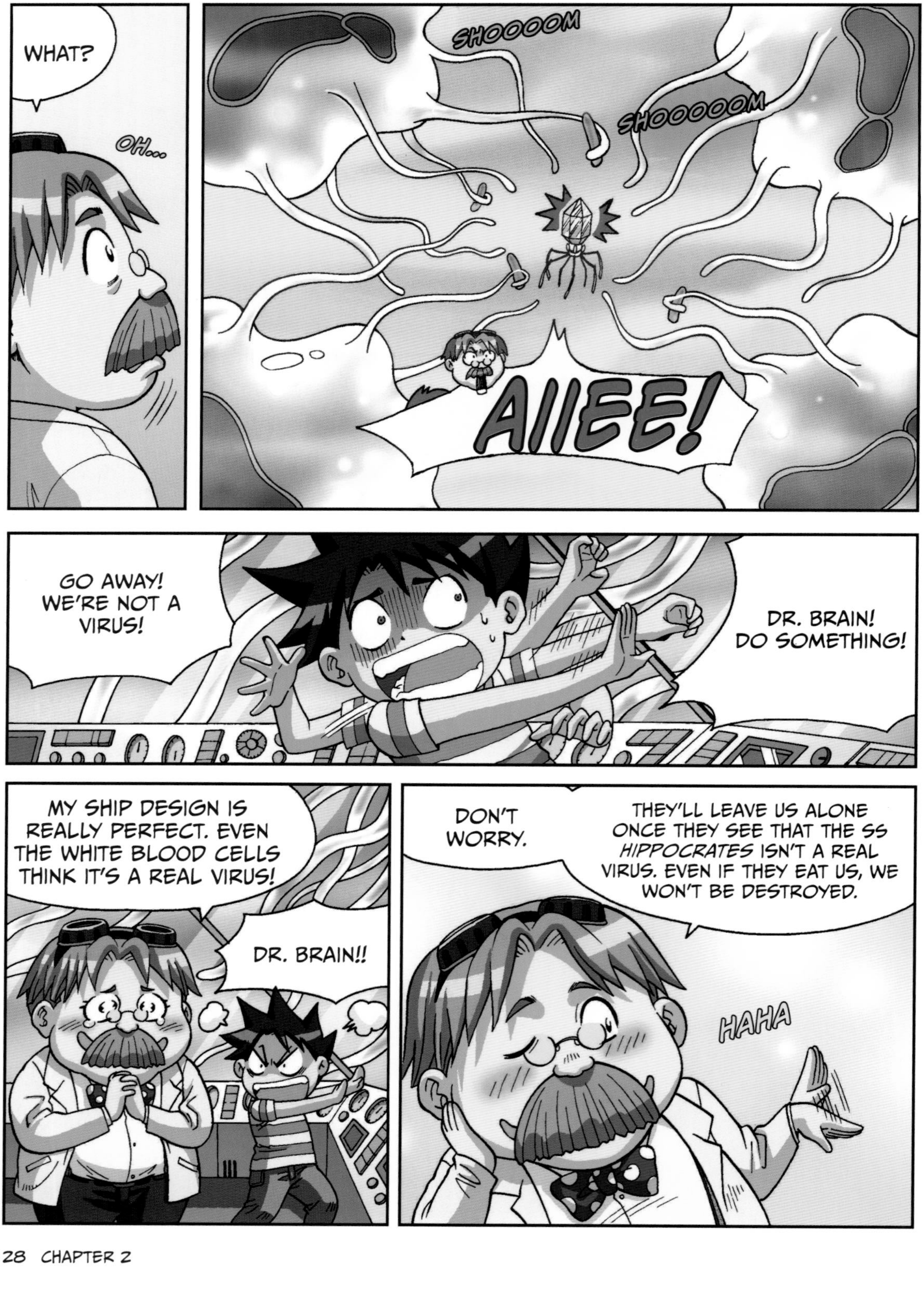
WHAT?
OH...
SHOOOOM
SHOOOOOM
AIIEE!
GO AWAY! WE'RE NOT A VIRUS!
DR. BRAIN! DO SOMETHING!
MY SHIP DESIGN IS REALLY PERFECT. EVEN THE WHITE BLOOD CELLS THINK IT'S A REAL VIRUS!
DR. BRAIN!!
DON'T WORRY.
THEY'LL LEAVE US ALONE ONCE THEY SEE THAT THE SS *HIPPOCRATES* ISN'T A REAL VIRUS. EVEN IF THEY EAT US, WE WON'T BE DESTROYED.
HAHA

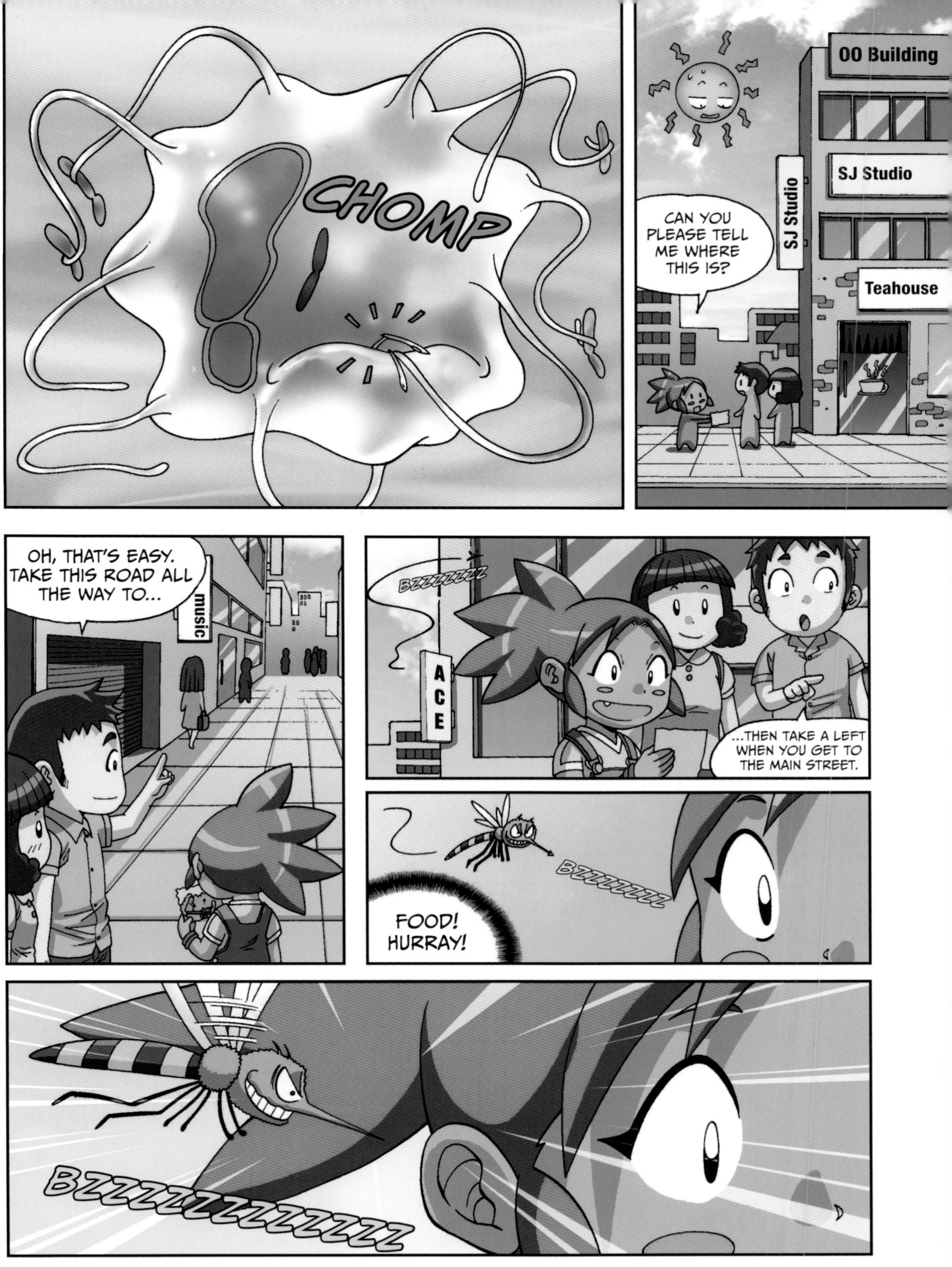
CHOMP
OO Building
SJ Studio
SJ Studio
Teahouse
CAN YOU PLEASE TELL ME WHERE THIS IS?
OH, THAT'S EASY. TAKE THIS ROAD ALL THE WAY TO...
music
BZZZZZZZ
ACE
...THEN TAKE A LEFT WHEN YOU GET TO THE MAIN STREET.
BZZZZZZZ
FOOD! HURRAY!
BZZZZZZZZZZZZZZZZ

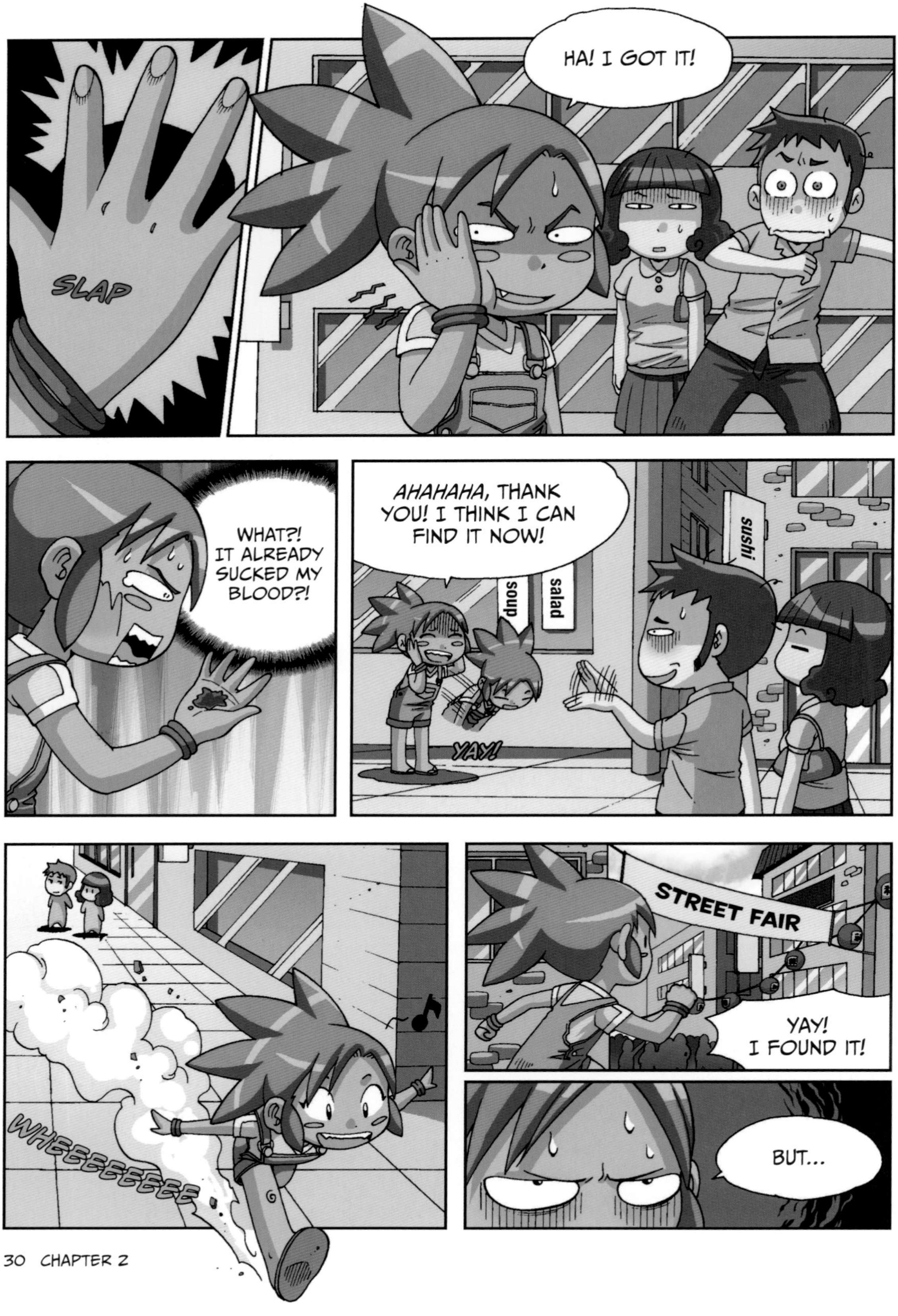
SLAP
HA! I GOT IT!
WHAT?! IT ALREADY SUCKED MY BLOOD?!
AHAHAHA, THANK YOU! I THINK I CAN FIND IT NOW!
sushi
salad
soup
YAY!
WHEEEEEEEEEE
STREET FAIR
YAY! I FOUND IT!
BUT...

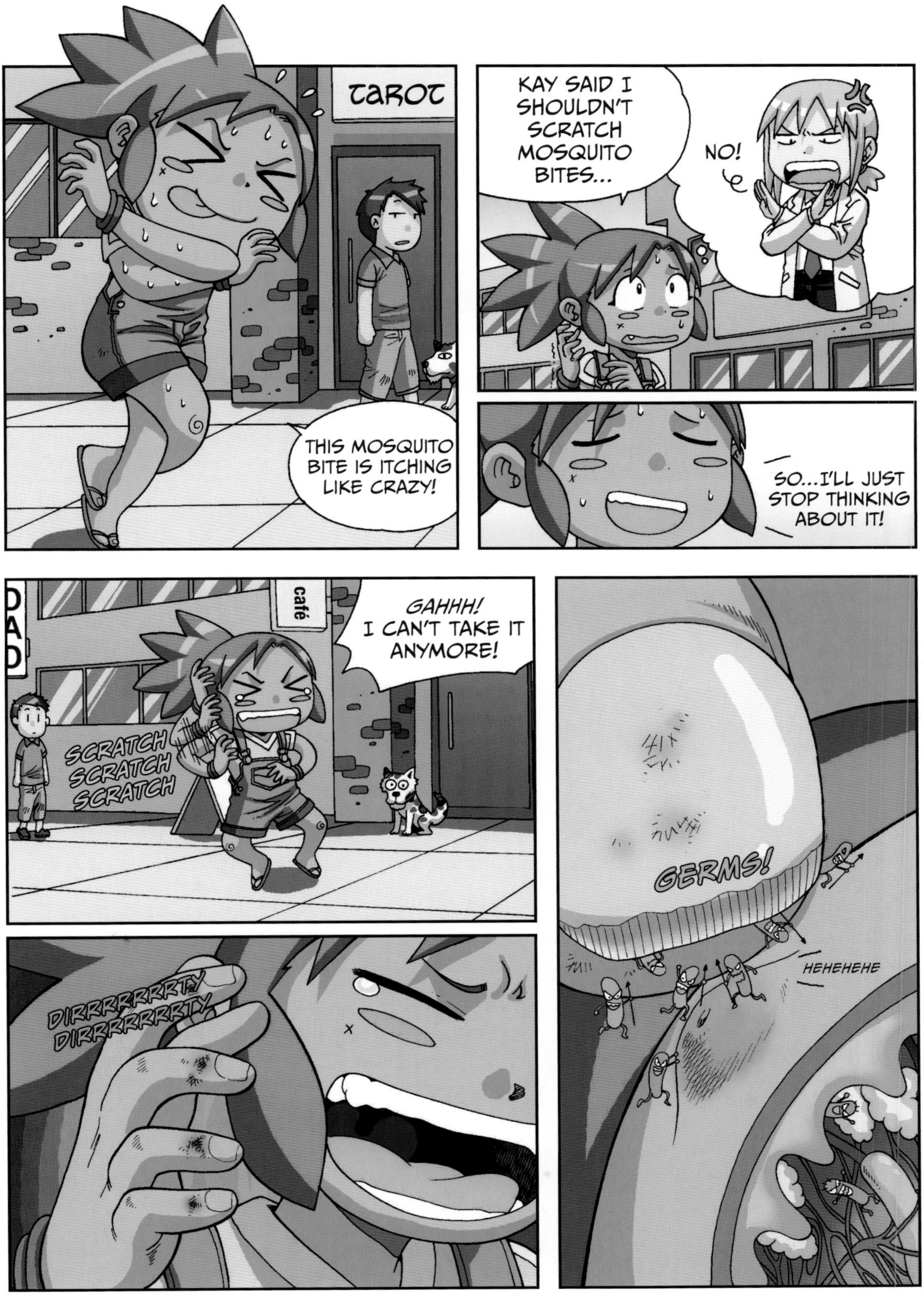
TAROT
THIS MOSQUITO BITE IS ITCHING LIKE CRAZY!
KAY SAID I SHOULDN'T SCRATCH MOSQUITO BITES...
NO!
SO...I'LL JUST STOP THINKING ABOUT IT!
café
GAHHH! I CAN'T TAKE IT ANYMORE!
SCRATCH SCRATCH SCRATCH
GERMS!
HEHEHEHE
DIRRRRRRRTY DIRRRRRRRTY

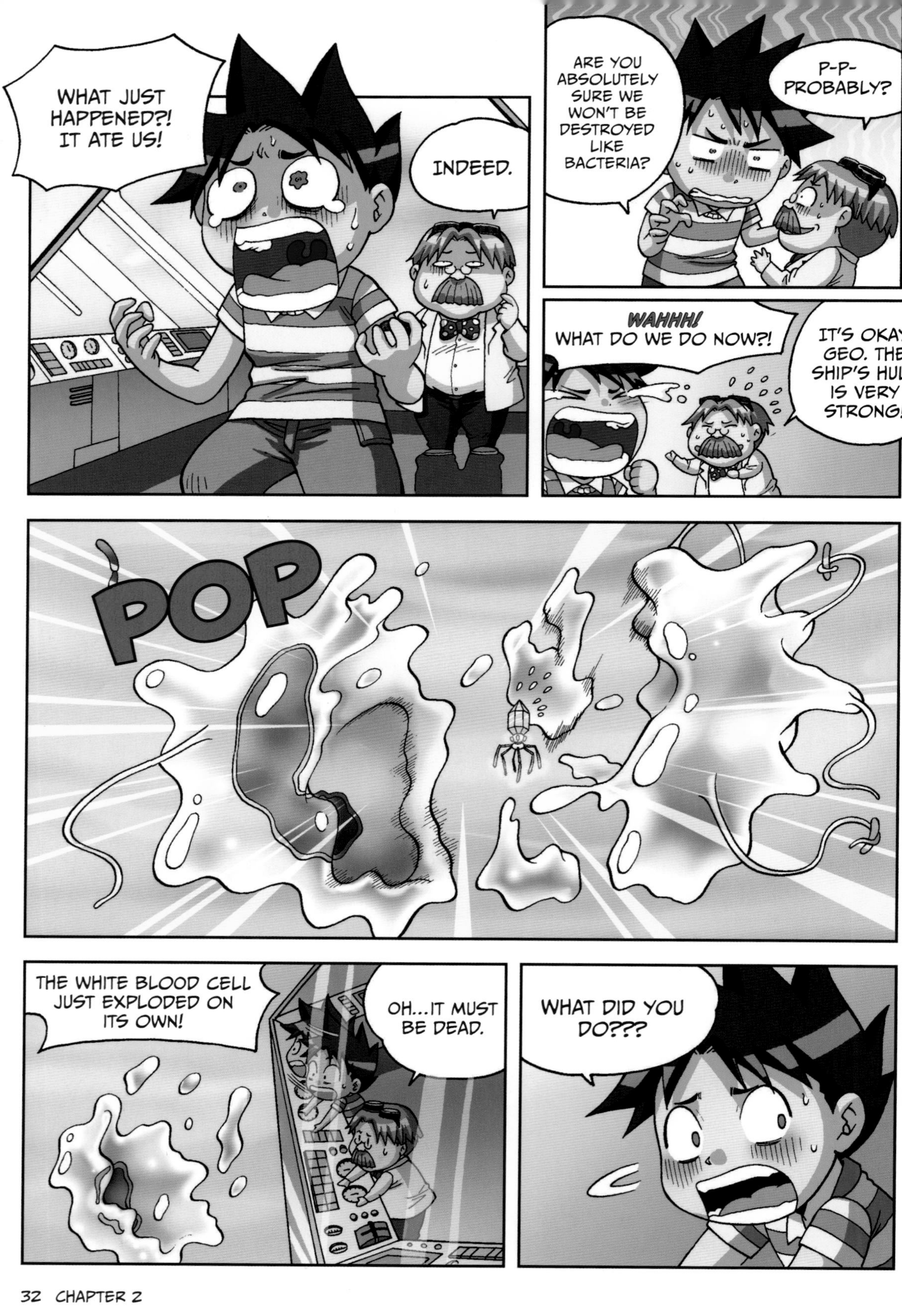
WHAT JUST HAPPENED?! IT ATE US!
INDEED.
ARE YOU ABSOLUTELY SURE WE WON'T BE DESTROYED LIKE BACTERIA?
P-P-PROBABLY?
WAHHH! WHAT DO WE DO NOW?!
IT'S OKAY, GEO. THE SHIP'S HULL IS VERY STRONG!
POP
THE WHITE BLOOD CELL JUST EXPLODED ON ITS OWN!
OH...IT MUST BE DEAD.
WHAT DID YOU DO???

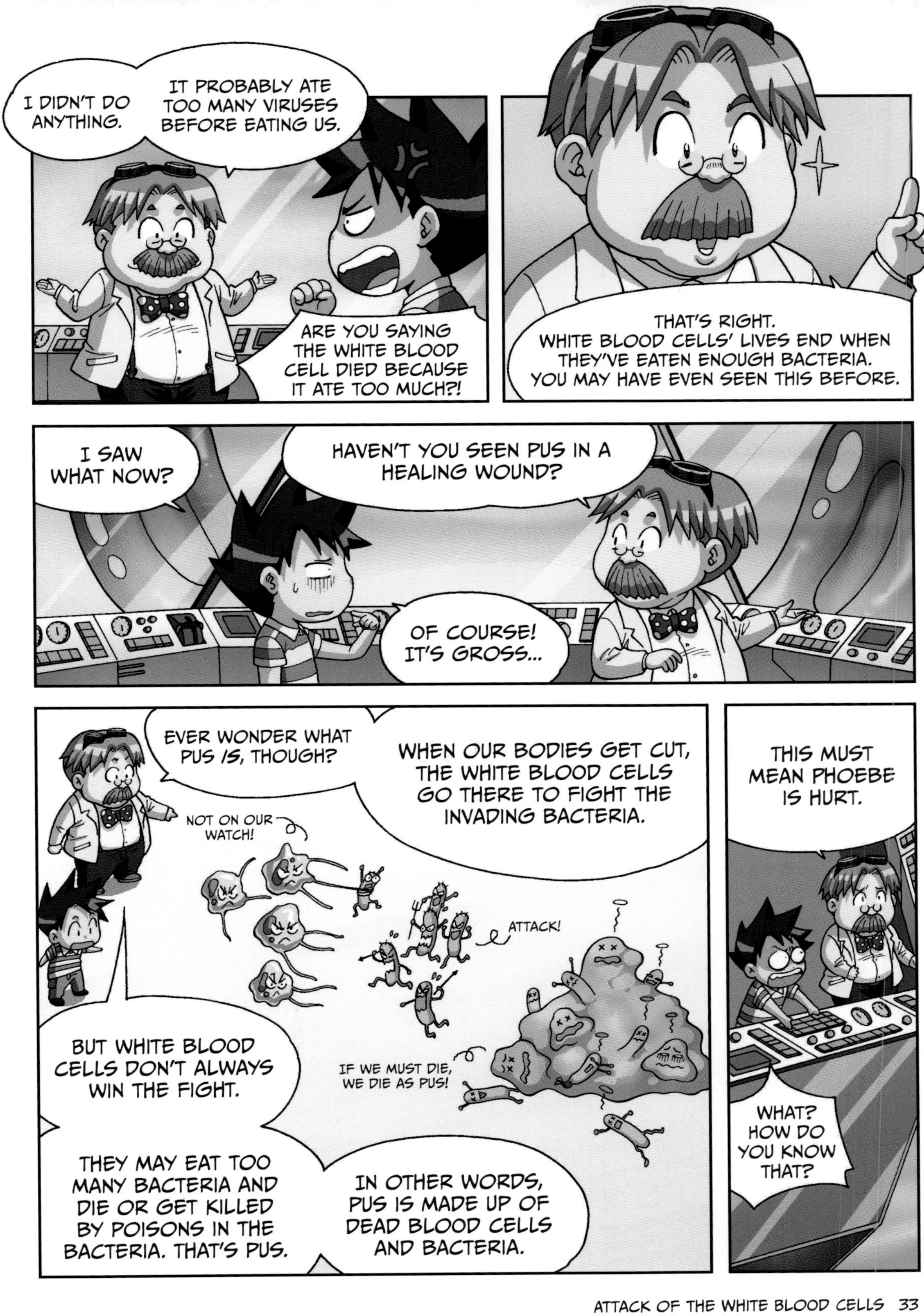
I DIDN'T DO ANYTHING.
IT PROBABLY ATE TOO MANY VIRUSES BEFORE EATING US.
ARE YOU SAYING THE WHITE BLOOD CELL DIED BECAUSE IT ATE TOO MUCH?!
THAT'S RIGHT. WHITE BLOOD CELLS' LIVES END WHEN THEY'VE EATEN ENOUGH BACTERIA. YOU MAY HAVE EVEN SEEN THIS BEFORE.
I SAW WHAT NOW?
HAVEN'T YOU SEEN PUS IN A HEALING WOUND?
OF COURSE! IT'S GROSS...
EVER WONDER WHAT PUS *IS*, THOUGH?
WHEN OUR BODIES GET CUT, THE WHITE BLOOD CELLS GO THERE TO FIGHT THE INVADING BACTERIA.
NOT ON OUR WATCH!
ATTACK!
BUT WHITE BLOOD CELLS DON'T ALWAYS WIN THE FIGHT.
IF WE MUST DIE, WE DIE AS PUS!
THEY MAY EAT TOO MANY BACTERIA AND DIE OR GET KILLED BY POISONS IN THE BACTERIA. THAT'S PUS.
IN OTHER WORDS, PUS IS MADE UP OF DEAD BLOOD CELLS AND BACTERIA.
THIS MUST MEAN PHOEBE IS HURT.
WHAT? HOW DO YOU KNOW THAT?

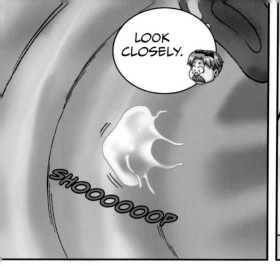

LOOK CLOSELY.

SHOOOOOOP

GASP

THE WHITE BLOOD CELLS ARE DISAPPEARING INTO THE WALL!

SHOOOOOOP

THEY'RE NOT DISAPPEARING. THEY'RE JUST PASSING THROUGH. WHITE BLOOD CELLS AREN'T LIKE RED BLOOD CELLS. WHITE BLOOD CELLS CAN CHANGE SHAPE AND GO THROUGH CELLS.

SHOOOP

WOW, REALLY?!

WHEN BACTERIA INVADE THROUGH A WOUND, THE NEARBY CELLS SEND A SIGNAL TO ALL THE WHITE BLOOD CELLS IN THE BODY.

THE WHITE BLOOD CELLS THAT RECEIVE THIS SIGNAL MOVE TO THE WOUND.

CALLING ALL NEARBY WHITE BLOOD CELLS!

AWOOGA AWOOGA

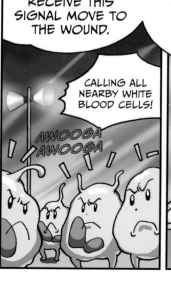

THE BODY THEN SENDS OUT HISTAMINE. HISTAMINE LOOSENS THE CAPILLARY WALLS SURROUNDING THE WOUND. THAT WAY, WHITE BLOOD CELLS CAN GET WHERE THEY NEED TO GO QUICKLY.

! PASS!

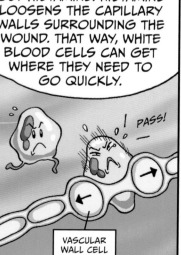

VASCULAR WALL CELL

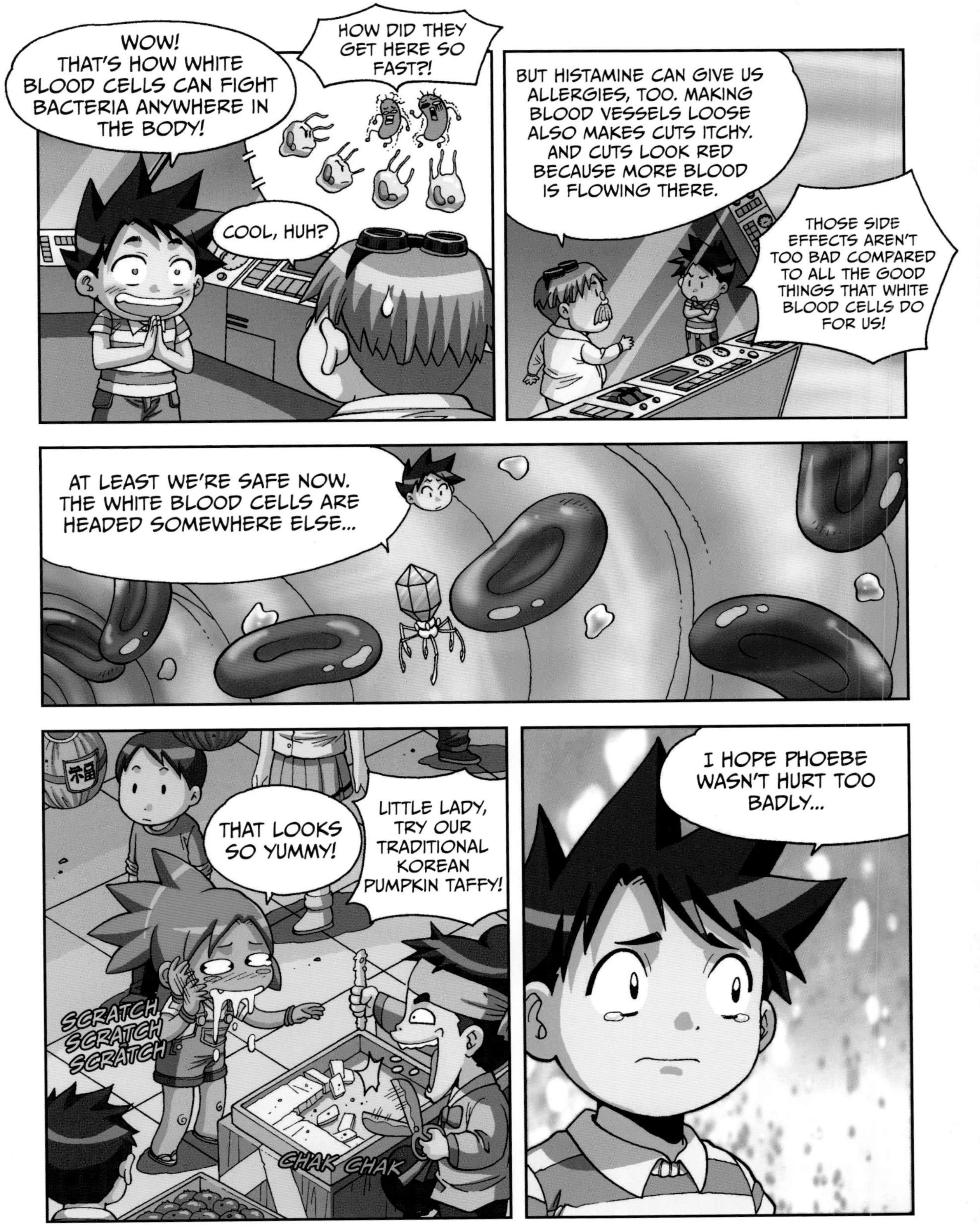
WOW! THAT'S HOW WHITE BLOOD CELLS CAN FIGHT BACTERIA ANYWHERE IN THE BODY!
HOW DID THEY GET HERE SO FAST?!
COOL, HUH?
BUT HISTAMINE CAN GIVE US ALLERGIES, TOO. MAKING BLOOD VESSELS LOOSE ALSO MAKES CUTS ITCHY. AND CUTS LOOK RED BECAUSE MORE BLOOD IS FLOWING THERE.
THOSE SIDE EFFECTS AREN'T TOO BAD COMPARED TO ALL THE GOOD THINGS THAT WHITE BLOOD CELLS DO FOR US!
AT LEAST WE'RE SAFE NOW. THE WHITE BLOOD CELLS ARE HEADED SOMEWHERE ELSE...
THAT LOOKS SO YUMMY!
LITTLE LADY, TRY OUR TRADITIONAL KOREAN PUMPKIN TAFFY!
SCRATCH SCRATCH SCRATCH
CHAK CHAK
I HOPE PHOEBE WASN'T HURT TOO BADLY...

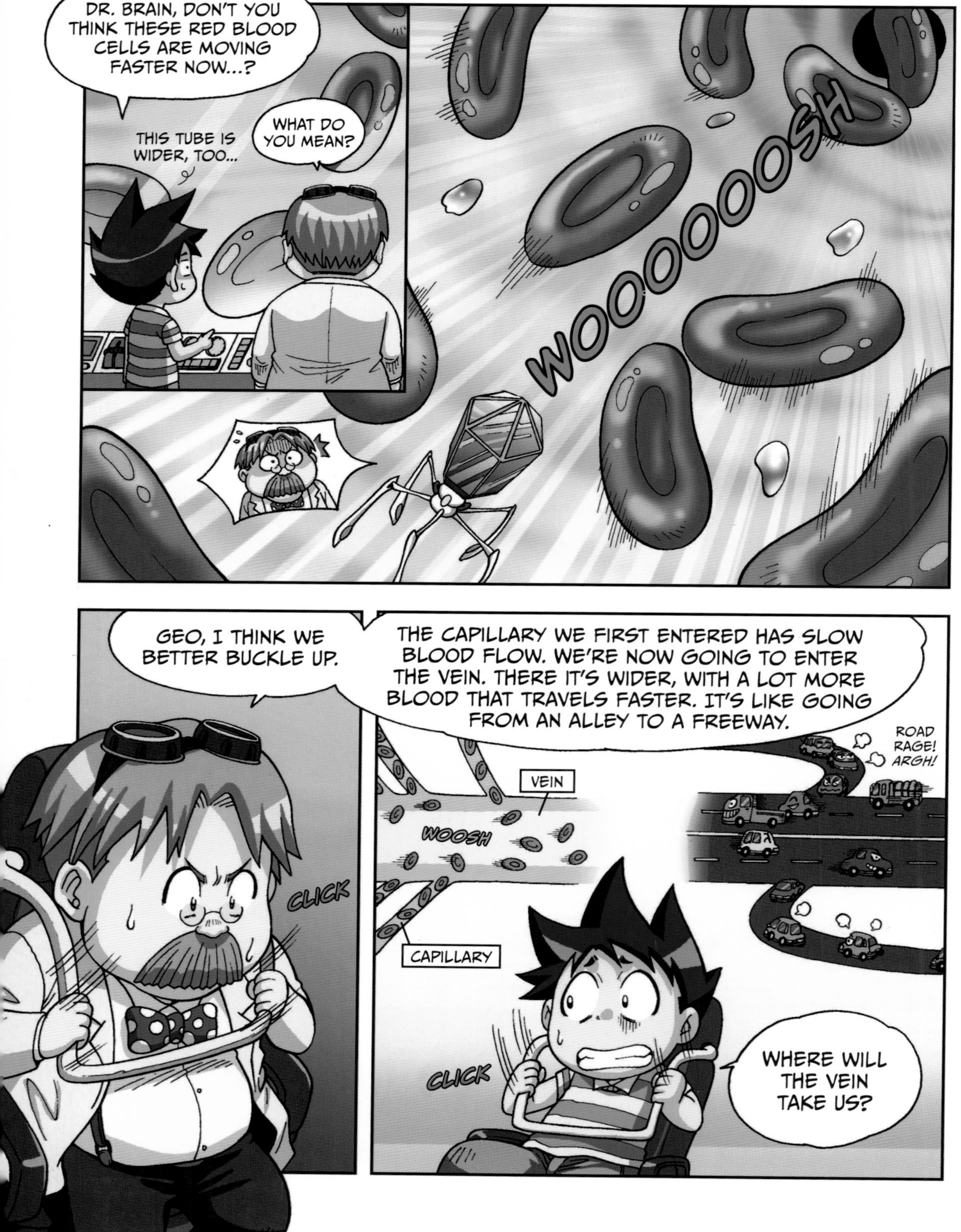
DR. BRAIN, DON'T YOU THINK THESE RED BLOOD CELLS ARE MOVING FASTER NOW...?
THIS TUBE IS WIDER, TOO...
WHAT DO YOU MEAN?
WOOOOOOOSH
GEO, I THINK WE BETTER BUCKLE UP.
THE CAPILLARY WE FIRST ENTERED HAS SLOW BLOOD FLOW. WE'RE NOW GOING TO ENTER THE VEIN. THERE IT'S WIDER, WITH A LOT MORE BLOOD THAT TRAVELS FASTER. IT'S LIKE GOING FROM AN ALLEY TO A FREEWAY.
VEIN
WOOSH
CAPILLARY
ROAD RAGE! ARGH!
CLICK
CLICK
WHERE WILL THE VEIN TAKE US?

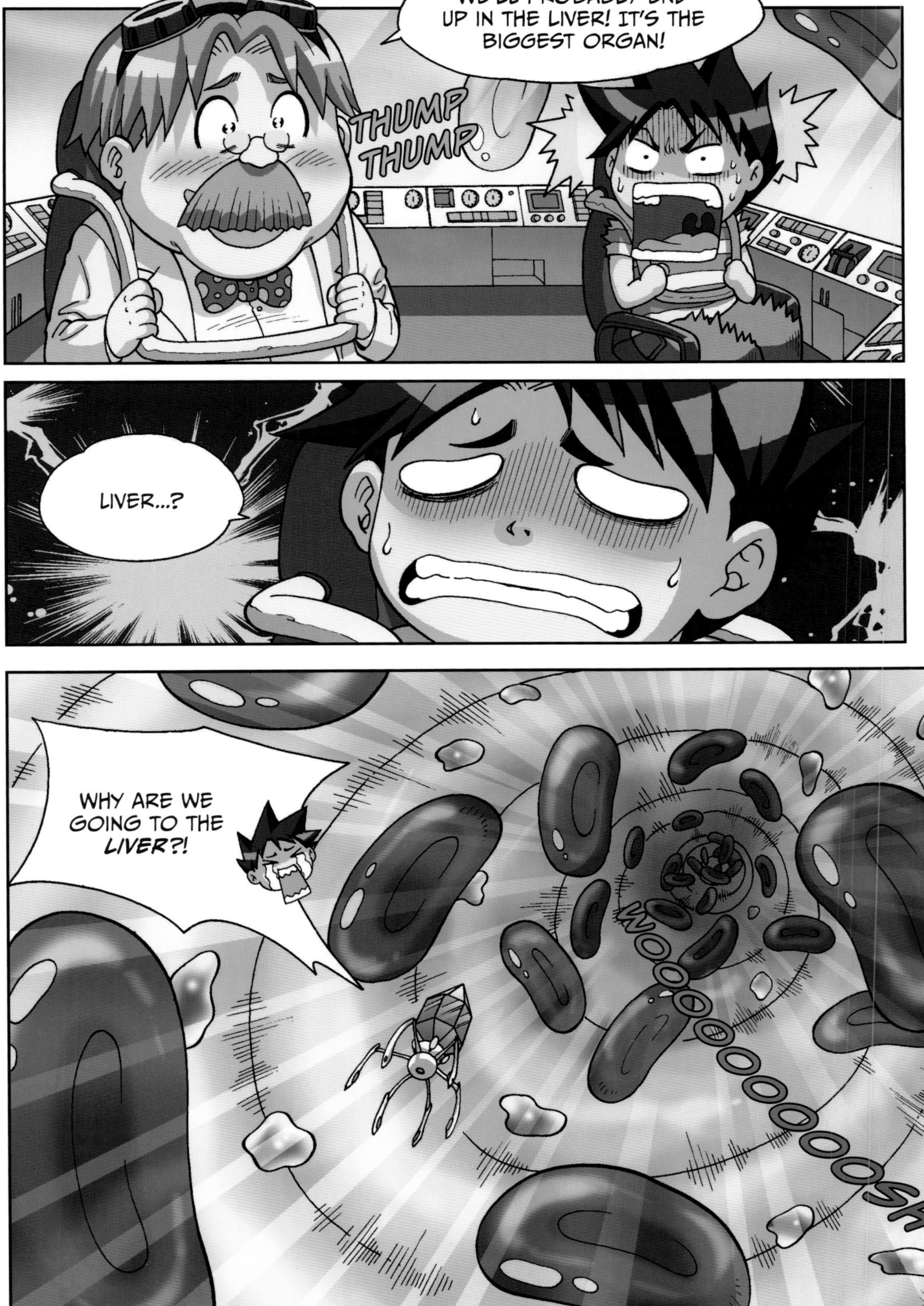
WE'LL PROBABLY END UP IN THE LIVER! IT'S THE BIGGEST ORGAN!
THUMP THUMP
LIVER...?
WHY ARE WE GOING TO THE *LIVER*?!
WOOOOOOOOOOOOOOSH

**CIRCULATORY
SYSTEM**

RED BLOOD CELLS

Red blood cells use a red protein called *hemo-globin* to transport oxygen. These blood cells are curved on both sides, which makes it easier for them to pass through narrow capillaries. But they are wide, too, and that helps them transport as much oxygen as possible. We have about 5 million red blood cells per microliter (a tiny droplet) of blood. A red blood cell lives for about 120 days. These cells can't regrow if they're damaged because they don't have a nucleus. Damaged or aged red blood cells are destroyed in the liver, spleen, and bone marrow. Their parts are recycled to create new blood cells.

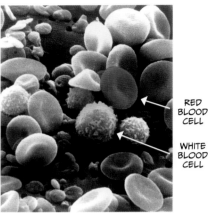

RED
BLOOD
CELL

WHITE
BLOOD
CELL

About 2 million red blood cells are created and destroyed every second. A sickness called anemia *can happen if you don't have enough red blood cells.*

PLATELETS

Platelets, which are fragments of blood cells, slow bleeding when you have a cut or wound. They clot the blood and make scabs. When platelets touch damaged blood vessels, they start their work. One part of clotting uses thrombin (a protease, which is a type of enzyme) that turns fibrinogen (a protein) into fibrin fibers. These fibers are thin and threadlike. They mix with blood cells and harden to create scabs. There are about 150,000 to 300,000 platelets in a droplet of blood. Without platelets, you can bruise easily and have lots of nosebleeds. Hemophilia, a group of diseases handed down from parent to child, can keep your platelets from working. It's dangerous because cuts can keep bleeding without stopping.

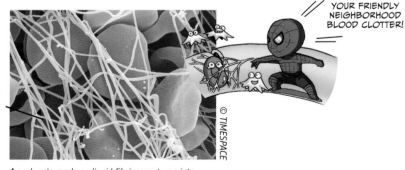

YOUR FRIENDLY
NEIGHBORHOOD
BLOOD CLOTTER!

FIBRIN

© TIMESPACE

A scab gets made as liquid fibrinogen turns into solid fibrin, thanks to platelets.

WHITE BLOOD CELLS

White blood cells protect the body from diseases. When bacteria or viruses enter the body, white blood cells swallow and destroy them or attack them with anti-bodies. Like an amoeba, white blood cells can change their size and shape. This special ability makes it easy for white blood cells to pass through the narrow gaps between cells to attack invaders.

There are about 6,000 to 8,000 white blood cells in a droplet of blood. They can be granulocytes or agranulocytes, depending on whether or not they have granules inside the cells. (When doctors see them under a microscope, granu-locytes are filled with little specks.) White blood cells belong to different groups based on the roles they play inside our bodies.

Types		Traits	Functions
Granulocytes		The most common kind of white blood cell. They have special immune granules inside.	• Neutrophils: Perform phagocytosis (eating bad bacteria) • Eosinophils: Defend against parasites • Basophils: Release inflammatory agents
Agranulocytes	**Lymphocytes**	Round cells that act directly against invaders.	• B Lymphocytes: Produce antibodies that block bacteria • T Lymphocytes: Direct immune activities, directly attack bacteria • Natural Killer Cells: Destroy infected and cancer cells
	Monocytes	Biggest type of white blood cell. They can be round or have a horseshoe-shaped nucleus.	• Macrophages: Eat bad bacteria, ask for help from lymphocytes • Dendritic Cells: Analyze bacteria, make immune activity go faster

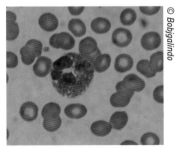

© Bobjgalindo

About 9 to 10 μm in diameter, slightly bigger than a red blood cell, eosinophils are part of allergic reactions.

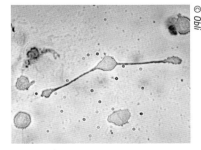

© Obli

As the biggest white blood cells, macrophages stretch their bodies to eat bacteria during phagocytosis.

A VISIT TO THE LIVER

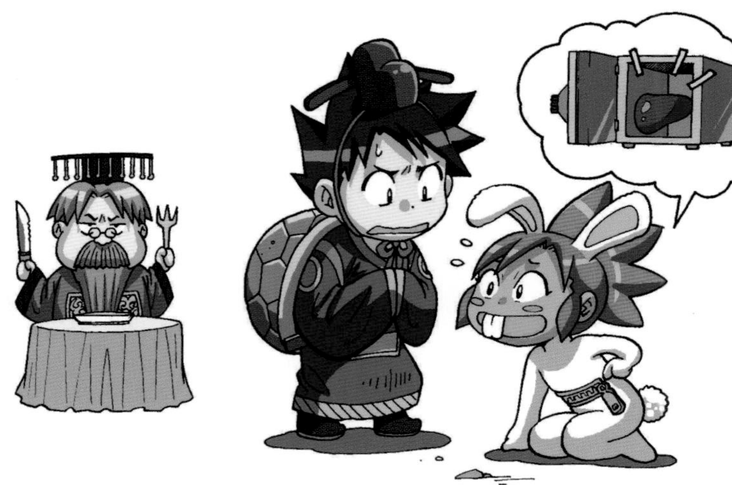

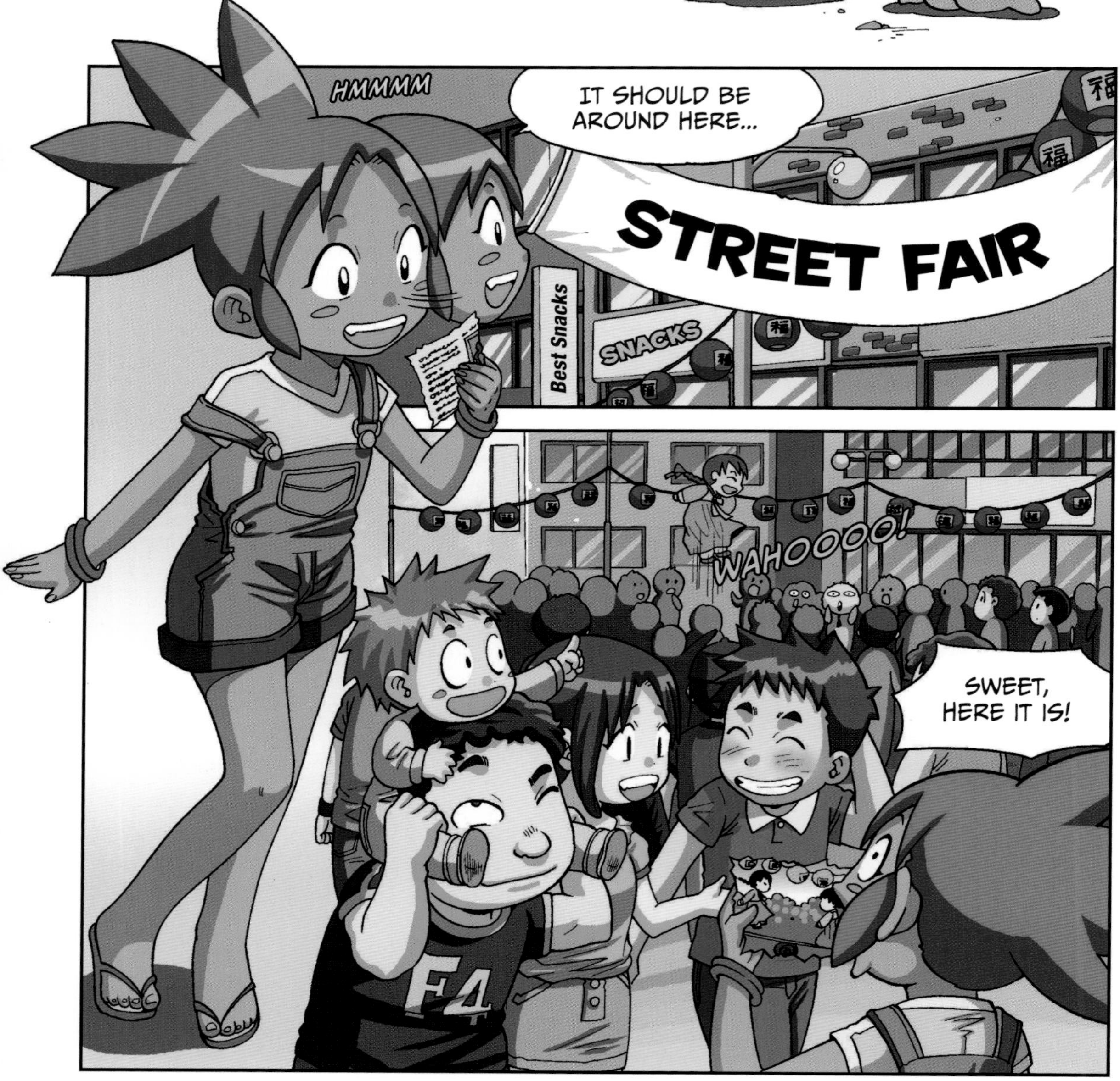
HMMMM
IT SHOULD BE AROUND HERE...
STREET FAIR
Best Snacks
SNACKS
WAHOOOOO!
SWEET, HERE IT IS!

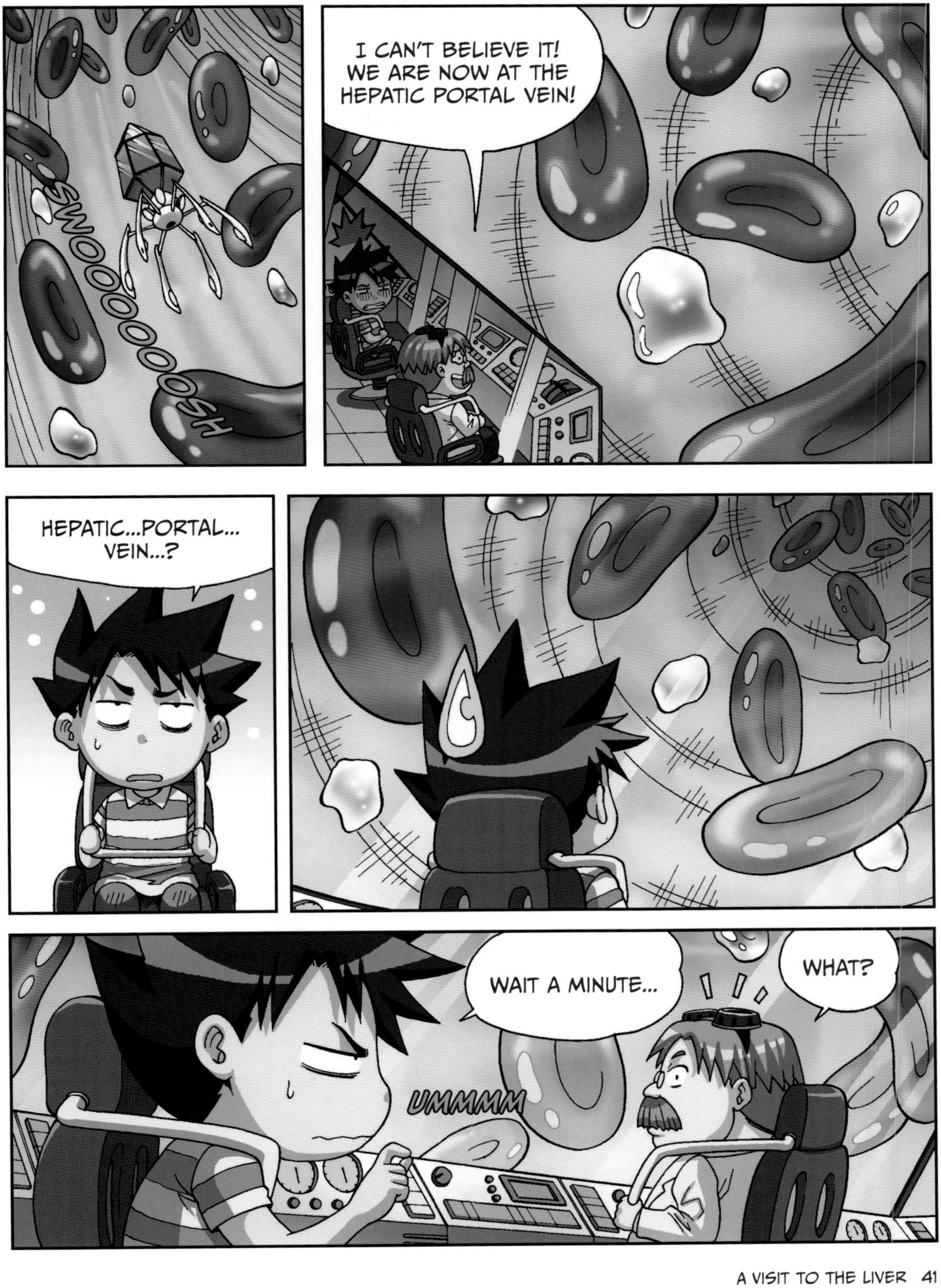
SWOOOOOOOSH
I CAN'T BELIEVE IT! WE ARE NOW AT THE HEPATIC PORTAL VEIN!
HEPATIC...PORTAL... VEIN...?
WAIT A MINUTE...
UMMMMM
WHAT?

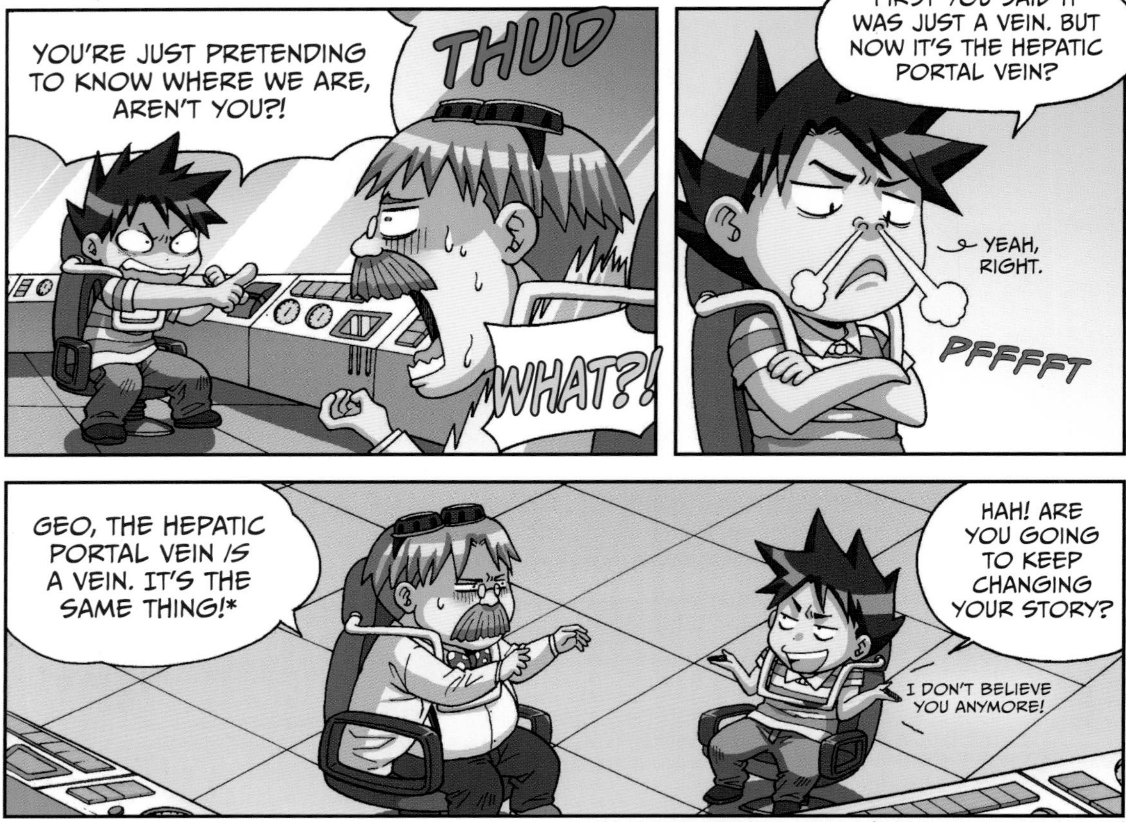
YOU'RE JUST PRETENDING TO KNOW WHERE WE ARE, AREN'T YOU?!
THUD
WHAT?!
FIRST YOU SAID IT WAS JUST A VEIN. BUT NOW IT'S THE HEPATIC PORTAL VEIN?
YEAH, RIGHT.
PFFFFT
GEO, THE HEPATIC PORTAL VEIN *IS* A VEIN. IT'S THE SAME THING!*
HAH! ARE YOU GOING TO KEEP CHANGING YOUR STORY?
I DON'T BELIEVE YOU ANYMORE!

* THE WORD *HEPATIC* MEANS "RELATED TO THE LIVER."

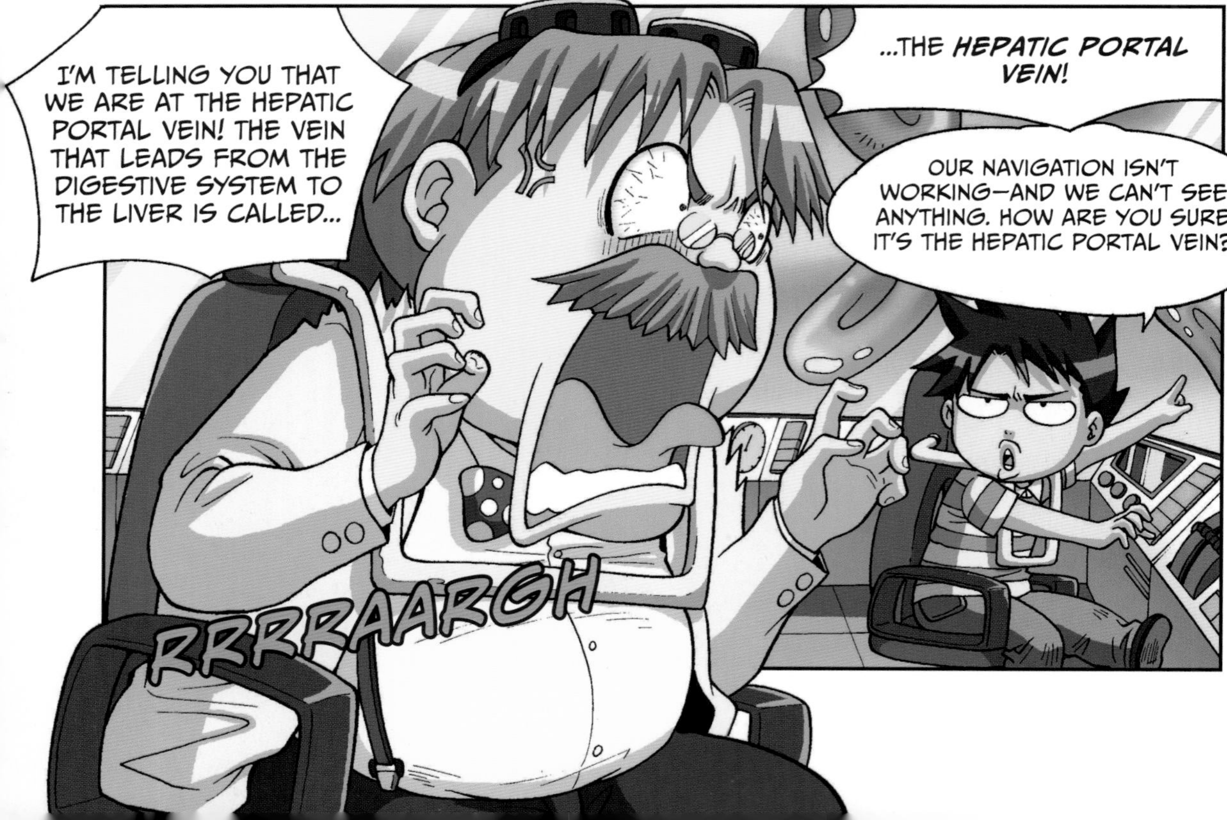
I'M TELLING YOU THAT WE ARE AT THE HEPATIC PORTAL VEIN! THE VEIN THAT LEADS FROM THE DIGESTIVE SYSTEM TO THE LIVER IS CALLED...
...THE ***HEPATIC PORTAL VEIN!***
OUR NAVIGATION ISN'T WORKING—AND WE CAN'T SEE ANYTHING. HOW ARE YOU SURE IT'S THE HEPATIC PORTAL VEIN?
RRRRAARGH

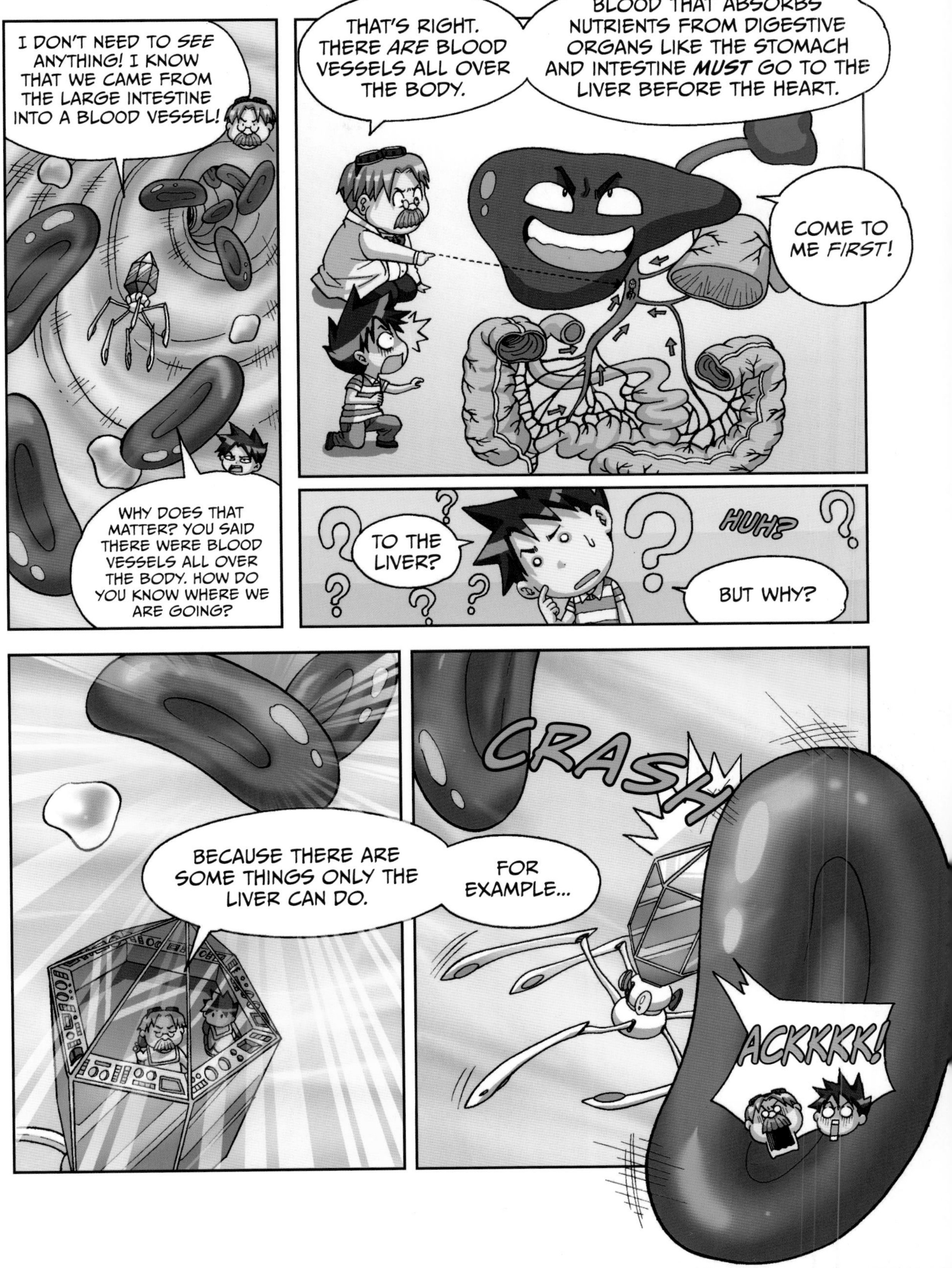
I DON'T NEED TO *SEE* ANYTHING! I KNOW THAT WE CAME FROM THE LARGE INTESTINE INTO A BLOOD VESSEL!
WHY DOES THAT MATTER? YOU SAID THERE WERE BLOOD VESSELS ALL OVER THE BODY. HOW DO YOU KNOW WHERE WE ARE GOING?
THAT'S RIGHT. THERE *ARE* BLOOD VESSELS ALL OVER THE BODY.
BLOOD THAT ABSORBS NUTRIENTS FROM DIGESTIVE ORGANS LIKE THE STOMACH AND INTESTINE ***MUST*** GO TO THE LIVER BEFORE THE HEART.
COME TO ME *FIRST*!
TO THE LIVER?
HUH?
BUT WHY?
BECAUSE THERE ARE SOME THINGS ONLY THE LIVER CAN DO.
FOR EXAMPLE...
CRASH
ACKKKK!

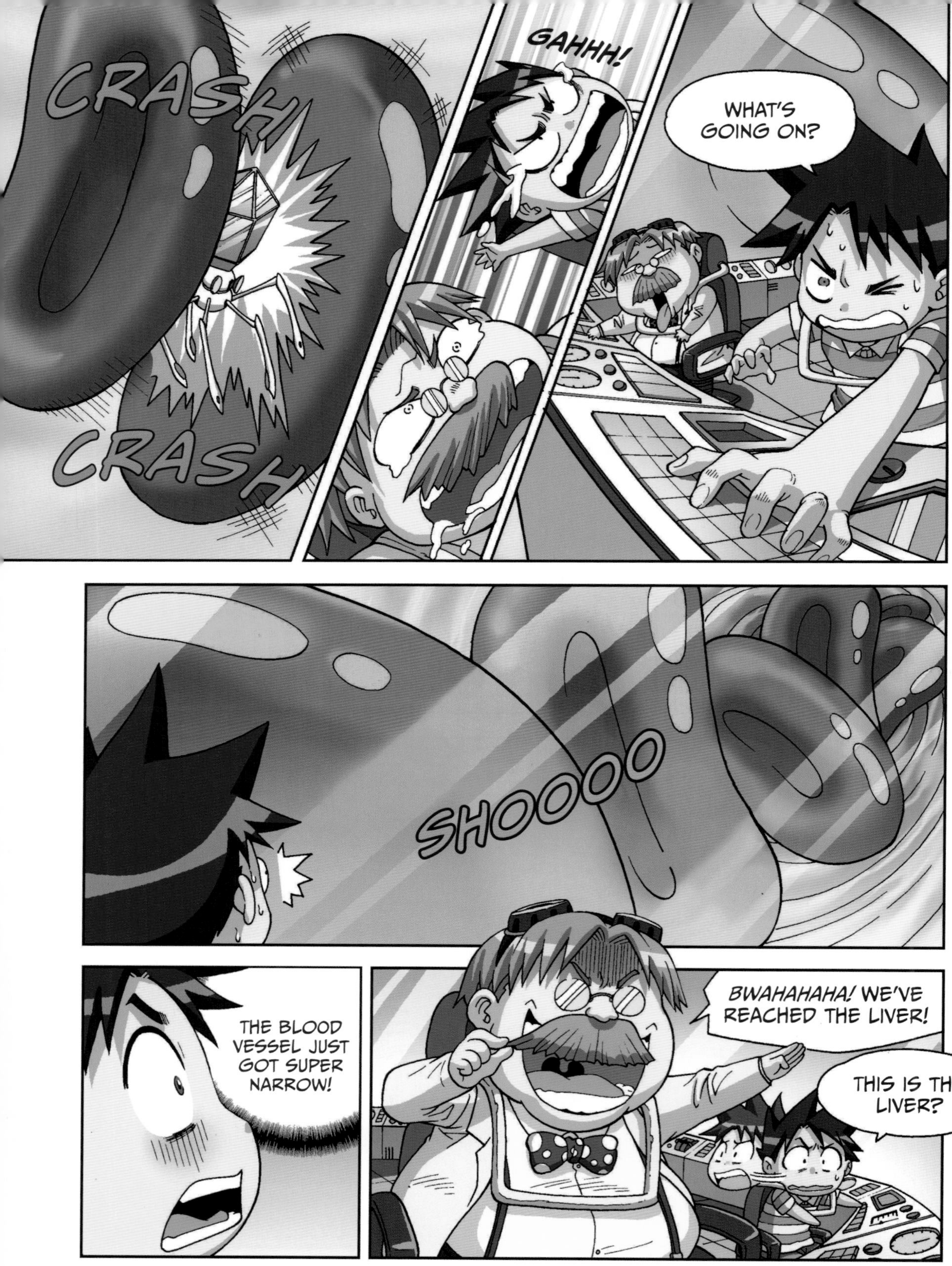
CRASH
CRASH
GAHHH!
WHAT'S GOING ON?
SHOOOO
THE BLOOD VESSEL JUST GOT SUPER NARROW!
BWAHAHAHA! WE'VE REACHED THE LIVER!
THIS IS THE LIVER?

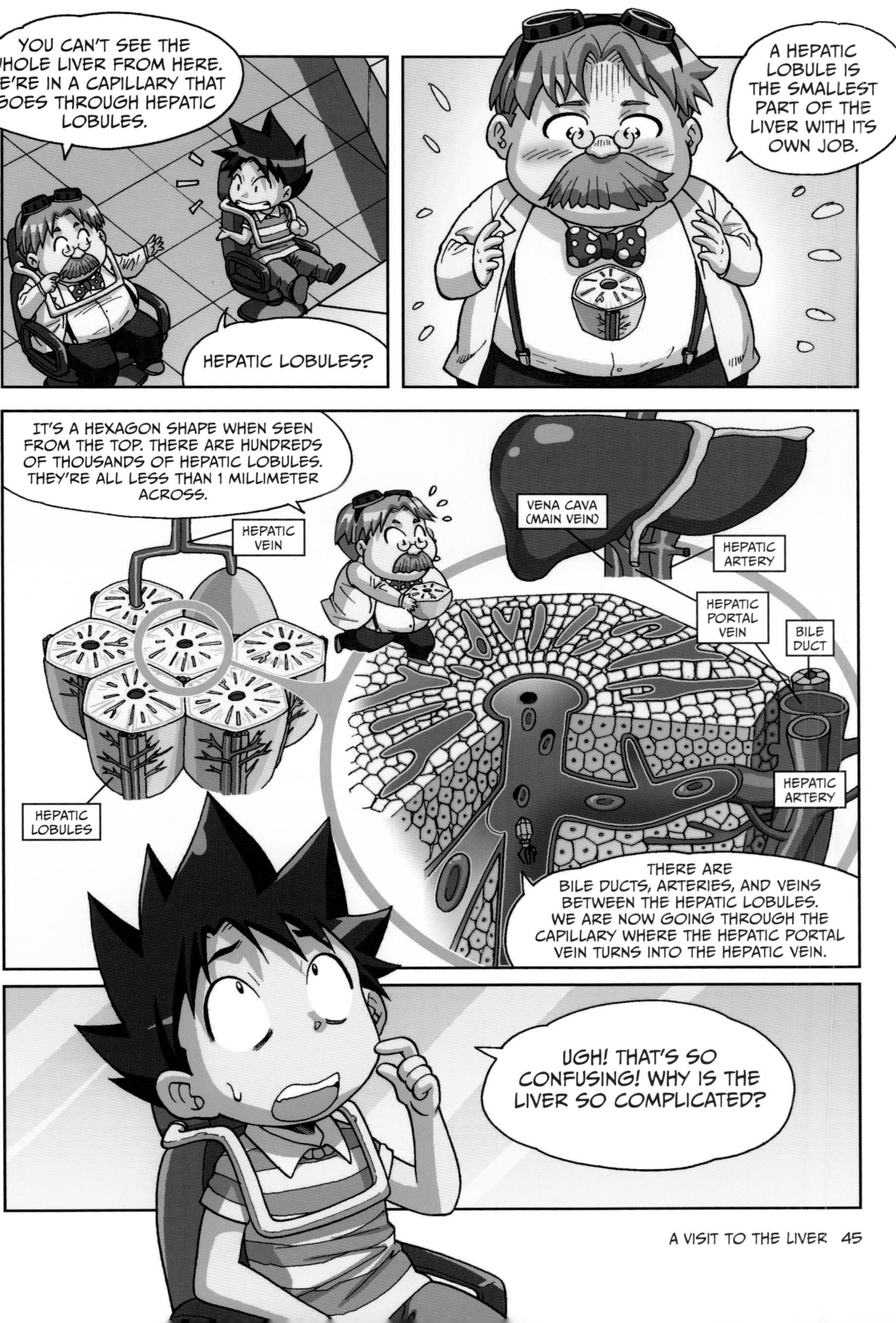
YOU CAN'T SEE THE WHOLE LIVER FROM HERE. WE'RE IN A CAPILLARY THAT GOES THROUGH HEPATIC LOBULES.
HEPATIC LOBULES?
A HEPATIC LOBULE IS THE SMALLEST PART OF THE LIVER WITH ITS OWN JOB.
IT'S A HEXAGON SHAPE WHEN SEEN FROM THE TOP. THERE ARE HUNDREDS OF THOUSANDS OF HEPATIC LOBULES. THEY'RE ALL LESS THAN 1 MILLIMETER ACROSS.
HEPATIC VEIN
VENA CAVA (MAIN VEIN)
HEPATIC ARTERY
HEPATIC PORTAL VEIN
BILE DUCT
HEPATIC ARTERY
HEPATIC LOBULES
THERE ARE BILE DUCTS, ARTERIES, AND VEINS BETWEEN THE HEPATIC LOBULES. WE ARE NOW GOING THROUGH THE CAPILLARY WHERE THE HEPATIC PORTAL VEIN TURNS INTO THE HEPATIC VEIN.
UGH! THAT'S SO CONFUSING! WHY IS THE LIVER SO COMPLICATED?

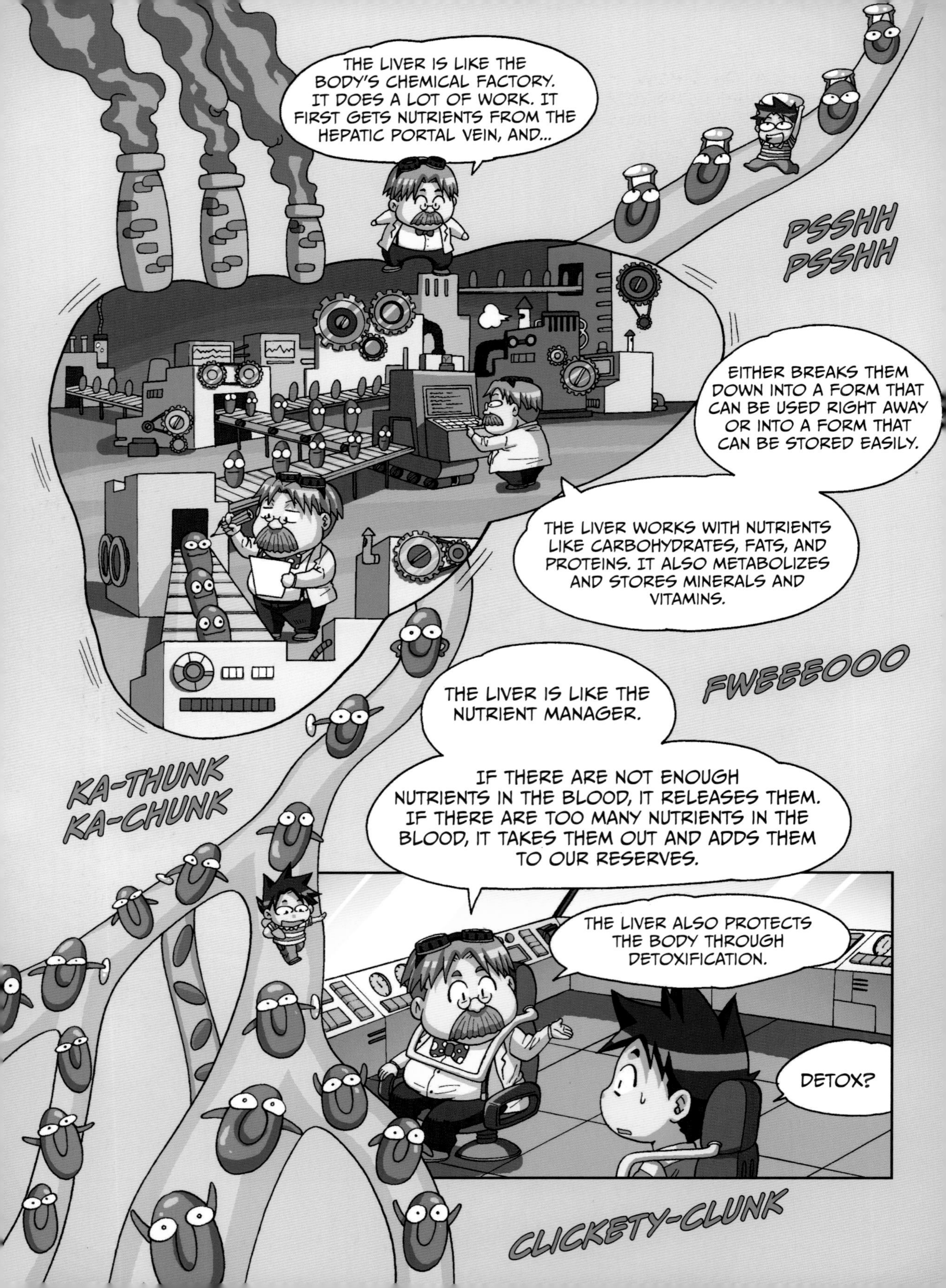
THE LIVER IS LIKE THE BODY'S CHEMICAL FACTORY. IT DOES A LOT OF WORK. IT FIRST GETS NUTRIENTS FROM THE HEPATIC PORTAL VEIN, AND...
PSSHH PSSHH
EITHER BREAKS THEM DOWN INTO A FORM THAT CAN BE USED RIGHT AWAY OR INTO A FORM THAT CAN BE STORED EASILY.
THE LIVER WORKS WITH NUTRIENTS LIKE CARBOHYDRATES, FATS, AND PROTEINS. IT ALSO METABOLIZES AND STORES MINERALS AND VITAMINS.
FWEEEOOO
THE LIVER IS LIKE THE NUTRIENT MANAGER.
IF THERE ARE NOT ENOUGH NUTRIENTS IN THE BLOOD, IT RELEASES THEM. IF THERE ARE TOO MANY NUTRIENTS IN THE BLOOD, IT TAKES THEM OUT AND ADDS THEM TO OUR RESERVES.
KA-THUNK KA-CHUNK
THE LIVER ALSO PROTECTS THE BODY THROUGH DETOXIFICATION.
DETOX?
CLICKETY-CLUNK

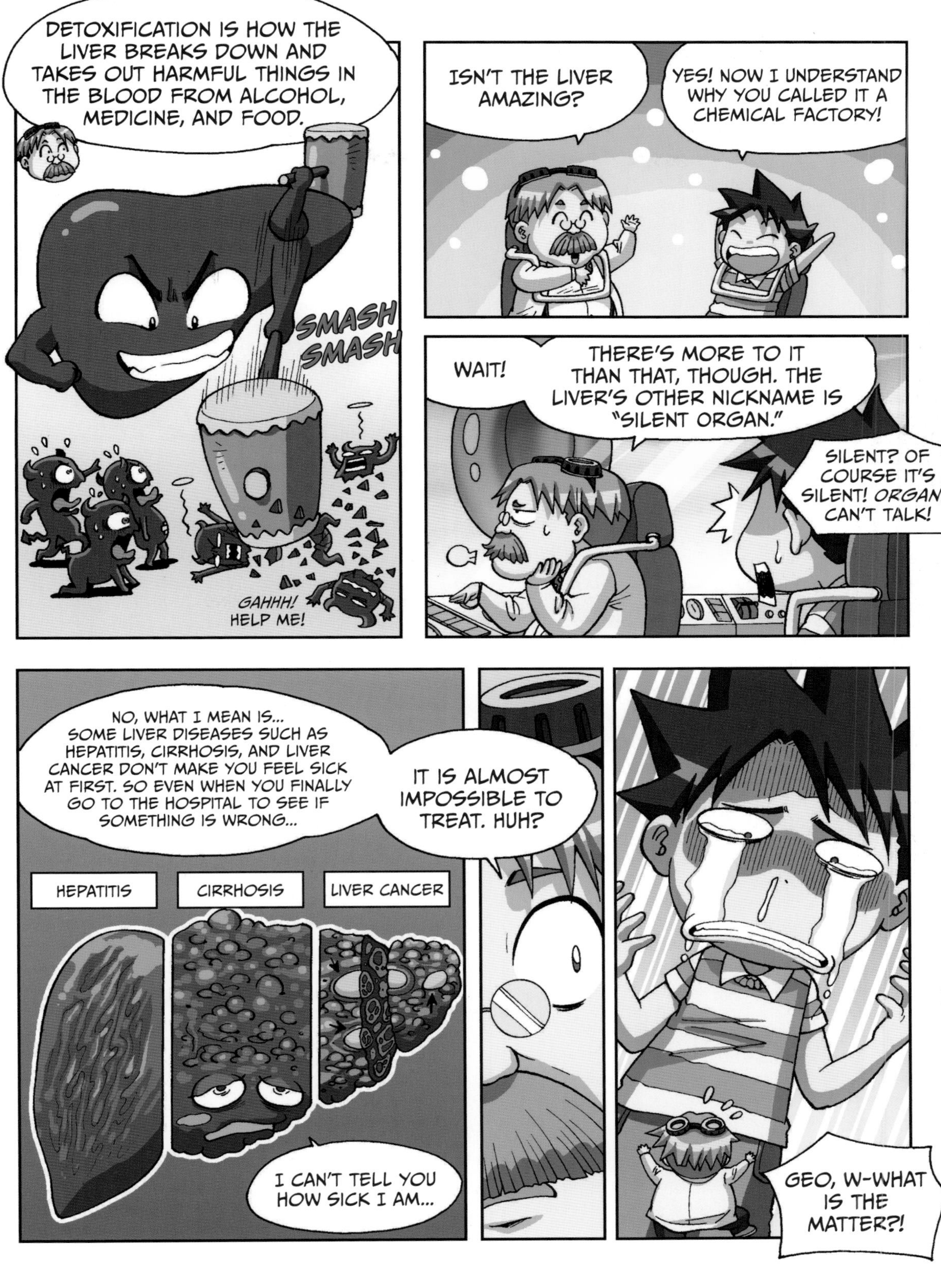
DETOXIFICATION IS HOW THE LIVER BREAKS DOWN AND TAKES OUT HARMFUL THINGS IN THE BLOOD FROM ALCOHOL, MEDICINE, AND FOOD.
SMASH SMASH
GAHHH! HELP ME!
ISN'T THE LIVER AMAZING?
YES! NOW I UNDERSTAND WHY YOU CALLED IT A CHEMICAL FACTORY!
WAIT!
THERE'S MORE TO IT THAN THAT, THOUGH. THE LIVER'S OTHER NICKNAME IS "SILENT ORGAN."
SILENT? OF COURSE IT'S SILENT! ORGANS CAN'T TALK!
NO, WHAT I MEAN IS... SOME LIVER DISEASES SUCH AS HEPATITIS, CIRRHOSIS, AND LIVER CANCER DON'T MAKE YOU FEEL SICK AT FIRST. SO EVEN WHEN YOU FINALLY GO TO THE HOSPITAL TO SEE IF SOMETHING IS WRONG...
IT IS ALMOST IMPOSSIBLE TO TREAT. HUH?
HEPATITIS
CIRRHOSIS
LIVER CANCER
I CAN'T TELL YOU HOW SICK I AM...
GEO, W-WHAT IS THE MATTER?!

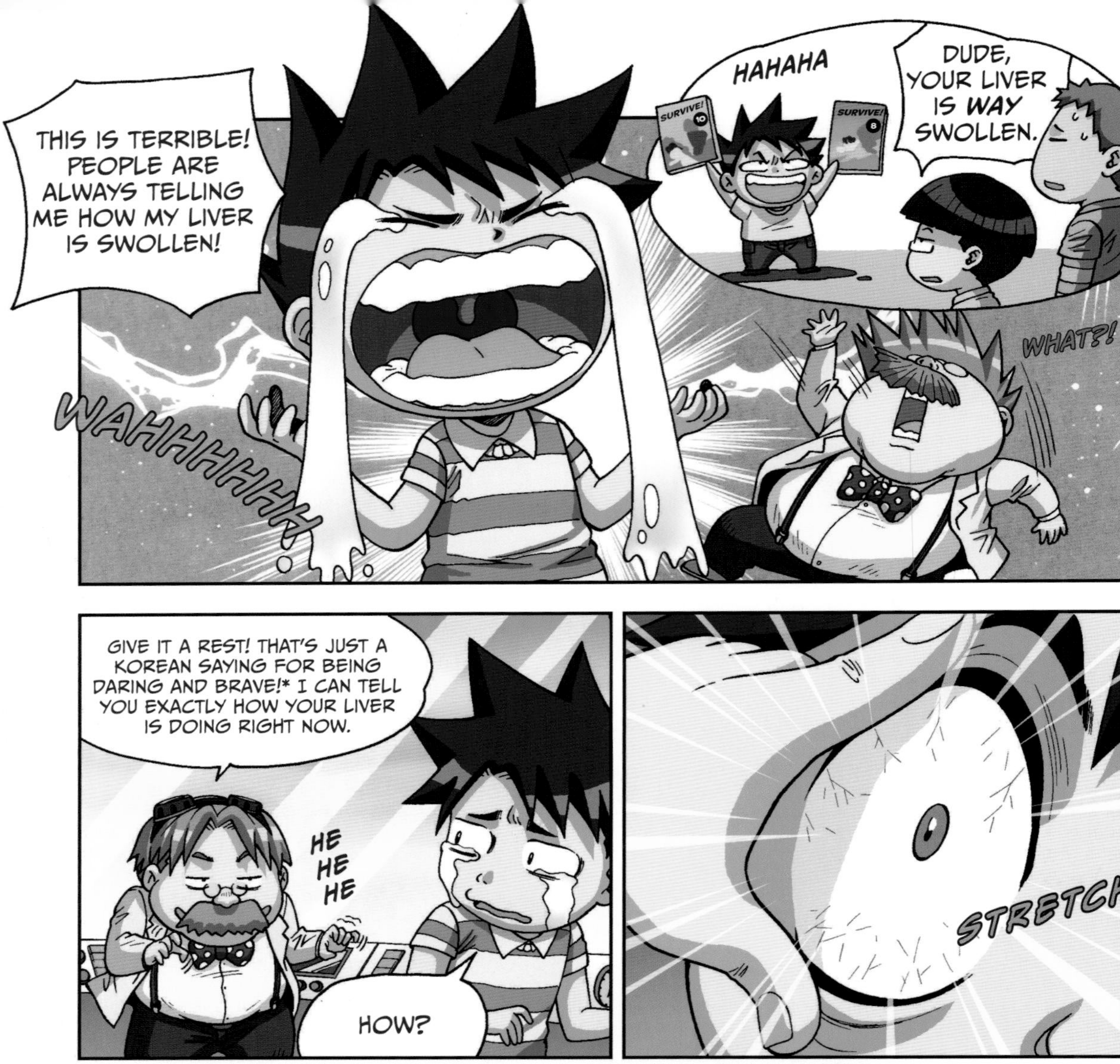
THIS IS TERRIBLE! PEOPLE ARE ALWAYS TELLING ME HOW MY LIVER IS SWOLLEN!
HAHAHA
SURVIVE!
SURVIVE!
DUDE, YOUR LIVER IS **WAY** SWOLLEN.
WAHHHHHHHH
WHAT?!
GIVE IT A REST! THAT'S JUST A KOREAN SAYING FOR BEING DARING AND BRAVE!* I CAN TELL YOU EXACTLY HOW YOUR LIVER IS DOING RIGHT NOW.
HE HE HE
HOW?
STRETCH

* THIS IS A LOT LIKE HOW SOME PEOPLE SAY "LILY-LIVERED" TO MEAN COWARDLY.

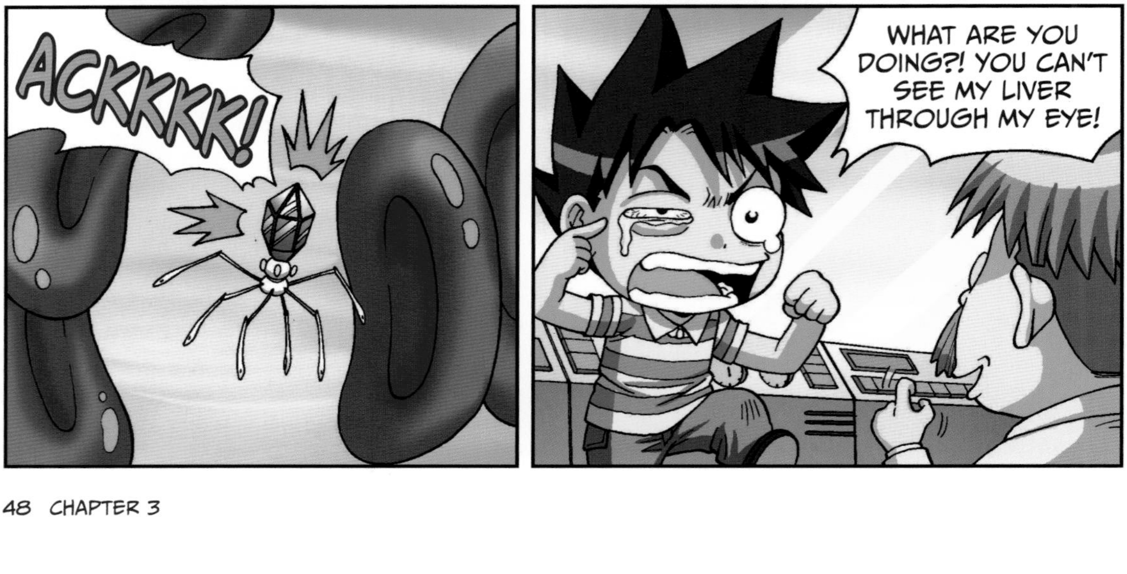
ACKKKK!
WHAT ARE YOU DOING?! YOU CAN'T SEE MY LIVER THROUGH MY EYE!

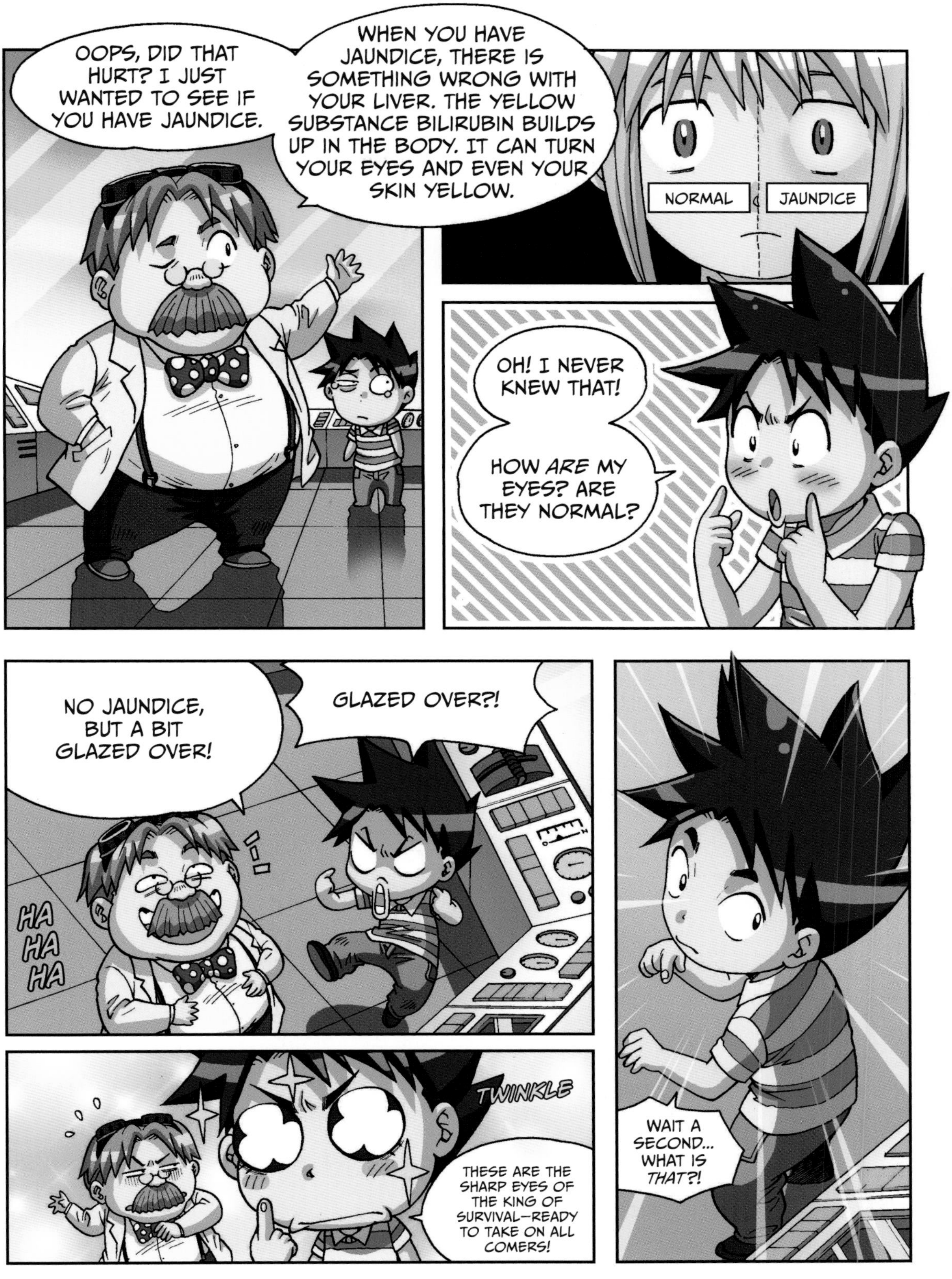
OOPS, DID THAT HURT? I JUST WANTED TO SEE IF YOU HAVE JAUNDICE.
WHEN YOU HAVE JAUNDICE, THERE IS SOMETHING WRONG WITH YOUR LIVER. THE YELLOW SUBSTANCE BILIRUBIN BUILDS UP IN THE BODY. IT CAN TURN YOUR EYES AND EVEN YOUR SKIN YELLOW.
NORMAL
JAUNDICE
OH! I NEVER KNEW THAT!
HOW *ARE* MY EYES? ARE THEY NORMAL?
NO JAUNDICE, BUT A BIT GLAZED OVER!
GLAZED OVER?!
HA HA HA
TWINKLE
THESE ARE THE SHARP EYES OF THE KING OF SURVIVAL—READY TO TAKE ON ALL COMERS!
WAIT A SECOND... WHAT IS *THAT*?!

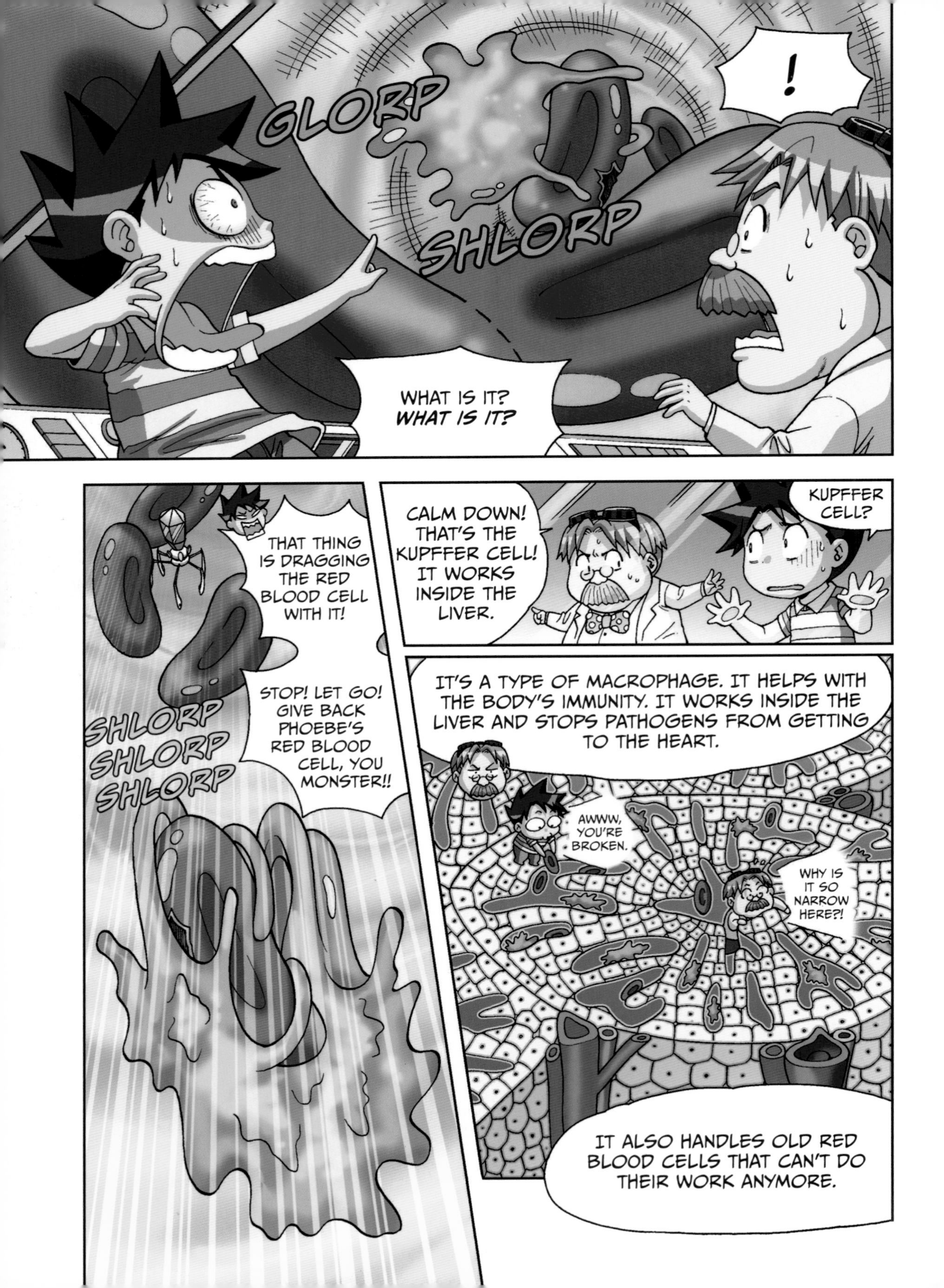
GLORP
SHLORP
!
WHAT IS IT? *WHAT IS IT?*
THAT THING IS DRAGGING THE RED BLOOD CELL WITH IT!
SHLORP SHLORP SHLORP
STOP! LET GO! GIVE BACK PHOEBE'S RED BLOOD CELL, YOU MONSTER!!
CALM DOWN! THAT'S THE KUPFFER CELL! IT WORKS INSIDE THE LIVER.
KUPFFER CELL?
IT'S A TYPE OF MACROPHAGE. IT HELPS WITH THE BODY'S IMMUNITY. IT WORKS INSIDE THE LIVER AND STOPS PATHOGENS FROM GETTING TO THE HEART.
AWWW, YOU'RE BROKEN.
WHY IS IT SO NARROW HERE?!
IT ALSO HANDLES OLD RED BLOOD CELLS THAT CAN'T DO THEIR WORK ANYMORE.

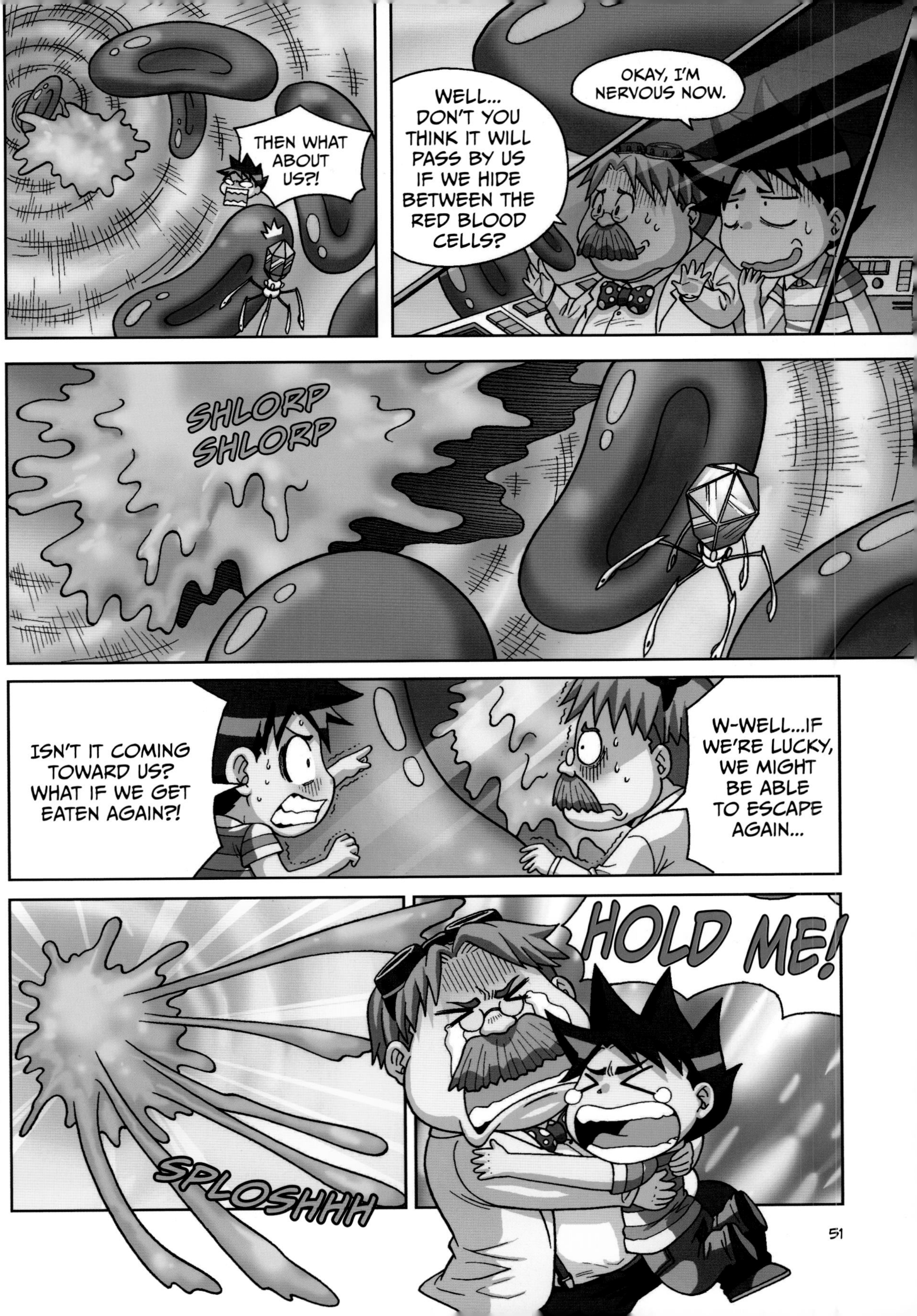
THEN WHAT ABOUT US?!
WELL... DON'T YOU THINK IT WILL PASS BY US IF WE HIDE BETWEEN THE RED BLOOD CELLS?
OKAY, I'M NERVOUS NOW.
SHLORP SHLORP
ISN'T IT COMING TOWARD US? WHAT IF WE GET EATEN AGAIN?!
W-WELL...IF WE'RE LUCKY, WE MIGHT BE ABLE TO ESCAPE AGAIN...
SPLOSHHH
HOLD ME!

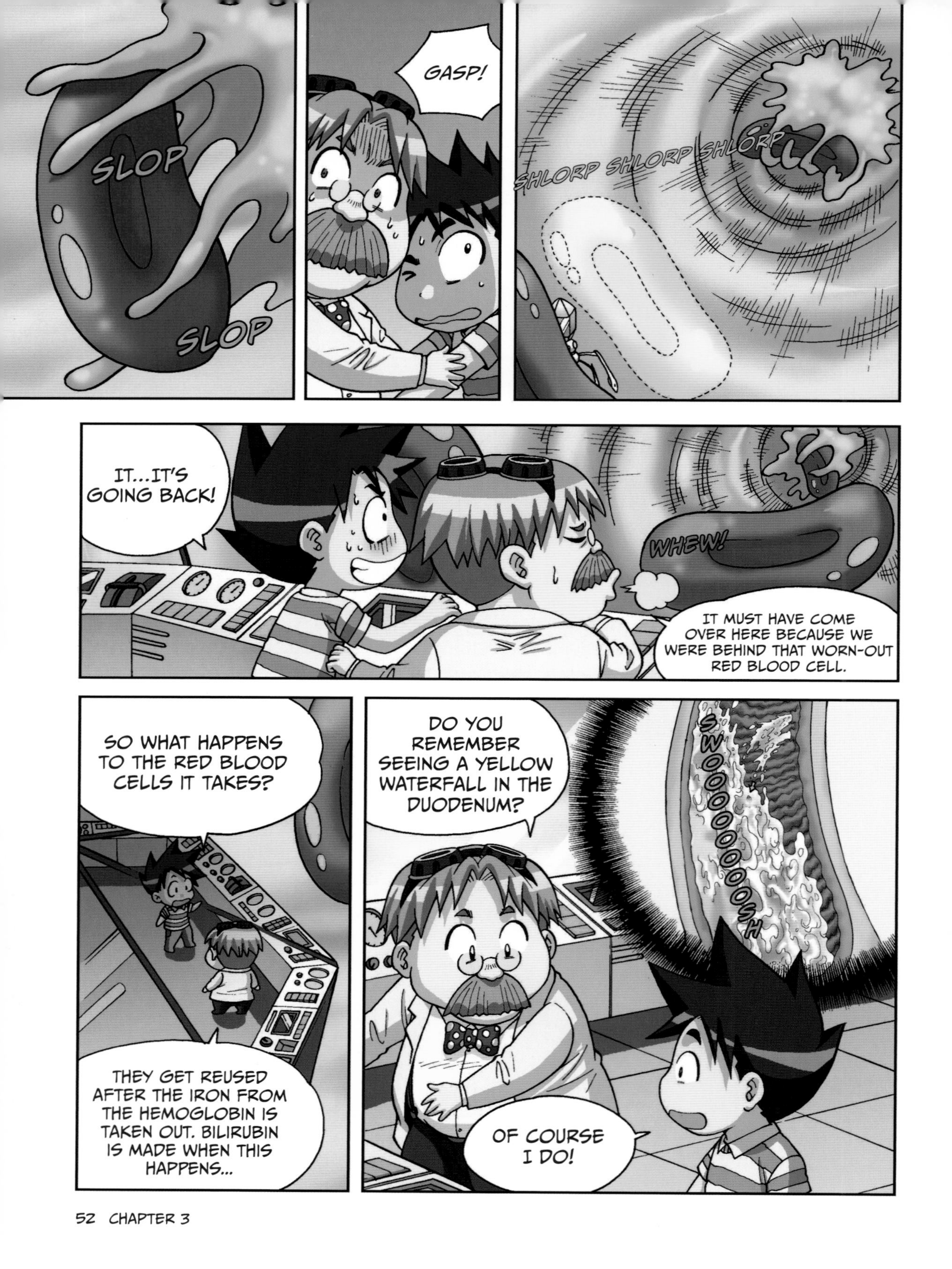
SLOP
SLOP
GASP!
SHLORP SHLORP SHLORP
IT...IT'S GOING BACK!
WHEW!
IT MUST HAVE COME OVER HERE BECAUSE WE WERE BEHIND THAT WORN-OUT RED BLOOD CELL.
SO WHAT HAPPENS TO THE RED BLOOD CELLS IT TAKES?
THEY GET REUSED AFTER THE IRON FROM THE HEMOGLOBIN IS TAKEN OUT. BILIRUBIN IS MADE WHEN THIS HAPPENS...
DO YOU REMEMBER SEEING A YELLOW WATERFALL IN THE DUODENUM?
SWOOOOOOOOSH
OF COURSE I DO!

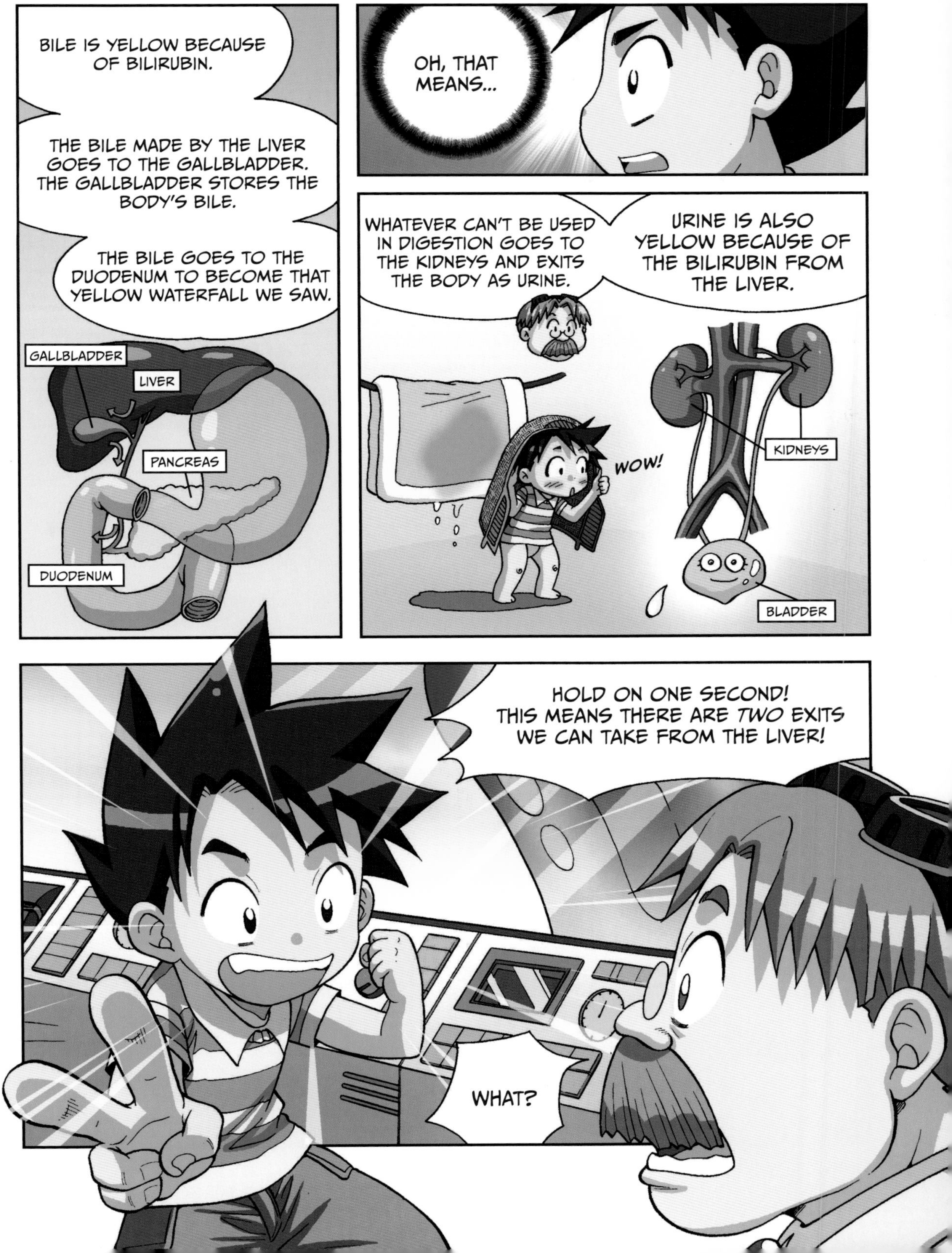

BILE IS YELLOW BECAUSE OF BILIRUBIN.
THE BILE MADE BY THE LIVER GOES TO THE GALLBLADDER. THE GALLBLADDER STORES THE BODY'S BILE.
THE BILE GOES TO THE DUODENUM TO BECOME THAT YELLOW WATERFALL WE SAW.
GALLBLADDER
LIVER
PANCREAS
DUODENUM
OH, THAT MEANS...
WHATEVER CAN'T BE USED IN DIGESTION GOES TO THE KIDNEYS AND EXITS THE BODY AS URINE.
URINE IS ALSO YELLOW BECAUSE OF THE BILIRUBIN FROM THE LIVER.
WOW!
KIDNEYS
BLADDER
HOLD ON ONE SECOND! THIS MEANS THERE ARE *TWO* EXITS WE CAN TAKE FROM THE LIVER!
WHAT?

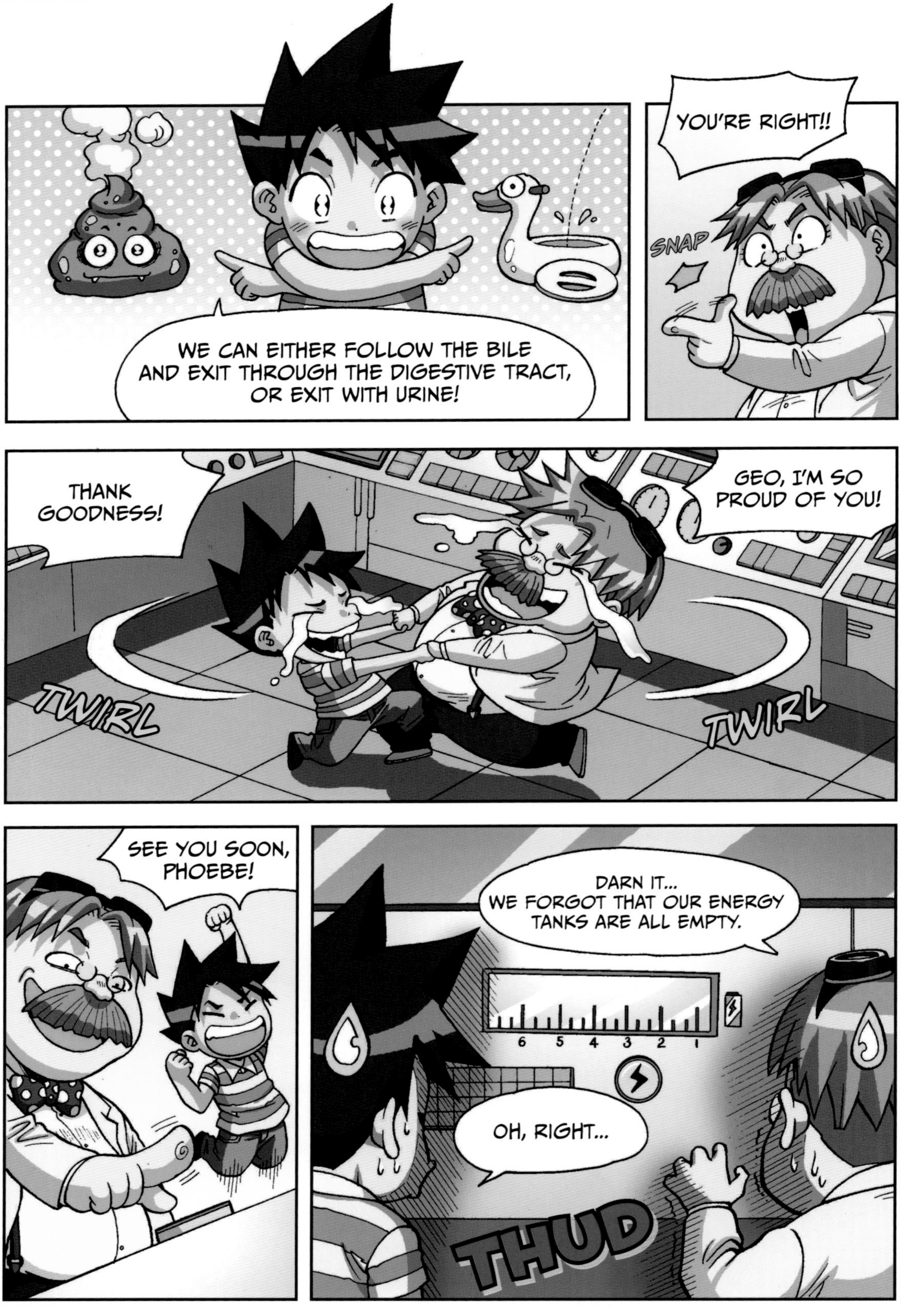
WE CAN EITHER FOLLOW THE BILE AND EXIT THROUGH THE DIGESTIVE TRACT, OR EXIT WITH URINE!
YOU'RE RIGHT!!
SNAP
THANK GOODNESS!
GEO, I'M SO PROUD OF YOU!
TWIRL
TWIRL
SEE YOU SOON, PHOEBE!
DARN IT... WE FORGOT THAT OUR ENERGY TANKS ARE ALL EMPTY.
6 5 4 3 2 1
OH, RIGHT...
THUD

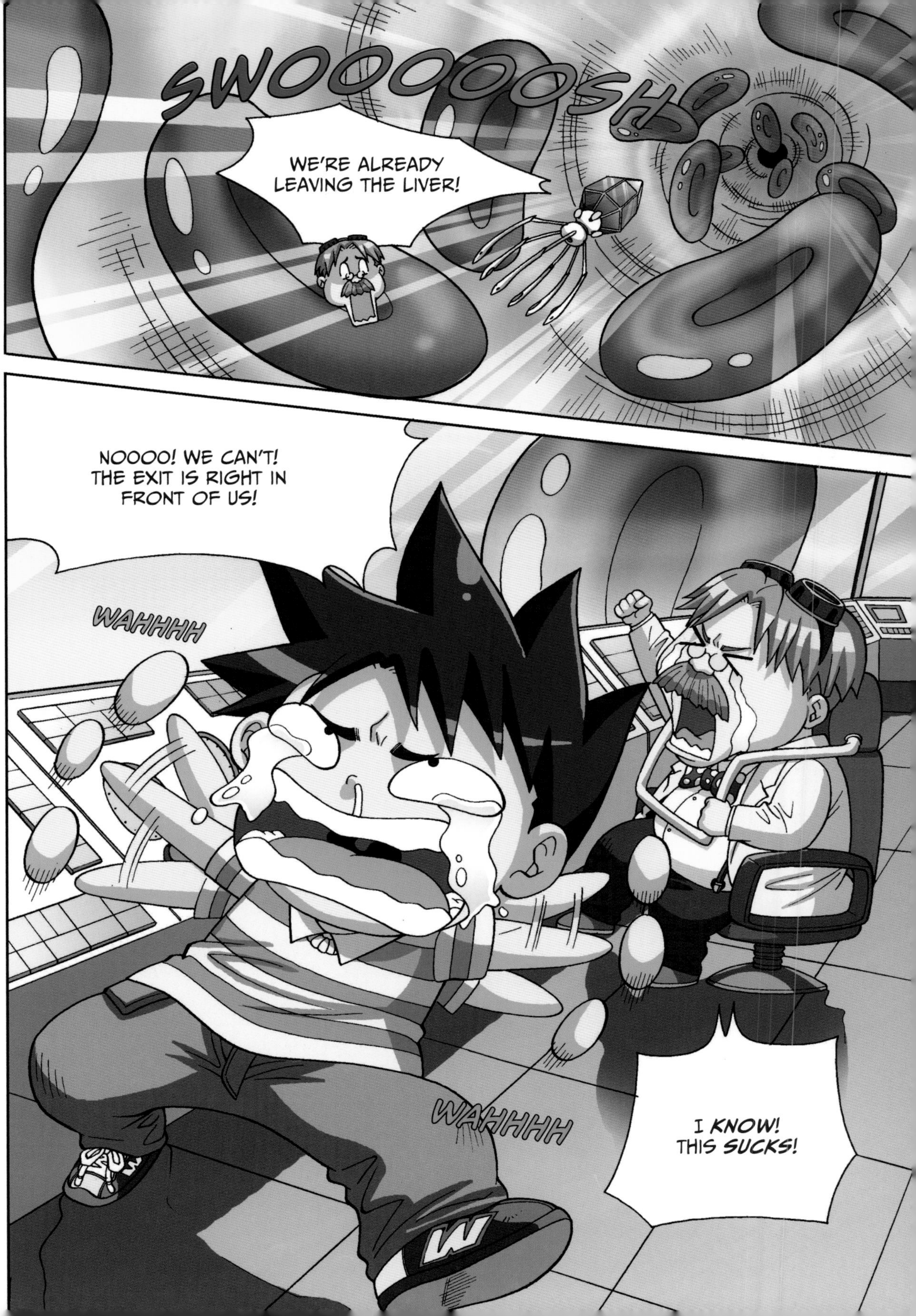
SWOOOOOSH
WE'RE ALREADY LEAVING THE LIVER!
NOOOO! WE CAN'T! THE EXIT IS RIGHT IN FRONT OF US!
WAHHHH
WAHHHH
I KNOW! THIS SUCKS!

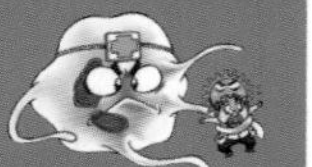

THE LIVER'S MANY JOBS

Although the liver is sometimes said to be part of the digestive system, it has over 500 different jobs in the human body. It uses thousands of enzymes and works with lots of different organs. Your liver is in charge of nutrient metabolism, detoxification, immune system support, hormone management, and many other crucial activities. No wonder Dr. Brain called it the chemical factory.

PROTECTING THE BODY

The human body naturally makes toxins like ammonia as it turns protein into energy. It can get very dangerous when outside toxins like alcohol or drugs are added to this. But the liver breaks down these harmful substances. What's left gets added to urine or bile in order to make sure we stay healthy. Almost everything we eat gets filtered through the liver.

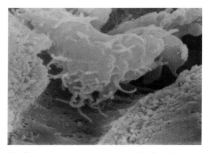

Kupffer cells are macrophages in the liver that eat viruses and break down old red blood cells.

The liver also helps out with the immune system. For example, Kupffer cells, a type of macrophage, eat bacteria.

PRODUCTION AND EXCRETION OF BILE

The liver makes 250–1,000 milliliters of bile a day. Bile is stored in the gall-bladder, which is right below the liver. Bile is mixed with pancreatic juice when food goes through the duodenum. Bile has enzymes that keep the intestine moving. It also breaks down and absorbs fats. An important part of bile is bilirubin. Bilirubin is made through the breakdown of old red blood cells. Yellow in color, it's what makes urine and a healing bruise look yellow. Sometimes, too much bilirubin builds up in the body. That can be a sign of a serious disease, such as some forms of hepatitis (or liver inflammation). It is called *jaundice*, and your skin and eyes can turn yellow.

METABOLISM AND OTHER JOBS

Metabolism stores, breaks down, and synthesizes the nutrients you eat to provide energy for the body. It also gets rid of any substances you don't need. In the human body, the liver plays the central role in metabolism. The liver stores and releases carbohydrates, protein, fat, and vitamins and minerals. It makes sure there is always the right amount of nutrients in the blood. The liver is important for other jobs in the body, too. It helps in hormone management and making materials for blood clotting. The liver is your largest internal organ and also one of the most important! A problem in the liver can hurt the entire body.

NO NUTRIENTS. SEND THEM OUT!
PLENTY OF NUTRIENTS. STORE THEM!

HEPATITIS

The liver comes across a lot of dangerous substances, so it's at high risk for diseases. Lucky for us, it doesn't often get sick and it recovers quickly. But you don't always feel sick when the liver has a disease.

Liver diseases can be divided into two groups. Acute diseases are brief and painful. Chronic diseases happen again and again. Hepatitis (liver inflammation) can start many ways, like with bacteria, viruses, or even toxins. Viral hepatitis is very well known (there are three kinds caused by three different viruses—Hepatitis A, B, and C) and can occur acutely or chronically. People with hepatitis have fevers, fatigue, weight loss, and jaundice.

	Hepatitis A	**Hepatitis B**	**Hepatitis C**
Route of Infection	Contaminated water, food	Blood transfusion, contaminated injection	Blood transfusion, contaminated injection
Liver Cancer Possibility	No	Yes	Yes
Preventive Vaccine	Yes	Yes	No
Medicine	No	Yes	Yes

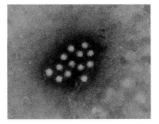

There's no medicine to cure Hepatitis A. Most people get better on their own in 2–6 months. And medications can make you feel better.

YOUR RESTLESS HEART

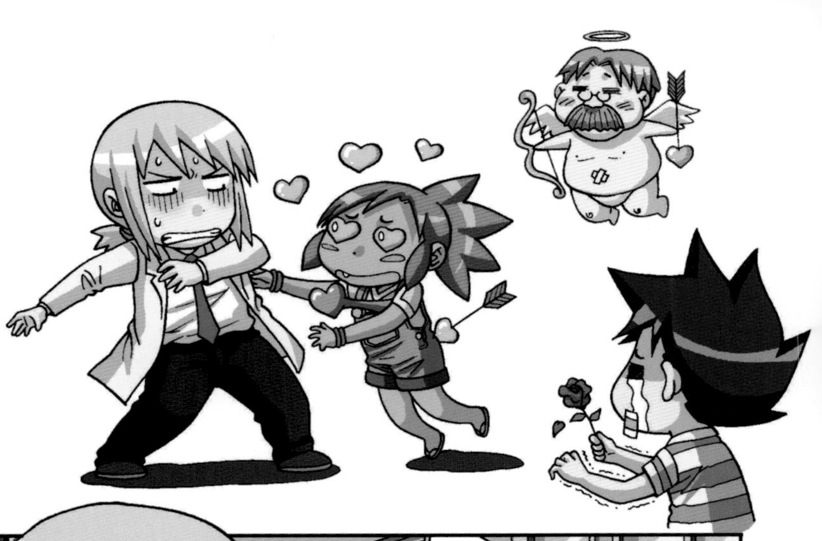

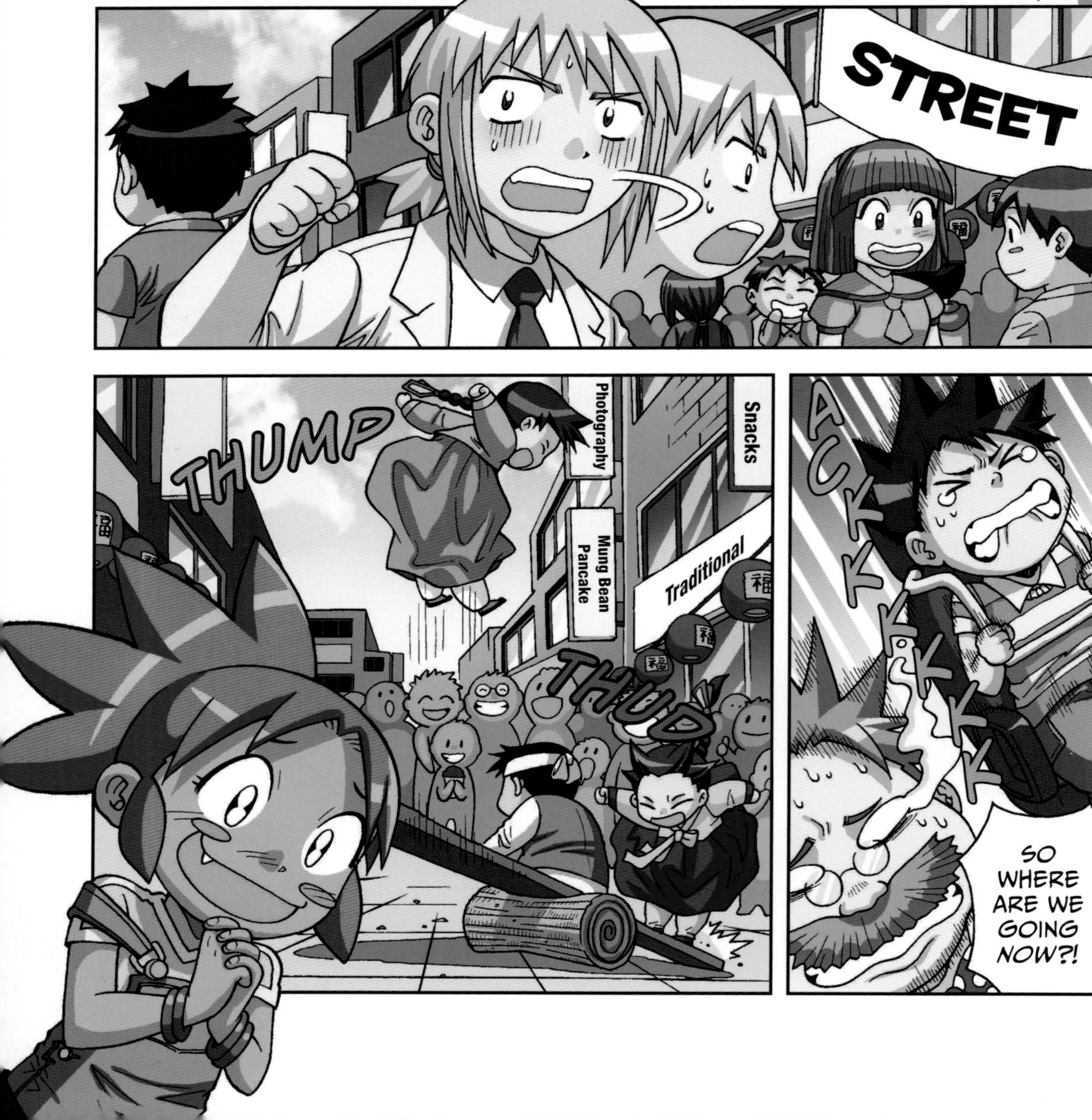
STREET
THUMP
Photography
Snacks
Mung Bean Pancake
Traditional
THUD
ACKKKKKK
SO WHERE ARE WE GOING *NOW?!*

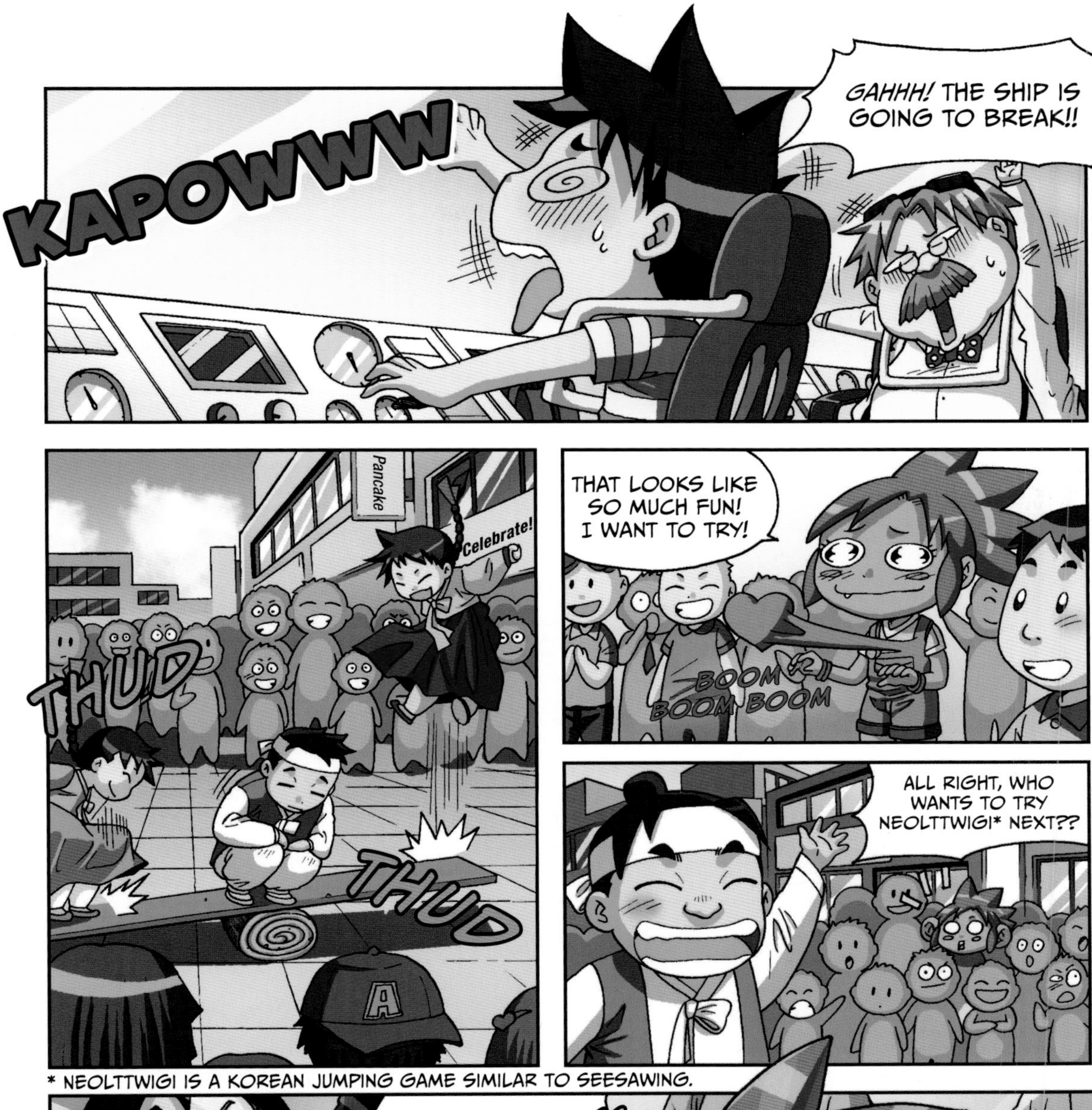
KAPOWWW
GAHHH! THE SHIP IS GOING TO BREAK!!
Pancake
Celebrate!
THUD
THUD
THAT LOOKS LIKE SO MUCH FUN! I WANT TO TRY!
BOOM BOOM BOOM
ALL RIGHT, WHO WANTS TO TRY NEOLTTWIGI* NEXT??

* NEOLTTWIGI IS A KOREAN JUMPING GAME SIMILAR TO SEESAWING.

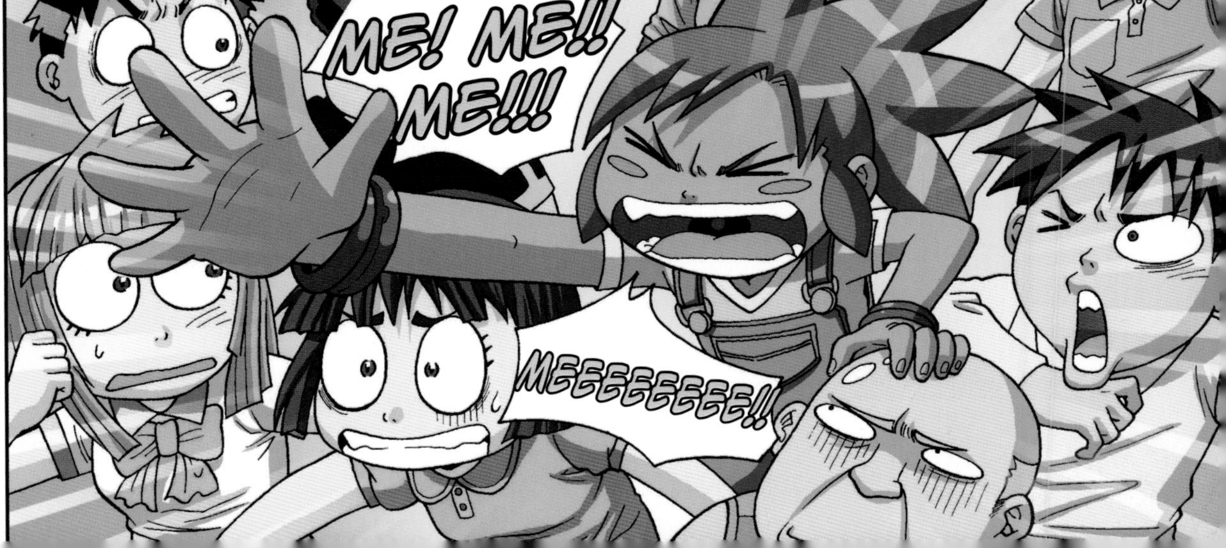
ME! ME!! ME!!!
MEEEEEEEEE!!

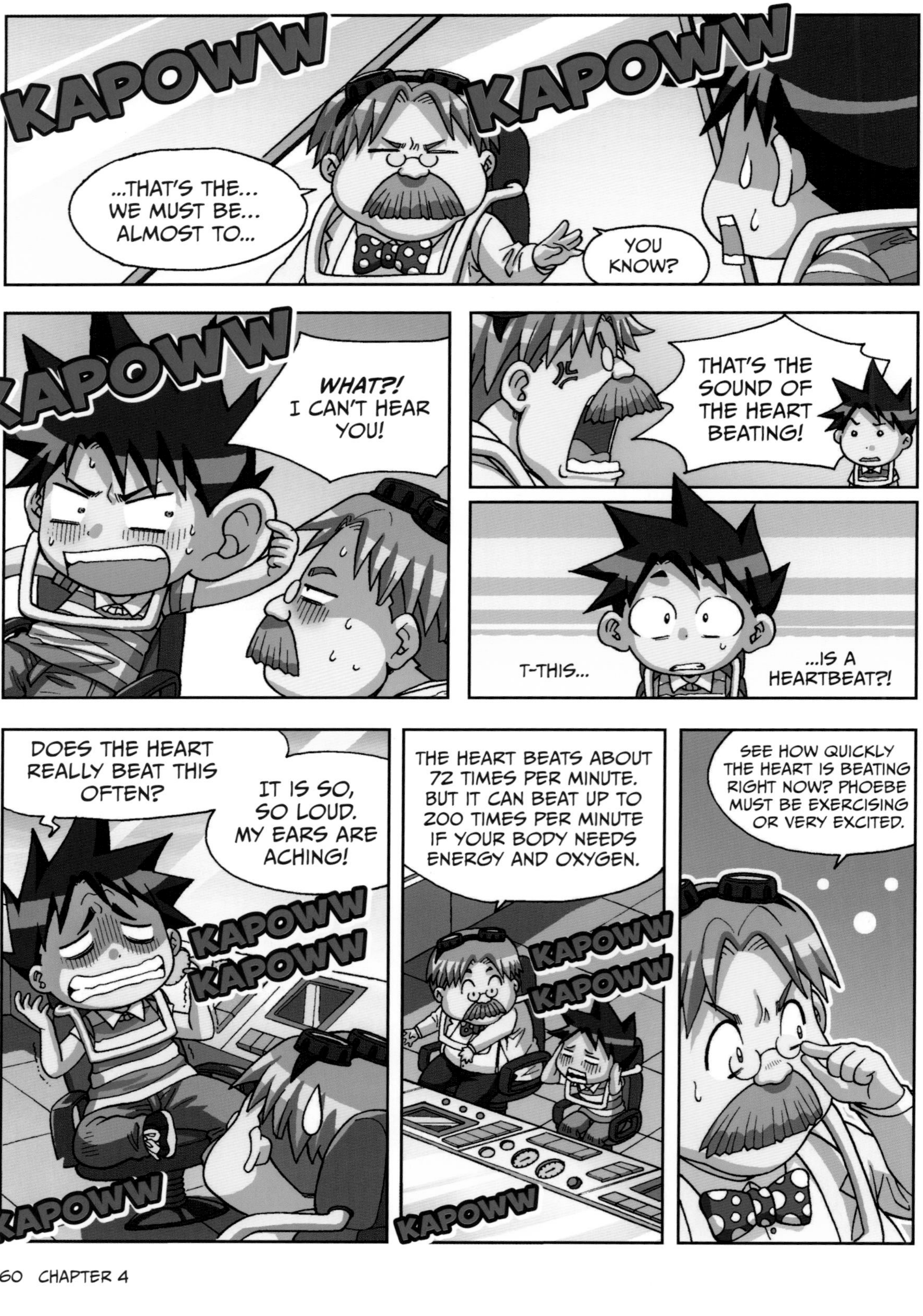
KAPOWW
KAPOWW
...THAT'S THE... WE MUST BE... ALMOST TO...
YOU KNOW?
KAPOWW
WHAT?! I CAN'T HEAR YOU!
THAT'S THE SOUND OF THE HEART BEATING!
T-THIS...
...IS A HEARTBEAT?!
DOES THE HEART REALLY BEAT THIS OFTEN?
IT IS SO, SO LOUD. MY EARS ARE ACHING!
KAPOWW
KAPOWW
KAPOWW
THE HEART BEATS ABOUT 72 TIMES PER MINUTE. BUT IT CAN BEAT UP TO 200 TIMES PER MINUTE IF YOUR BODY NEEDS ENERGY AND OXYGEN.
KAPOWW
KAPOWW
KAPOWW
SEE HOW QUICKLY THE HEART IS BEATING RIGHT NOW? PHOEBE MUST BE EXERCISING OR VERY EXCITED.

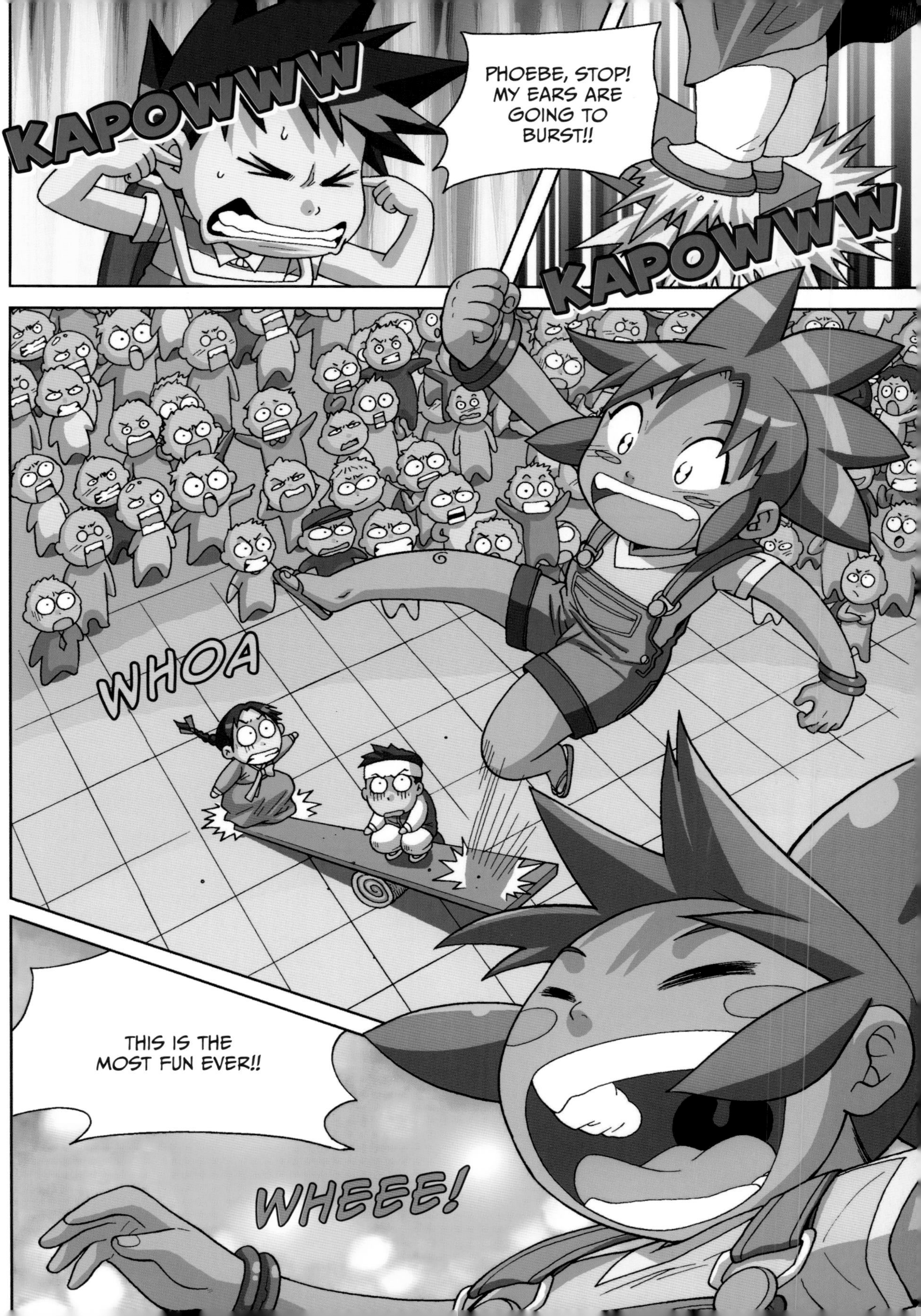
KAPOWWW
PHOEBE, STOP! MY EARS ARE GOING TO BURST!!
KAPOWWW
WHOA
THIS IS THE MOST FUN EVER!!
WHEEEE!

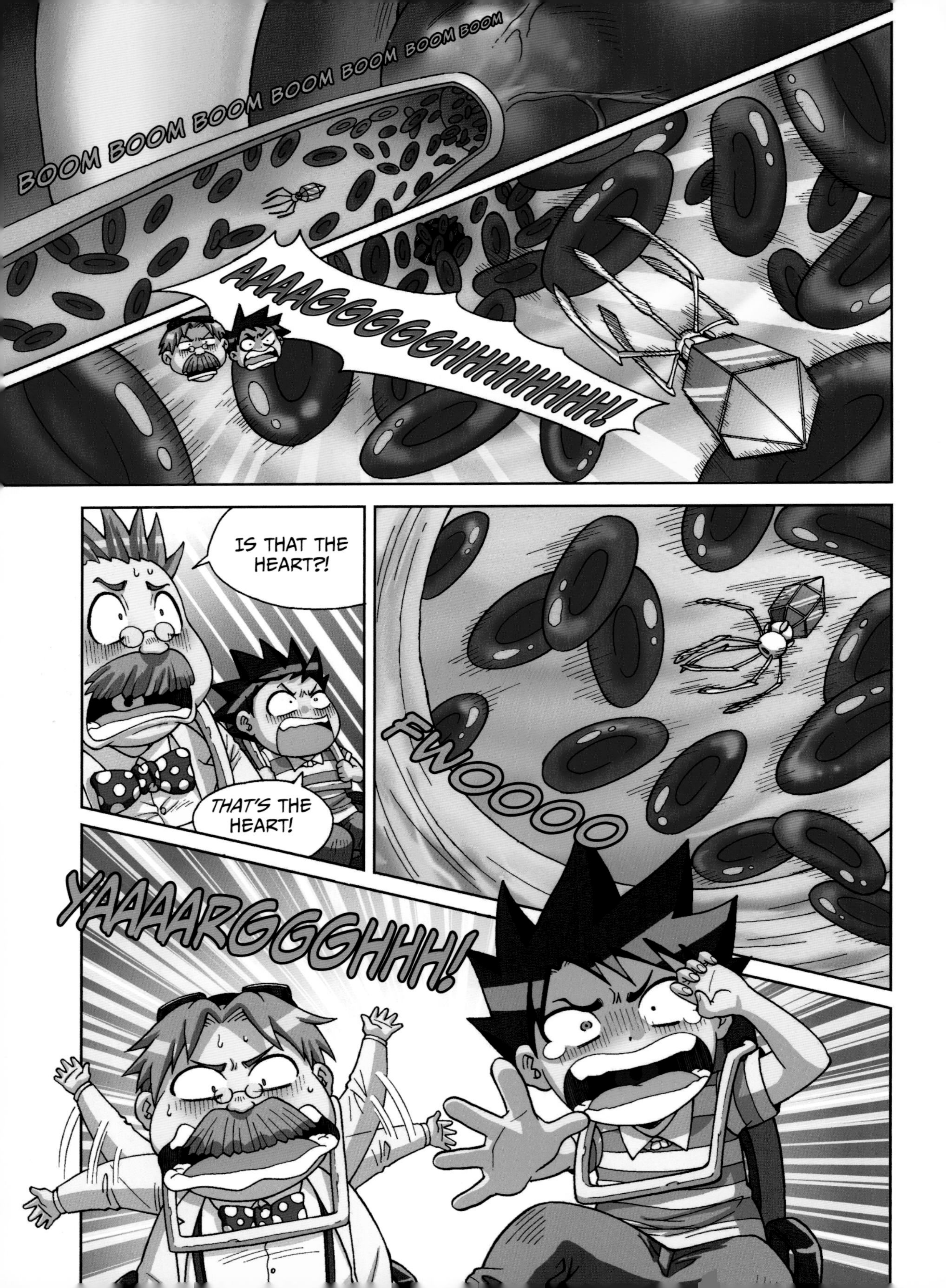
BOOM BOOM BOOM BOOM BOOM BOOM BOOM
AAAAGGGGGGHHHHHHHH!
IS THAT THE HEART?!
THAT'S THE HEART!
FWOOOOO
YAAAARGGGHHH!

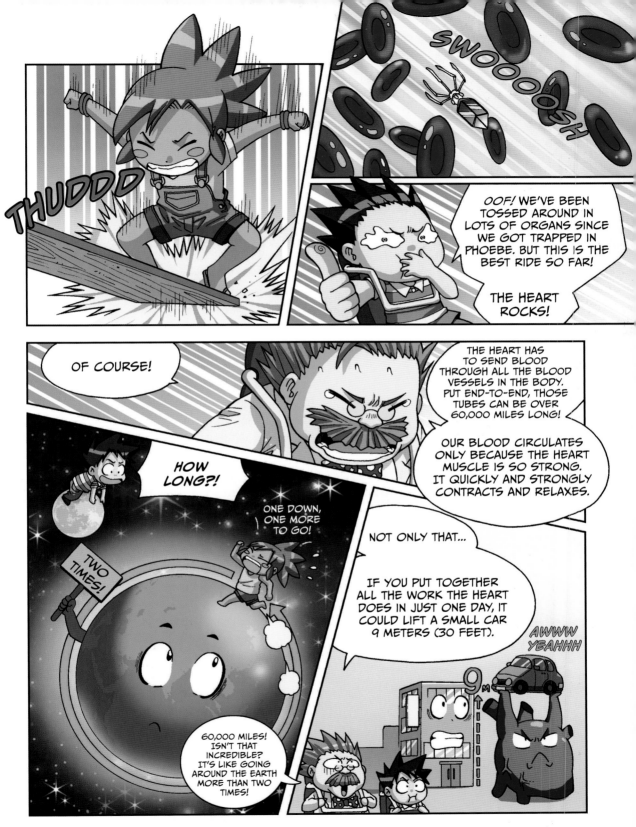

SWOOOOSH

THUDDD

OOF! WE'VE BEEN TOSSED AROUND IN LOTS OF ORGANS SINCE WE GOT TRAPPED IN PHOEBE. BUT THIS IS THE BEST RIDE SO FAR!

THE HEART ROCKS!

OF COURSE!

THE HEART HAS TO SEND BLOOD THROUGH ALL THE BLOOD VESSELS IN THE BODY. PUT END-TO-END, THOSE TUBES CAN BE OVER 60,000 MILES LONG!

OUR BLOOD CIRCULATES ONLY BECAUSE THE HEART MUSCLE IS SO STRONG. IT QUICKLY AND STRONGLY CONTRACTS AND RELAXES.

HOW LONG?!

ONE DOWN, ONE MORE TO GO!

TWO TIMES!

NOT ONLY THAT...

IF YOU PUT TOGETHER ALL THE WORK THE HEART DOES IN JUST ONE DAY, IT COULD LIFT A SMALL CAR 9 METERS (30 FEET).

AWWW YEAHHH

9m

60,000 MILES! ISN'T THAT INCREDIBLE? IT'S LIKE GOING AROUND THE EARTH MORE THAN TWO TIMES!

SWOOOOOOSH
KAPOWW
TINK
TUNK
TONK
SAVE US!!!

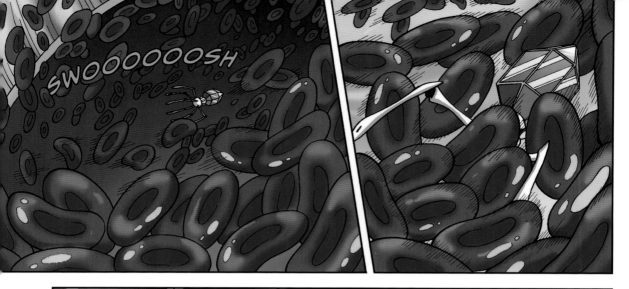

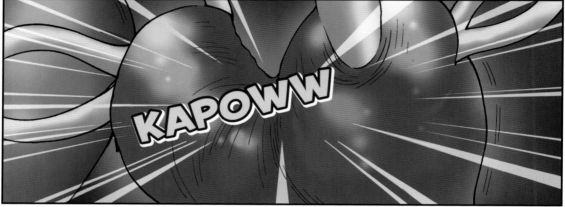

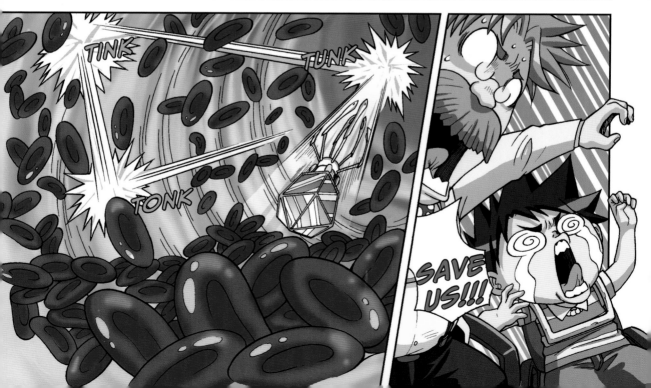

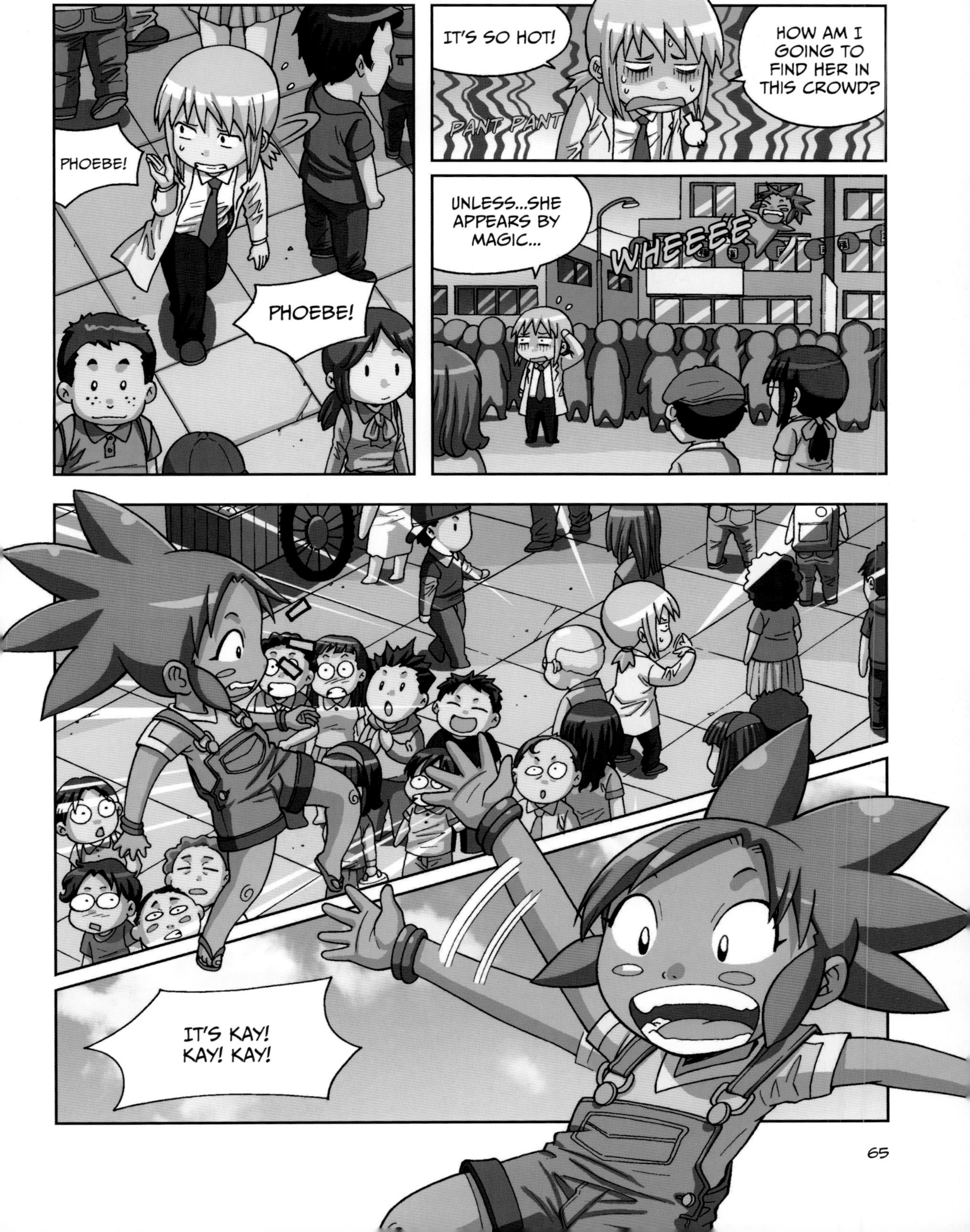
PHOEBE!
PHOEBE!
IT'S SO HOT!
HOW AM I GOING TO FIND HER IN THIS CROWD?
PANT PANT
UNLESS...SHE APPEARS BY MAGIC...
WHEEEE
IT'S KAY! KAY! KAY!

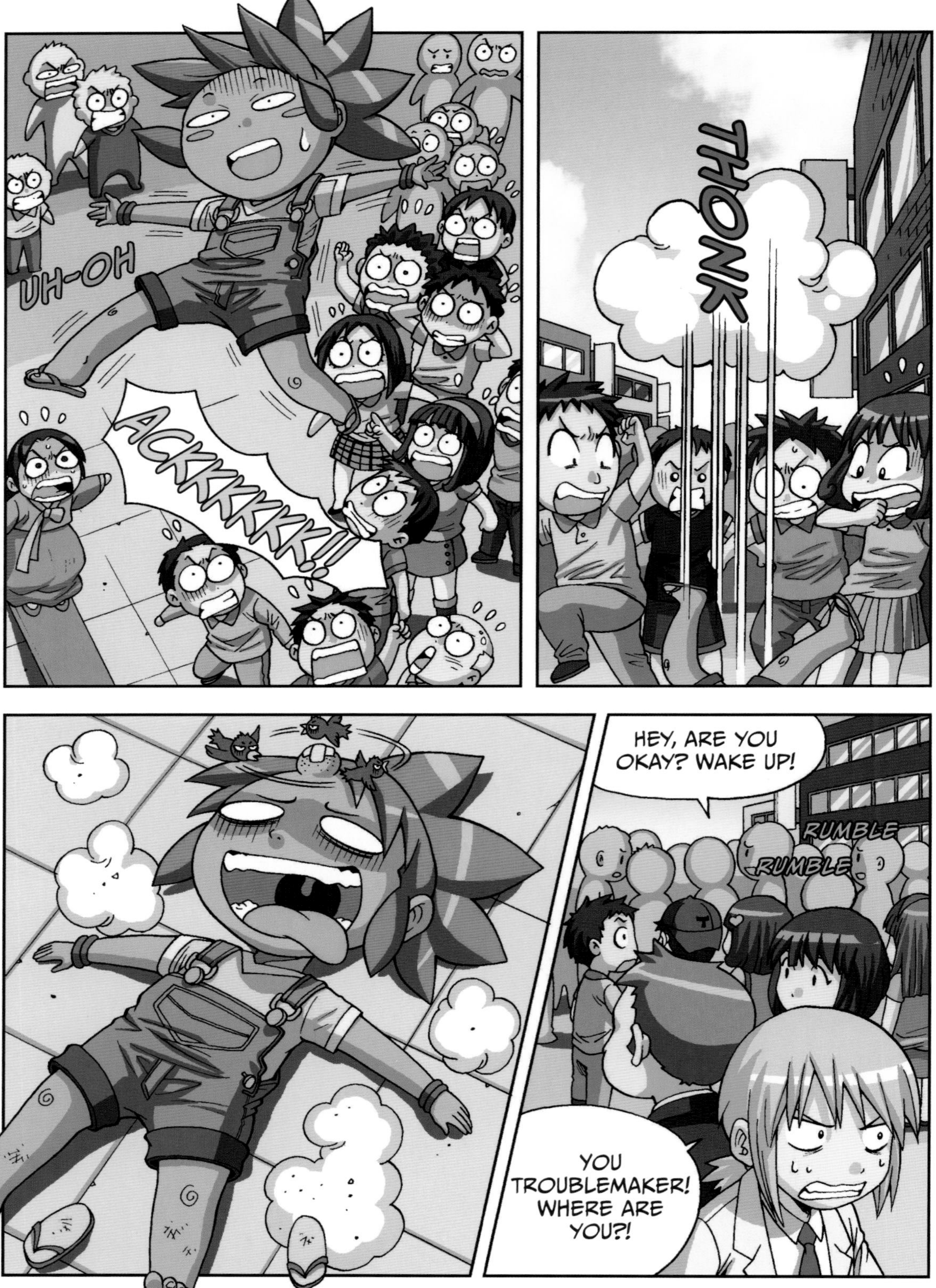
UH-OH
ACKKKKKK!!
THONK
HEY, ARE YOU OKAY? WAKE UP!
RUMBLE
RUMBLE
YOU TROUBLEMAKER! WHERE ARE YOU?!

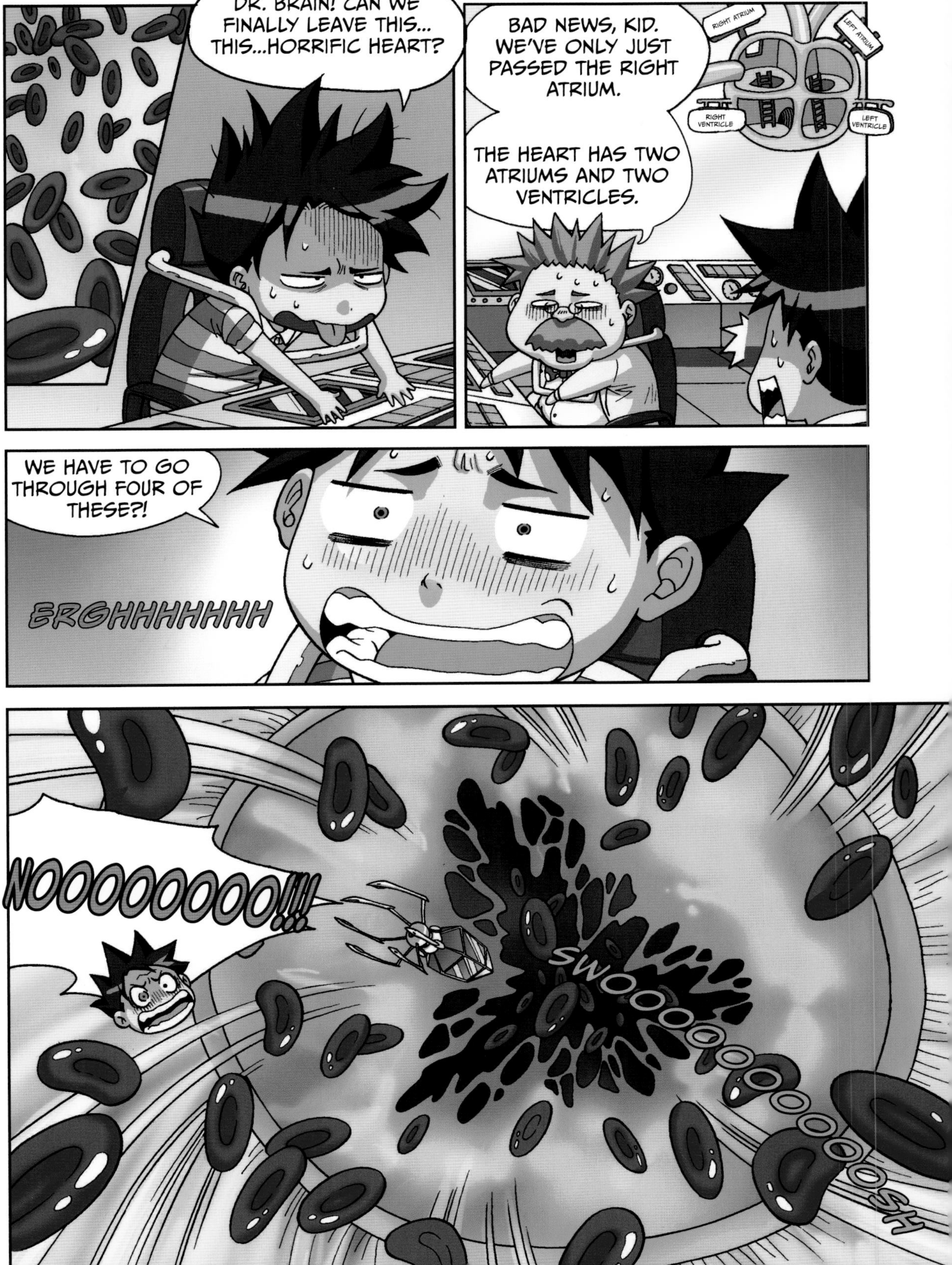
DR. BRAIN! CAN WE FINALLY LEAVE THIS... THIS...HORRIFIC HEART?
BAD NEWS, KID. WE'VE ONLY JUST PASSED THE RIGHT ATRIUM.
THE HEART HAS TWO ATRIUMS AND TWO VENTRICLES.
RIGHT ATRIUM
LEFT ATRIUM
RIGHT VENTRICLE
LEFT VENTRICLE
WE HAVE TO GO THROUGH FOUR OF THESE?!
ERGHHHHHHH
NOOOOOOOO!!!
SWOOOOOOOOOOOOOSH

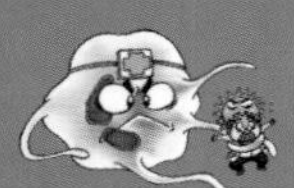

CIRCULATORY
SYSTEM

YOUR SUPER POWERFUL HEART!

The heart beats about 72 times a minute. That's 100,000 times a day! It sends 5 liters of blood throughout the entire body. The heart of a 70-year-old person has beat 2.6 billion times and circulated 180 million liters of blood! So what is the secret behind your endlessly beating heart?

HOW YOUR HEART BEATS

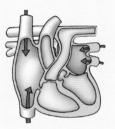
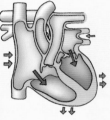
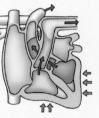

❶ Blood that has already circulated the body enters the right atrium. Oxygen-rich blood from the lungs enters the left atrium.

❷ When the ventricle expands and the atrium contracts, blood enters the ventricle through the open valves.

❸ When the ventricle contracts, the blood from the right ventricle goes through the artery to the lungs. Blood from the left ventricle goes through the whole body.

THE HEART'S AUTOMATIC TIMER

You can't make your heart stop, slow down, or beat faster just by thinking about it. The heart beats on its own with its own electrical rhythm because it has pacemaker cells. They control how fast the heart beats, which is called the *heart rate*.

In the right atrium, the sinoatrial node sends electrical signals to the rest of the heart. It's this node's job to keep the heartbeat steady.

The autonomic nervous system helps control the heartbeat, too. The autonomic nervous system makes adrenaline when we get excited or angry, which makes the heart beat faster. Exercise also increases your heart rate. When we rest, acetylcholine is secreted to slow down the heart rate.

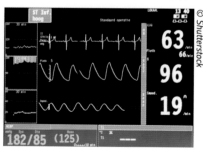
© Shutterstock

The electrocardiogram measures the electrical signals that the nodes make. This provides important information about a person's heart and heartbeat.

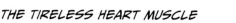

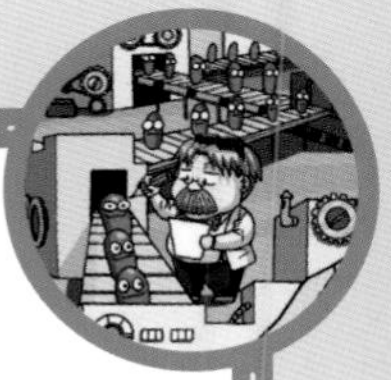

THE TIRELESS HEART MUSCLE

Could you bend your arms or legs 100,000 times in one day? Even professional athletes can't do that.

The heart can. It doesn't tire out because it is such a strong muscle. The heart muscle has the advantage of both striated muscles that are quick and strong (like those that move our arms and legs) and smooth muscles, which keep the internal organs moving all the time. The short moment of rest the heart gets between each heartbeat is all it needs to recover.

I STOP, I DIE!
KEEP RUNNING, BABY!

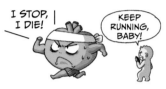

EVOLUTION OF THE HEART IN VERTEBRATES

If you look at the hearts of vertebrates (animals with backbones), you can see that over time bodies have learned how to use oxygen in better and better ways.

A fish, the first of the vertebrates, has a heart with one ventricle and one atrium. There is no difference between arteries and veins, which is very inefficient.

Amphibians have a heart with two atriums and one ventricle. Oxygen-deficient venous blood and oxygen-rich arterial blood enter a frog's heart separately, but when they exit the heart, the two mix together and cause a drop in the overall oxygen level in the blood that circulates the body.

Reptiles have two atriums and two incomplete ventricles. In other words, there is a passage between the two ventricles. Blood from the veins and arteries is mixed a little when the blood leaves the heart.

Lastly, birds and mammals have two atriums and two ventricles. They are totally separated. The blood going to the lungs and to the body doesn't mix at all, so blood with the most oxygen flows throughout the body.

LUNGS
HEART
BODY
OXYGEN-RICH ARTERIAL BLOOD
OXYGEN-DEFICIENT VENOUS BLOOD
MIX OF ARTERIAL BLOOD AND VENOUS BLOOD
AMPHIBIANS (2 ATRIUMS, 1 VENTRICLE)
REPTILES (2 ATRIUMS, 2 INCOMPLETE VENTRICLES)
MAMMALS (2 ATRIUMS, 2 VENTRICLES)

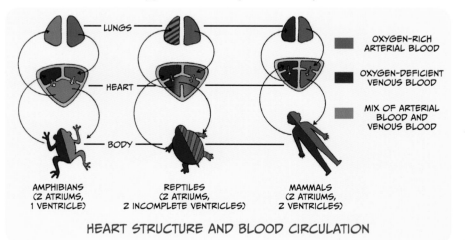

HEART STRUCTURE AND BLOOD CIRCULATION

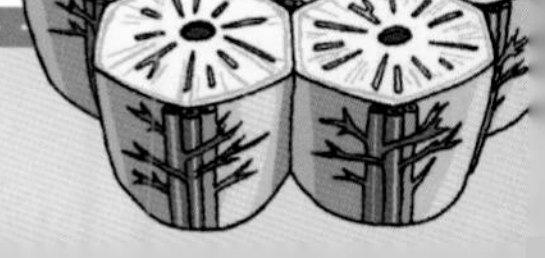

RESPIRATORY ARREST

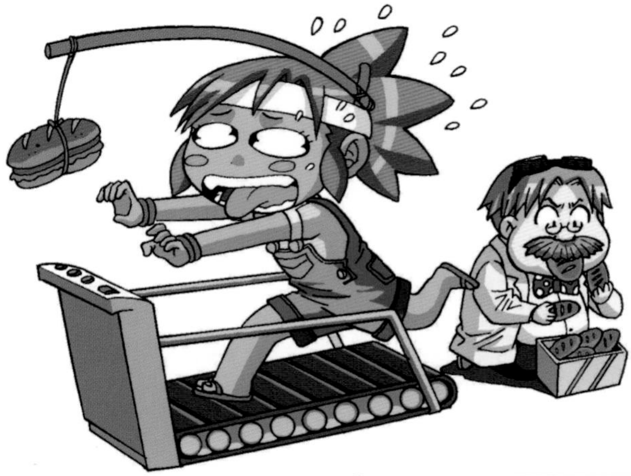

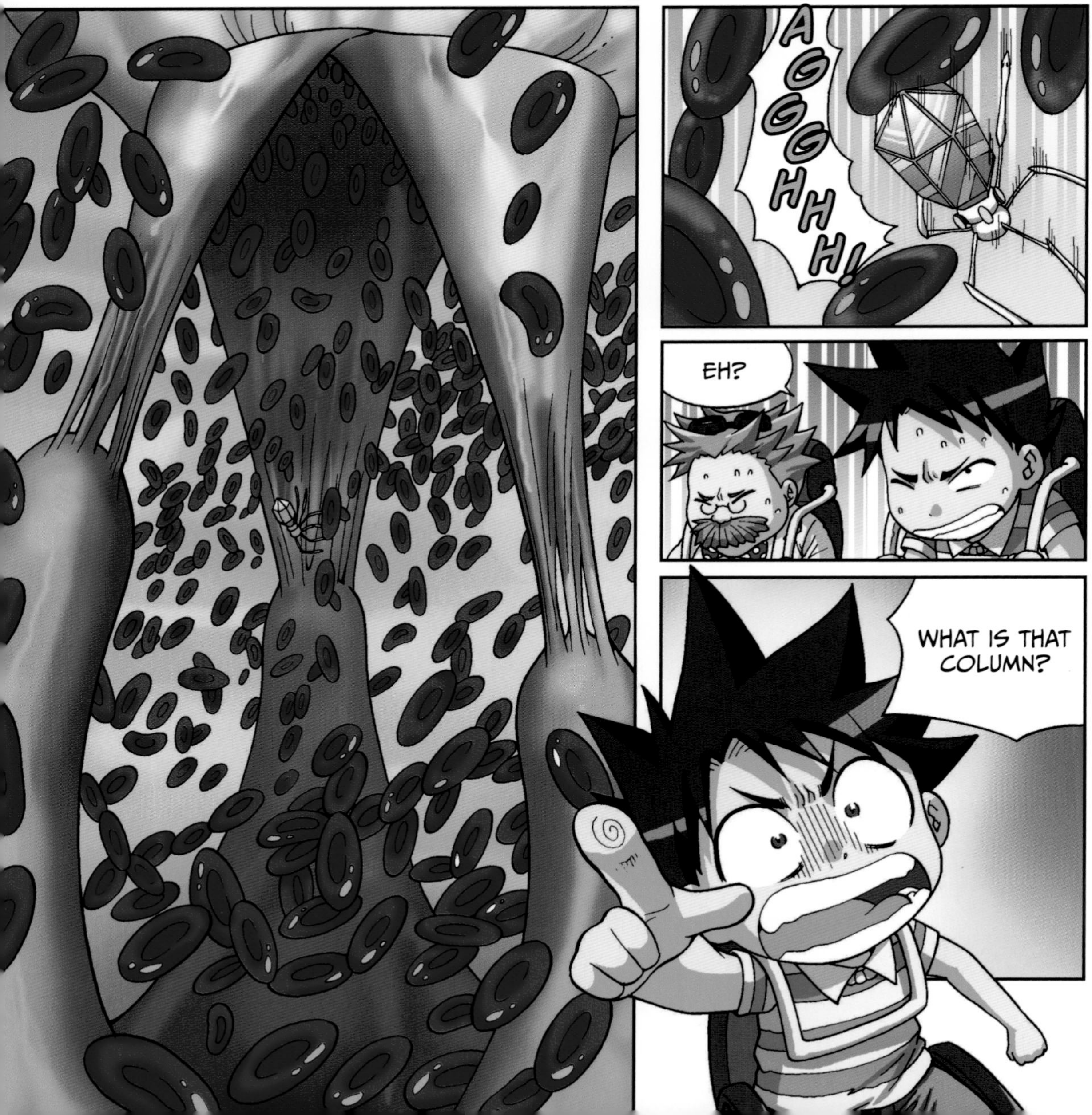

AGGGHHH!
EH?
WHAT IS THAT COLUMN?

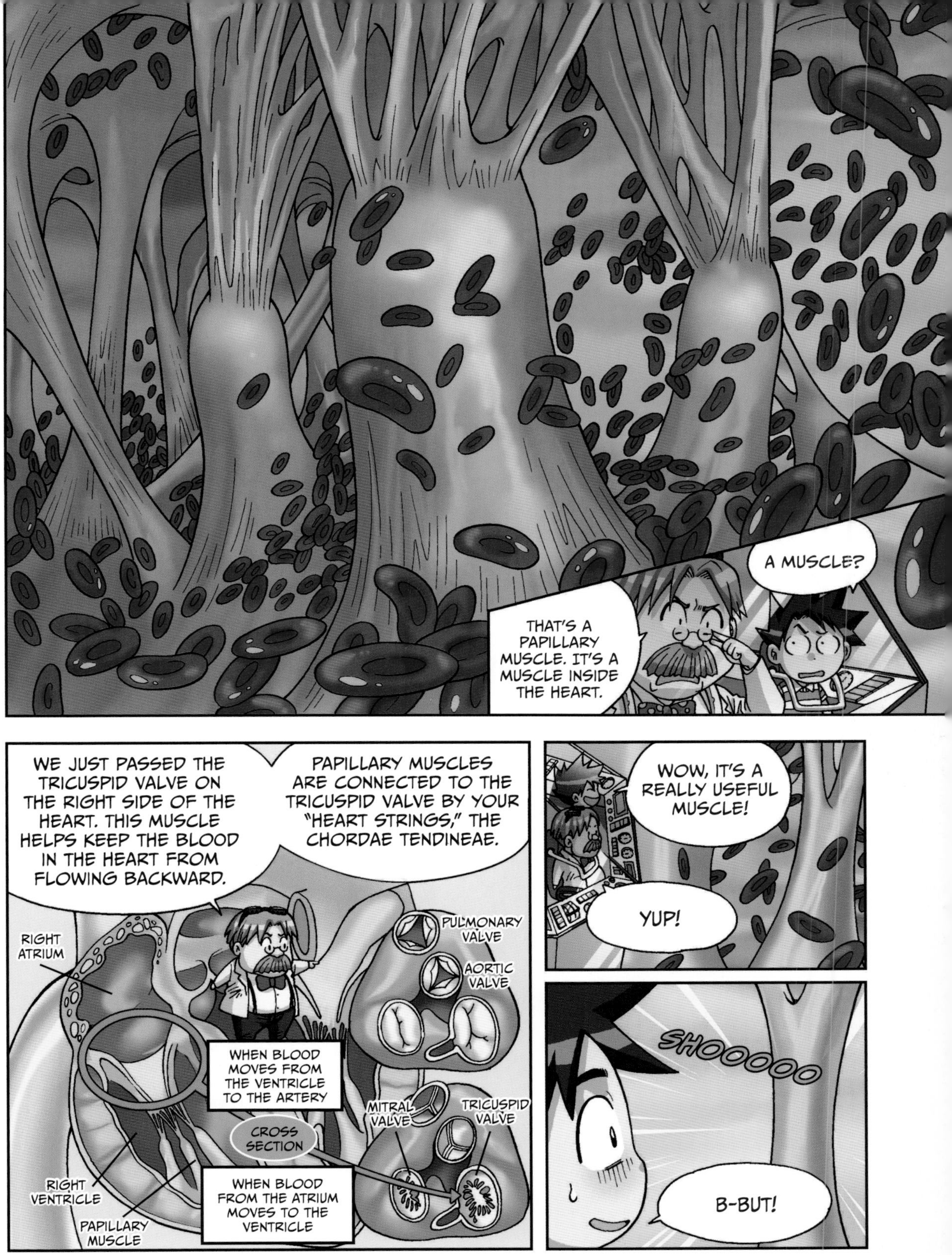
A MUSCLE?
THAT'S A PAPILLARY MUSCLE. IT'S A MUSCLE INSIDE THE HEART.
WE JUST PASSED THE TRICUSPID VALVE ON THE RIGHT SIDE OF THE HEART. THIS MUSCLE HELPS KEEP THE BLOOD IN THE HEART FROM FLOWING BACKWARD.
PAPILLARY MUSCLES ARE CONNECTED TO THE TRICUSPID VALVE BY YOUR "HEART STRINGS," THE CHORDAE TENDINEAE.
RIGHT ATRIUM
PULMONARY VALVE
AORTIC VALVE
WHEN BLOOD MOVES FROM THE VENTRICLE TO THE ARTERY
MITRAL VALVE
TRICUSPID VALVE
CROSS SECTION
RIGHT VENTRICLE
PAPILLARY MUSCLE
WHEN BLOOD FROM THE ATRIUM MOVES TO THE VENTRICLE
WOW, IT'S A REALLY USEFUL MUSCLE!
YUP!
SHOOOOOO
B-BUT!

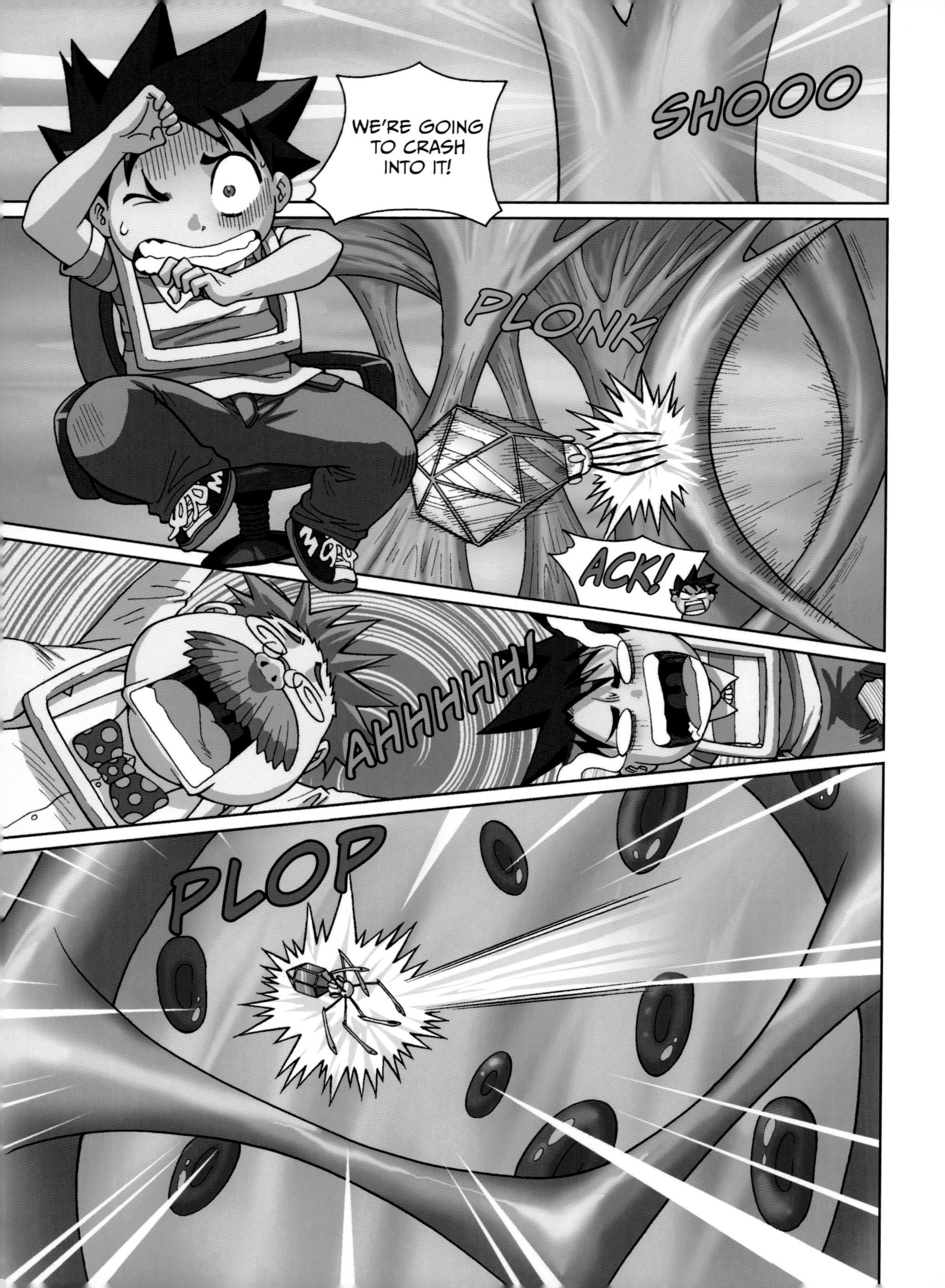
WE'RE GOING TO CRASH INTO IT!
SHOOO
PLONK
ACK!
AHHHHHH!
PLOP

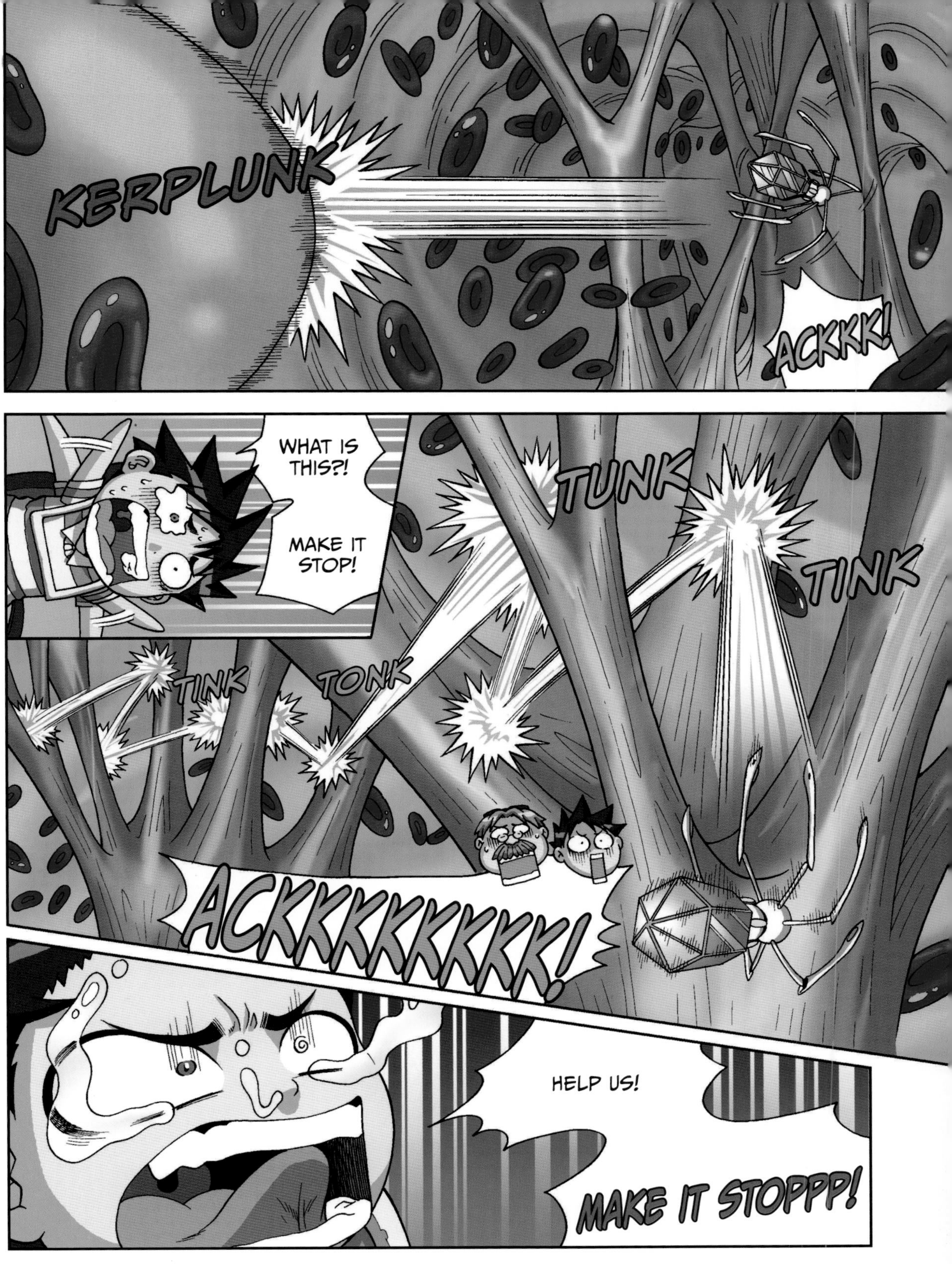
KERPLUNK
ACKKK!
WHAT IS THIS?!
MAKE IT STOP!
TUNK
TINK
TINK
TONK
ACKKKKKKKK!
HELP US!
MAKE IT STOPPP!

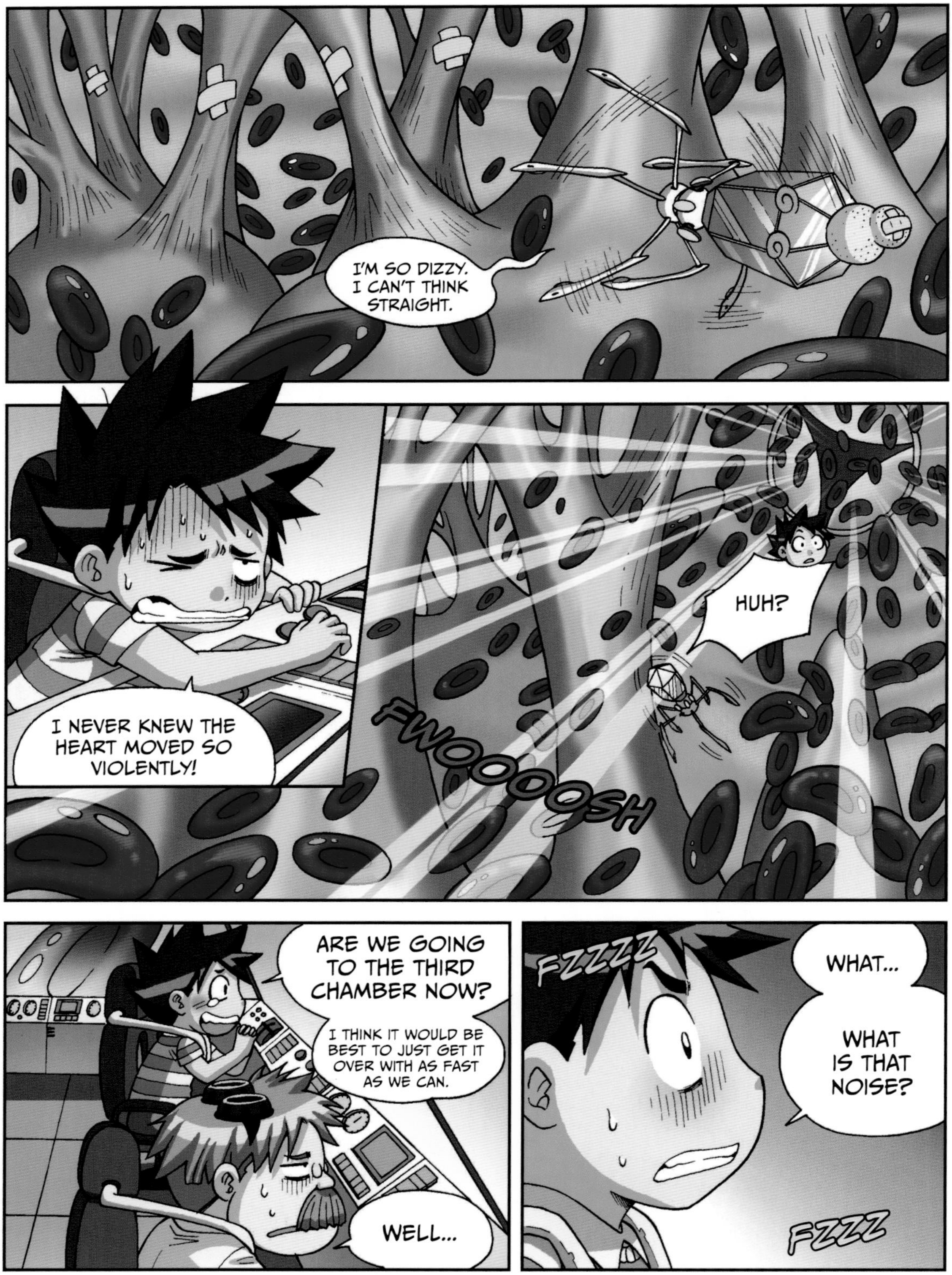
I'M SO DIZZY. I CAN'T THINK STRAIGHT.
I NEVER KNEW THE HEART MOVED SO VIOLENTLY!
FWOOOOOSH
HUH?
ARE WE GOING TO THE THIRD CHAMBER NOW?
I THINK IT WOULD BE BEST TO JUST GET IT OVER WITH AS FAST AS WE CAN.
WELL...
FZZZZ
WHAT...
WHAT IS THAT NOISE?
FZZZ

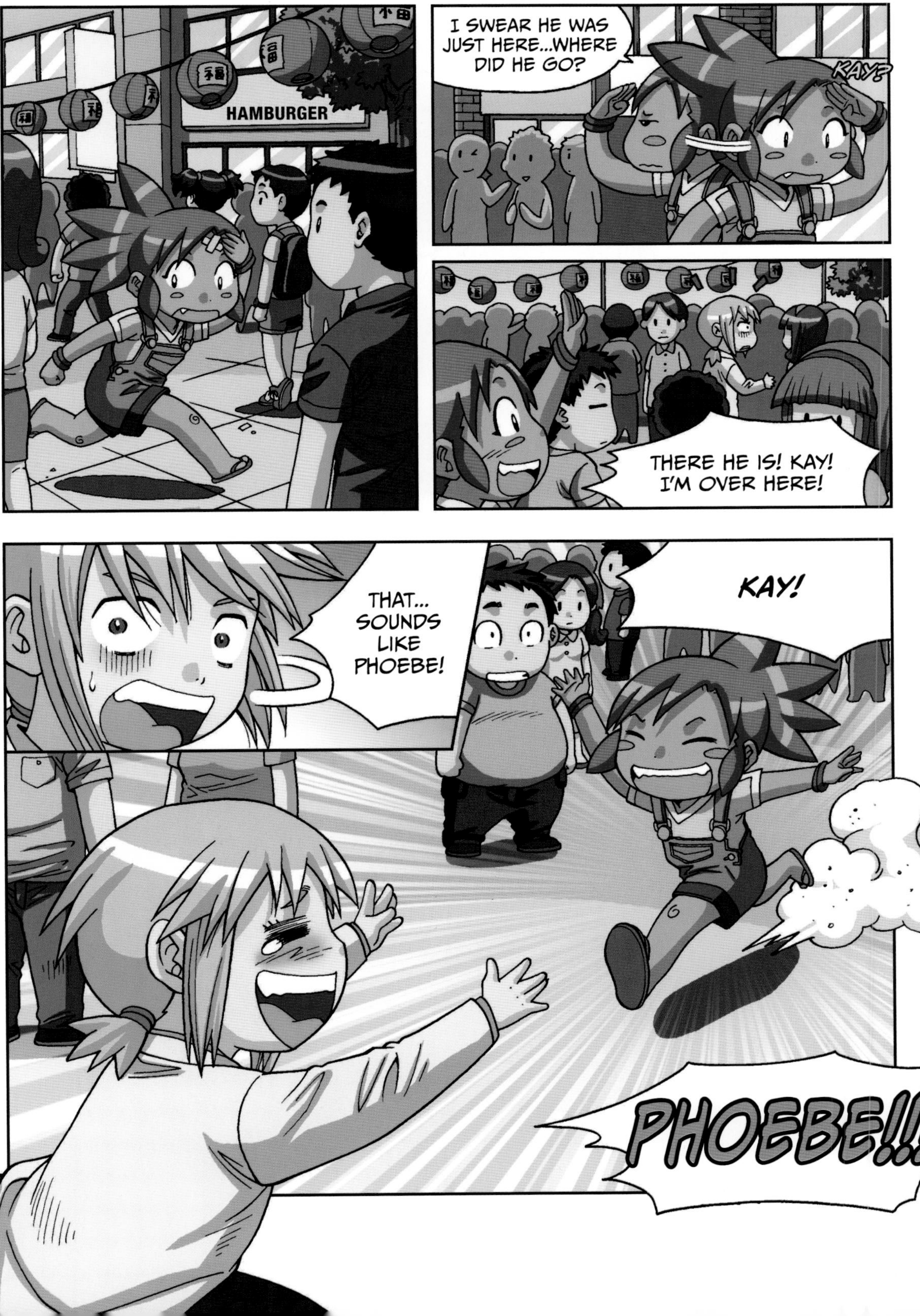
HAMBURGER
I SWEAR HE WAS JUST HERE...WHERE DID HE GO?
KAY?
THERE HE IS! KAY! I'M OVER HERE!
THAT... SOUNDS LIKE PHOEBE!
KAY!
PHOEBE!!!

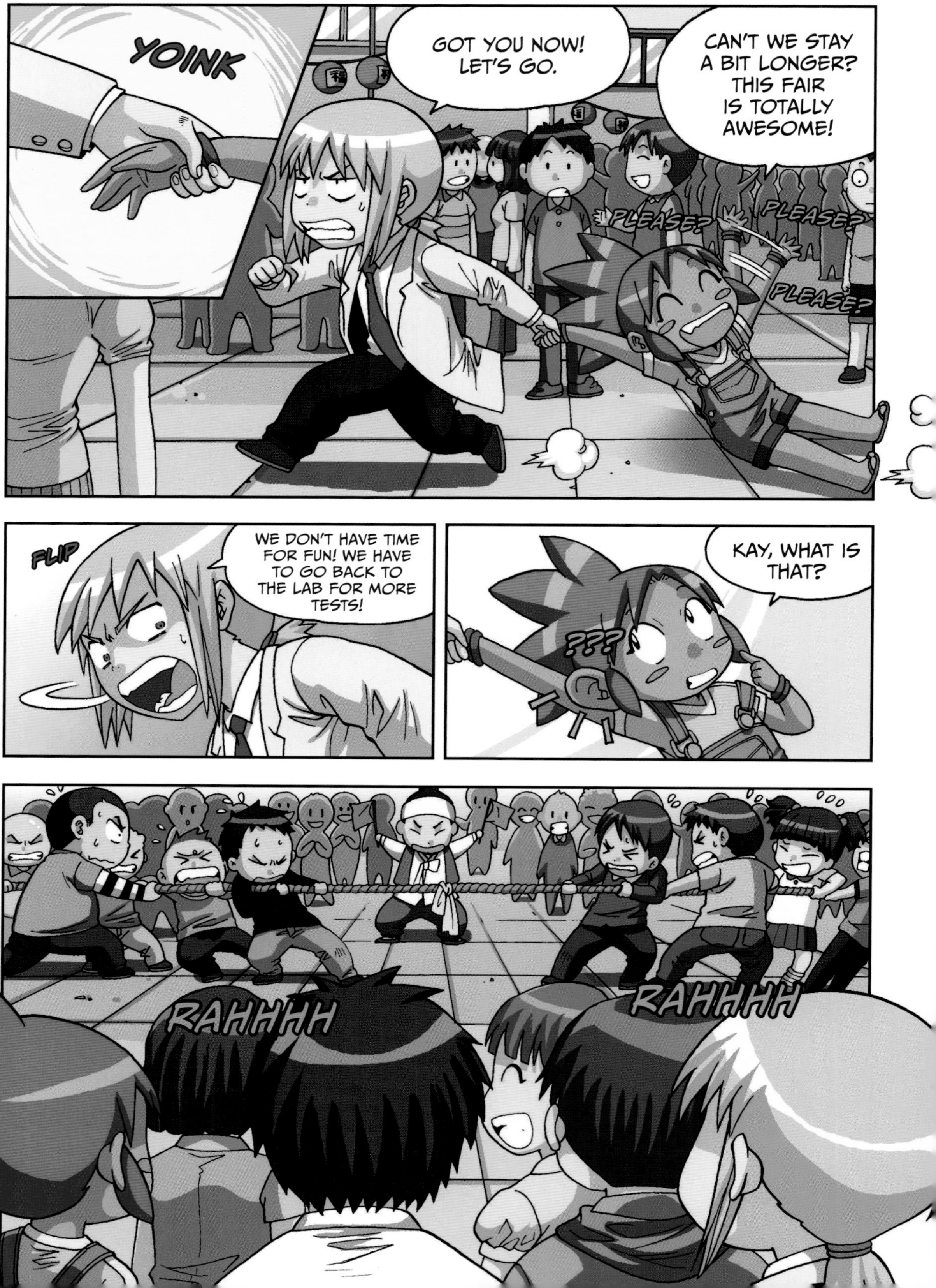
YOINK
GOT YOU NOW! LET'S GO.
CAN'T WE STAY A BIT LONGER? THIS FAIR IS TOTALLY AWESOME!
PLEASE?
PLEASE?
PLEASE?
FLIP
WE DON'T HAVE TIME FOR FUN! WE HAVE TO GO BACK TO THE LAB FOR MORE TESTS!
KAY, WHAT IS THAT?
???
RAHHHH
RAHHHH

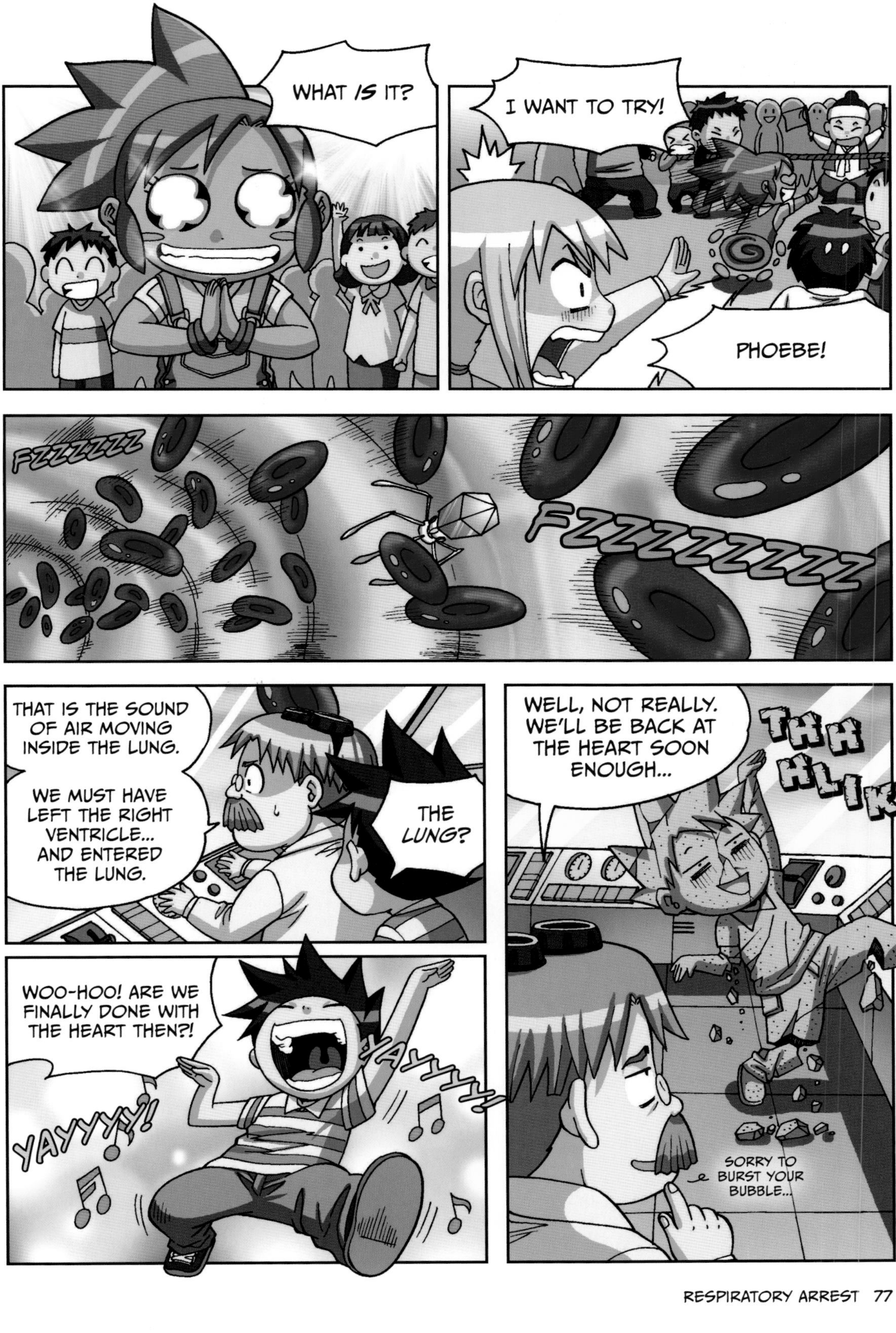
WHAT IS IT?
I WANT TO TRY!
PHOEBE!
FZZZZZZ
FZZZZZZZZZZ
THAT IS THE SOUND OF AIR MOVING INSIDE THE LUNG.
WE MUST HAVE LEFT THE RIGHT VENTRICLE... AND ENTERED THE LUNG.
THE LUNG?
WOO-HOO! ARE WE FINALLY DONE WITH THE HEART THEN?!
YAYYYY!
YAYYYY!
WELL, NOT REALLY. WE'LL BE BACK AT THE HEART SOON ENOUGH...
THH HLIK
SORRY TO BURST YOUR BUBBLE...

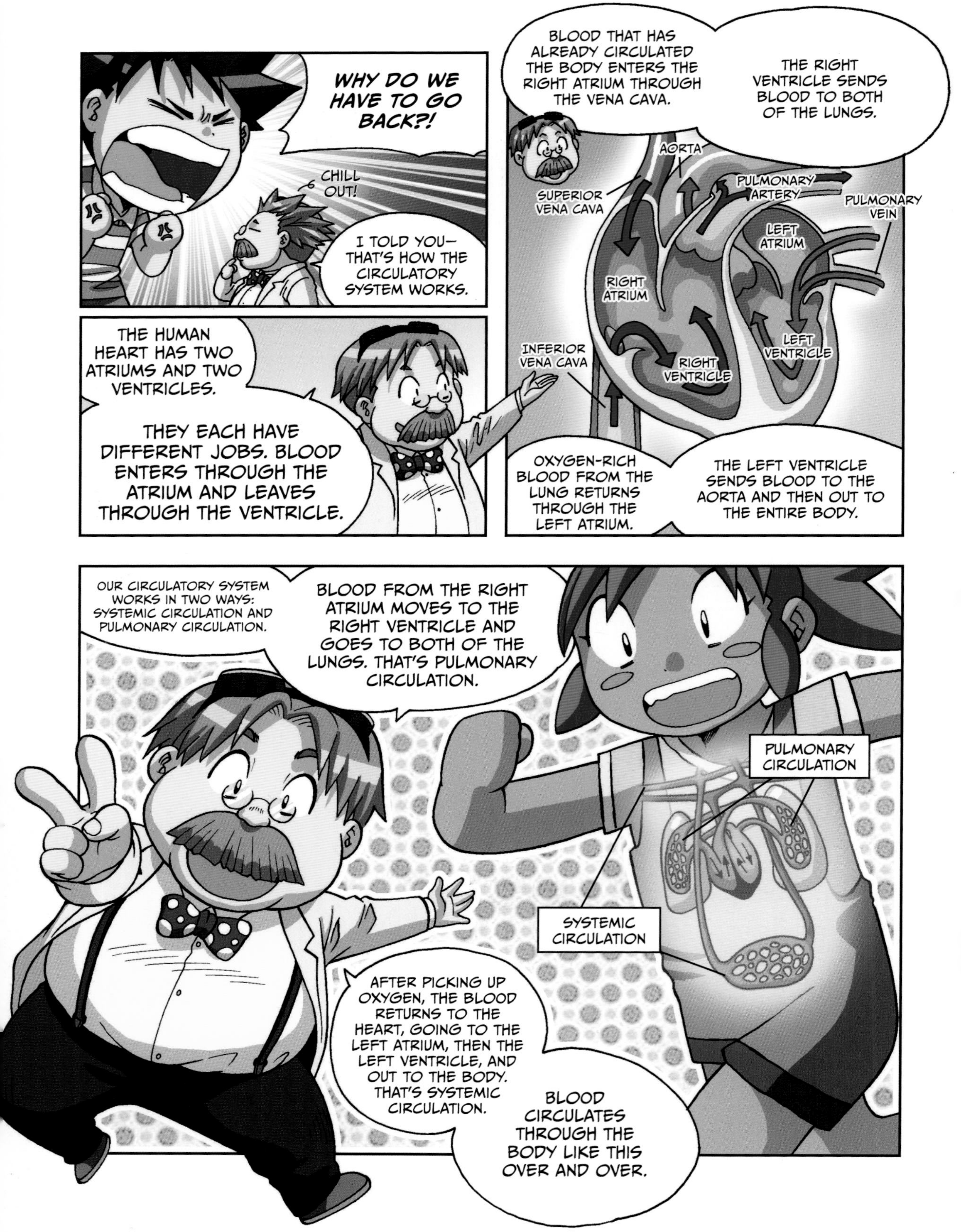
WHY DO WE HAVE TO GO BACK?!
CHILL OUT!
I TOLD YOU—THAT'S HOW THE CIRCULATORY SYSTEM WORKS.
BLOOD THAT HAS ALREADY CIRCULATED THE BODY ENTERS THE RIGHT ATRIUM THROUGH THE VENA CAVA.
THE RIGHT VENTRICLE SENDS BLOOD TO BOTH OF THE LUNGS.
AORTA
SUPERIOR VENA CAVA
PULMONARY ARTERY
PULMONARY VEIN
LEFT ATRIUM
RIGHT ATRIUM
INFERIOR VENA CAVA
RIGHT VENTRICLE
LEFT VENTRICLE
THE HUMAN HEART HAS TWO ATRIUMS AND TWO VENTRICLES.
THEY EACH HAVE DIFFERENT JOBS. BLOOD ENTERS THROUGH THE ATRIUM AND LEAVES THROUGH THE VENTRICLE.
OXYGEN-RICH BLOOD FROM THE LUNG RETURNS THROUGH THE LEFT ATRIUM.
THE LEFT VENTRICLE SENDS BLOOD TO THE AORTA AND THEN OUT TO THE ENTIRE BODY.
OUR CIRCULATORY SYSTEM WORKS IN TWO WAYS: SYSTEMIC CIRCULATION AND PULMONARY CIRCULATION.
BLOOD FROM THE RIGHT ATRIUM MOVES TO THE RIGHT VENTRICLE AND GOES TO BOTH OF THE LUNGS. THAT'S PULMONARY CIRCULATION.
PULMONARY CIRCULATION
SYSTEMIC CIRCULATION
AFTER PICKING UP OXYGEN, THE BLOOD RETURNS TO THE HEART, GOING TO THE LEFT ATRIUM, THEN THE LEFT VENTRICLE, AND OUT TO THE BODY. THAT'S SYSTEMIC CIRCULATION.
BLOOD CIRCULATES THROUGH THE BODY LIKE THIS OVER AND OVER.

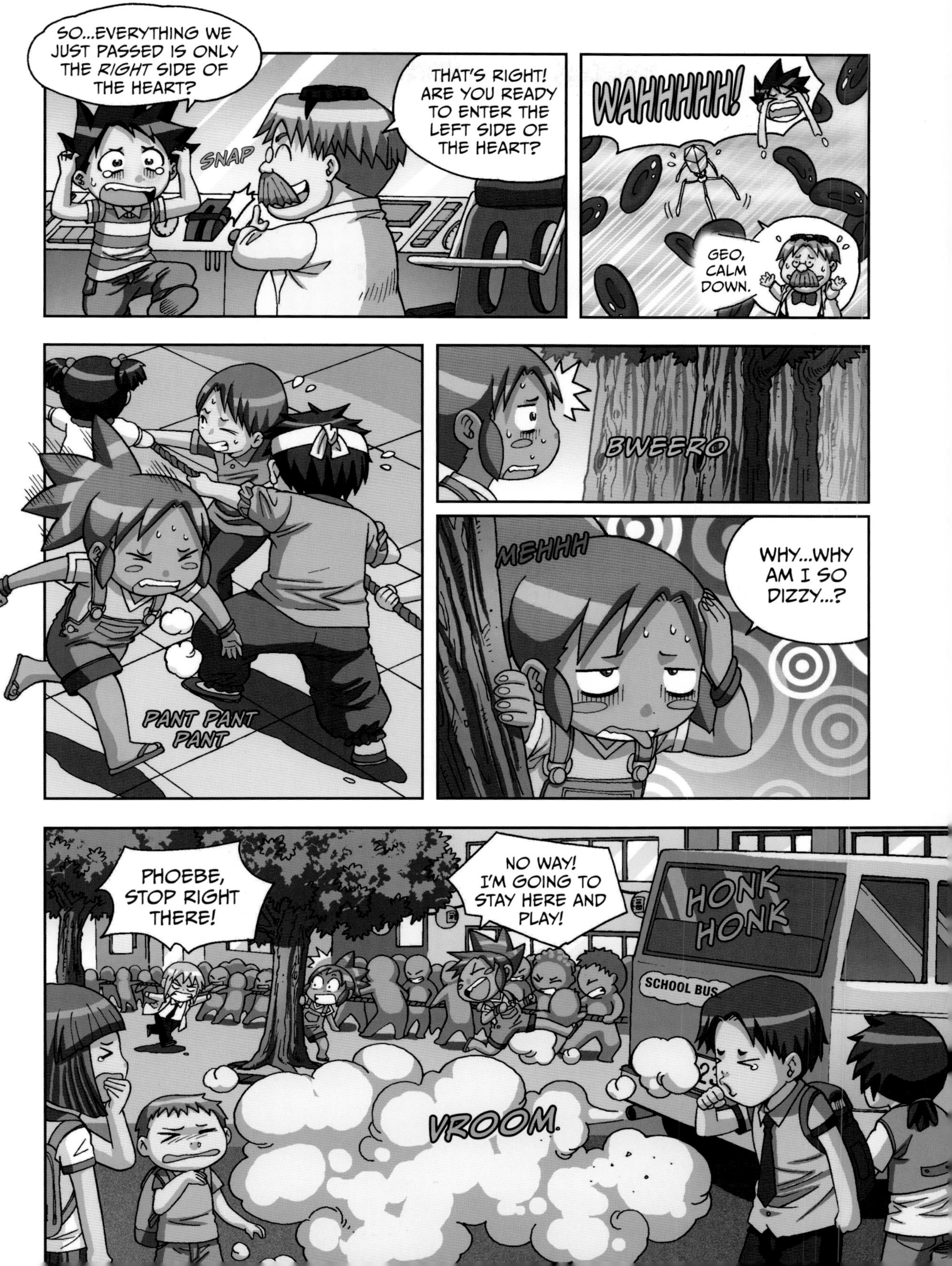
SO...EVERYTHING WE JUST PASSED IS ONLY THE *RIGHT* SIDE OF THE HEART?
SNAP
THAT'S RIGHT! ARE YOU READY TO ENTER THE LEFT SIDE OF THE HEART?
WAHHHHH!
GEO, CALM DOWN.
BWEERO
PANT PANT PANT
MEHHH
WHY...WHY AM I SO DIZZY...?
PHOEBE, STOP RIGHT THERE!
NO WAY! I'M GOING TO STAY HERE AND PLAY!
HONK HONK
SCHOOL BUS
VROOM

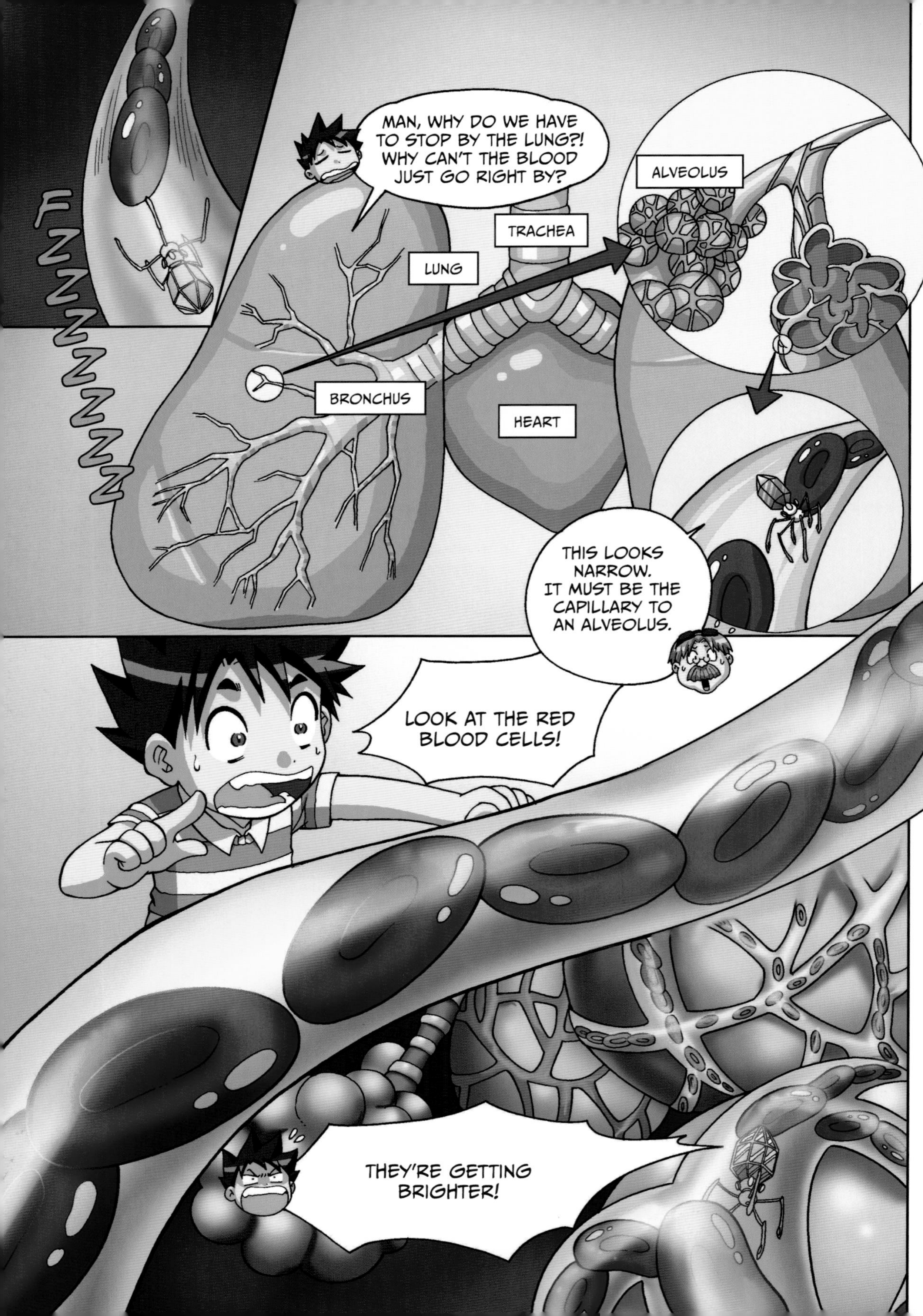
F Z Z Z Z Z Z Z Z Z
MAN, WHY DO WE HAVE TO STOP BY THE LUNG?! WHY CAN'T THE BLOOD JUST GO RIGHT BY?
ALVEOLUS
TRACHEA
LUNG
BRONCHUS
HEART
THIS LOOKS NARROW. IT MUST BE THE CAPILLARY TO AN ALVEOLUS.
LOOK AT THE RED BLOOD CELLS!
THEY'RE GETTING BRIGHTER!

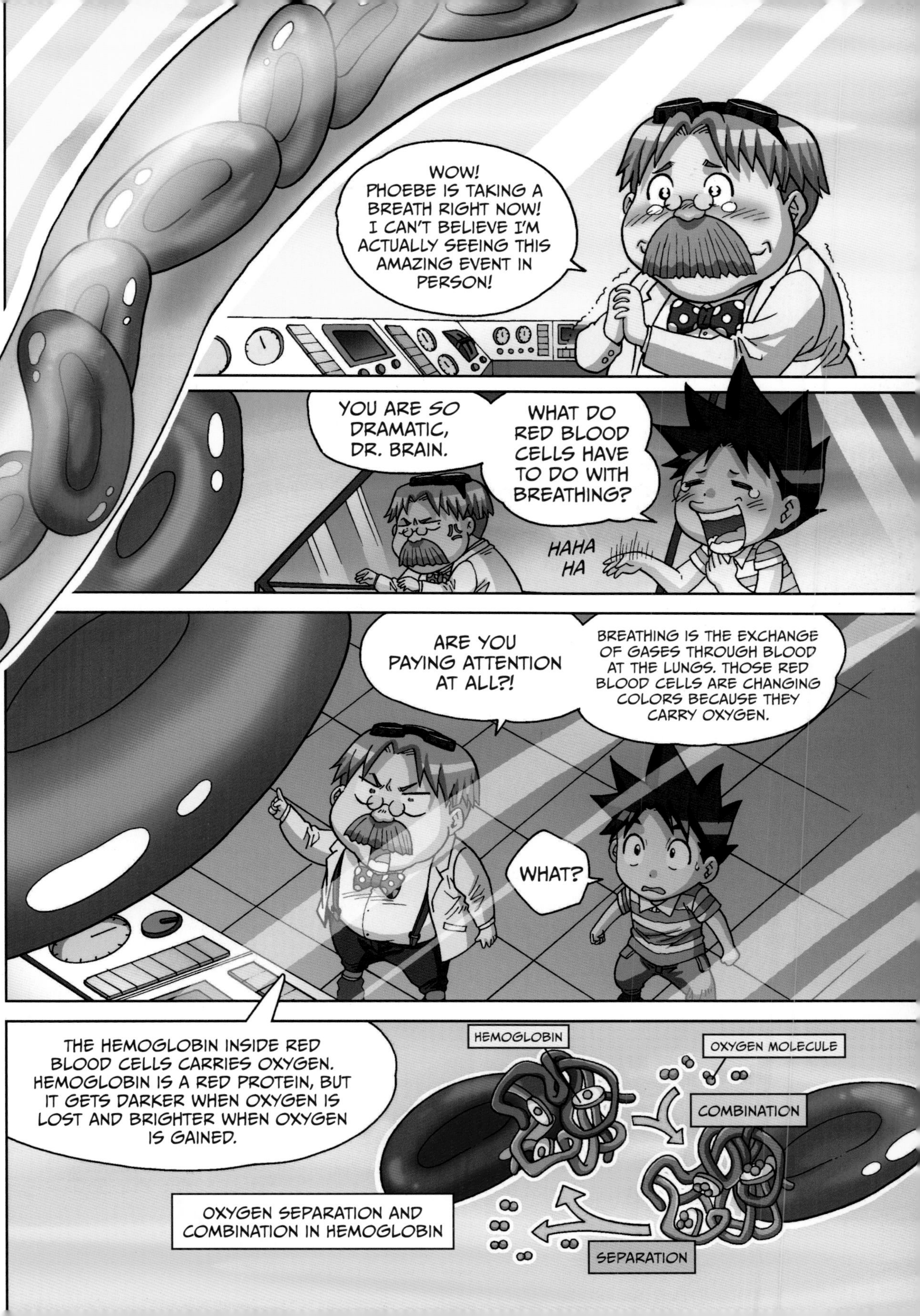

WOW! PHOEBE IS TAKING A BREATH RIGHT NOW! I CAN'T BELIEVE I'M ACTUALLY SEEING THIS AMAZING EVENT IN PERSON!
YOU ARE SO DRAMATIC, DR. BRAIN.
WHAT DO RED BLOOD CELLS HAVE TO DO WITH BREATHING?
HAHA HA
ARE YOU PAYING ATTENTION AT ALL?!
BREATHING IS THE EXCHANGE OF GASES THROUGH BLOOD AT THE LUNGS. THOSE RED BLOOD CELLS ARE CHANGING COLORS BECAUSE THEY CARRY OXYGEN.
WHAT?
THE HEMOGLOBIN INSIDE RED BLOOD CELLS CARRIES OXYGEN. HEMOGLOBIN IS A RED PROTEIN, BUT IT GETS DARKER WHEN OXYGEN IS LOST AND BRIGHTER WHEN OXYGEN IS GAINED.
HEMOGLOBIN
OXYGEN MOLECULE
COMBINATION
SEPARATION
OXYGEN SEPARATION AND COMBINATION IN HEMOGLOBIN

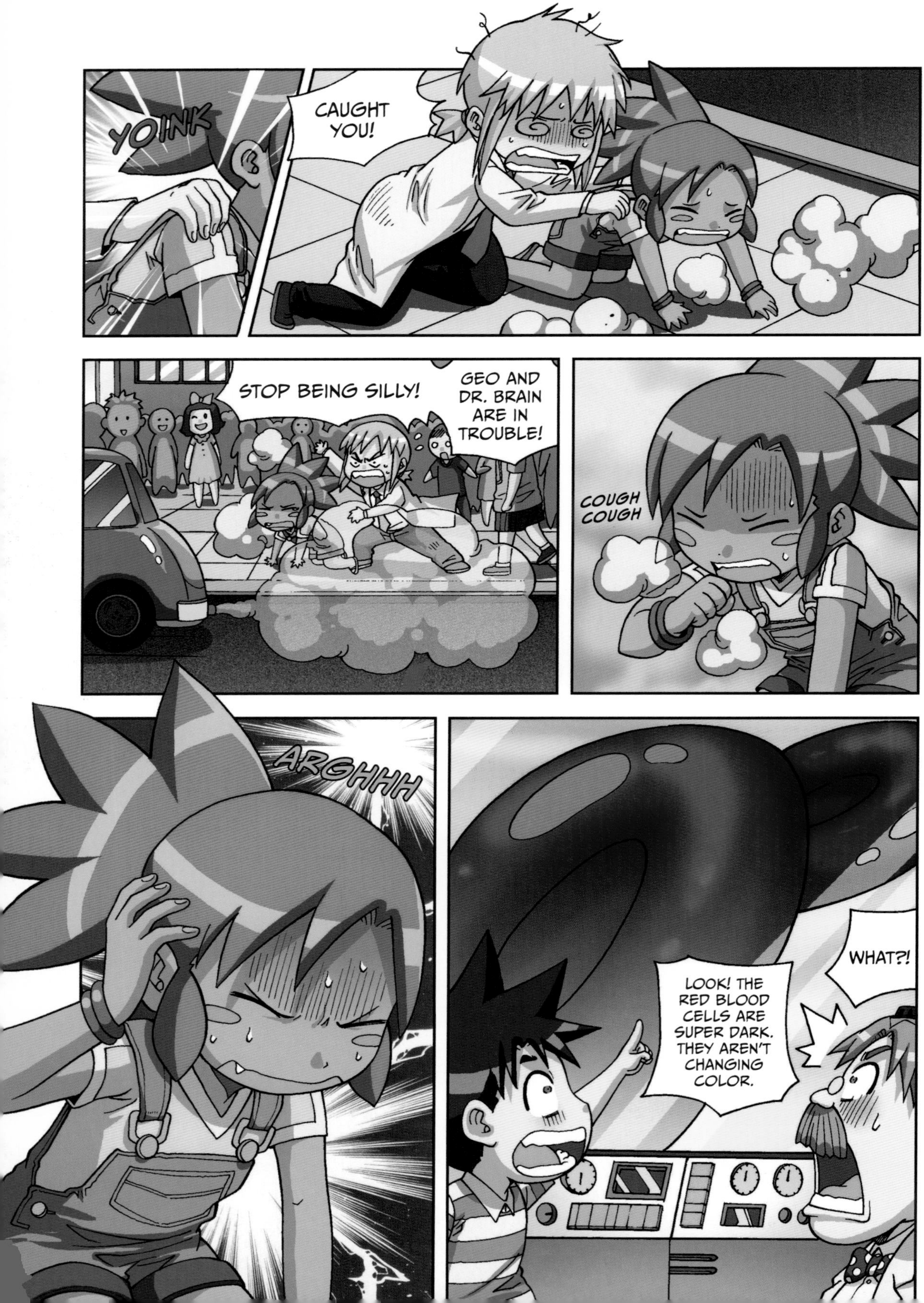
YOINK
CAUGHT YOU!
STOP BEING SILLY!
GEO AND DR. BRAIN ARE IN TROUBLE!
COUGH COUGH
ARGHHH
WHAT?!
LOOK! THE RED BLOOD CELLS ARE SUPER DARK. THEY AREN'T CHANGING COLOR.

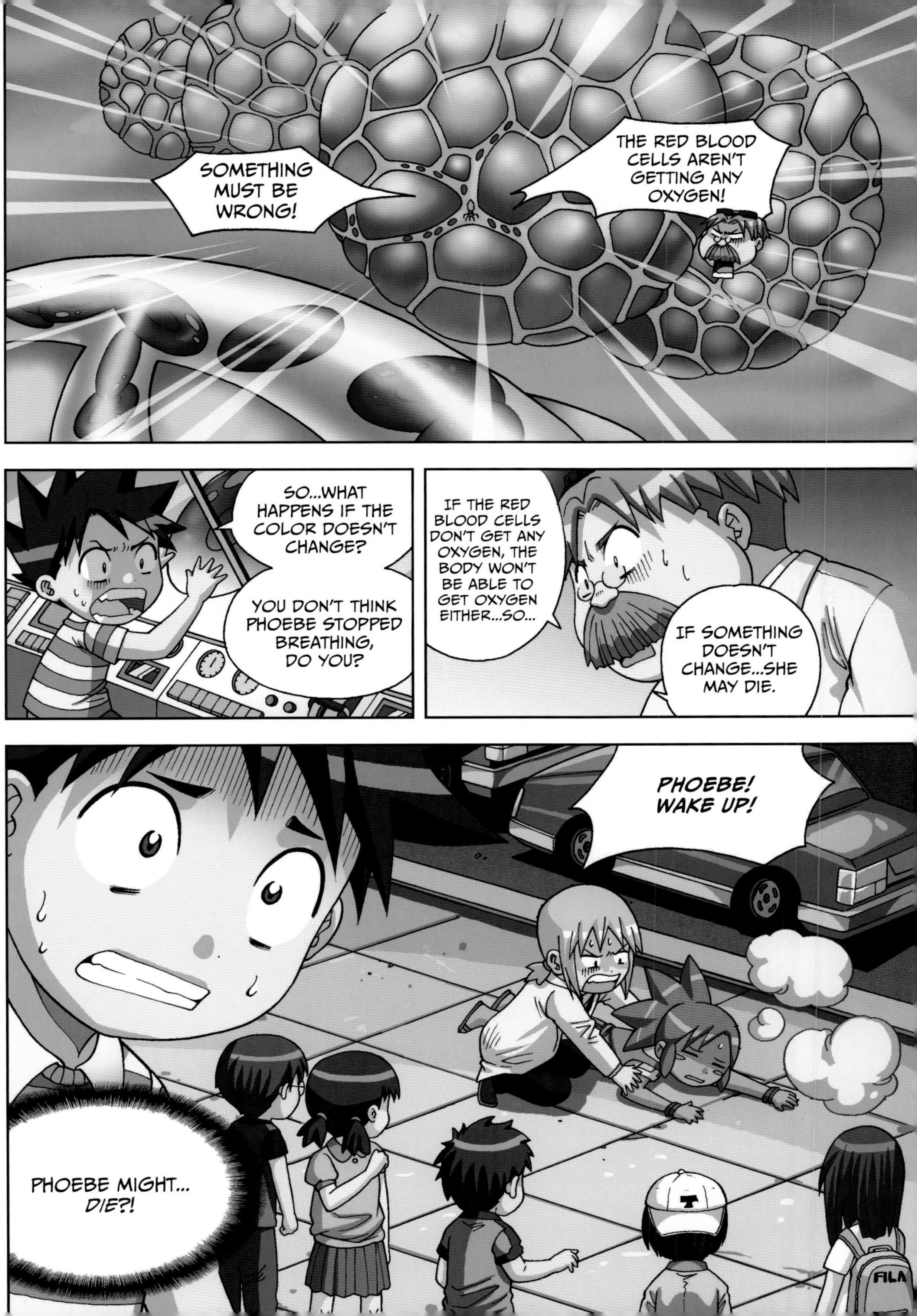
SOMETHING MUST BE WRONG!
THE RED BLOOD CELLS AREN'T GETTING ANY OXYGEN!
SO...WHAT HAPPENS IF THE COLOR DOESN'T CHANGE?
YOU DON'T THINK PHOEBE STOPPED BREATHING, DO YOU?
IF THE RED BLOOD CELLS DON'T GET ANY OXYGEN, THE BODY WON'T BE ABLE TO GET OXYGEN EITHER...SO...
IF SOMETHING DOESN'T CHANGE...SHE MAY DIE.
PHOEBE! WAKE UP!
PHOEBE MIGHT... DIE?!
FILA

THE TRACHEA AND LUNGS

When you breathe, you constantly use your trachea and lungs, breathing in (inhaling) oxygen and breathing out (exhaling) carbon dioxide. Your trachea is the tube in your throat that leads to your lungs. Every breath you take goes into the trachea and then to the lungs. About 10,000 liters of air pass through the trachea every day! When you breathe in, the air meets your blood at the lungs and the blood brings oxygen to your muscles and organs. At the same time, the blood lets go of carbon dioxide, which is released when you exhale. We call this exchange of gases *respiration*.

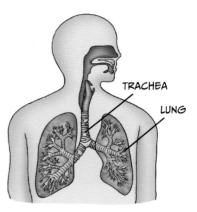

TRACHEA

LUNG

KEEPING THE TRACHEA CLEAN

Your trachea is shaped like a hose that is 15 centimeters long (about 6 inches) and 2–3 centimeters across (about 1 inch). The trachea is lined with cells that make mucus and cells that have cilia, which are little hairlike projections. The mucus keeps your airways moist and traps particles and bacteria you breathe in. The cilia work to "sweep" the mucus upward, along with everything it brings with it. This mixture can be coughed out or swallowed down the esophagus, where stomach acid kills all the bacteria. If the mucus-making cells in the trachea are damaged, it can cause a dry cough.

© Charles Daghlian

PTOOIE!

DUST AND BACTERIA ENTER THROUGH THE TRACHEA AND MIX WITH MUCUS TO FORM PHLEGM.

PHOEBE! DON'T SPIT IN PUBLIC!

Tracheal cilia move particles and bacteria that entered the throat along with air, so you can cough them out.

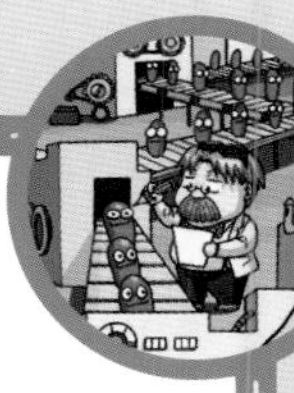

STRUCTURE AND FUNCTIONS OF THE LUNGS

You have two lungs, one on either side of the heart. They take up most of the chest. They are wrapped in a thin membrane called *pleura* that helps the lungs to hold air like a plastic bag. The diaphragm below the lungs moves up and down to help with the breathing process.

The tiny alveolus is where most of the oxygen and carbon dioxide exchange happens—each lung has hundreds of millions of alveoli. Red blood cells from the capillaries around the alveolus meet the air, let carbon dioxide go, and absorb oxygen. A single alveolus is about 0.1 millimeters across. If you laid out all 700 million alveoli, they would take up 70 square meters. That's 30 times larger than the outside of the human body.

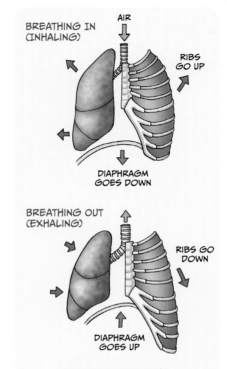

BREATHING IN (INHALING)
AIR
RIBS GO UP
DIAPHRAGM GOES DOWN
BREATHING OUT (EXHALING)
RIBS GO DOWN
DIAPHRAGM GOES UP

HOW WE BREATHE

HOW TO STOP HICCUPS

Hiccups happen when the diaphragm below the lungs has a spasm. If the diaphragm suddenly contracts (and has nothing to do with breathing), air comes into the body quickly. Then your vocal cords close, which makes the *hic* noise. Hiccups usually stop within 30 minutes but can last for a few days. There is a man in the *Guinness Book of World Records* who had hiccups from 1922 to 1990 (that's 68 years)! You can get hiccups from overeating, stomach ulcers, liver problems, esophagitis, alcohol, problems with the brain, some drugs, and even anxiety. Home cures, like drinking cold water, sticking your tongue out, and holding your breath, can treat light hiccups. In the worst cases, people need surgery to cut the nerve of the diaphragm.

HICCUP HICCUP
HOW ABOUT NOW? ARE THEY GONE?

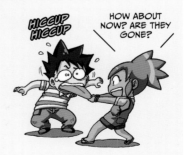

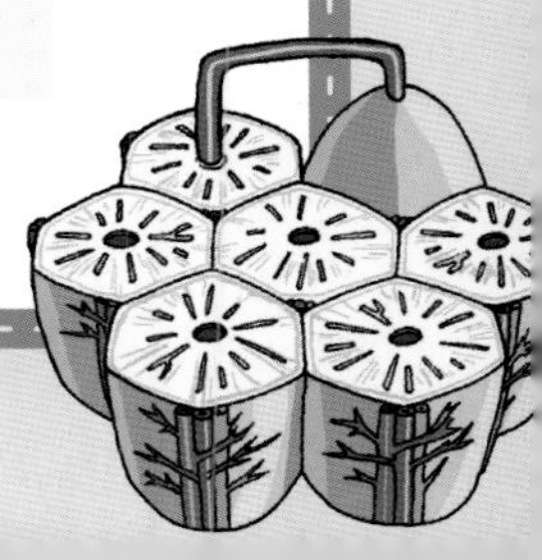

KAY'S CRISIS

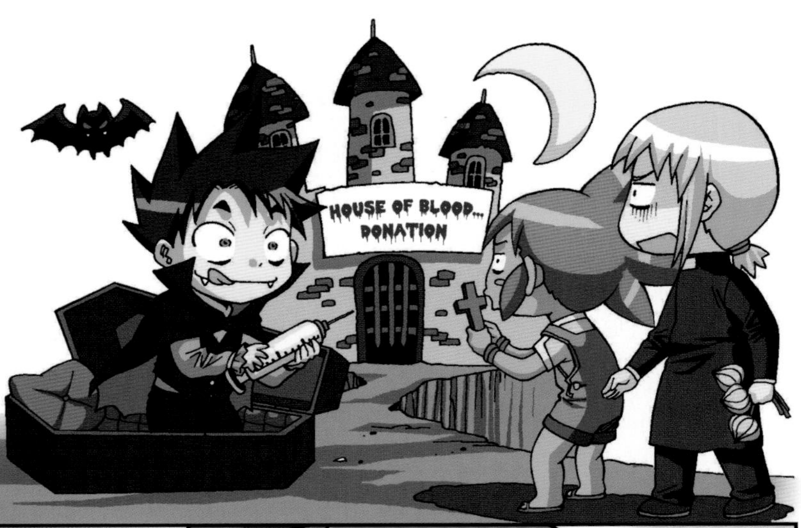
HOUSE OF BLOOD... DONATION

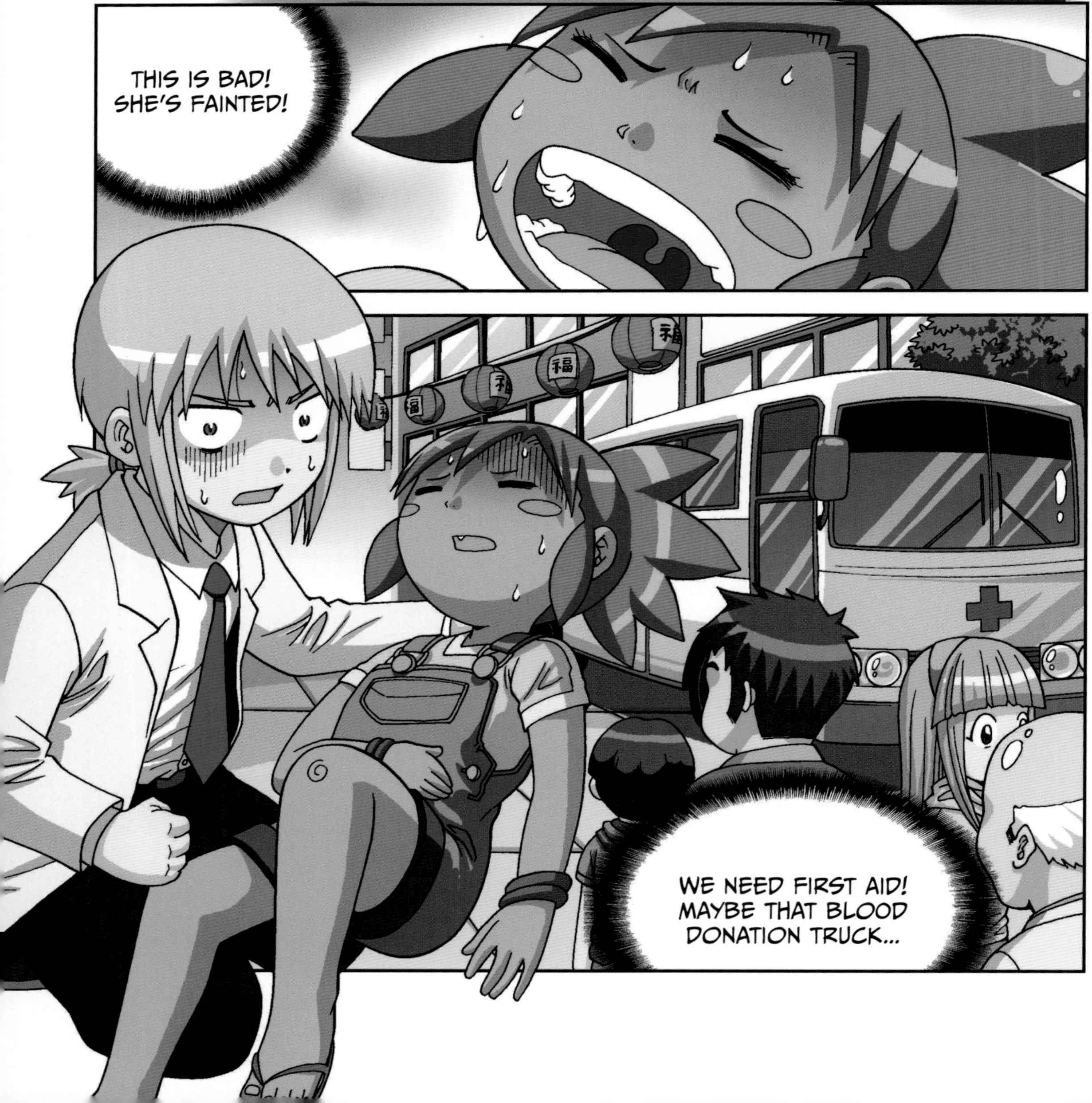
THIS IS BAD! SHE'S FAINTED!
WE NEED FIRST AID! MAYBE THAT BLOOD DONATION TRUCK...

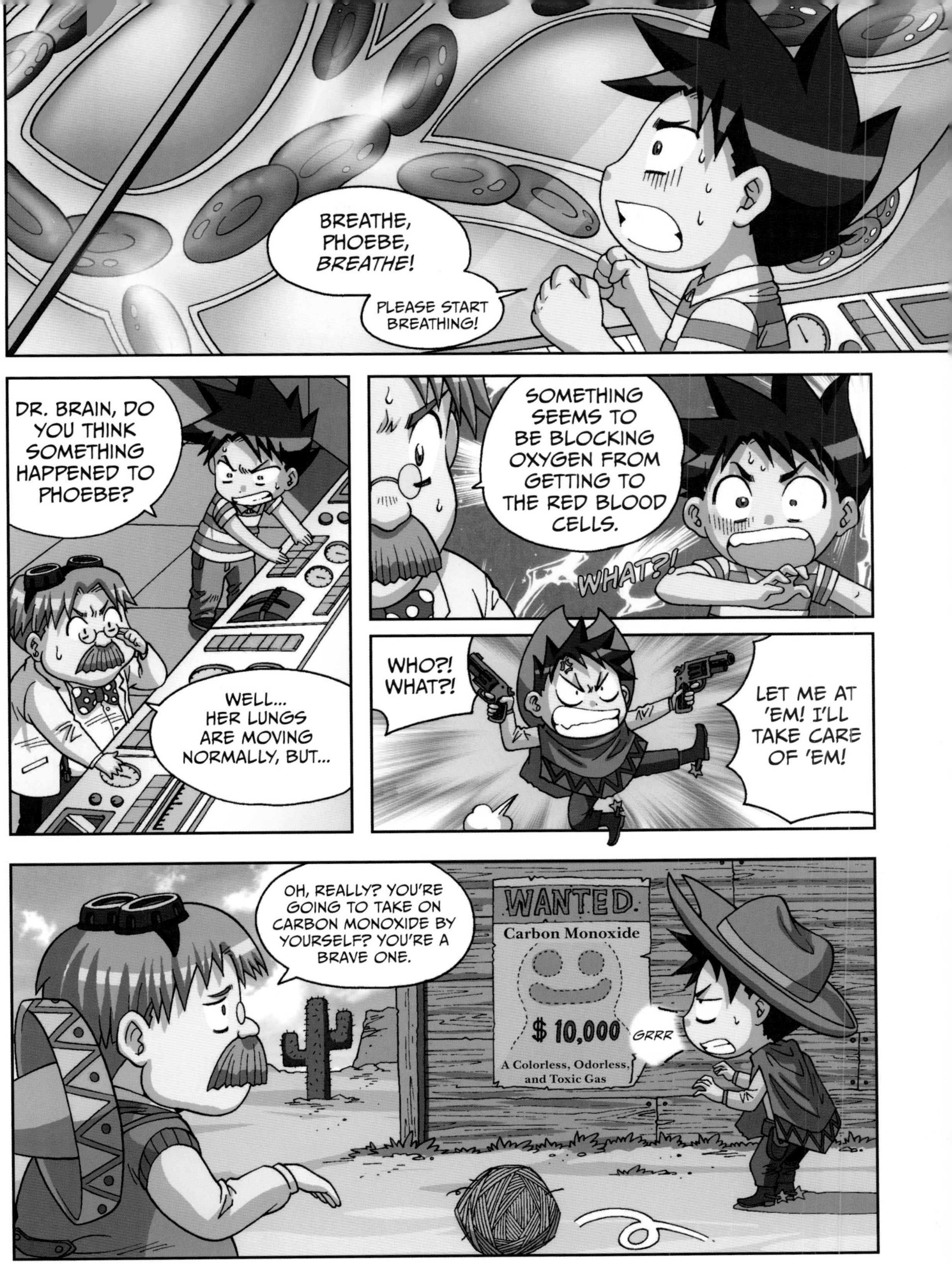
BREATHE, PHOEBE, BREATHE!
PLEASE START BREATHING!
DR. BRAIN, DO YOU THINK SOMETHING HAPPENED TO PHOEBE?
WELL... HER LUNGS ARE MOVING NORMALLY, BUT...
SOMETHING SEEMS TO BE BLOCKING OXYGEN FROM GETTING TO THE RED BLOOD CELLS.
WHAT?!
WHO?! WHAT?!
LET ME AT 'EM! I'LL TAKE CARE OF 'EM!
OH, REALLY? YOU'RE GOING TO TAKE ON CARBON MONOXIDE BY YOURSELF? YOU'RE A BRAVE ONE.
WANTED
Carbon Monoxide
$ 10,000
A Colorless, Odorless, and Toxic Gas
GRRR

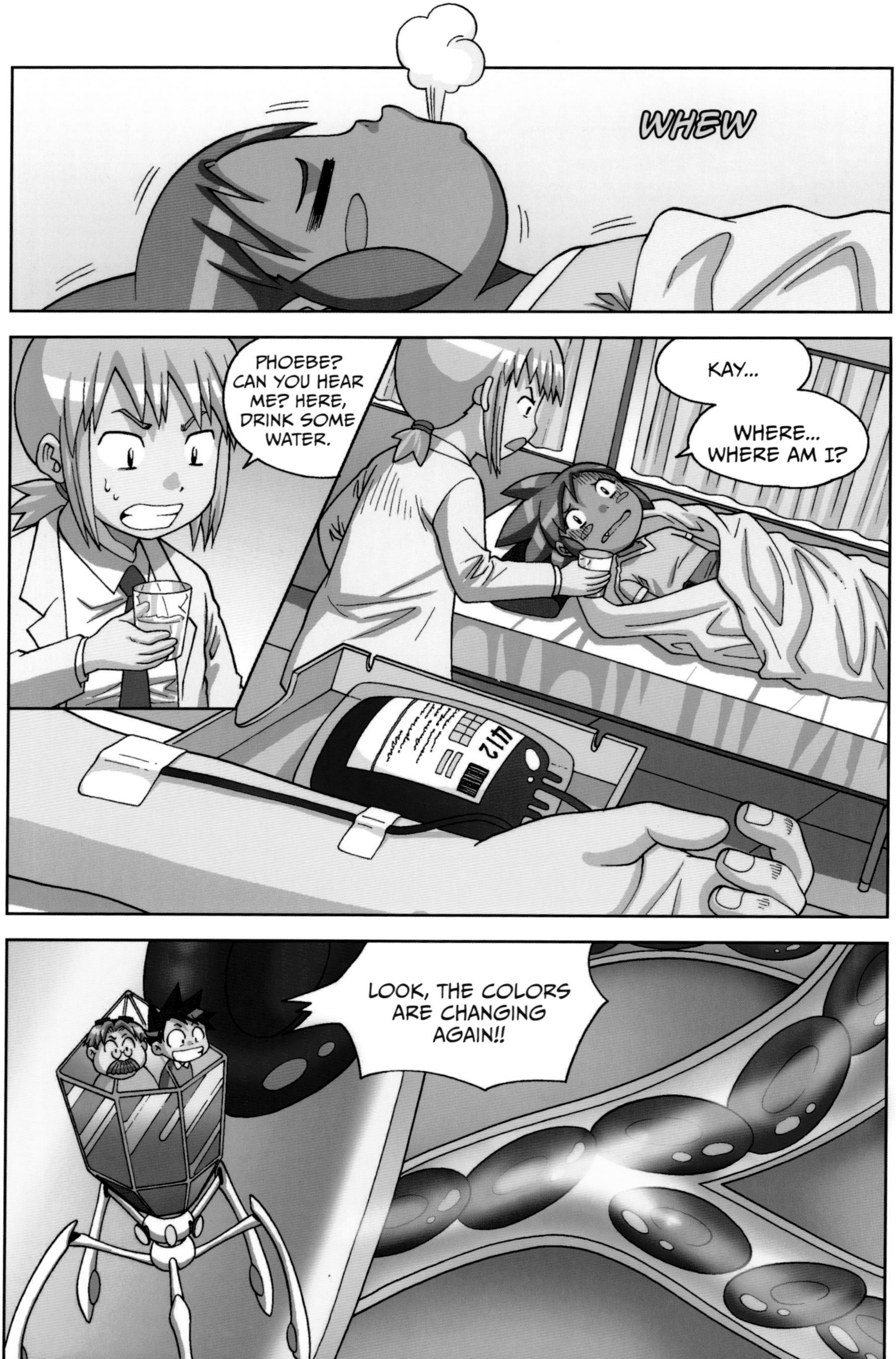
WHEW
PHOEBE? CAN YOU HEAR ME? HERE, DRINK SOME WATER.
KAY...
WHERE... WHERE AM I?
4412
LOOK, THE COLORS ARE CHANGING AGAIN!!

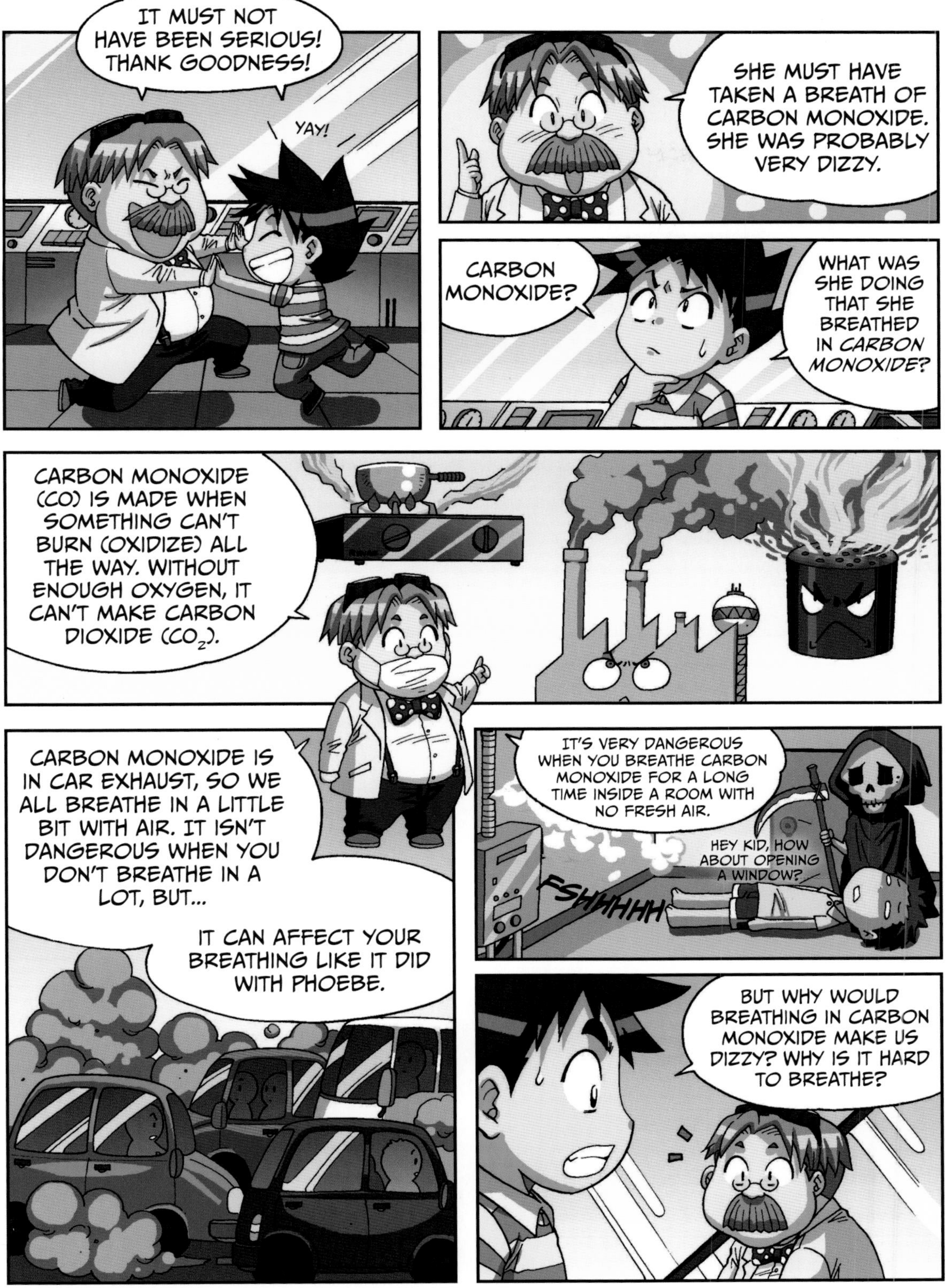
IT MUST NOT HAVE BEEN SERIOUS! THANK GOODNESS!
YAY!
SHE MUST HAVE TAKEN A BREATH OF CARBON MONOXIDE. SHE WAS PROBABLY VERY DIZZY.
CARBON MONOXIDE?
WHAT WAS SHE DOING THAT SHE BREATHED IN *CARBON MONOXIDE*?
CARBON MONOXIDE (CO) IS MADE WHEN SOMETHING CAN'T BURN (OXIDIZE) ALL THE WAY. WITHOUT ENOUGH OXYGEN, IT CAN'T MAKE CARBON DIOXIDE (CO_2).
CARBON MONOXIDE IS IN CAR EXHAUST, SO WE ALL BREATHE IN A LITTLE BIT WITH AIR. IT ISN'T DANGEROUS WHEN YOU DON'T BREATHE IN A LOT, BUT...
IT CAN AFFECT YOUR BREATHING LIKE IT DID WITH PHOEBE.
IT'S VERY DANGEROUS WHEN YOU BREATHE CARBON MONOXIDE FOR A LONG TIME INSIDE A ROOM WITH NO FRESH AIR.
HEY KID, HOW ABOUT OPENING A WINDOW?
FSHHHHHH
BUT WHY WOULD BREATHING IN CARBON MONOXIDE MAKE US DIZZY? WHY IS IT HARD TO BREATHE?

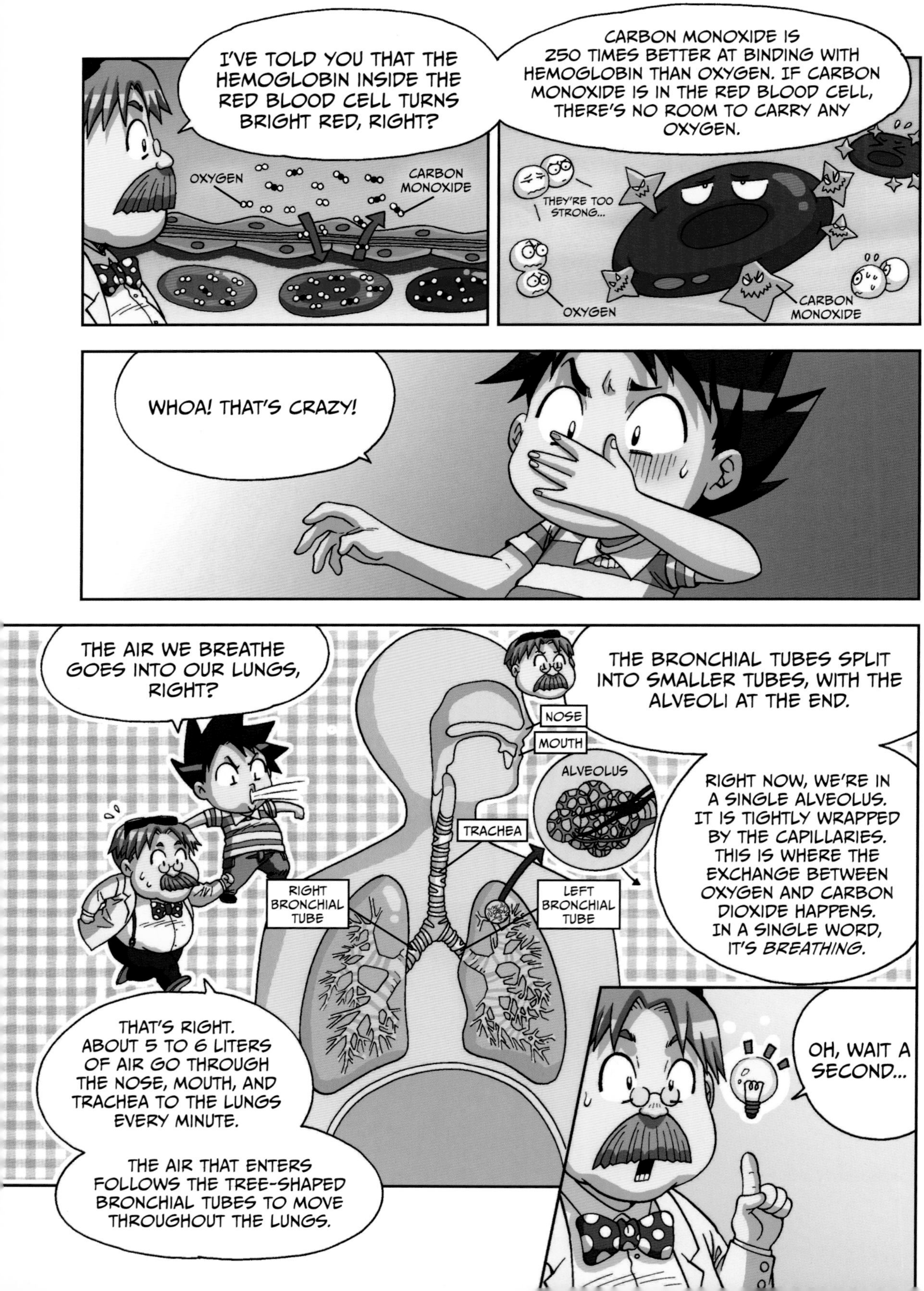
I'VE TOLD YOU THAT THE HEMOGLOBIN INSIDE THE RED BLOOD CELL TURNS BRIGHT RED, RIGHT?
OXYGEN
CARBON MONOXIDE
CARBON MONOXIDE IS 250 TIMES BETTER AT BINDING WITH HEMOGLOBIN THAN OXYGEN. IF CARBON MONOXIDE IS IN THE RED BLOOD CELL, THERE'S NO ROOM TO CARRY ANY OXYGEN.
THEY'RE TOO STRONG...
OXYGEN
CARBON MONOXIDE
WHOA! THAT'S CRAZY!
THE AIR WE BREATHE GOES INTO OUR LUNGS, RIGHT?
THE BRONCHIAL TUBES SPLIT INTO SMALLER TUBES, WITH THE ALVEOLI AT THE END.
NOSE
MOUTH
ALVEOLUS
TRACHEA
RIGHT BRONCHIAL TUBE
LEFT BRONCHIAL TUBE
RIGHT NOW, WE'RE IN A SINGLE ALVEOLUS. IT IS TIGHTLY WRAPPED BY THE CAPILLARIES. THIS IS WHERE THE EXCHANGE BETWEEN OXYGEN AND CARBON DIOXIDE HAPPENS. IN A SINGLE WORD, IT'S *BREATHING*.
THAT'S RIGHT. ABOUT 5 TO 6 LITERS OF AIR GO THROUGH THE NOSE, MOUTH, AND TRACHEA TO THE LUNGS EVERY MINUTE.
THE AIR THAT ENTERS FOLLOWS THE TREE-SHAPED BRONCHIAL TUBES TO MOVE THROUGHOUT THE LUNGS.
OH, WAIT A SECOND...

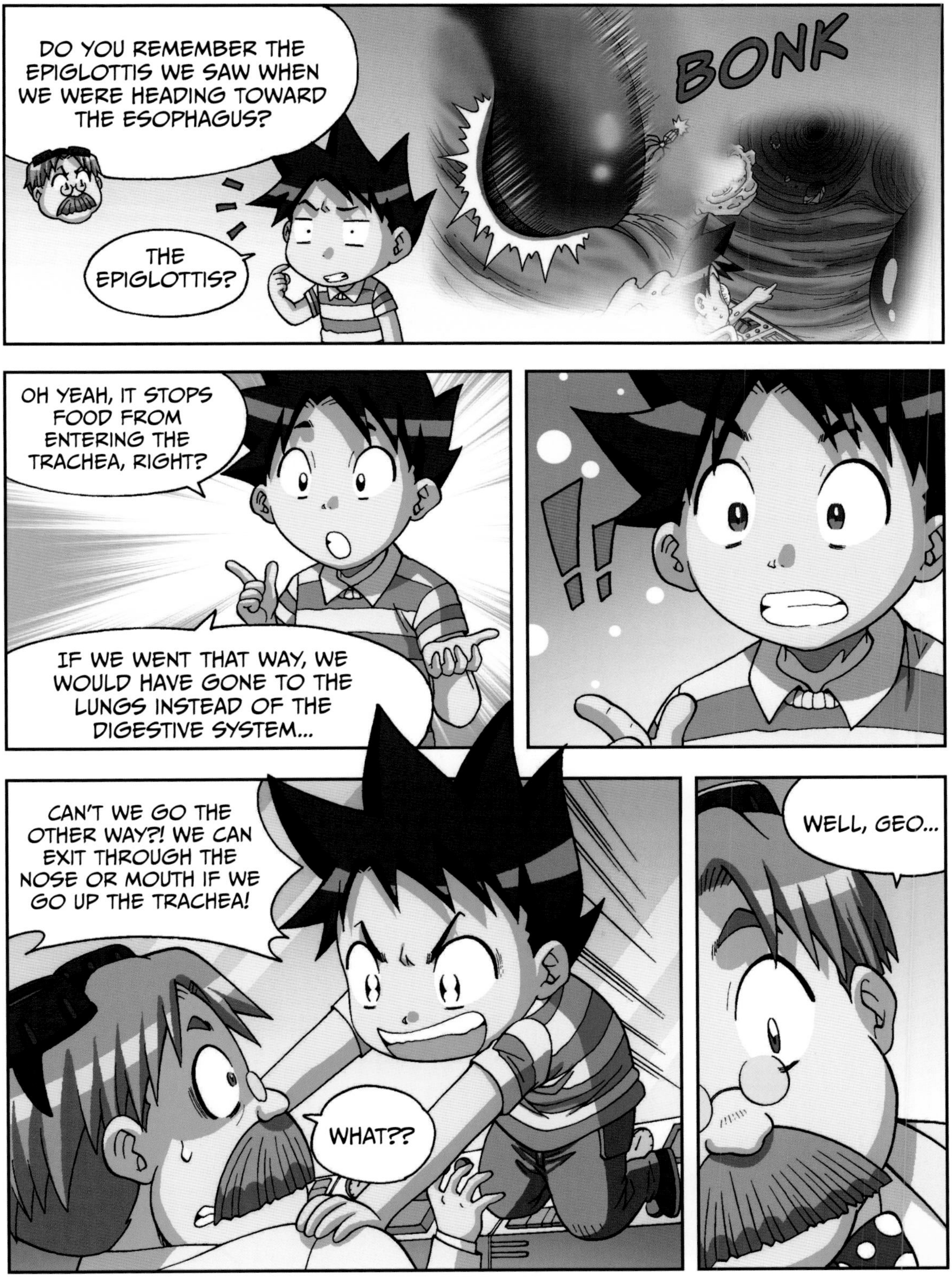
DO YOU REMEMBER THE EPIGLOTTIS WE SAW WHEN WE WERE HEADING TOWARD THE ESOPHAGUS?
BONK
THE EPIGLOTTIS?
OH YEAH, IT STOPS FOOD FROM ENTERING THE TRACHEA, RIGHT?
IF WE WENT THAT WAY, WE WOULD HAVE GONE TO THE LUNGS INSTEAD OF THE DIGESTIVE SYSTEM...
CAN'T WE GO THE OTHER WAY?! WE CAN EXIT THROUGH THE NOSE OR MOUTH IF WE GO UP THE TRACHEA!
WHAT??
WELL, GEO...

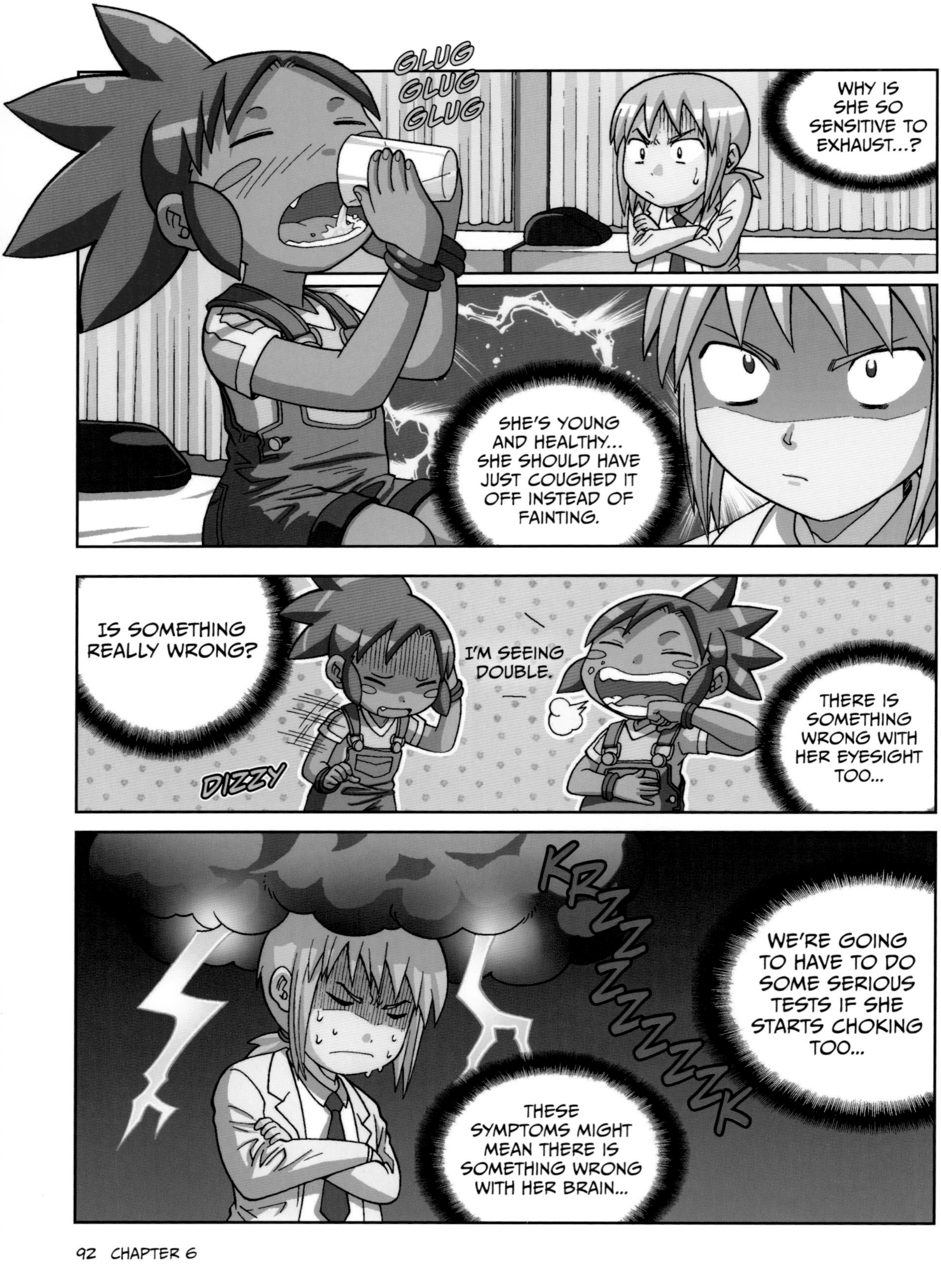
GLUG GLUG GLUG
WHY IS SHE SO SENSITIVE TO EXHAUST...?
SHE'S YOUNG AND HEALTHY... SHE SHOULD HAVE JUST COUGHED IT OFF INSTEAD OF FAINTING.
IS SOMETHING REALLY WRONG?
I'M SEEING DOUBLE.
DIZZY
THERE IS SOMETHING WRONG WITH HER EYESIGHT TOO...
KRZZZZZZZK
WE'RE GOING TO HAVE TO DO SOME SERIOUS TESTS IF SHE STARTS CHOKING TOO...
THESE SYMPTOMS MIGHT MEAN THERE IS SOMETHING WRONG WITH HER BRAIN...

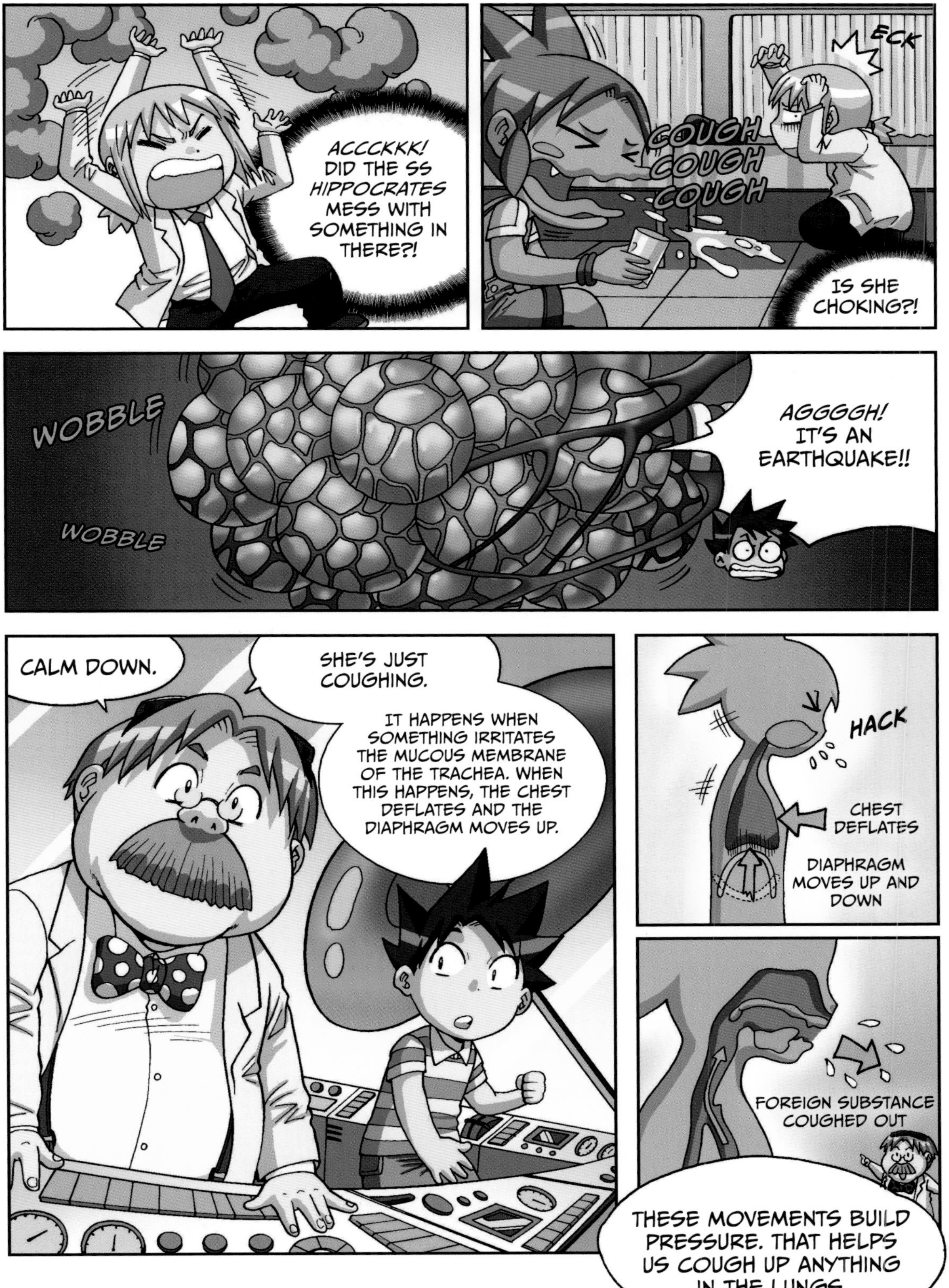
ACCCKKK! DID THE SS HIPPOCRATES MESS WITH SOMETHING IN THERE?!
ECK
COUGH COUGH COUGH
IS SHE CHOKING?!
WOBBLE
WOBBLE
AGGGGH! IT'S AN EARTHQUAKE!!
CALM DOWN.
SHE'S JUST COUGHING.
IT HAPPENS WHEN SOMETHING IRRITATES THE MUCOUS MEMBRANE OF THE TRACHEA. WHEN THIS HAPPENS, THE CHEST DEFLATES AND THE DIAPHRAGM MOVES UP.
HACK
CHEST DEFLATES
DIAPHRAGM MOVES UP AND DOWN
FOREIGN SUBSTANCE COUGHED OUT
THESE MOVEMENTS BUILD PRESSURE. THAT HELPS US COUGH UP ANYTHING IN THE LUNGS.

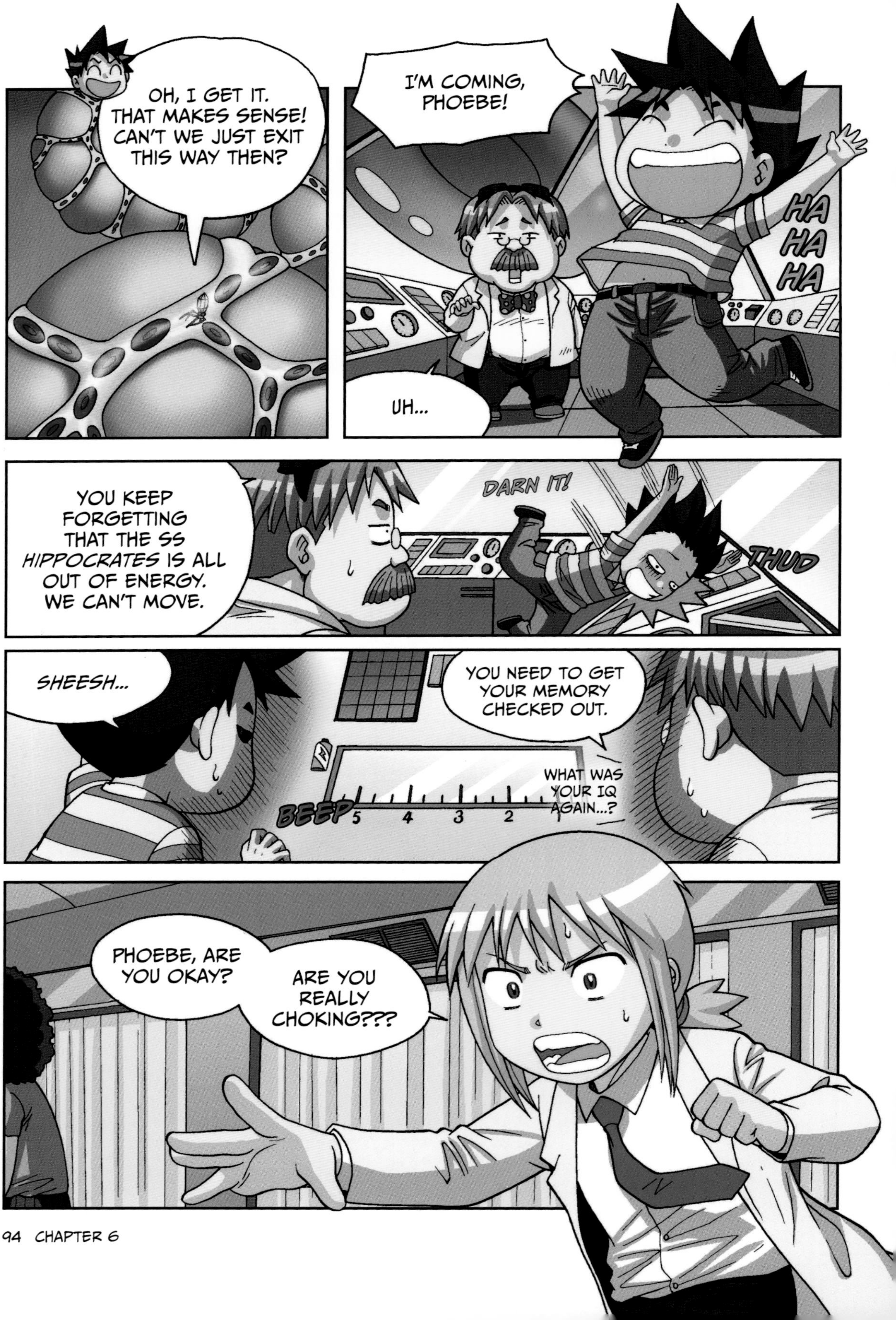
OH, I GET IT. THAT MAKES SENSE! CAN'T WE JUST EXIT THIS WAY THEN?
I'M COMING, PHOEBE!
HA HA HA
UH...
YOU KEEP FORGETTING THAT THE SS *HIPPOCRATES* IS ALL OUT OF ENERGY. WE CAN'T MOVE.
DARN IT!
THUD
SHEESH...
YOU NEED TO GET YOUR MEMORY CHECKED OUT.
WHAT WAS YOUR IQ AGAIN...?
BEEP
5 4 3 2 1
PHOEBE, ARE YOU OKAY?
ARE YOU REALLY CHOKING???

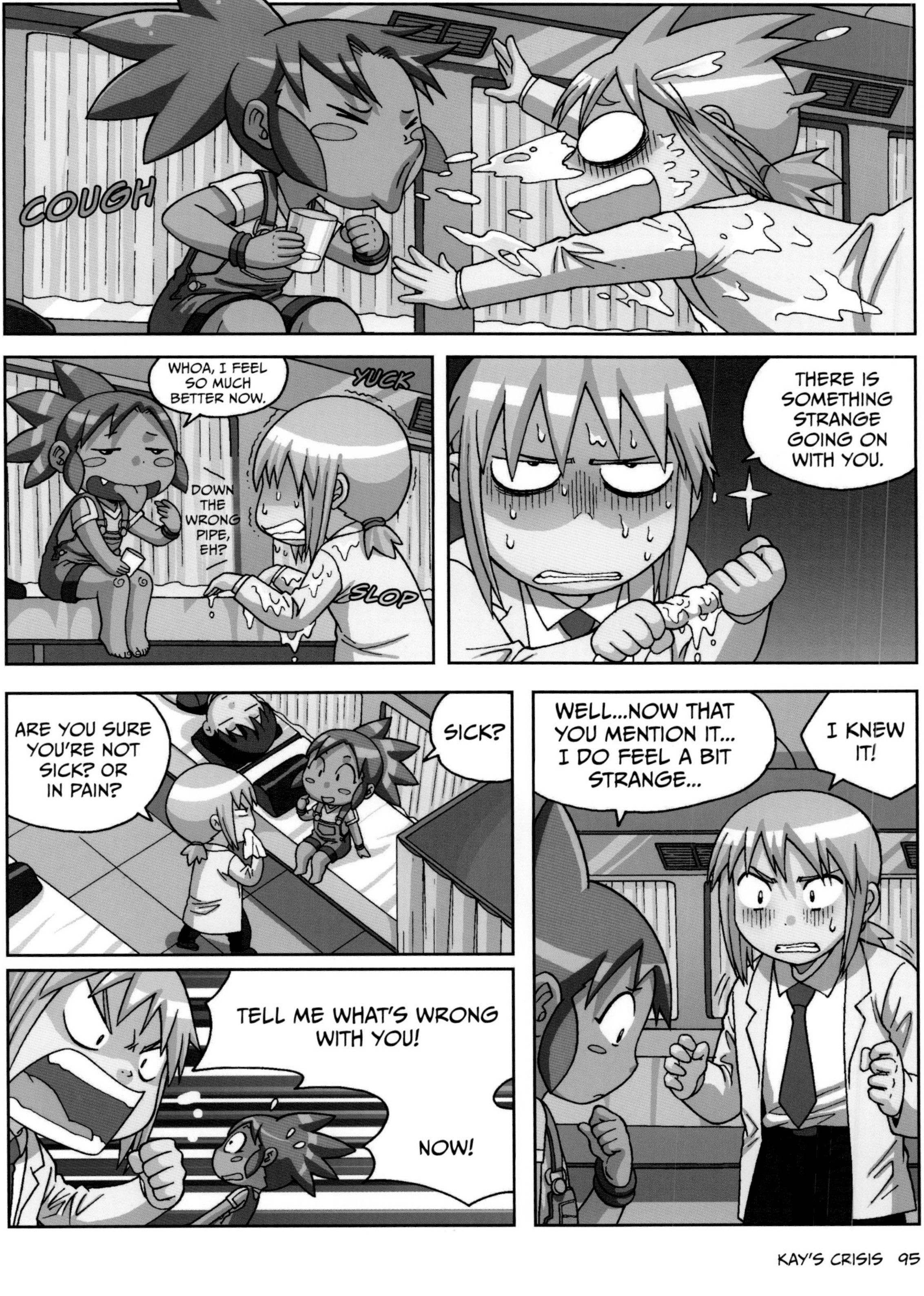
COUGH
WHOA, I FEEL SO MUCH BETTER NOW.
YUCK
DOWN THE WRONG PIPE, EH?
SLOP
THERE IS SOMETHING STRANGE GOING ON WITH YOU.
ARE YOU SURE YOU'RE NOT SICK? OR IN PAIN?
SICK?
WELL...NOW THAT YOU MENTION IT... I DO FEEL A BIT STRANGE...
I KNEW IT!
TELL ME WHAT'S WRONG WITH YOU!
NOW!

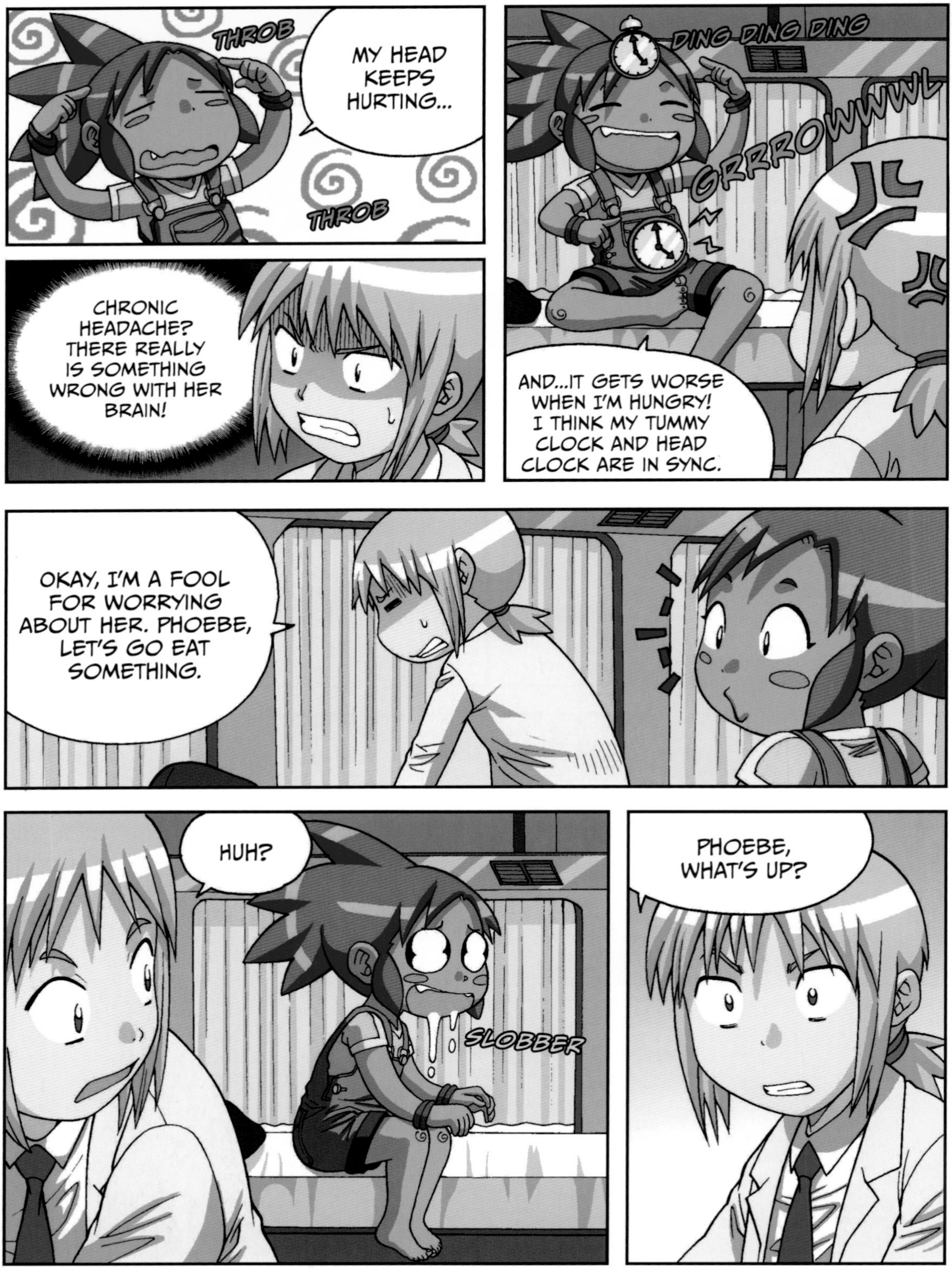
THROB
MY HEAD KEEPS HURTING...
THROB
DING DING DING
GRRROWWWL
CHRONIC HEADACHE? THERE REALLY IS SOMETHING WRONG WITH HER BRAIN!
AND...IT GETS WORSE WHEN I'M HUNGRY! I THINK MY TUMMY CLOCK AND HEAD CLOCK ARE IN SYNC.
OKAY, I'M A FOOL FOR WORRYING ABOUT HER. PHOEBE, LET'S GO EAT SOMETHING.
HUH?
SLOBBER
PHOEBE, WHAT'S UP?

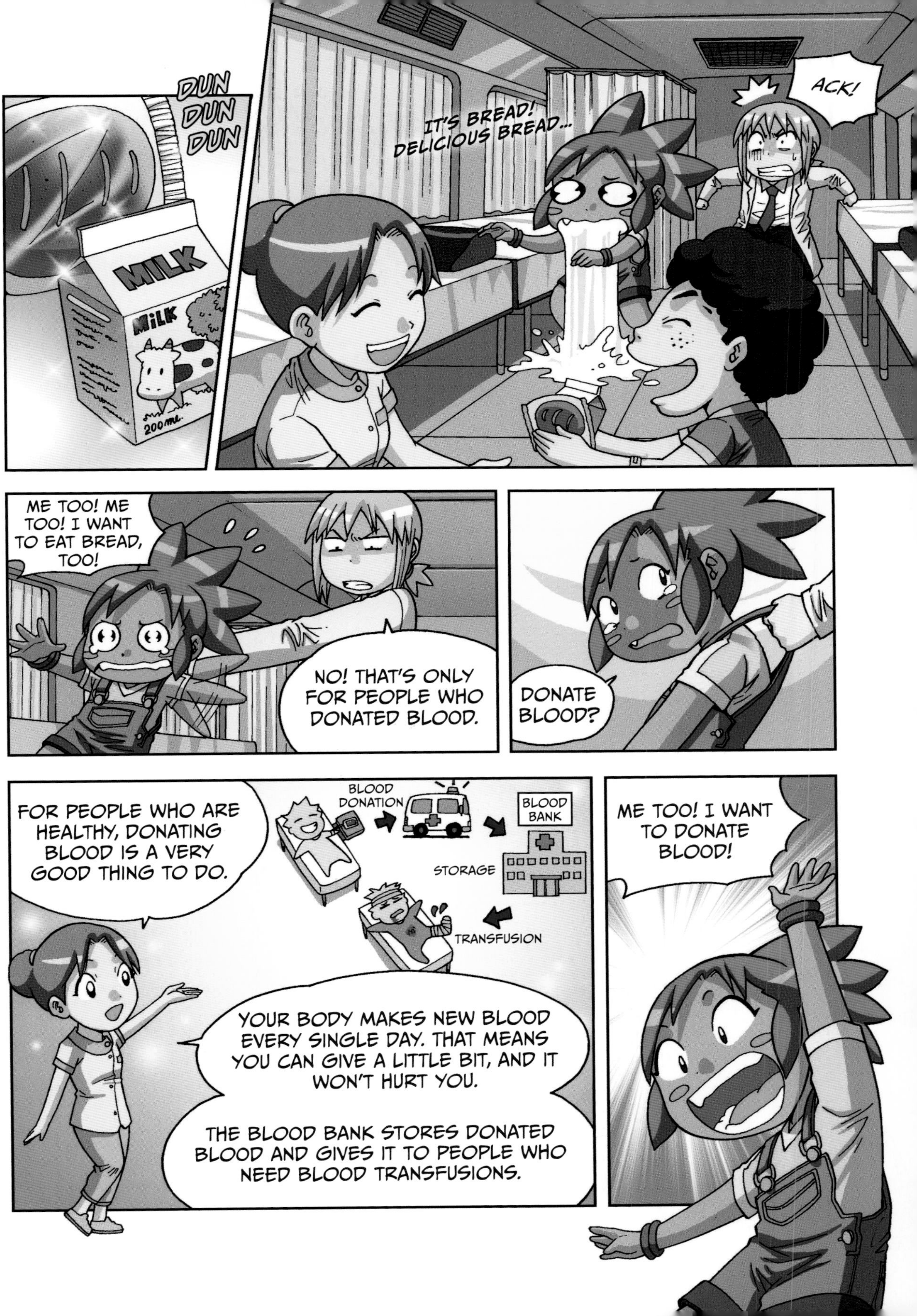
DUN DUN DUN
MILK
MILK
200ml.
IT'S BREAD! DELICIOUS BREAD...
ACK!
ME TOO! ME TOO! I WANT TO EAT BREAD, TOO!
NO! THAT'S ONLY FOR PEOPLE WHO DONATED BLOOD.
DONATE BLOOD?
FOR PEOPLE WHO ARE HEALTHY, DONATING BLOOD IS A VERY GOOD THING TO DO.
BLOOD DONATION
BLOOD BANK
STORAGE
TRANSFUSION
YOUR BODY MAKES NEW BLOOD EVERY SINGLE DAY. THAT MEANS YOU CAN GIVE A LITTLE BIT, AND IT WON'T HURT YOU.
THE BLOOD BANK STORES DONATED BLOOD AND GIVES IT TO PEOPLE WHO NEED BLOOD TRANSFUSIONS.
ME TOO! I WANT TO DONATE BLOOD!

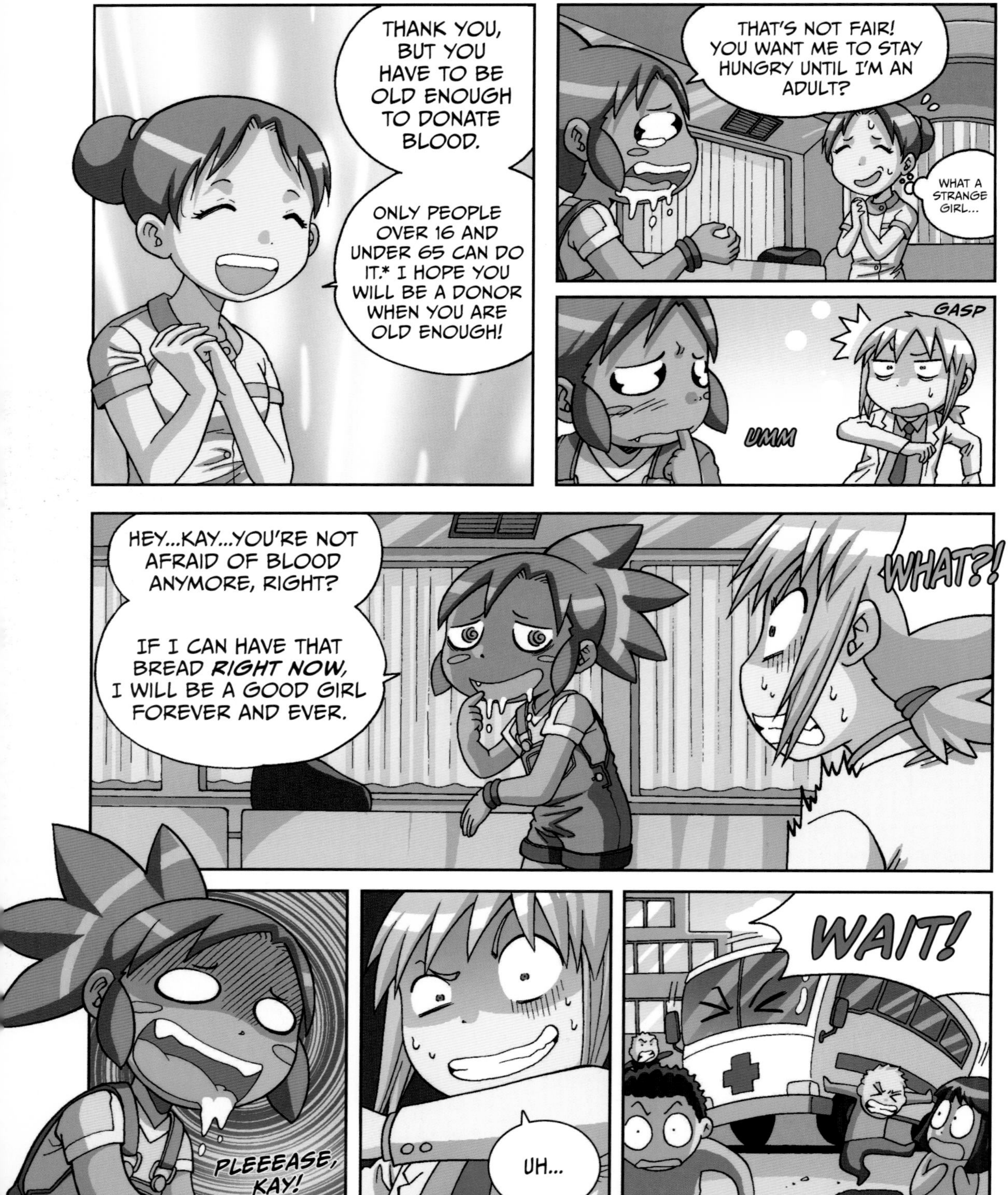
THANK YOU, BUT YOU HAVE TO BE OLD ENOUGH TO DONATE BLOOD.
ONLY PEOPLE OVER 16 AND UNDER 65 CAN DO IT.* I HOPE YOU WILL BE A DONOR WHEN YOU ARE OLD ENOUGH!
THAT'S NOT FAIR! YOU WANT ME TO STAY HUNGRY UNTIL I'M AN ADULT?
WHAT A STRANGE GIRL...
GASP
UMM
HEY...KAY...YOU'RE NOT AFRAID OF BLOOD ANYMORE, RIGHT?
IF I CAN HAVE THAT BREAD RIGHT NOW, I WILL BE A GOOD GIRL FOREVER AND EVER.
WHAT?!
PLEEEASE, KAY!
UH...
WAIT!

* DIFFERENT STATES (AND COUNTRIES) HAVE DIFFERENT RULES ABOUT BLOOD DONATION. READ MORE ABOUT BLOOD DONATIONS AT *HTTP://REDCROSSBLOOD.ORG/*.

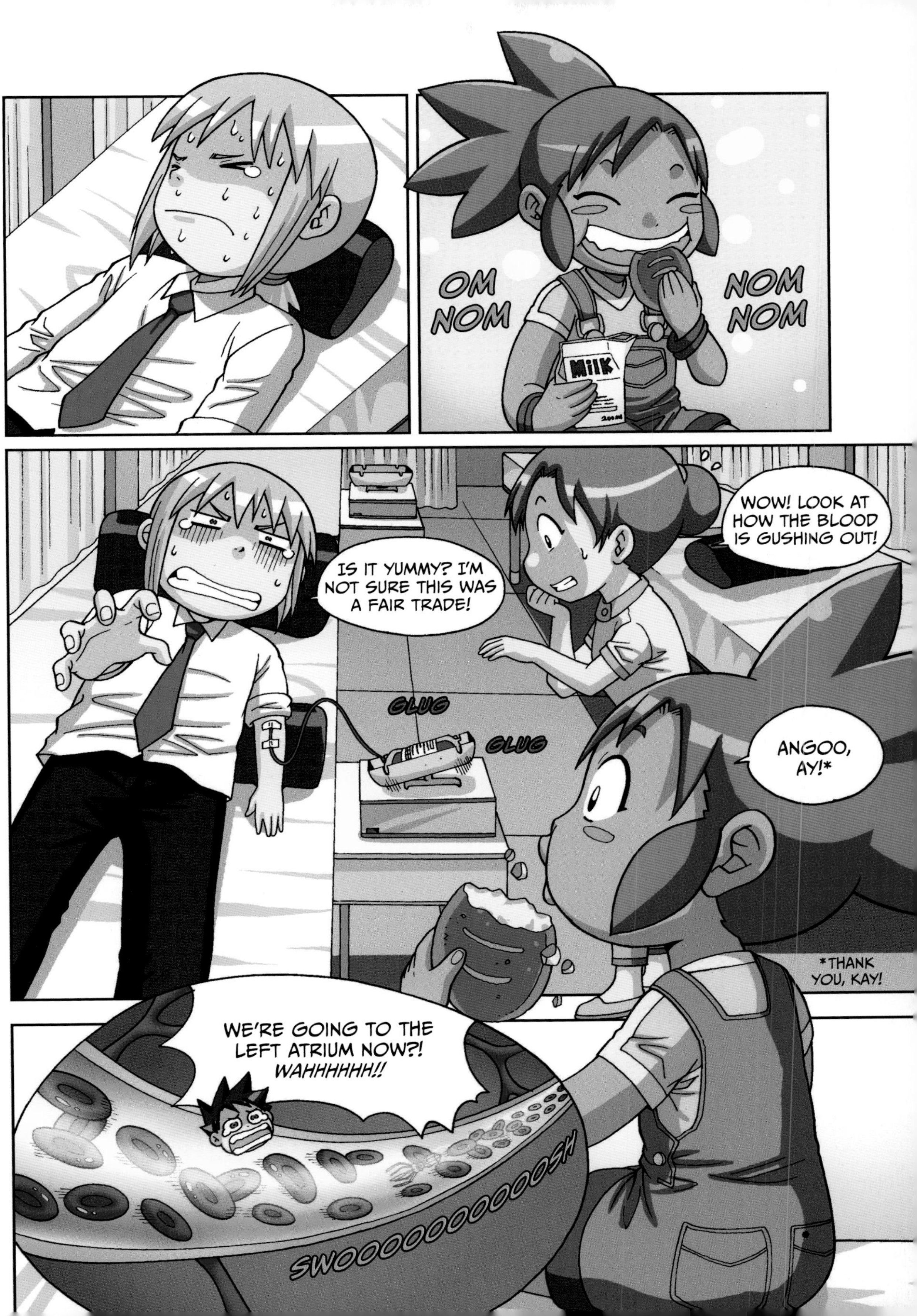
OM NOM
NOM NOM
MILK
IS IT YUMMY? I'M NOT SURE THIS WAS A FAIR TRADE!
WOW! LOOK AT HOW THE BLOOD IS GUSHING OUT!
GLUG
GLUG
ANGOO, AY!*
*THANK YOU, KAY!
WE'RE GOING TO THE LEFT ATRIUM NOW?! WAHHHHHH!!
SWOOOOOOOOOOOOSH

CIRCULATORY SYSTEM

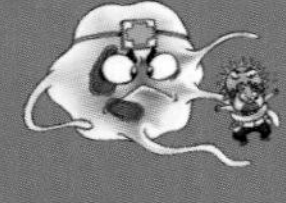

UNDERSTANDING BLOOD TYPES

When people get in an accident or have surgery, they can lose a lot of blood, which is very dangerous or even fatal. Doctors can give patients a blood transfusion to replace the blood they've lost. But the blood used in transfusions must be as close a match as possible to the patient's blood.

DISCOVERY OF BLOOD TYPES

Today getting a blood transfusion is a simple and safe medical procedure, but it used to be like gambling with your life. Most of the patients who received blood transfusions had blood clots and died from poor blood circulation. At first, everyone thought this problem was because of diseases like rheumatism or tuberculosis. The mystery was finally solved after an Austrian scientist named Karl Landsteiner discovered blood types in the early 20th century. He noticed that when blood from two different people mixed, the blood clumped together. This is an immune response known as *agglutination*. From that, he was able to discover the three main blood types: A, B, and O.

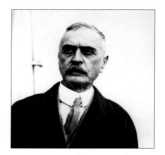

Karl Landsteiner (1868–1943) received the Nobel Prize in Physiology or Medicine in 1930 for his discovery of blood types.

Since then, it has become common knowledge that people have different blood types. This was the beginning of safe blood transfusions and saved many many lives.

A, B, AND O BLOOD TYPES AND RH FACTOR

When people have Type A blood, that means their red blood cells have the A antigen, an immune marker. Their blood plasma (the fluid that the cells float in) has B antibodies. People with Type B blood, on the other hand, have B antigens in their cells and A antibodies in their blood plasma. If you give Type A blood to a patient with Type B blood, the patient's A antibodies will attack the Type A blood. The same thing happens in reverse if you tried to transfuse Type B blood into a person with Type A blood.

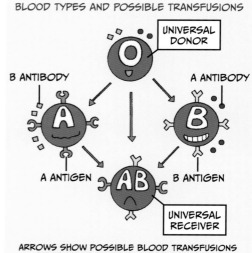

BLOOD TYPES AND POSSIBLE TRANSFUSIONS

UNIVERSAL DONOR
O
B ANTIBODY
A ANTIBODY
A
B
A ANTIGEN
B ANTIGEN
AB
UNIVERSAL RECEIVER

ARROWS SHOW POSSIBLE BLOOD TRANSFUSIONS (EACH BLOOD TYPE CAN ALSO DONATE TO A PERSON WITH THE SAME BLOOD TYPE.)

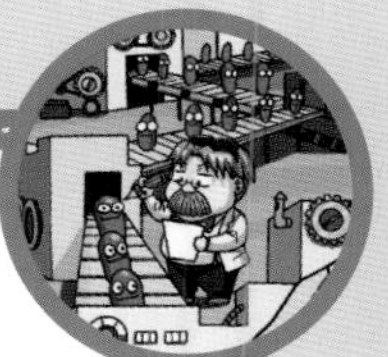

Type O blood has no A or B antigens, but in the plasma, there are A and B antibodies. That means that people with Type O blood can donate to anyone—but they can only receive Type O blood in return. People with Type AB blood have both antigens but no A or B antibodies. They can receive any kind of blood.

Also, doctors have to think about another kind of blood type system when matching blood. This system is called *Rh*, a grouping of 50 antigens. People are either Rh positive (Rh+) or Rh negative (Rh–). Matching the Rh factor is important, as a mismatch can cause bad immune reactions, just like an ABO mismatch.

The biggest problem that doctors face with this blood type is with pregnant women and their babies. If a woman is Rh– and her baby is Rh+, the mother's antigens can start making antigens against Rh+. This means the baby's blood is being attacked! Babies can become very sick and even die from this. Luckily, we have medicine that keeps this from happening. Doctors always check pregnant women for this blood type.

HEREDITY OF BLOOD TYPES

Each parent passes down one of the A, B, or O blood types to their children. The child's blood type is made by mixing the genes from the parents.

Parents' Blood Types	O × O =	A × O *or* A × A =	B × O *or* B × B =	O × AB =	A × AB, B × AB, *or* AB × AB =	A × B =
Child's Type	O	A *or* O	B *or* O	A *or* B	A, B, *or* AB	A, B, O, *or* AB

SAVING LIVES BY DONATING BLOOD

Blood is donated by healthy people for free. Most adults have about 10 pints of blood, so they can donate a pint of blood to help others without hurting themselves at all. To be safe, the donated blood is first tested for diseases like hepatitis, and then it is stored in the blood bank for patients who need it later. There's still no substitute for real blood, so doctors (and patients!) must rely on donors.

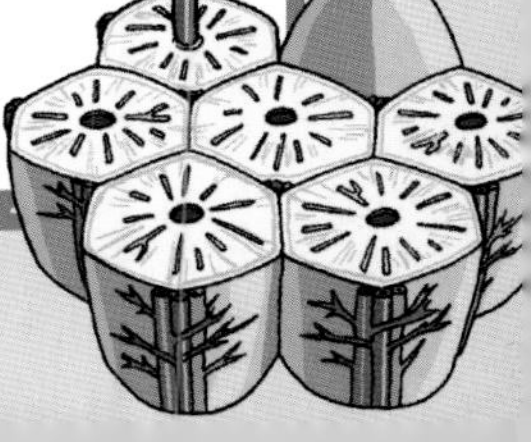

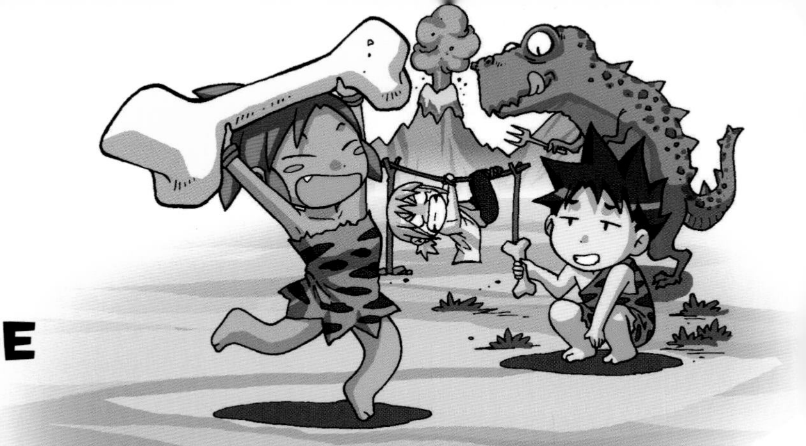

PHOEBE'S HEMORRHAGE

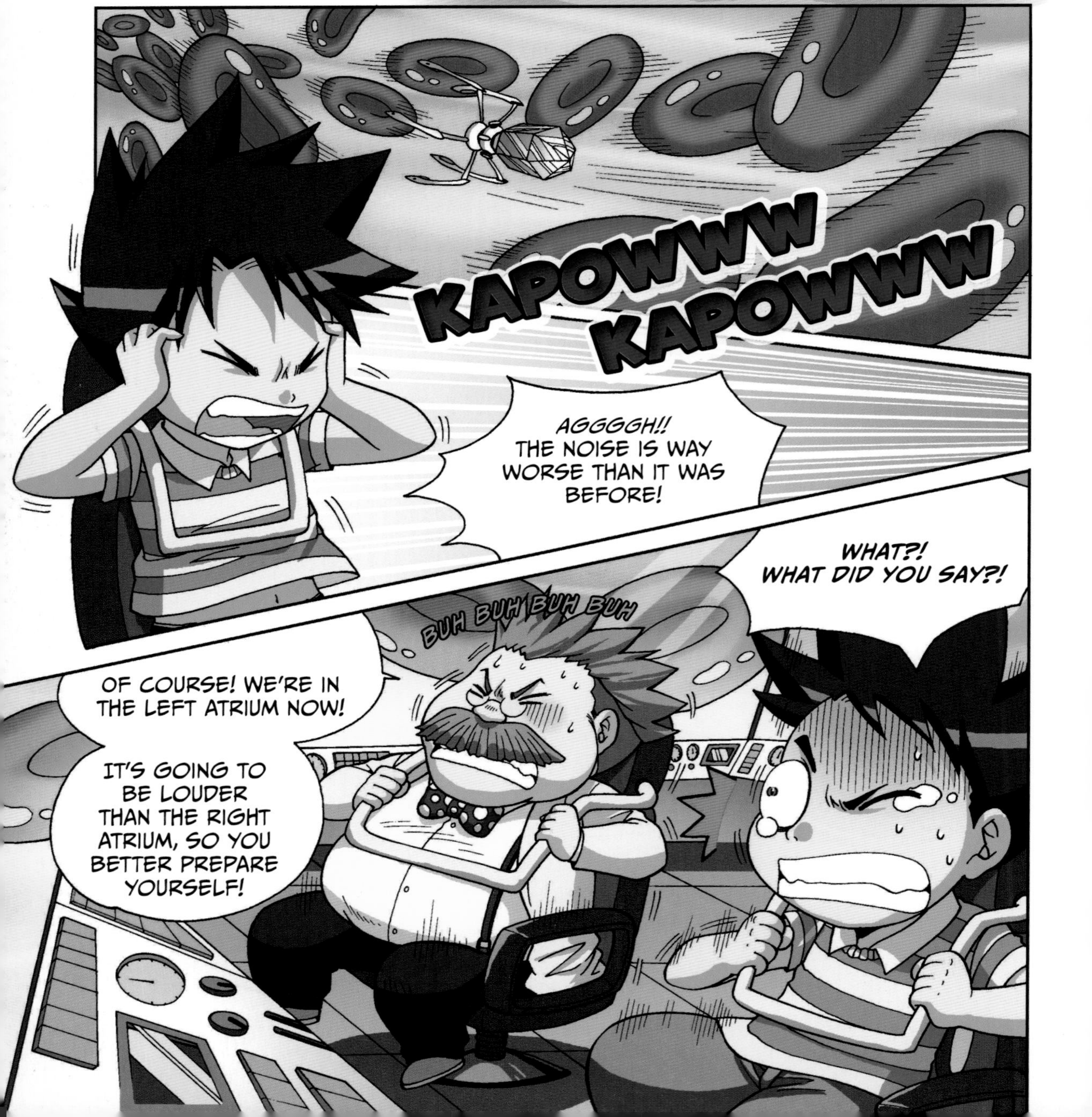
KAPOWWW
KAPOWWW
AGGGGH!! THE NOISE IS WAY WORSE THAN IT WAS BEFORE!
WHAT?! WHAT DID YOU SAY?!
BUH BUH BUH BUH
OF COURSE! WE'RE IN THE LEFT ATRIUM NOW!
IT'S GOING TO BE LOUDER THAN THE RIGHT ATRIUM, SO YOU BETTER PREPARE YOURSELF!

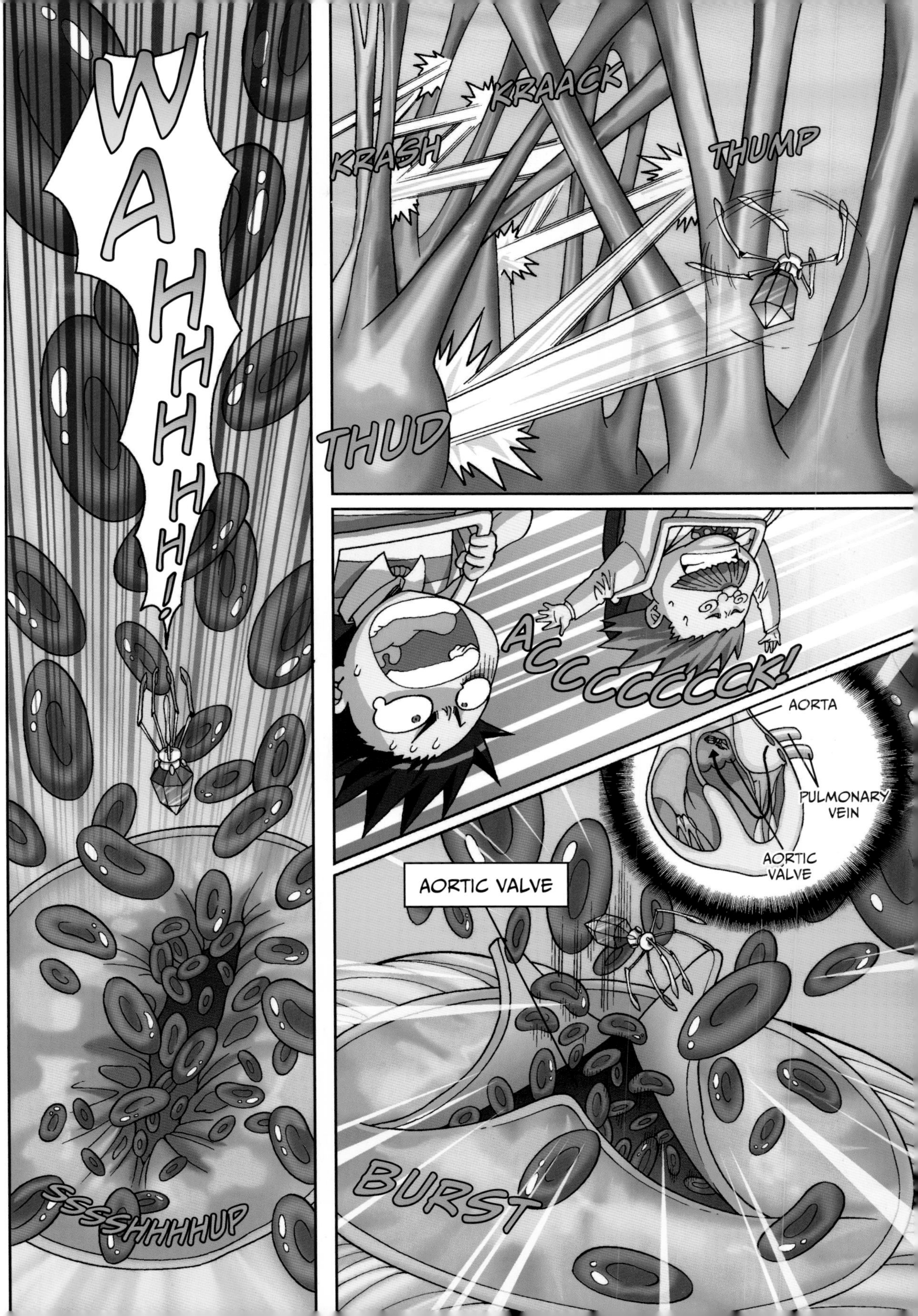
WAHHHHHH!
SSSSHHHHUP
KRASH
KRAACK
THUMP
THUD
ACCCCCCCCK!
AORTA
PULMONARY VEIN
AORTIC VALVE
AORTIC VALVE
BURST

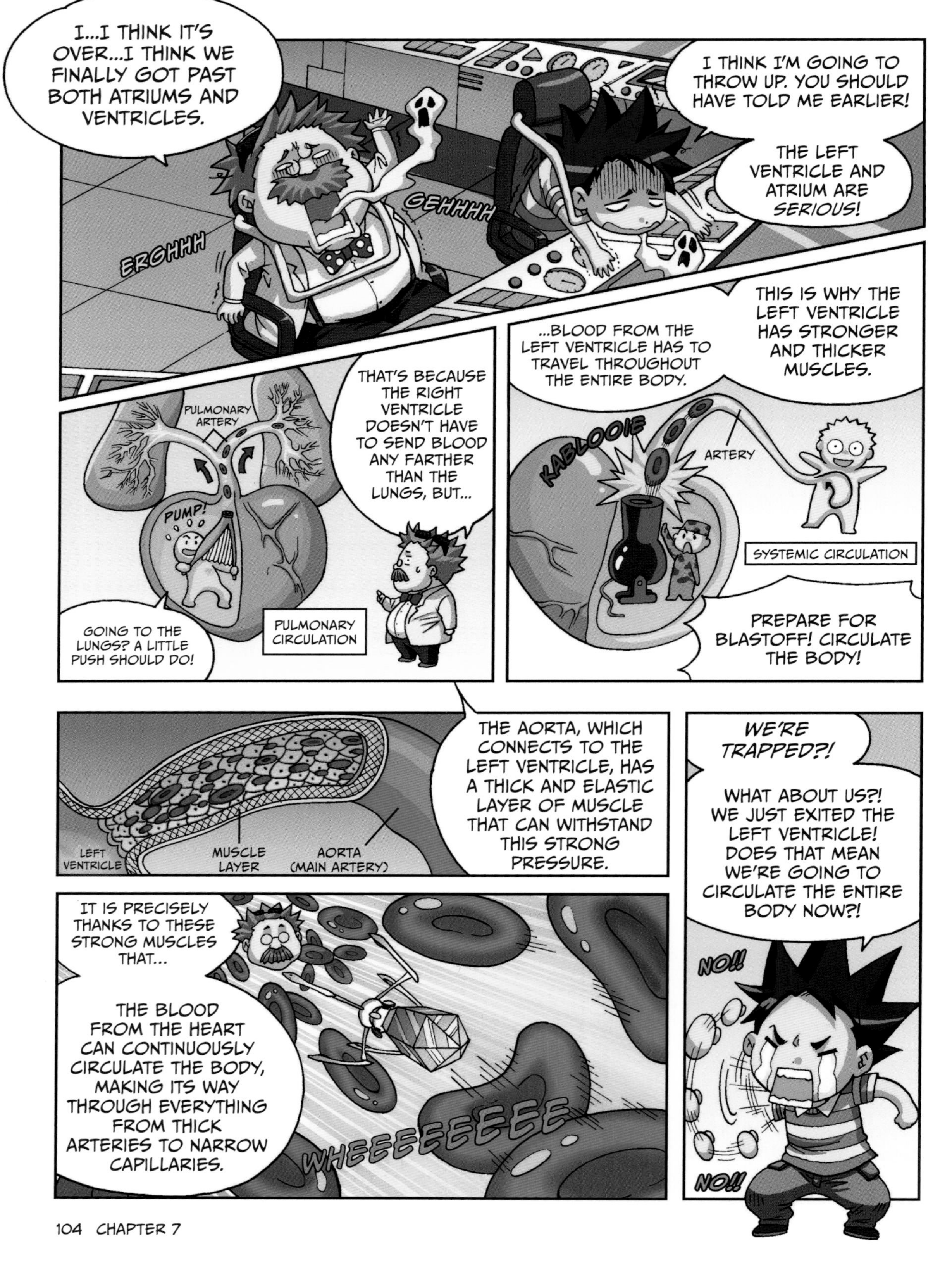

I...I THINK IT'S OVER...I THINK WE FINALLY GOT PAST BOTH ATRIUMS AND VENTRICLES.
ERGHHH
GEHHHH
I THINK I'M GOING TO THROW UP. YOU SHOULD HAVE TOLD ME EARLIER!
THE LEFT VENTRICLE AND ATRIUM ARE *SERIOUS*!
PULMONARY ARTERY
THAT'S BECAUSE THE RIGHT VENTRICLE DOESN'T HAVE TO SEND BLOOD ANY FARTHER THAN THE LUNGS, BUT...
PUMP!
GOING TO THE LUNGS? A LITTLE PUSH SHOULD DO!
PULMONARY CIRCULATION
...BLOOD FROM THE LEFT VENTRICLE HAS TO TRAVEL THROUGHOUT THE ENTIRE BODY.
THIS IS WHY THE LEFT VENTRICLE HAS STRONGER AND THICKER MUSCLES.
KABLOOIE
ARTERY
SYSTEMIC CIRCULATION
PREPARE FOR BLASTOFF! CIRCULATE THE BODY!
LEFT VENTRICLE
MUSCLE LAYER
AORTA (MAIN ARTERY)
THE AORTA, WHICH CONNECTS TO THE LEFT VENTRICLE, HAS A THICK AND ELASTIC LAYER OF MUSCLE THAT CAN WITHSTAND THIS STRONG PRESSURE.
IT IS PRECISELY THANKS TO THESE STRONG MUSCLES THAT...
THE BLOOD FROM THE HEART CAN CONTINUOUSLY CIRCULATE THE BODY, MAKING ITS WAY THROUGH EVERYTHING FROM THICK ARTERIES TO NARROW CAPILLARIES.
WHEEEEEEEEE
WE'RE TRAPPED?!
WHAT ABOUT US?! WE JUST EXITED THE LEFT VENTRICLE! DOES THAT MEAN WE'RE GOING TO CIRCULATE THE ENTIRE BODY NOW?!
NO!!
NO!!

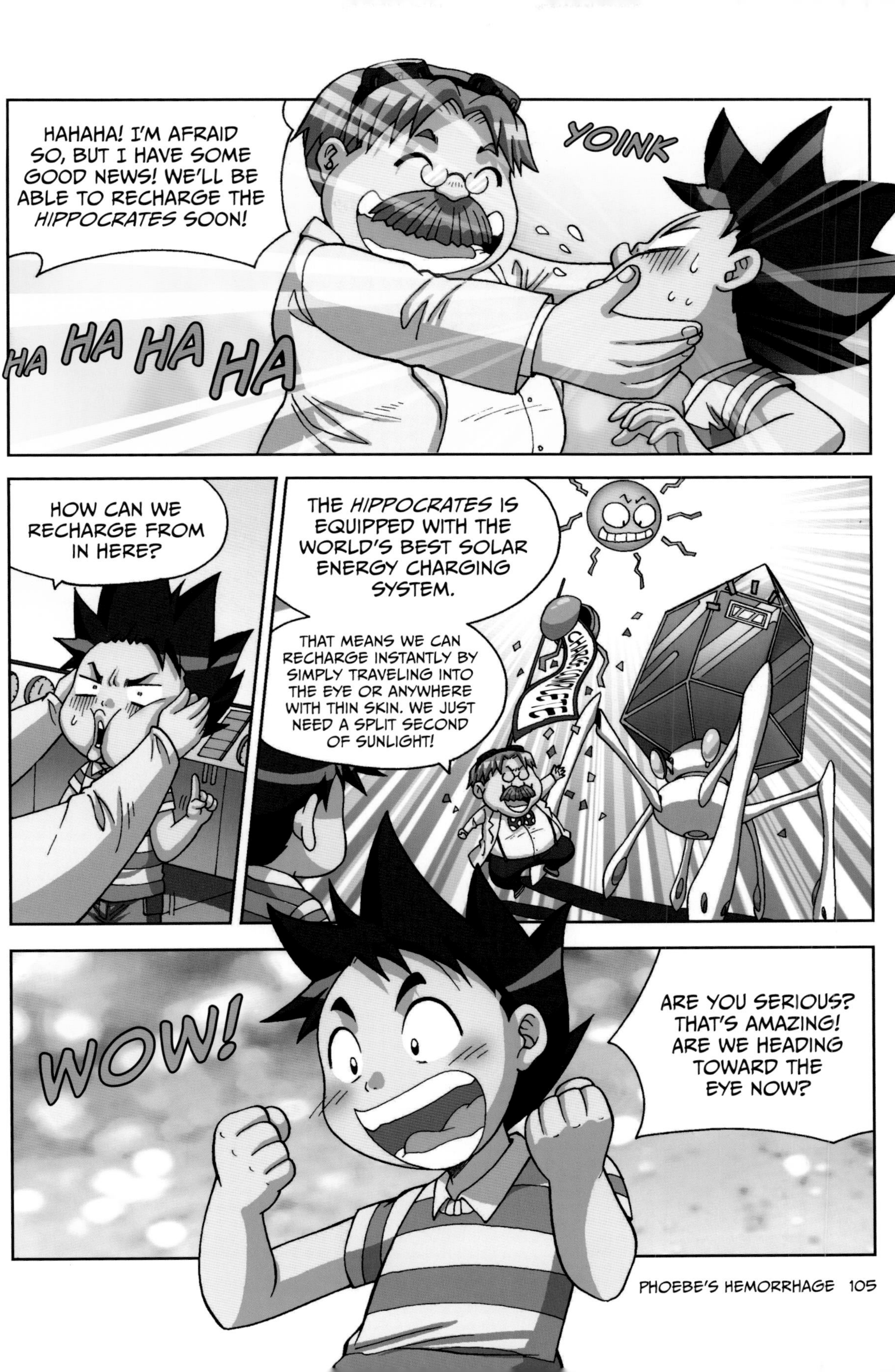
HAHAHA! I'M AFRAID SO, BUT I HAVE SOME GOOD NEWS! WE'LL BE ABLE TO RECHARGE THE *HIPPOCRATES* SOON!
YOINK
HA HA HA HA HA
HOW CAN WE RECHARGE FROM IN HERE?
THE *HIPPOCRATES* IS EQUIPPED WITH THE WORLD'S BEST SOLAR ENERGY CHARGING SYSTEM.
THAT MEANS WE CAN RECHARGE INSTANTLY BY SIMPLY TRAVELING INTO THE EYE OR ANYWHERE WITH THIN SKIN. WE JUST NEED A SPLIT SECOND OF SUNLIGHT!
CHARGE COMPLETE
WOW!
ARE YOU SERIOUS? THAT'S AMAZING! ARE WE HEADING TOWARD THE EYE NOW?

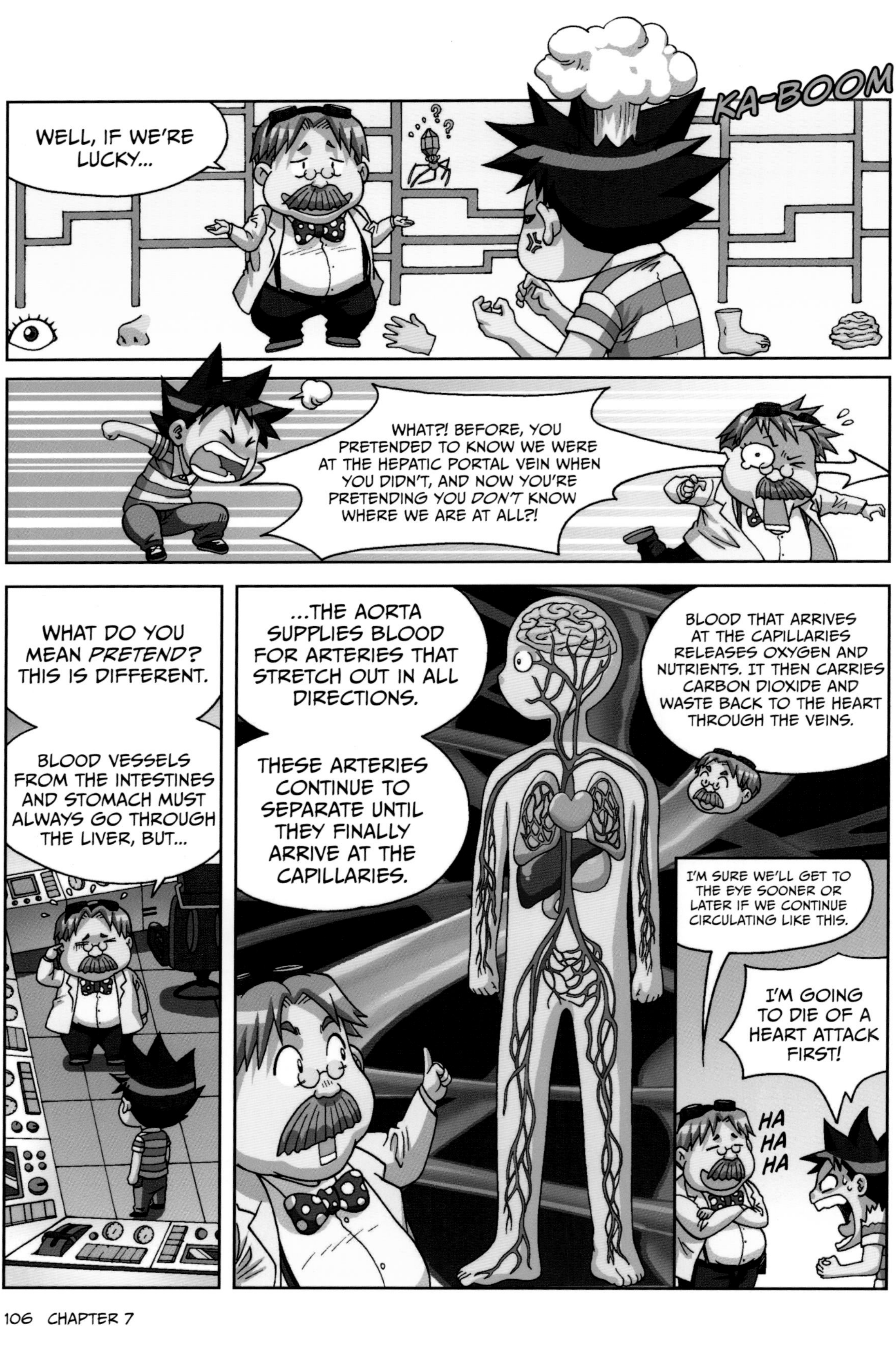
KA-BOOM
WELL, IF WE'RE LUCKY...
WHAT?! BEFORE, YOU PRETENDED TO KNOW WE WERE AT THE HEPATIC PORTAL VEIN WHEN YOU DIDN'T, AND NOW YOU'RE PRETENDING YOU *DON'T* KNOW WHERE WE ARE AT ALL?!
WHAT DO YOU MEAN *PRETEND*? THIS IS DIFFERENT.
BLOOD VESSELS FROM THE INTESTINES AND STOMACH MUST ALWAYS GO THROUGH THE LIVER, BUT...
...THE AORTA SUPPLIES BLOOD FOR ARTERIES THAT STRETCH OUT IN ALL DIRECTIONS.
THESE ARTERIES CONTINUE TO SEPARATE UNTIL THEY FINALLY ARRIVE AT THE CAPILLARIES.
BLOOD THAT ARRIVES AT THE CAPILLARIES RELEASES OXYGEN AND NUTRIENTS. IT THEN CARRIES CARBON DIOXIDE AND WASTE BACK TO THE HEART THROUGH THE VEINS.
I'M SURE WE'LL GET TO THE EYE SOONER OR LATER IF WE CONTINUE CIRCULATING LIKE THIS.
I'M GOING TO DIE OF A HEART ATTACK FIRST!
HA HA HA

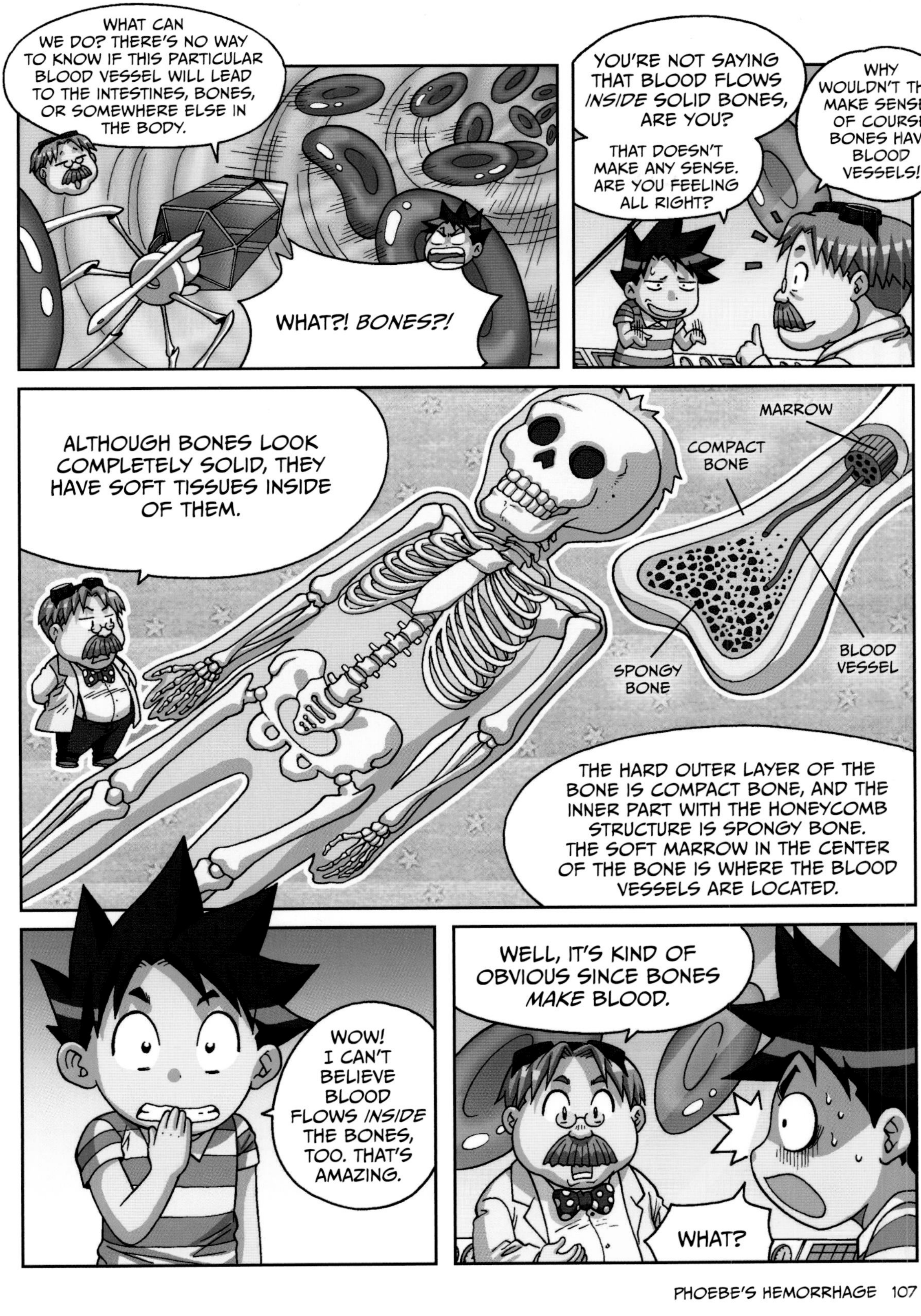

WHAT CAN WE DO? THERE'S NO WAY TO KNOW IF THIS PARTICULAR BLOOD VESSEL WILL LEAD TO THE INTESTINES, BONES, OR SOMEWHERE ELSE IN THE BODY.
WHAT?! BONES?!
YOU'RE NOT SAYING THAT BLOOD FLOWS INSIDE SOLID BONES, ARE YOU?
THAT DOESN'T MAKE ANY SENSE. ARE YOU FEELING ALL RIGHT?
WHY WOULDN'T THAT MAKE SENSE? OF COURSE BONES HAVE BLOOD VESSELS!
ALTHOUGH BONES LOOK COMPLETELY SOLID, THEY HAVE SOFT TISSUES INSIDE OF THEM.
MARROW
COMPACT BONE
SPONGY BONE
BLOOD VESSEL
THE HARD OUTER LAYER OF THE BONE IS COMPACT BONE, AND THE INNER PART WITH THE HONEYCOMB STRUCTURE IS SPONGY BONE. THE SOFT MARROW IN THE CENTER OF THE BONE IS WHERE THE BLOOD VESSELS ARE LOCATED.
WOW! I CAN'T BELIEVE BLOOD FLOWS INSIDE THE BONES, TOO. THAT'S AMAZING.
WELL, IT'S KIND OF OBVIOUS SINCE BONES MAKE BLOOD.
WHAT?

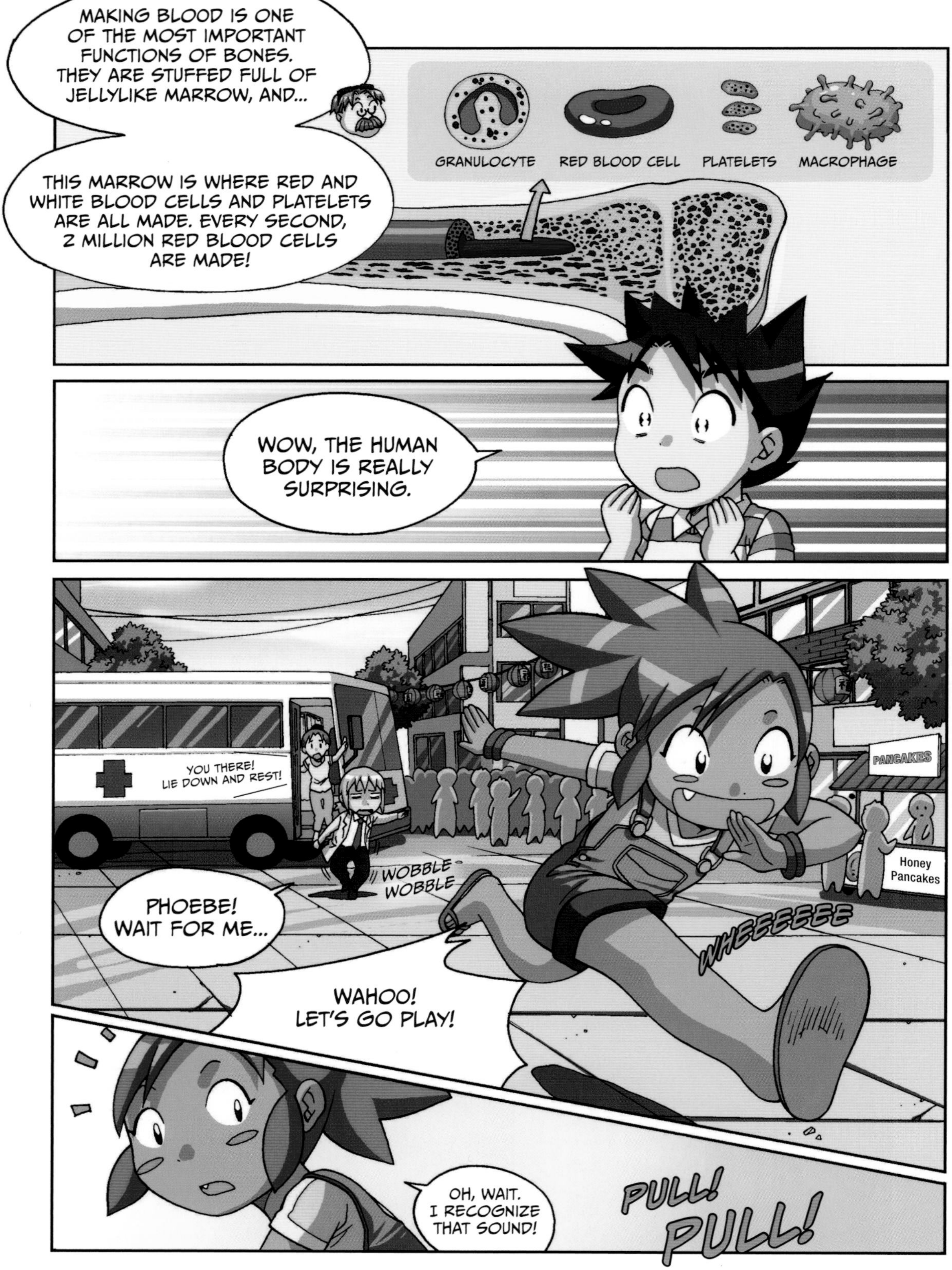

MAKING BLOOD IS ONE OF THE MOST IMPORTANT FUNCTIONS OF BONES. THEY ARE STUFFED FULL OF JELLYLIKE MARROW, AND...
THIS MARROW IS WHERE RED AND WHITE BLOOD CELLS AND PLATELETS ARE ALL MADE. EVERY SECOND, 2 MILLION RED BLOOD CELLS ARE MADE!
GRANULOCYTE
RED BLOOD CELL
PLATELETS
MACROPHAGE
WOW, THE HUMAN BODY IS REALLY SURPRISING.
YOU THERE! LIE DOWN AND REST!
PANCAKES
Honey Pancakes
WOBBLE WOBBLE
PHOEBE! WAIT FOR ME...
WHEEEEEEE
WAHOO! LET'S GO PLAY!
OH, WAIT. I RECOGNIZE THAT SOUND!
PULL! PULL!

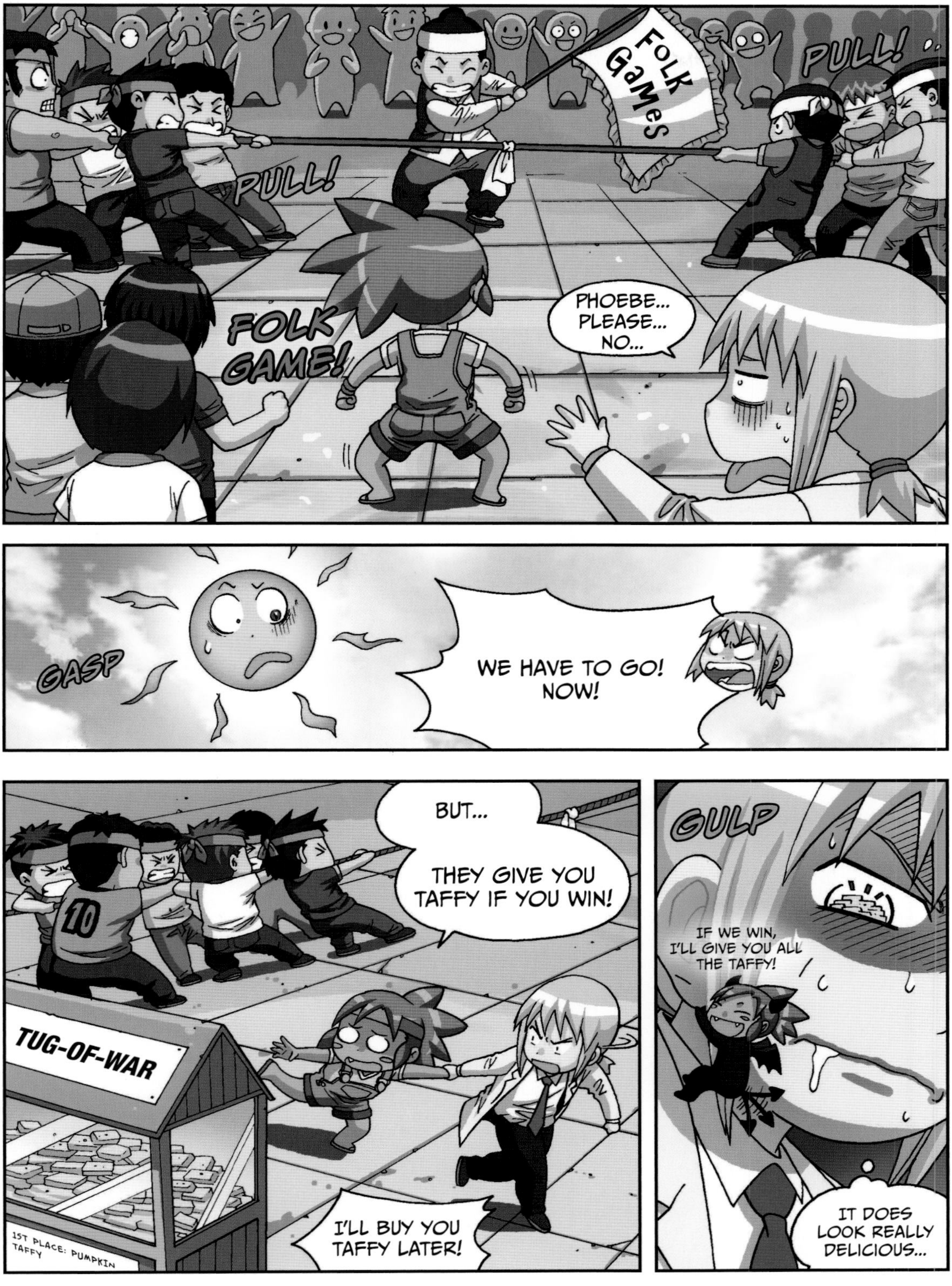
FOLK GAMES
PULL!
PULL!
FOLK GAME!
PHOEBE... PLEASE... NO...
GASP
WE HAVE TO GO! NOW!
BUT...
THEY GIVE YOU TAFFY IF YOU WIN!
TUG-OF-WAR
1ST PLACE: PUMPKIN TAFFY
I'LL BUY YOU TAFFY LATER!
GULP
IF WE WIN, I'LL GIVE YOU ALL THE TAFFY!
IT DOES LOOK REALLY DELICIOUS...

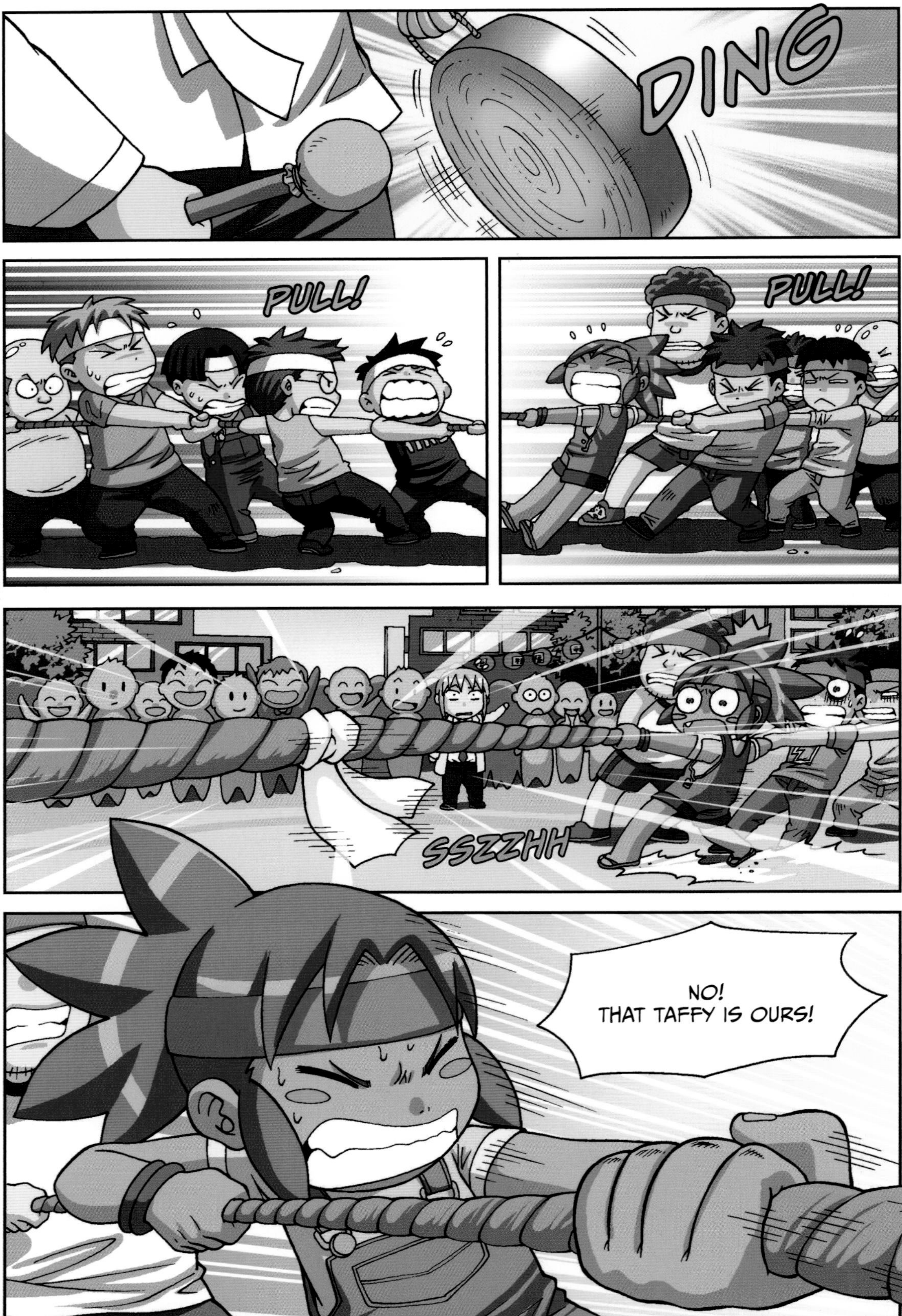
DING
PULL!
PULL!
SSZZHH
NO!
THAT TAFFY IS OURS!

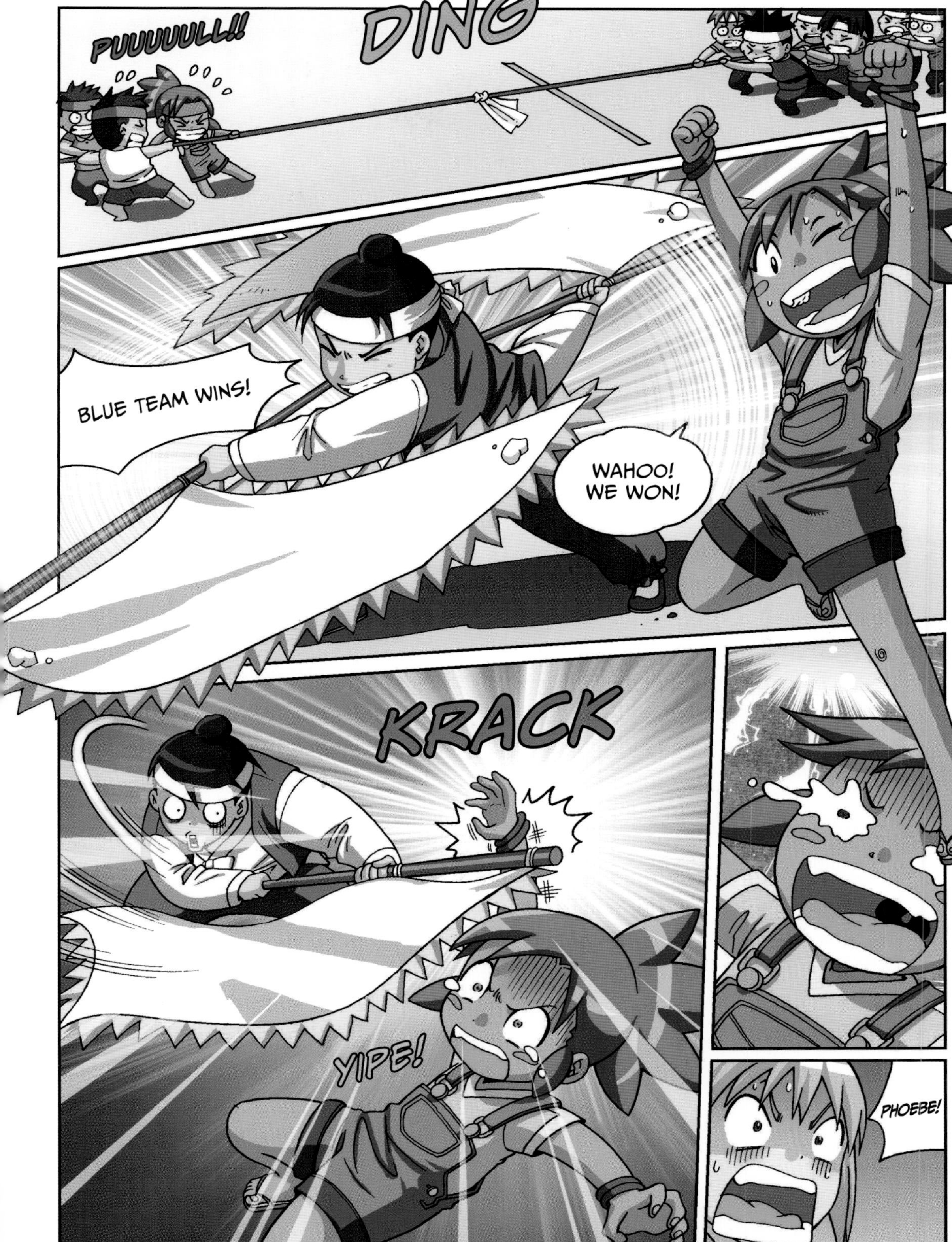

PUUUUULL!!
DING
BLUE TEAM WINS!
WAHOO! WE WON!
KRACK
YIPE!
PHOEBE!

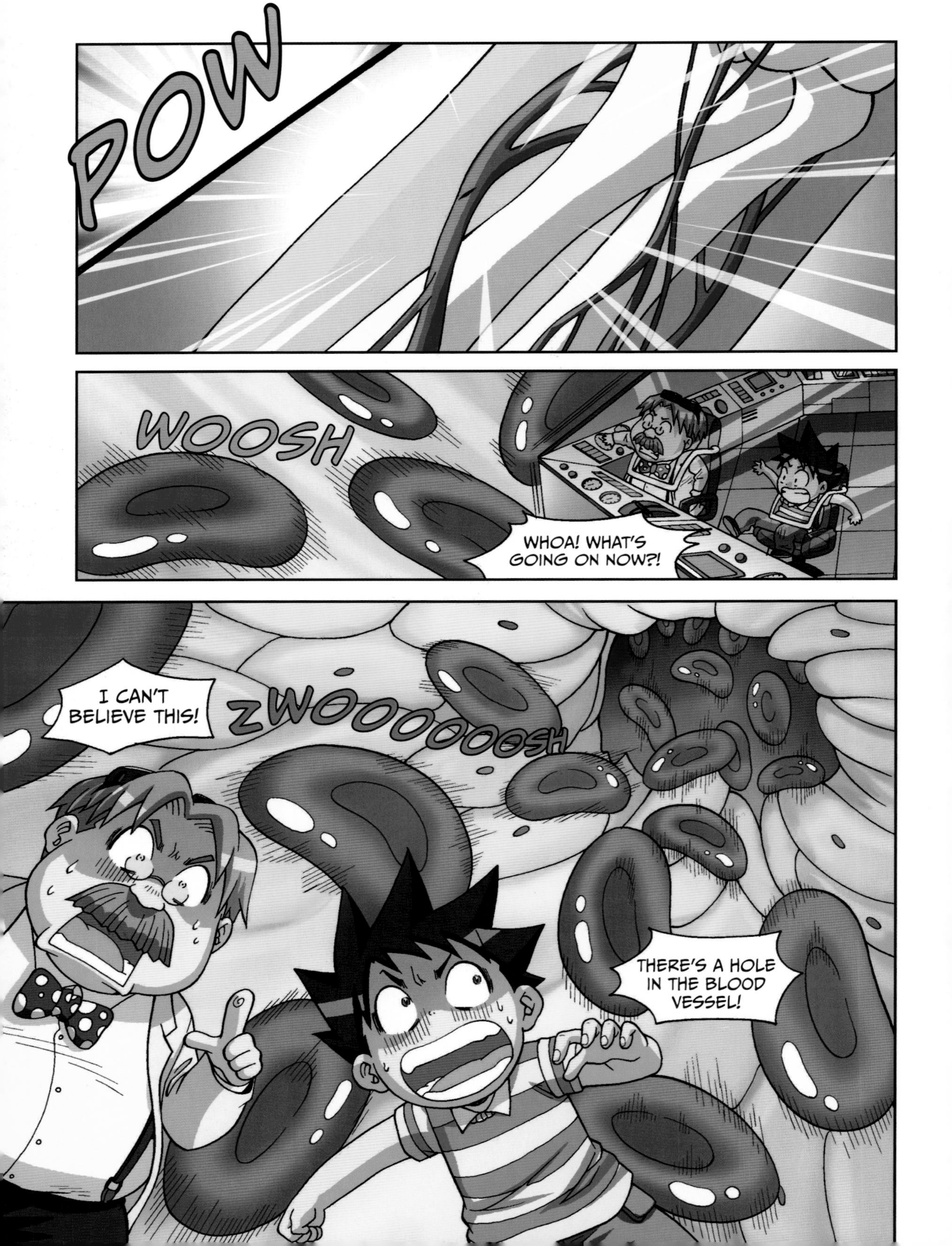
POW
WOOSH
WHOA! WHAT'S GOING ON NOW?!
I CAN'T BELIEVE THIS!
ZWOOOOOOOSH
THERE'S A HOLE IN THE BLOOD VESSEL!

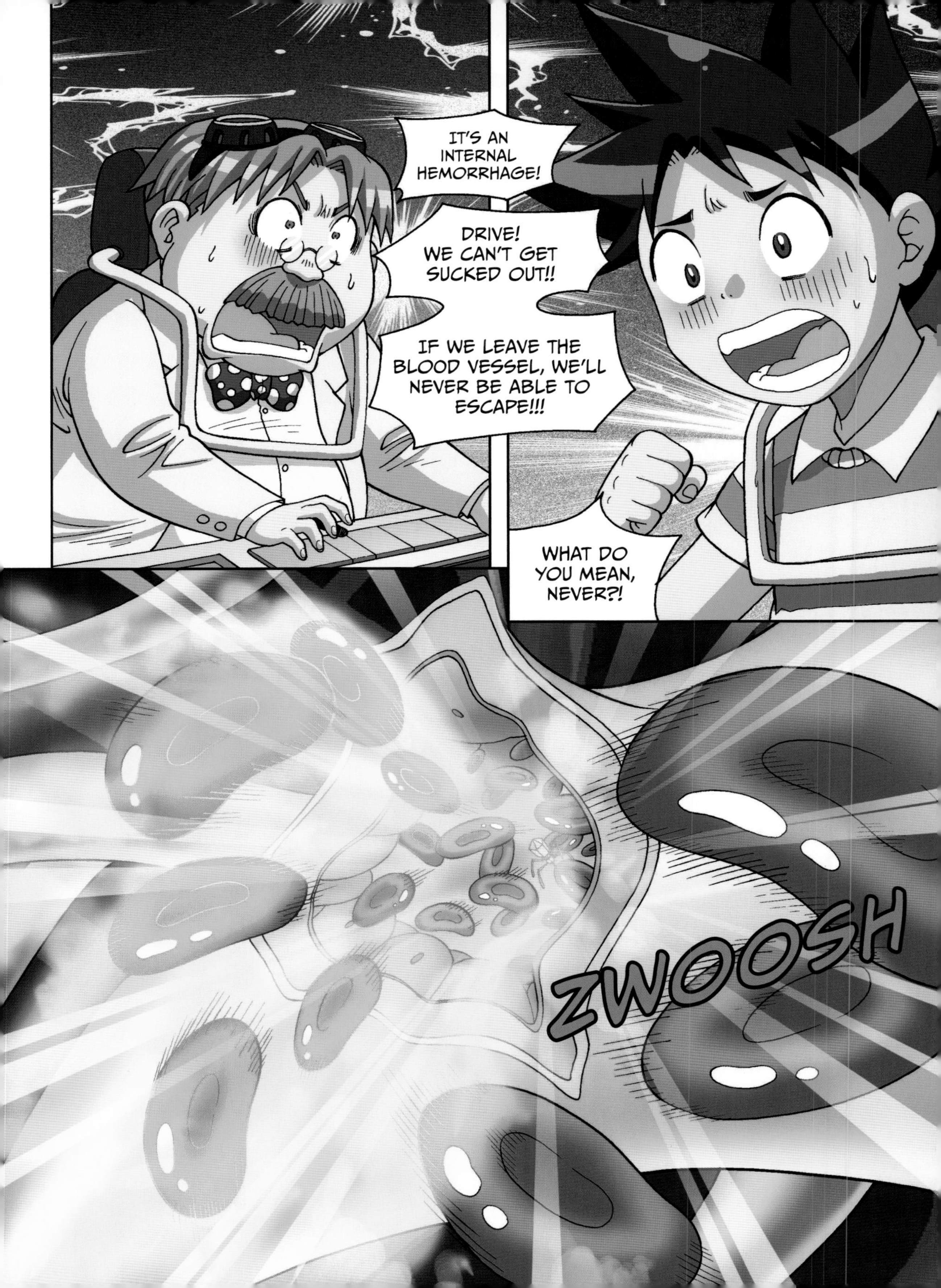
IT'S AN INTERNAL HEMORRHAGE!
DRIVE! WE CAN'T GET SUCKED OUT!!
IF WE LEAVE THE BLOOD VESSEL, WE'LL NEVER BE ABLE TO ESCAPE!!!
WHAT DO YOU MEAN, NEVER?!
ZWOOSH

THE SUPER-FLEXIBLE SKELETAL SYSTEM

The skeletal system is made up of the bones, cartilage, and joints that, together, maintain the framework of the human body. Humans have between 250 and 350 bones at birth, but many of these bones, such as the skull bones, fuse together as time goes on. By adulthood, the human body has 206 bones.

WHAT'S IN YOUR BONES?

The bones supporting our bodies have a unique structure. The outer parts of bones are made of compact bone. This hard, dense layer gives the bones weight and strength. Underneath this layer is spongy bone, a matrix of hollow cells that help to make bones lightweight and elastic. Deep within the bone is a hollow cavity containing the much softer bone marrow, which is composed of fat cells and is also where blood cells are created.

While bones are very hard, their unique structure also allows them to bend a little bit. Bones are in charge of supporting our muscles, bearing our weight, protecting internal organs (like the brain and heart) from damage, allowing movement through the use of joints, and creating blood cells.

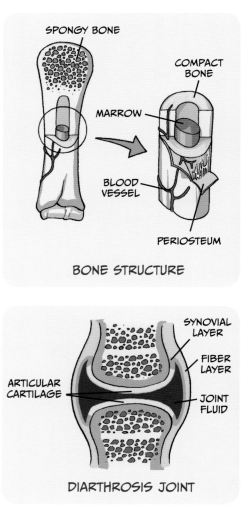

SPONGY BONE
COMPACT BONE
MARROW
BLOOD VESSEL
PERIOSTEUM

BONE STRUCTURE

JOINT STRUCTURE AND TYPES

We call the connection between a bone and another bone a *joint*. We are able to move our fingers, arms, and legs freely thanks to our joints. Depending on whether we can move them, joints are called either *diarthrosis joints* or *synarthrosis joints*. Diarthrosis joints are found in the bendy parts of the body, such as the knees and shoulders. The bones that form this type of joint are not directly connected with each other. There is a space between them that is filled with joint fluid and a joint membrane, allowing you to freely bend and straighten the joint. Synarthrosis joints cannot be moved because the bones making up these joints are connected by strongly adhesive fibrous tissue.

SYNOVIAL LAYER
FIBER LAYER
ARTICULAR CARTILAGE
JOINT FLUID

DIARTHROSIS JOINT

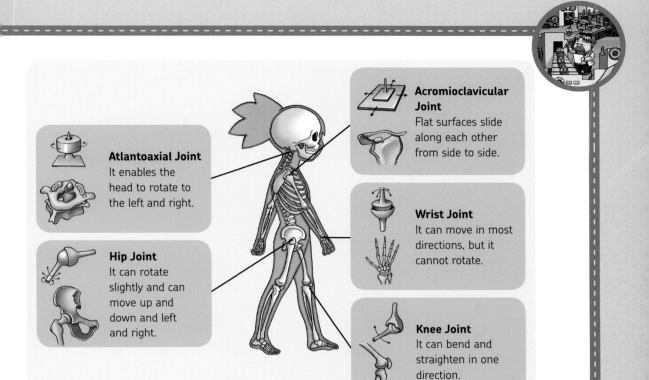

Atlantoaxial Joint
It enables the head to rotate to the left and right.
Hip Joint
It can rotate slightly and can move up and down and left and right.
Acromioclavicular Joint
Flat surfaces slide along each other from side to side.
Wrist Joint
It can move in most directions, but it cannot rotate.
Knee Joint
It can bend and straighten in one direction.

DIFFERENT KINDS OF DIARTHROSIS JOINTS

EPIPHYSEAL PLATE (GROWTH PLATE)

An epiphyseal plate, also known as a *growth plate*, is where a bone can grow. It is located at the end of bones directly connected to a joint. These plates are in our arms, legs, hands, feet, and back. Bone growth is a complicated process that involves nutrition, hormones, and even a good night's sleep.

Growth plate at the end of the knee joint

WHY AREN'T I TALLER?
BECAUSE YOU'RE READING BLOGS AT NIGHT INSTEAD OF SLEEPING!

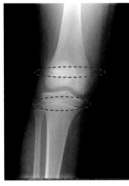

THE SS HIPPOCRATES BOUNCES BACK

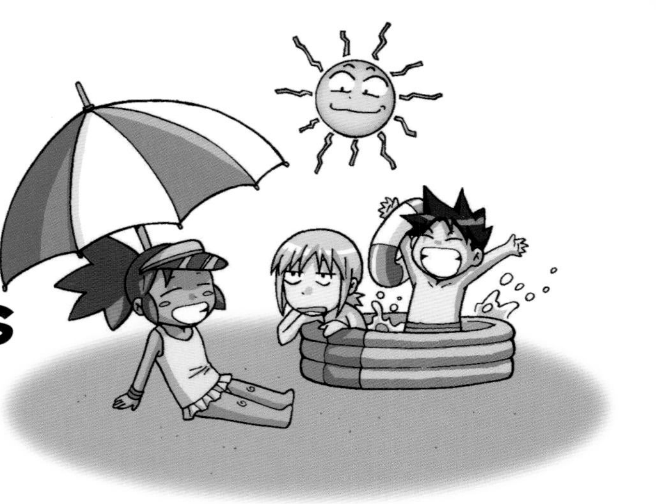

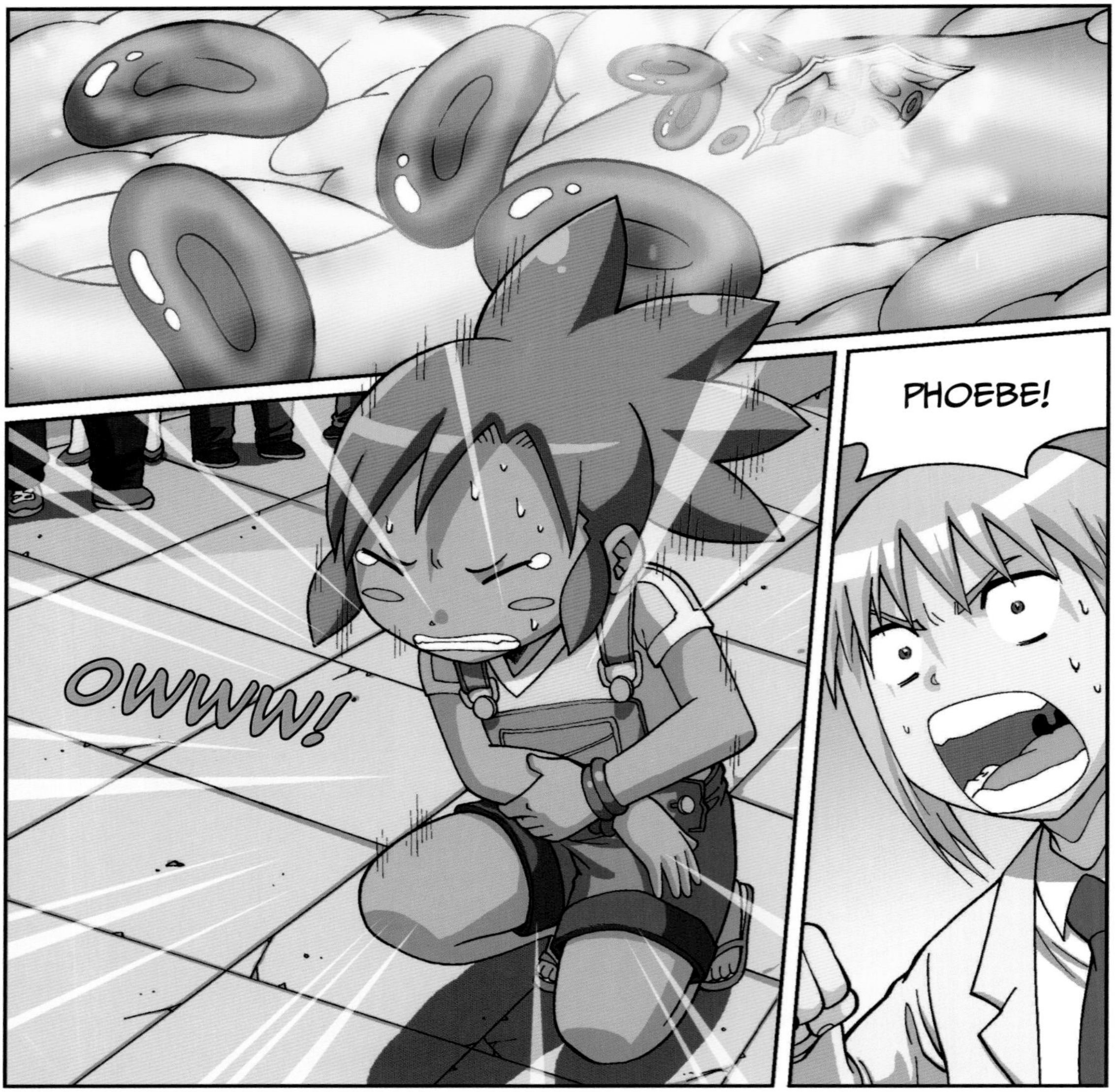
OWWW!
PHOEBE!

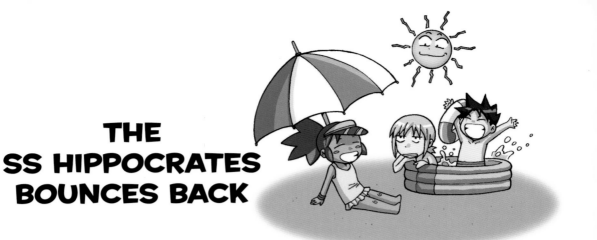

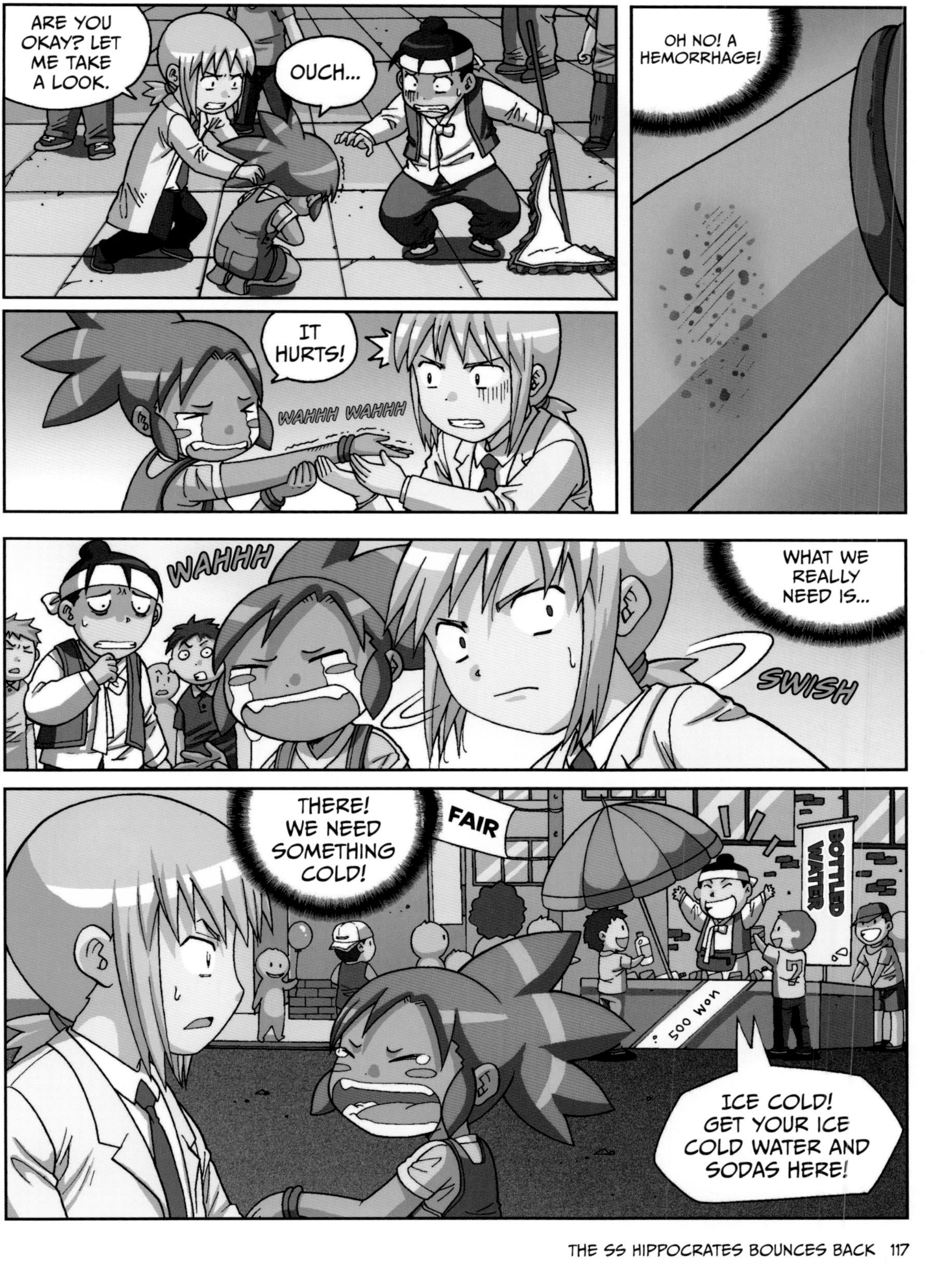
ARE YOU OKAY? LET ME TAKE A LOOK.
OUCH...
OH NO! A HEMORRHAGE!
IT HURTS!
WAHHH WAHHH
WAHHH
WHAT WE REALLY NEED IS...
SWISH
THERE! WE NEED SOMETHING COLD!
FAIR
BOTTLED WATER
500 won
ICE COLD! GET YOUR ICE COLD WATER AND SODAS HERE!

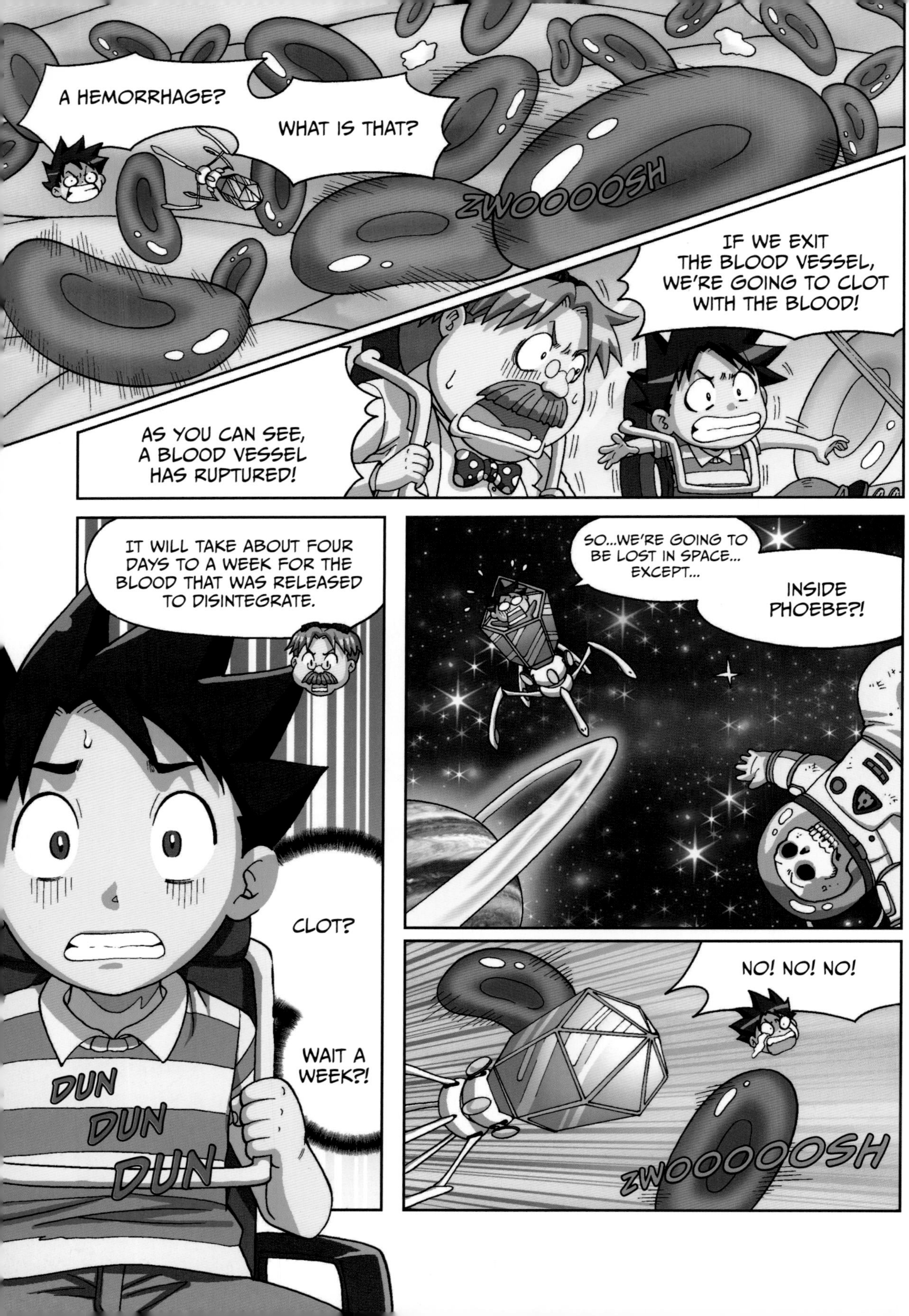
A HEMORRHAGE?
WHAT IS THAT?
ZWOOOOOSH
IF WE EXIT THE BLOOD VESSEL, WE'RE GOING TO CLOT WITH THE BLOOD!
AS YOU CAN SEE, A BLOOD VESSEL HAS RUPTURED!
IT WILL TAKE ABOUT FOUR DAYS TO A WEEK FOR THE BLOOD THAT WAS RELEASED TO DISINTEGRATE.
CLOT?
WAIT A WEEK?!
DUN DUN DUN
SO...WE'RE GOING TO BE LOST IN SPACE... EXCEPT...
INSIDE PHOEBE?!
NO! NO! NO!
ZWOOOOOSH

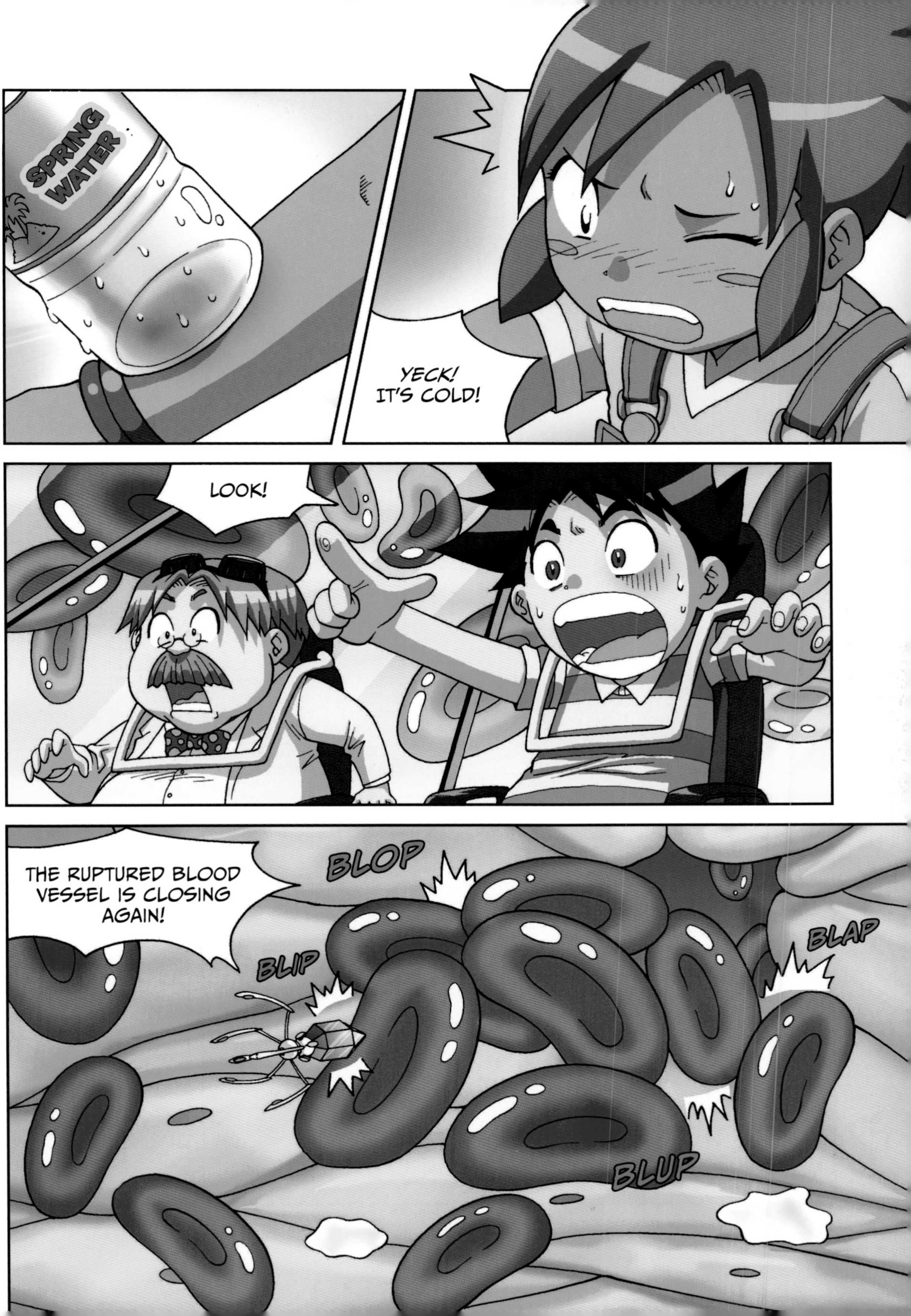
SPRING WATER
YECK! IT'S COLD!
LOOK!
THE RUPTURED BLOOD VESSEL IS CLOSING AGAIN!
BLOP
BLAP
BLIP
BLUP

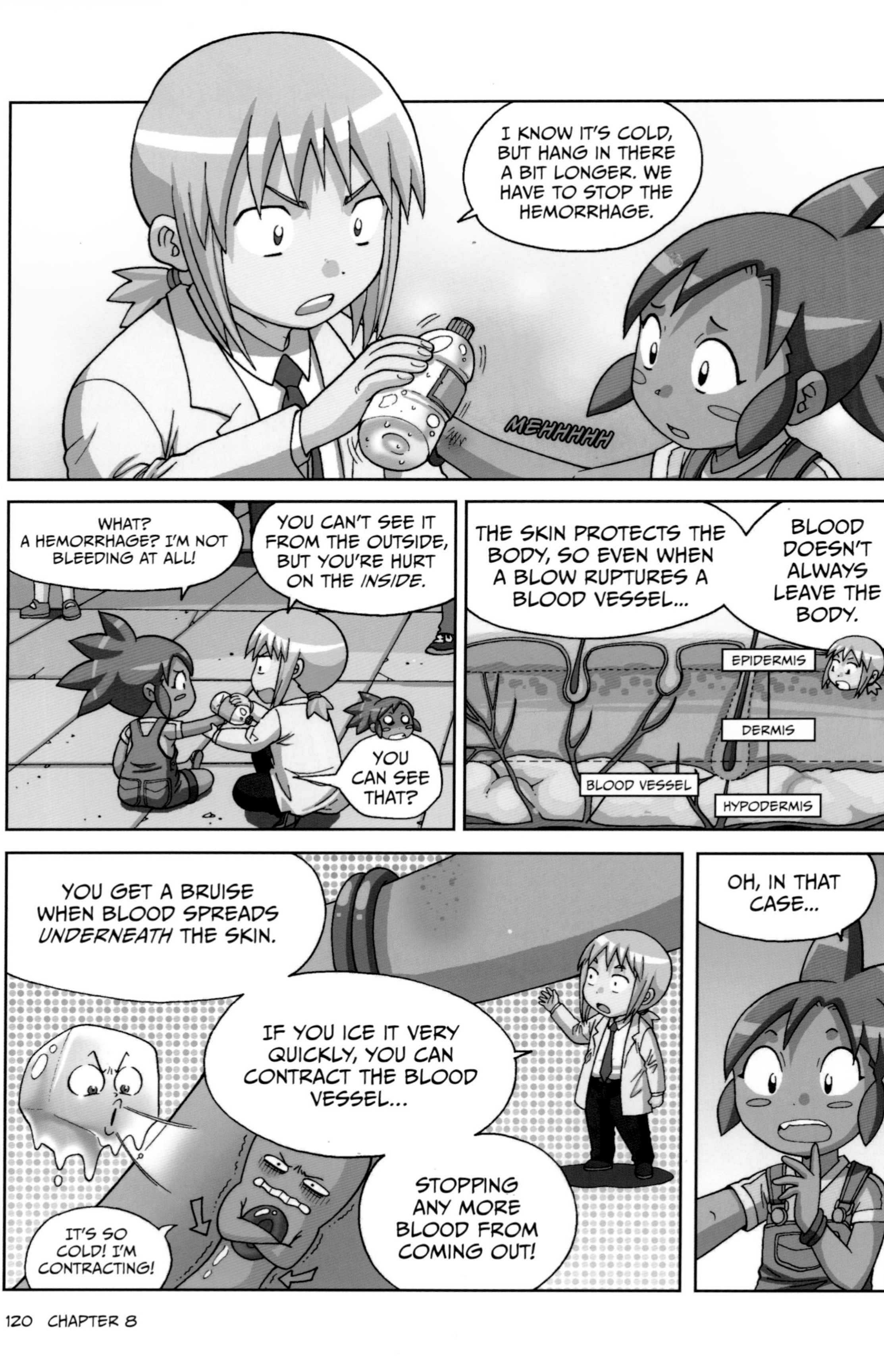
I KNOW IT'S COLD, BUT HANG IN THERE A BIT LONGER. WE HAVE TO STOP THE HEMORRHAGE.
MEHHHHH
WHAT? A HEMORRHAGE? I'M NOT BLEEDING AT ALL!
YOU CAN'T SEE IT FROM THE OUTSIDE, BUT YOU'RE HURT ON THE *INSIDE*.
YOU CAN SEE THAT?
THE SKIN PROTECTS THE BODY, SO EVEN WHEN A BLOW RUPTURES A BLOOD VESSEL...
BLOOD DOESN'T ALWAYS LEAVE THE BODY.
EPIDERMIS
DERMIS
BLOOD VESSEL
HYPODERMIS
YOU GET A BRUISE WHEN BLOOD SPREADS *UNDERNEATH* THE SKIN.
IF YOU ICE IT VERY QUICKLY, YOU CAN CONTRACT THE BLOOD VESSEL...
STOPPING ANY MORE BLOOD FROM COMING OUT!
IT'S SO COLD! I'M CONTRACTING!
OH, IN THAT CASE...

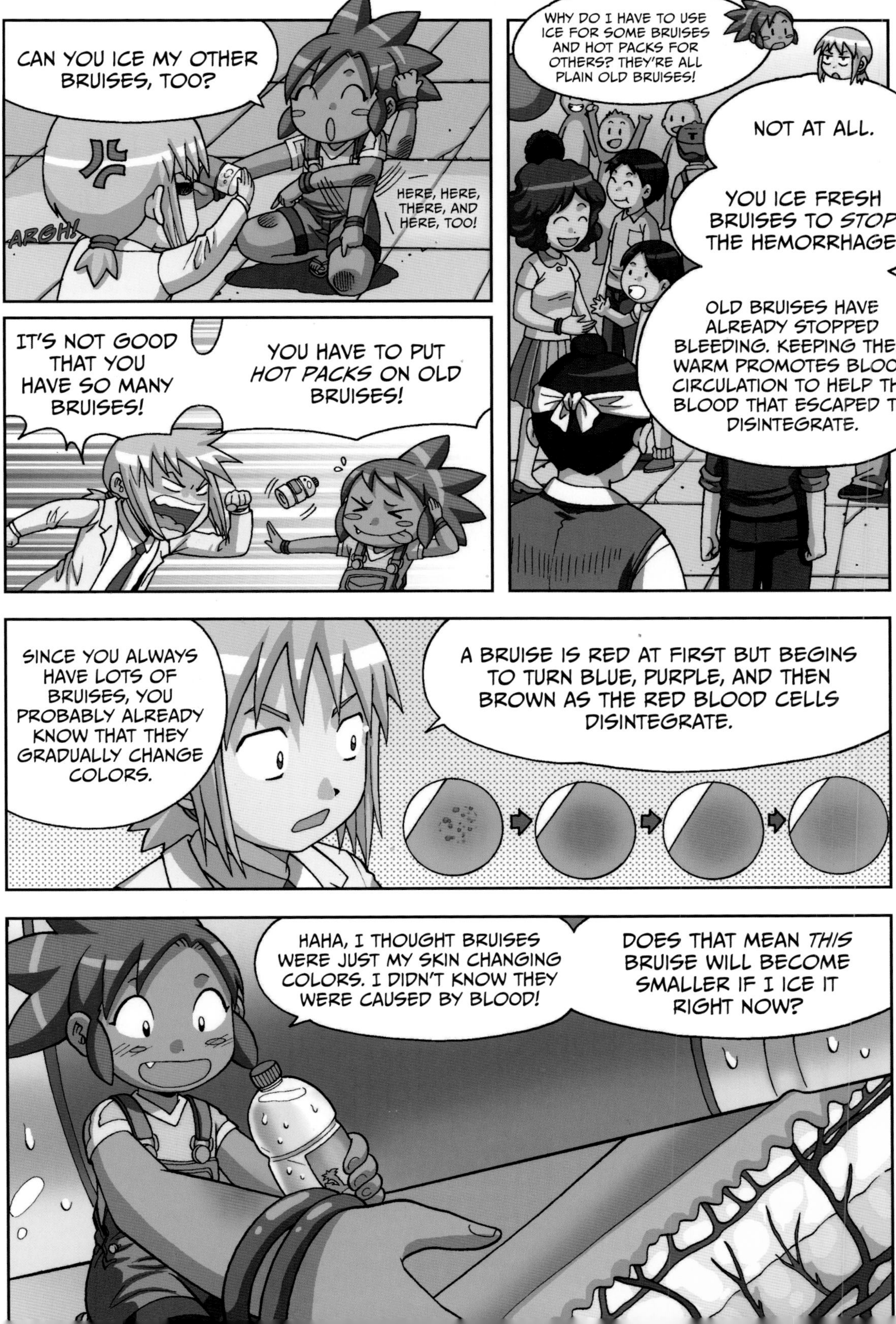
CAN YOU ICE MY OTHER BRUISES, TOO?
ARGH!
HERE, HERE, THERE, AND HERE, TOO!
IT'S NOT GOOD THAT YOU HAVE SO MANY BRUISES!
YOU HAVE TO PUT *HOT PACKS* ON OLD BRUISES!
WHY DO I HAVE TO USE ICE FOR SOME BRUISES AND HOT PACKS FOR OTHERS? THEY'RE ALL PLAIN OLD BRUISES!
NOT AT ALL.
YOU ICE FRESH BRUISES TO *STOP* THE HEMORRHAGE.
OLD BRUISES HAVE ALREADY STOPPED BLEEDING. KEEPING THEM WARM PROMOTES BLOOD CIRCULATION TO HELP THE BLOOD THAT ESCAPED TO DISINTEGRATE.
SINCE YOU ALWAYS HAVE LOTS OF BRUISES, YOU PROBABLY ALREADY KNOW THAT THEY GRADUALLY CHANGE COLORS.
A BRUISE IS RED AT FIRST BUT BEGINS TO TURN BLUE, PURPLE, AND THEN BROWN AS THE RED BLOOD CELLS DISINTEGRATE.
HAHA, I THOUGHT BRUISES WERE JUST MY SKIN CHANGING COLORS. I DIDN'T KNOW THEY WERE CAUSED BY BLOOD!
DOES THAT MEAN *THIS* BRUISE WILL BECOME SMALLER IF I ICE IT RIGHT NOW?

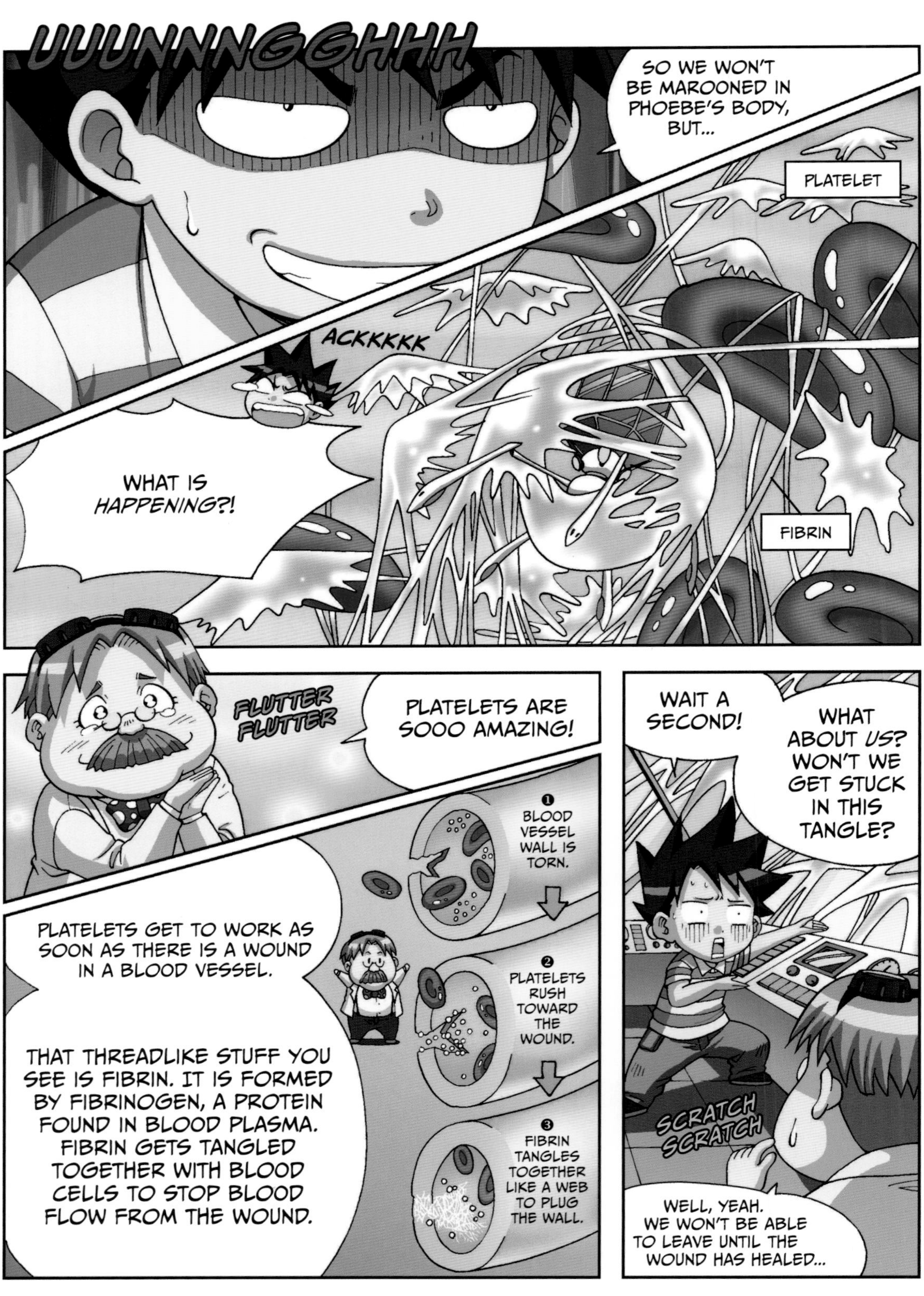
UUUNNNGGHHH
SO WE WON'T BE MAROONED IN PHOEBE'S BODY, BUT...
PLATELET
ACKKKKK
WHAT IS *HAPPENING?!*
FIBRIN
FLUTTER FLUTTER
PLATELETS ARE SOOO AMAZING!
1 BLOOD VESSEL WALL IS TORN.
2 PLATELETS RUSH TOWARD THE WOUND.
3 FIBRIN TANGLES TOGETHER LIKE A WEB TO PLUG THE WALL.
PLATELETS GET TO WORK AS SOON AS THERE IS A WOUND IN A BLOOD VESSEL.
THAT THREADLIKE STUFF YOU SEE IS FIBRIN. IT IS FORMED BY FIBRINOGEN, A PROTEIN FOUND IN BLOOD PLASMA. FIBRIN GETS TANGLED TOGETHER WITH BLOOD CELLS TO STOP BLOOD FLOW FROM THE WOUND.
WAIT A SECOND!
WHAT ABOUT *US*? WON'T WE GET STUCK IN THIS TANGLE?
SCRATCH SCRATCH
WELL, YEAH. WE WON'T BE ABLE TO LEAVE UNTIL THE WOUND HAS HEALED...

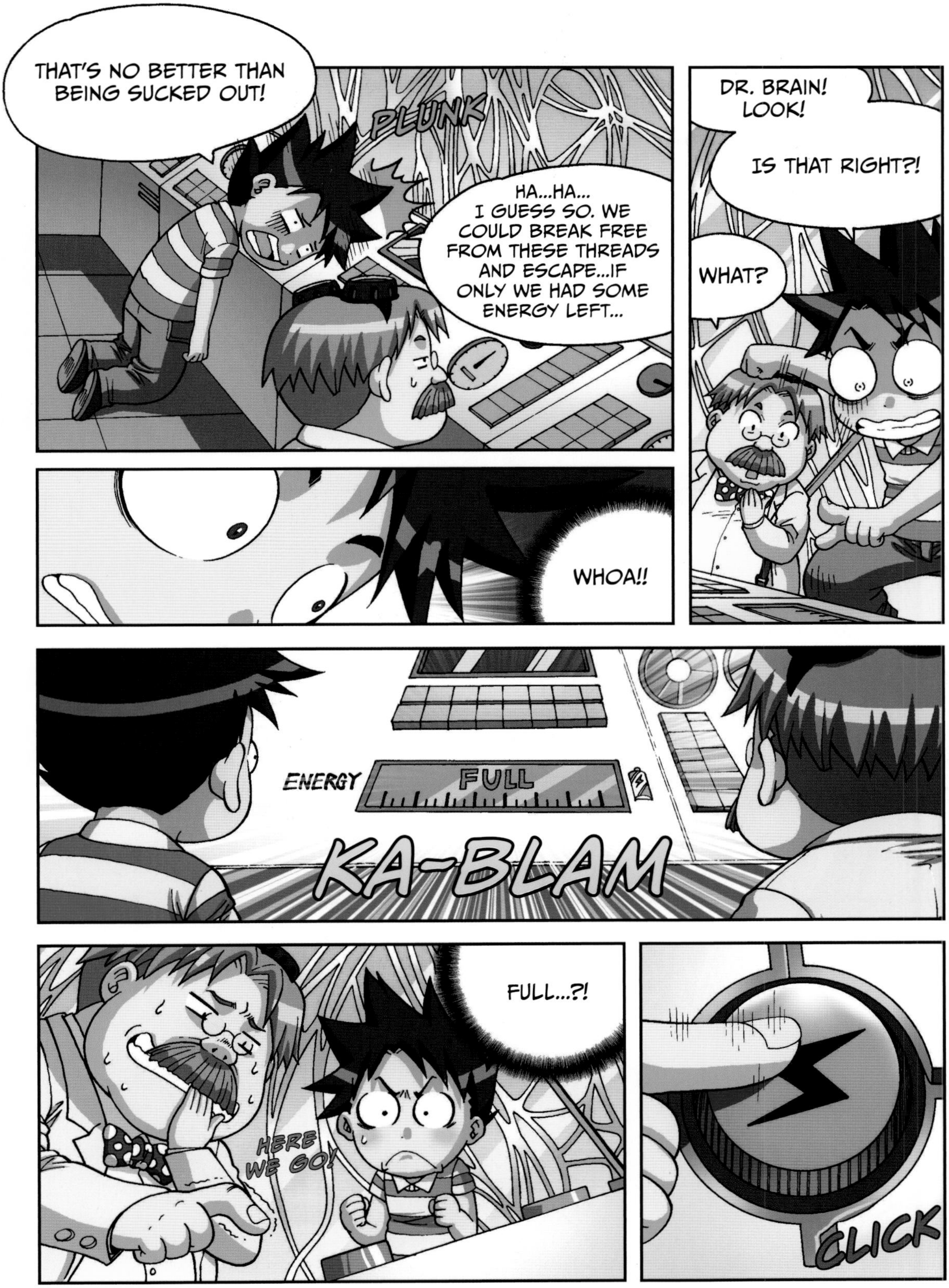
THAT'S NO BETTER THAN BEING SUCKED OUT!
PLUNK
HA...HA... I GUESS SO. WE COULD BREAK FREE FROM THESE THREADS AND ESCAPE...IF ONLY WE HAD SOME ENERGY LEFT...
DR. BRAIN! LOOK!
IS THAT RIGHT?!
WHAT?
WHOA!!
ENERGY
FULL
KA-BLAM
FULL...?!
HERE WE GO!
CLICK

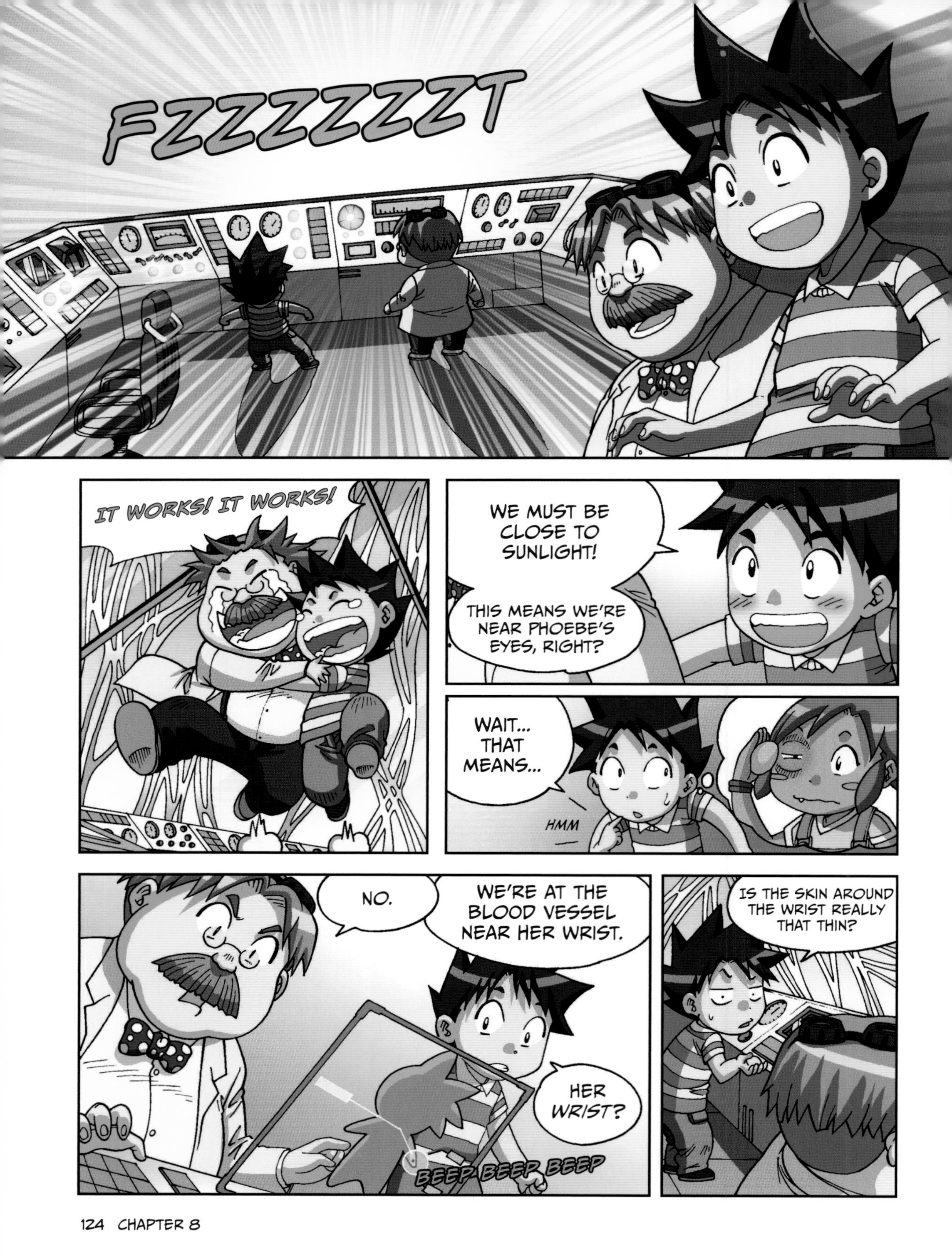
FZZZZZZZT
IT WORKS! IT WORKS!
WE MUST BE CLOSE TO SUNLIGHT!
THIS MEANS WE'RE NEAR PHOEBE'S EYES, RIGHT?
WAIT... THAT MEANS...
HMM
NO.
WE'RE AT THE BLOOD VESSEL NEAR HER WRIST.
HER WRIST?
BEEP BEEP BEEP
IS THE SKIN AROUND THE WRIST REALLY THAT THIN?

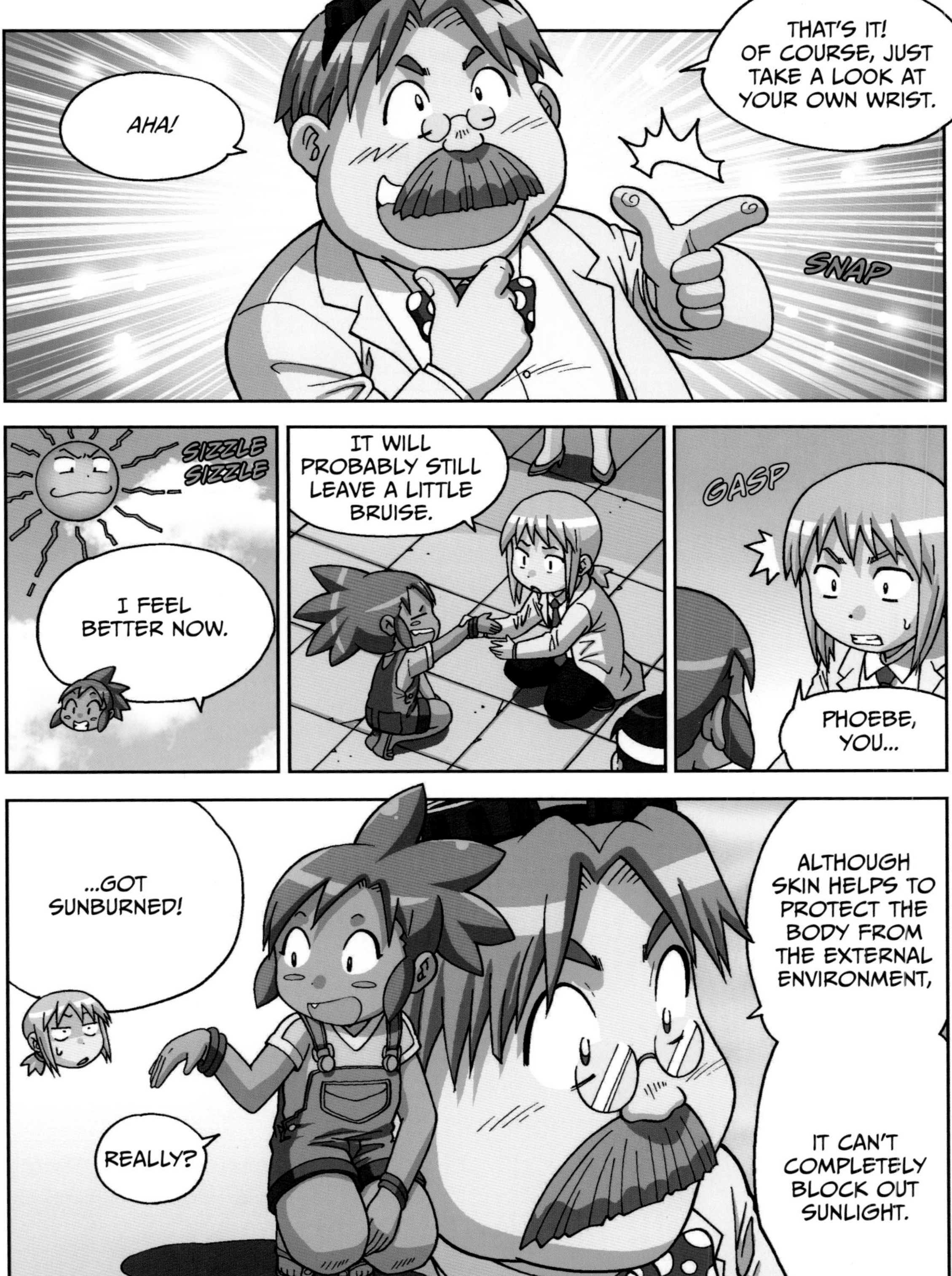
AHA!
THAT'S IT! OF COURSE, JUST TAKE A LOOK AT YOUR OWN WRIST.
SNAP
SIZZLE SIZZLE
I FEEL BETTER NOW.
IT WILL PROBABLY STILL LEAVE A LITTLE BRUISE.
GASP
PHOEBE, YOU...
...GOT SUNBURNED!
REALLY?
ALTHOUGH SKIN HELPS TO PROTECT THE BODY FROM THE EXTERNAL ENVIRONMENT,
IT CAN'T COMPLETELY BLOCK OUT SUNLIGHT.

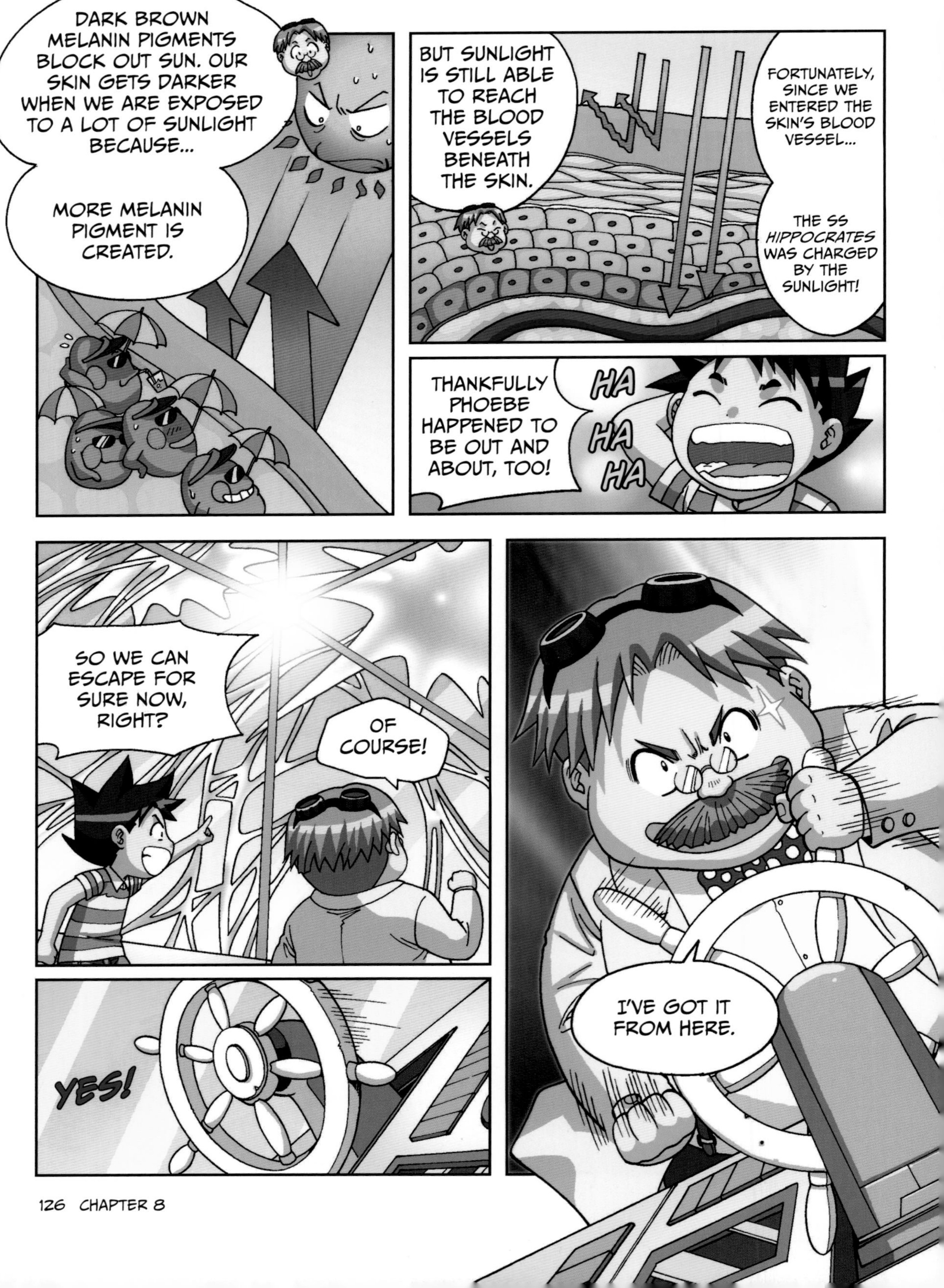
DARK BROWN MELANIN PIGMENTS BLOCK OUT SUN. OUR SKIN GETS DARKER WHEN WE ARE EXPOSED TO A LOT OF SUNLIGHT BECAUSE...
MORE MELANIN PIGMENT IS CREATED.
BUT SUNLIGHT IS STILL ABLE TO REACH THE BLOOD VESSELS BENEATH THE SKIN.
FORTUNATELY, SINCE WE ENTERED THE SKIN'S BLOOD VESSEL...
THE SS *HIPPOCRATES* WAS CHARGED BY THE SUNLIGHT!
THANKFULLY PHOEBE HAPPENED TO BE OUT AND ABOUT, TOO!
HA HA HA
SO WE CAN ESCAPE FOR SURE NOW, RIGHT?
OF COURSE!
YES!
I'VE GOT IT FROM HERE.

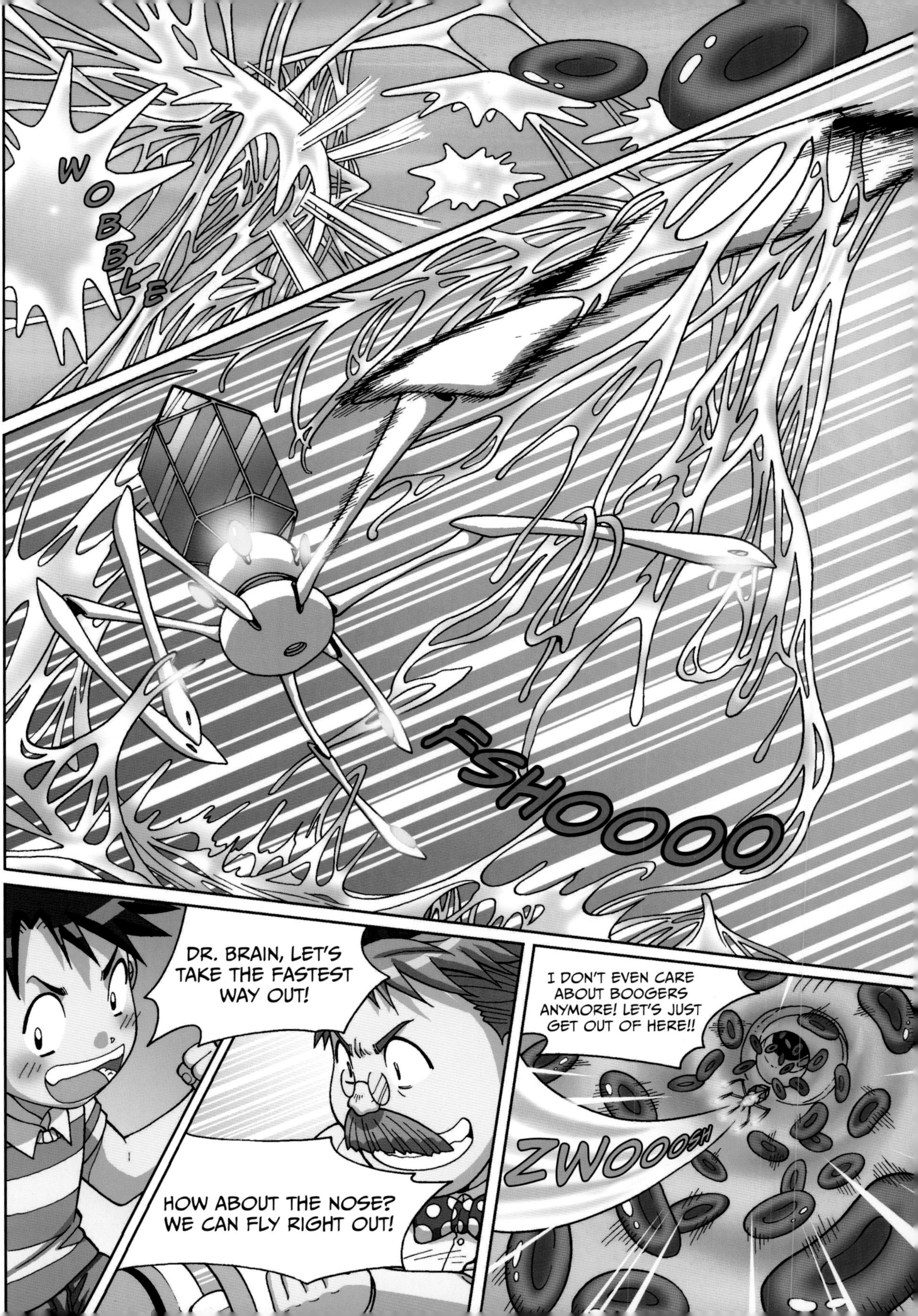
WOBBLE
FSHOOOO
DR. BRAIN, LET'S TAKE THE FASTEST WAY OUT!
HOW ABOUT THE NOSE? WE CAN FLY RIGHT OUT!
I DON'T EVEN CARE ABOUT BOOGERS ANYMORE! LET'S JUST GET OUT OF HERE!!
ZWOOOOSH

THE SKIN WE'RE IN

I DIDN'T KNOW THE SKIN HAS THIS AWESOME PROTECTIVE FUNCTION!

The skin is the outermost layer of the human body. If we didn't have skin, we would not be able to survive because we'd be exposed to all sorts of harmful bacteria and other dangerous things. Skin is a thin tissue, only about 2 or 3 millimeters thick. Although it's thin, there's a lot of it. If you consider the skin to be an "organ," it would be the largest organ in our bodies. Our skin is like armor!

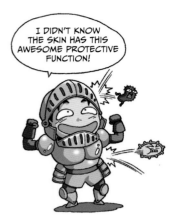

THE LAYERS OF YOUR SKIN

Skin is composed of three layers: epidermis, dermis, and hypodermis (also called *subcutaneous tissue*). Dead skin cells covering the outside of the epidermis prevent moisture from escaping the skin and protect the body from external stimuli and bacteria. The dermis, located just below the epidermis, contains collagen and elastic fibers that maintain the elasticity of the skin and support the epidermis. The dermis also has tissues with nerves, sweat glands, hair follicles, and even sensory receptors (which allow you to feel cold, heat, and pain). In addition, the dermis supplies oxygen and nutrients to various tissues through the blood vessels. Just a bit deeper is the hypodermis, a fatty layer that helps to maintain body temperature and softens blows to the body.

SKIN STRUCTURE
PORE
EPIDERMIS
SENSORY NERVE ENDING
ARRECTOR PILI MUSCLE
SEBACEOUS GLAND
CONNECTIVE TISSUE
DERMIS
HAIR FOLLICLE
FAT CELL
SWEAT GLAND
HYPODERMIS
BLOOD VESSEL

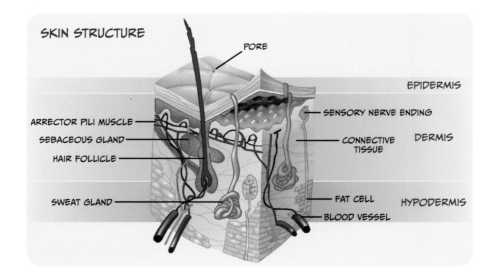

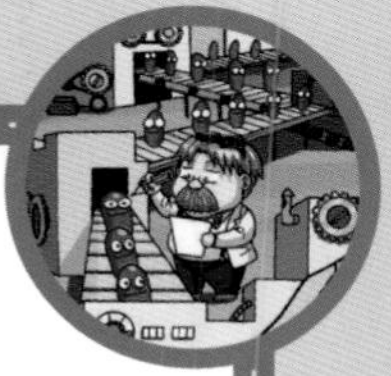

FINGERNAILS, GLANDS, AND HAIR

There are also several types of appendages with roots in the skin, including fingernails, toenails, hair, and glands that secrete sweat and oil.

Fingernails and toenails protect the ends of our fingers and toes and help us to grab objects.

Hair grows out of the follicles on the dermis at a rate of about 2 millimeters each week. The visible part of hair is composed of dead cells, and it helps protect the body from cold and heat. Furthermore, the roots of the hair come into contact with the skin's nerves, heightening the sensitivity of the skin.

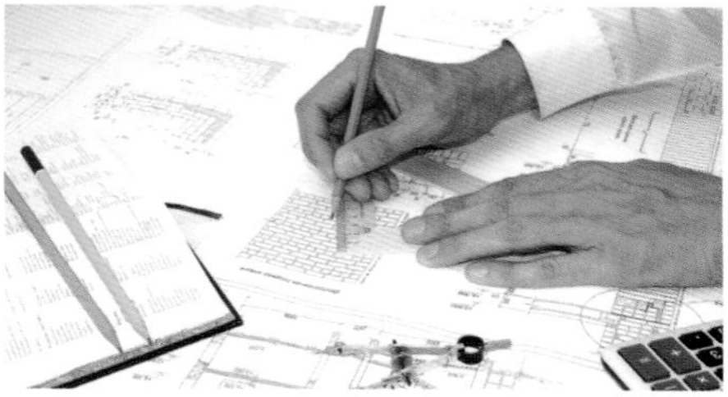

© Shutterstock

Fingernails help us with fine motor skills.

Glands in the skin include sebaceous glands and sweat glands. The oiliness created by sebaceous glands helps to repel water and maintain the flexibility of skin and hair. Sweat prevents skin from drying and keeps the body cool as the sweat evaporates.

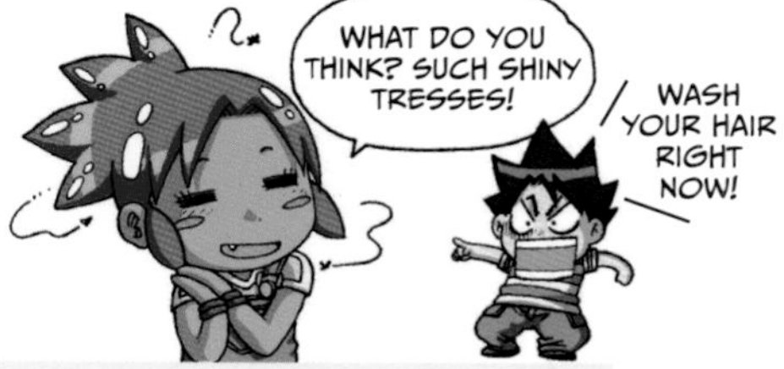
WHAT DO YOU THINK? SUCH SHINY TRESSES!
WASH YOUR HAIR RIGHT NOW!

SKIN AND ULTRAVIOLET RAYS

Skin color is different from person to person because each individual has different amounts of melanin, a pigment in the skin. Melanin is made in melanocytes, a type of cell located in the epidermis (specifically, in the stratum basale, which is the lower level of the epidermis).

You can't see ultraviolet (UV) rays with the naked eye, but these rays contain stronger energy than visible light. A moderate amount of UV rays from the sun will create vitamin D in the skin and can be good for you, but an excessive amount of sunlight will make the skin age more quickly and create spots and wrinkles. In serious cases, too much sun will cause skin diseases like melanoma and other types of skin cancer. That's why it's a good idea to use sunscreen to avoid sunburn, no matter your skin tone.

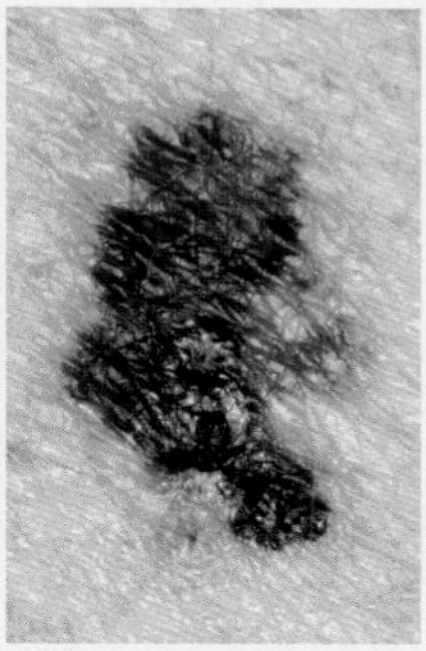

Melanoma is the most dangerous form of skin cancer. UV rays damage melanocytes and cause them to mutate and multiply. The mass production of melanin is what causes the brown or black color.

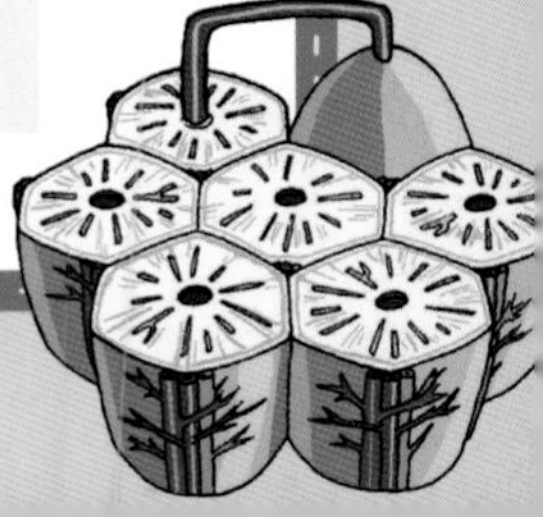

ESCAPE?

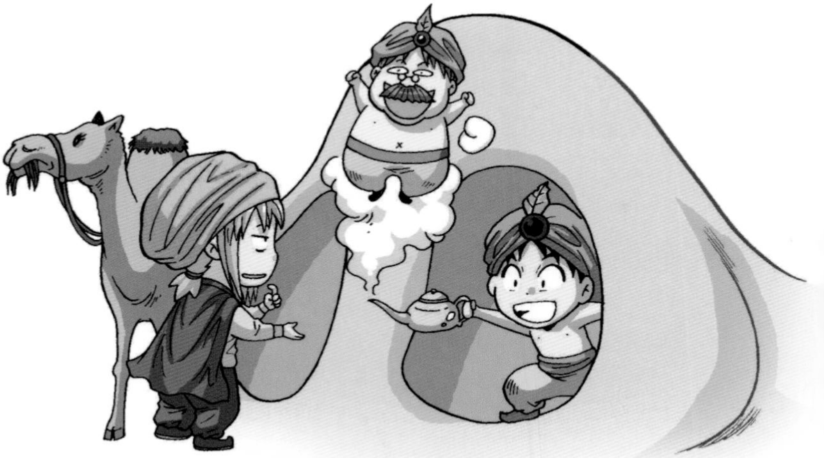

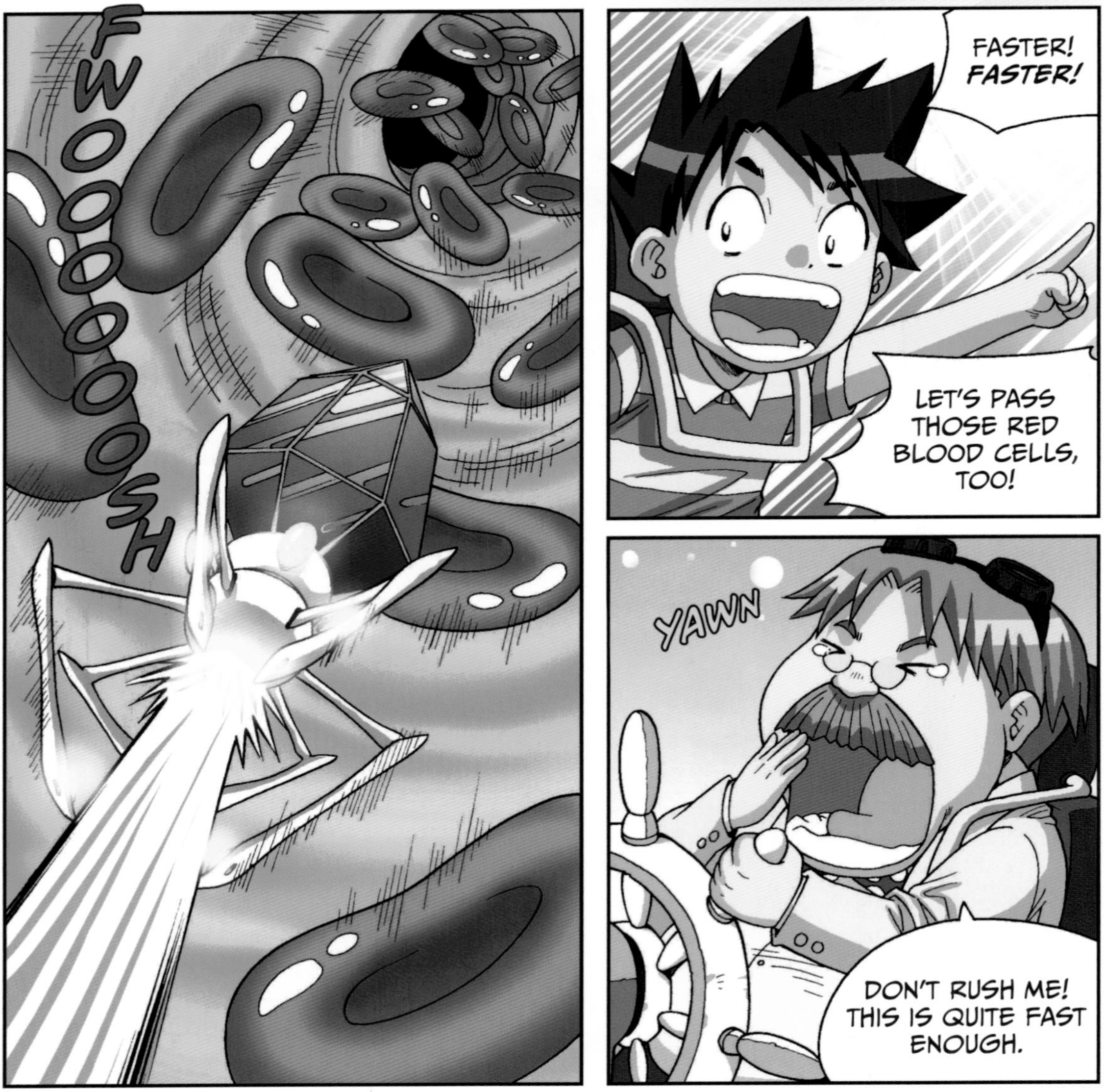
FWOOOOOOOSH
FASTER! FASTER!
LET'S PASS THOSE RED BLOOD CELLS, TOO!
YAWN
DON'T RUSH ME! THIS IS QUITE FAST ENOUGH.

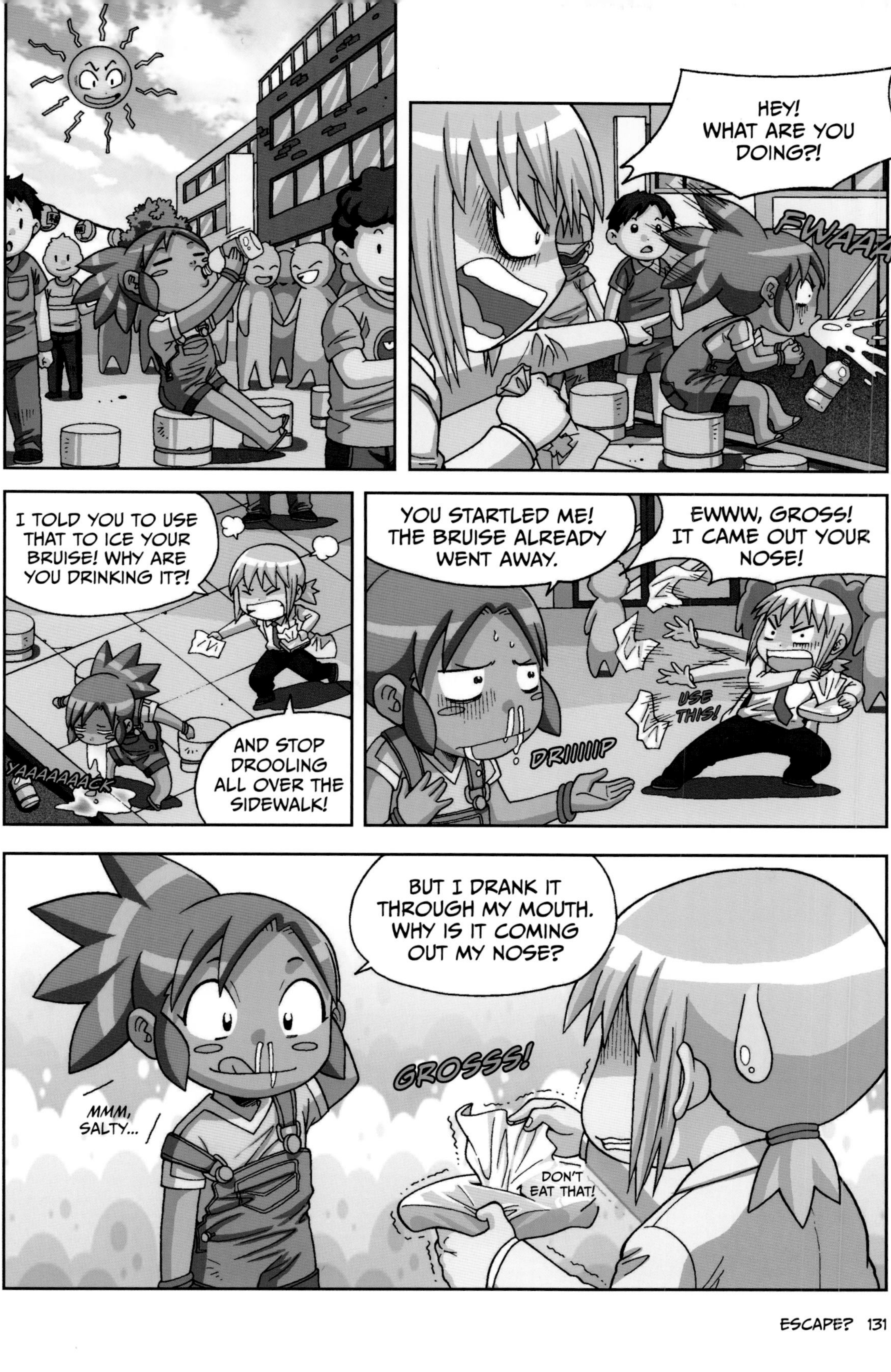
HEY! WHAT ARE YOU DOING?!
FWAAAA
I TOLD YOU TO USE THAT TO ICE YOUR BRUISE! WHY ARE YOU DRINKING IT?!
AND STOP DROOLING ALL OVER THE SIDEWALK!
YAAAAAAACK
YOU STARTLED ME! THE BRUISE ALREADY WENT AWAY.
EWWW, GROSS! IT CAME OUT YOUR NOSE!
USE THIS!
DRIIIIIP
BUT I DRANK IT THROUGH MY MOUTH. WHY IS IT COMING OUT MY NOSE?
GROSSS!
MMM, SALTY...
DON'T EAT THAT!

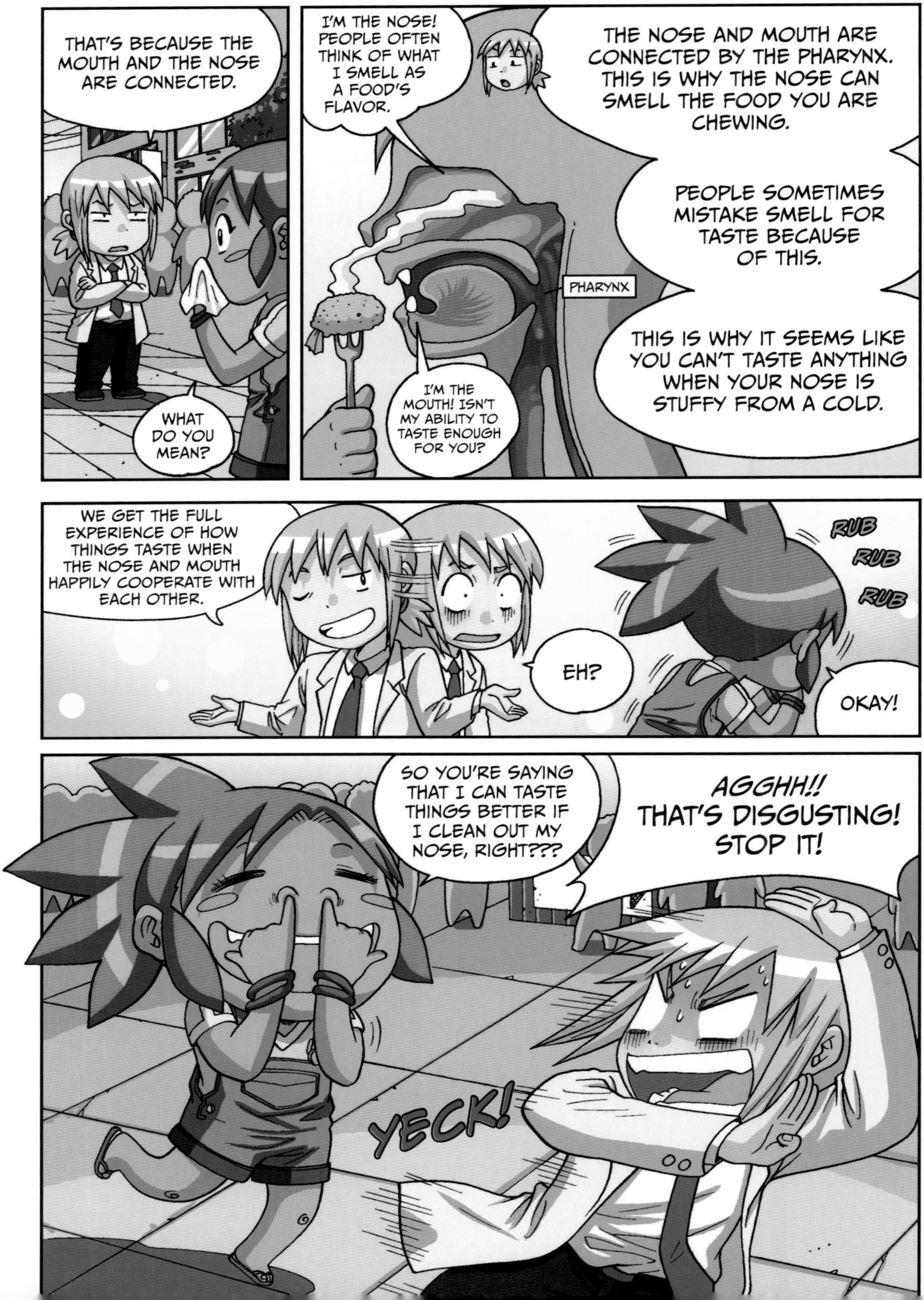
THAT'S BECAUSE THE MOUTH AND THE NOSE ARE CONNECTED.
WHAT DO YOU MEAN?
I'M THE NOSE! PEOPLE OFTEN THINK OF WHAT I SMELL AS A FOOD'S FLAVOR.
I'M THE MOUTH! ISN'T MY ABILITY TO TASTE ENOUGH FOR YOU?
PHARYNX
THE NOSE AND MOUTH ARE CONNECTED BY THE PHARYNX. THIS IS WHY THE NOSE CAN SMELL THE FOOD YOU ARE CHEWING.
PEOPLE SOMETIMES MISTAKE SMELL FOR TASTE BECAUSE OF THIS.
THIS IS WHY IT SEEMS LIKE YOU CAN'T TASTE ANYTHING WHEN YOUR NOSE IS STUFFY FROM A COLD.
WE GET THE FULL EXPERIENCE OF HOW THINGS TASTE WHEN THE NOSE AND MOUTH HAPPILY COOPERATE WITH EACH OTHER.
EH?
RUB
RUB
RUB
OKAY!
SO YOU'RE SAYING THAT I CAN TASTE THINGS BETTER IF I CLEAN OUT MY NOSE, RIGHT???
AGGHH!! THAT'S DISGUSTING! STOP IT!
YECK!

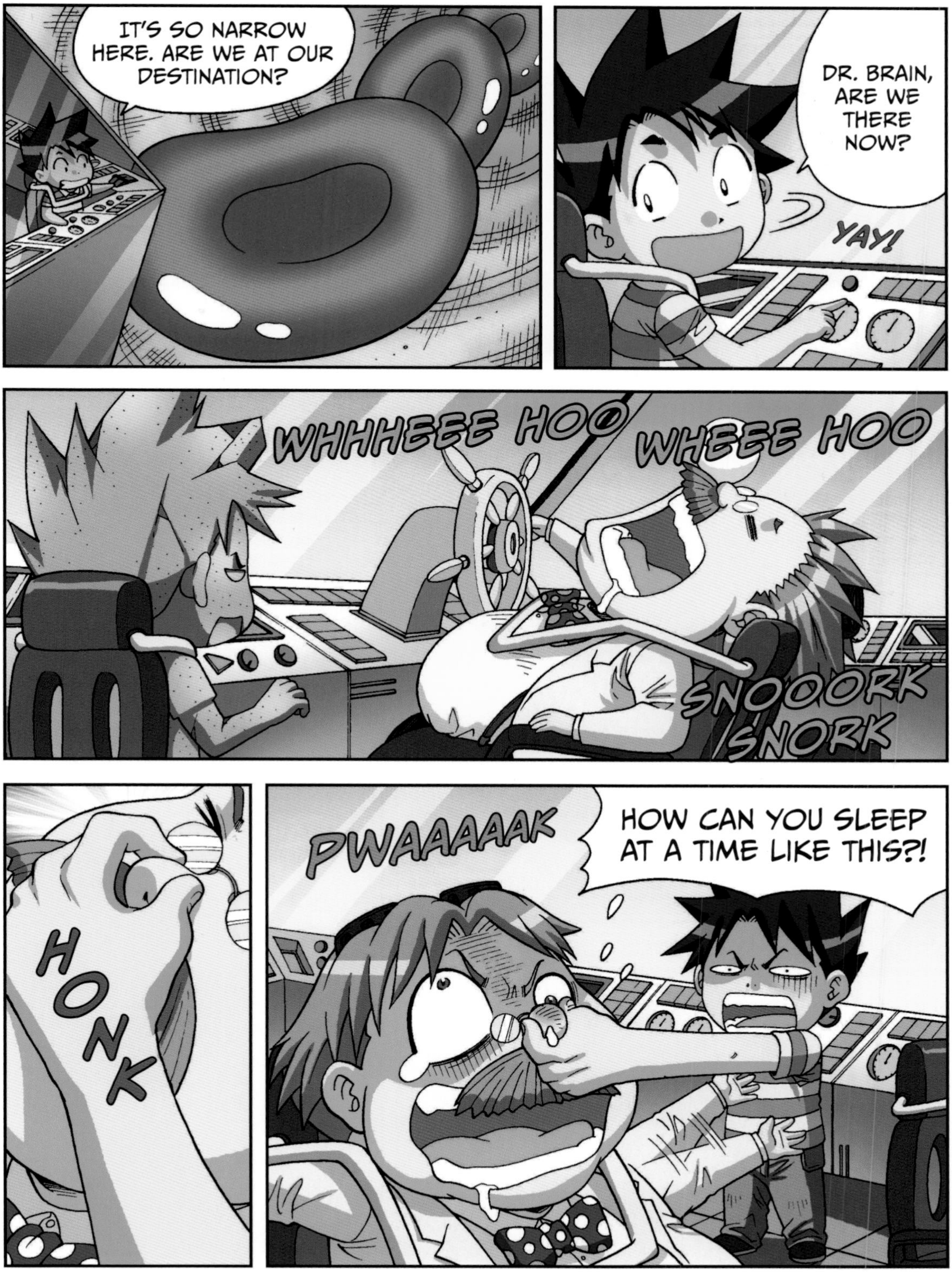
IT'S SO NARROW HERE. ARE WE AT OUR DESTINATION?
DR. BRAIN, ARE WE THERE NOW?
YAY!
WHHHEEE HOO
WHEEE HOO
SNOOORK SNORK
HONK
PWAAAAAK
HOW CAN YOU SLEEP AT A TIME LIKE THIS?!

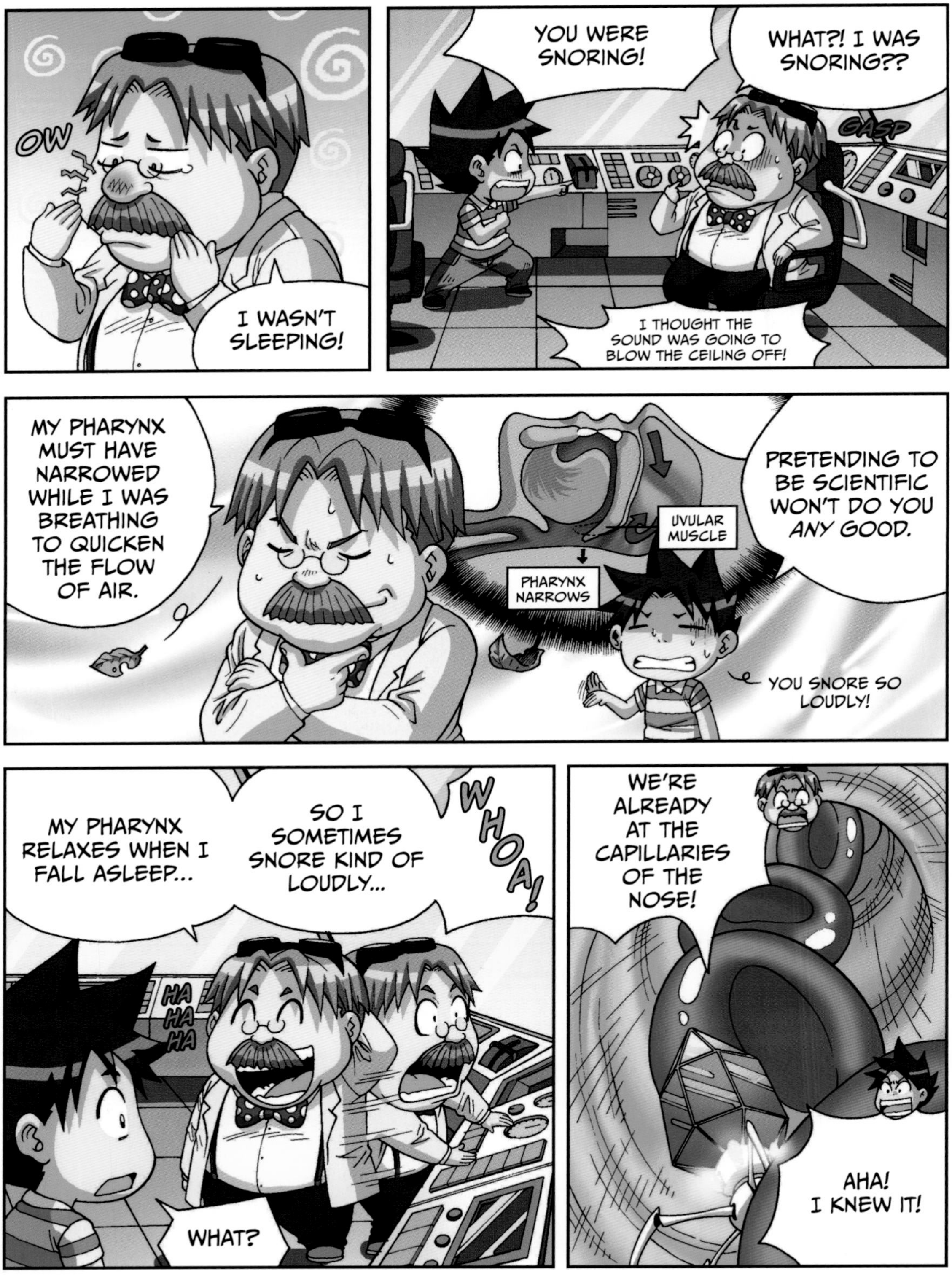
OW
I WASN'T SLEEPING!
YOU WERE SNORING!
WHAT?! I WAS SNORING??
GASP
I THOUGHT THE SOUND WAS GOING TO BLOW THE CEILING OFF!
MY PHARYNX MUST HAVE NARROWED WHILE I WAS BREATHING TO QUICKEN THE FLOW OF AIR.
UVULAR MUSCLE
PHARYNX NARROWS
PRETENDING TO BE SCIENTIFIC WON'T DO YOU ANY GOOD.
YOU SNORE SO LOUDLY!
MY PHARYNX RELAXES WHEN I FALL ASLEEP...
SO I SOMETIMES SNORE KIND OF LOUDLY...
HA HA HA
WHOA!
WHAT?
WE'RE ALREADY AT THE CAPILLARIES OF THE NOSE!
AHA! I KNEW IT!

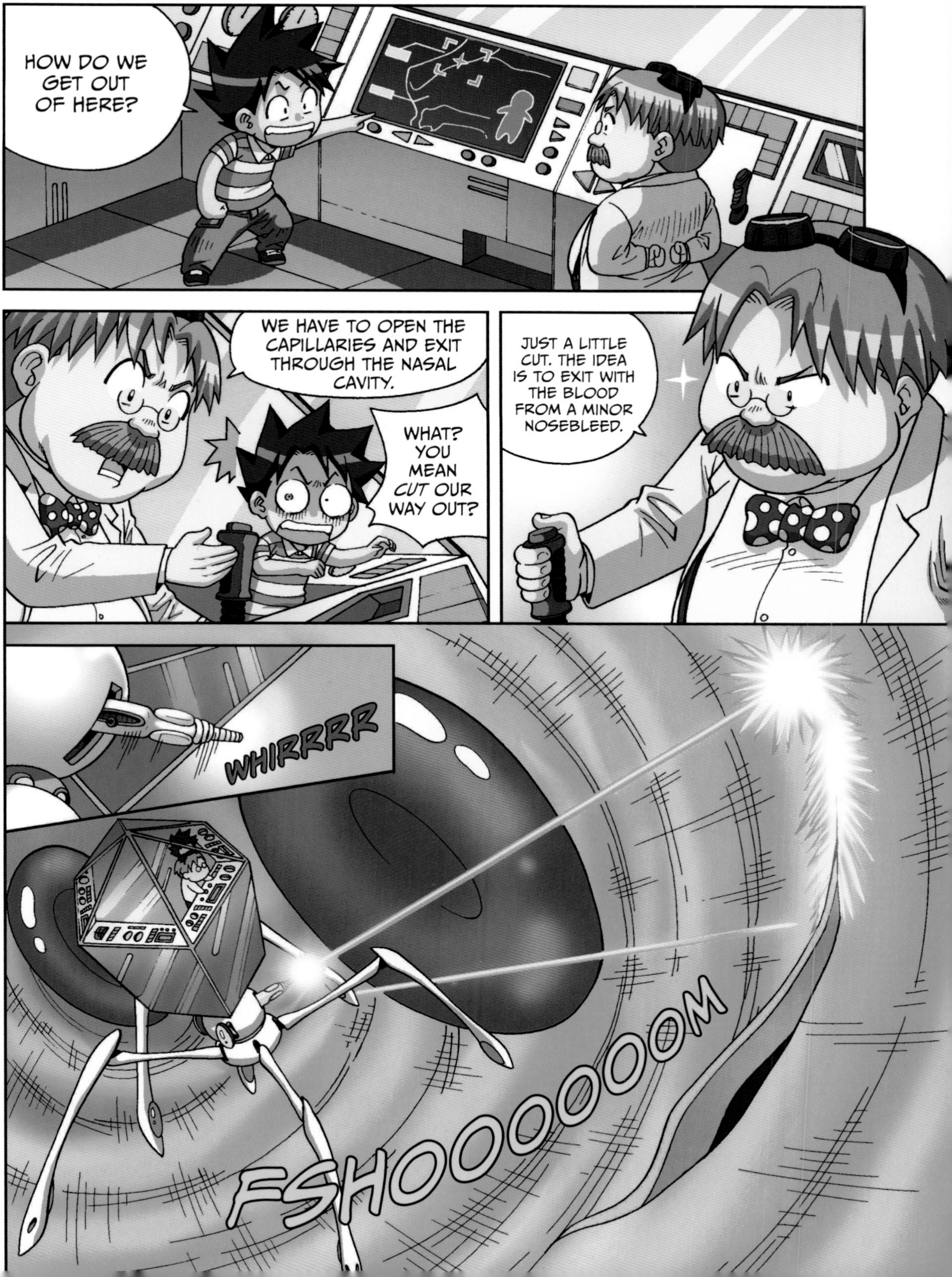
HOW DO WE GET OUT OF HERE?
WE HAVE TO OPEN THE CAPILLARIES AND EXIT THROUGH THE NASAL CAVITY.
WHAT? YOU MEAN *CUT* OUR WAY OUT?
JUST A LITTLE CUT. THE IDEA IS TO EXIT WITH THE BLOOD FROM A MINOR NOSEBLEED.
WHIRRRR
FSHOOOOOOOM

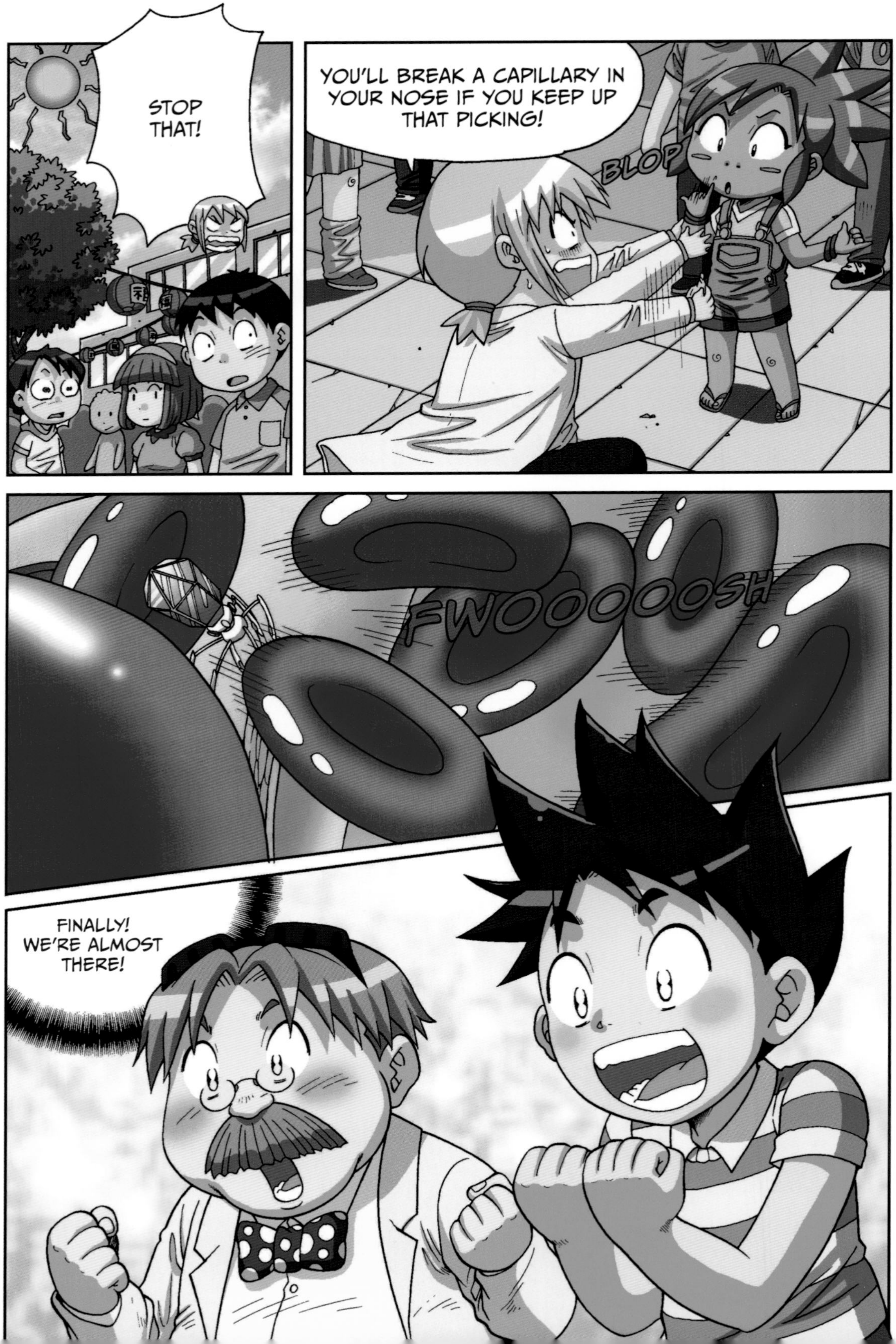
STOP THAT!
YOU'LL BREAK A CAPILLARY IN YOUR NOSE IF YOU KEEP UP THAT PICKING!
BLOP
FWOOOOOOSH
FINALLY! WE'RE ALMOST THERE!

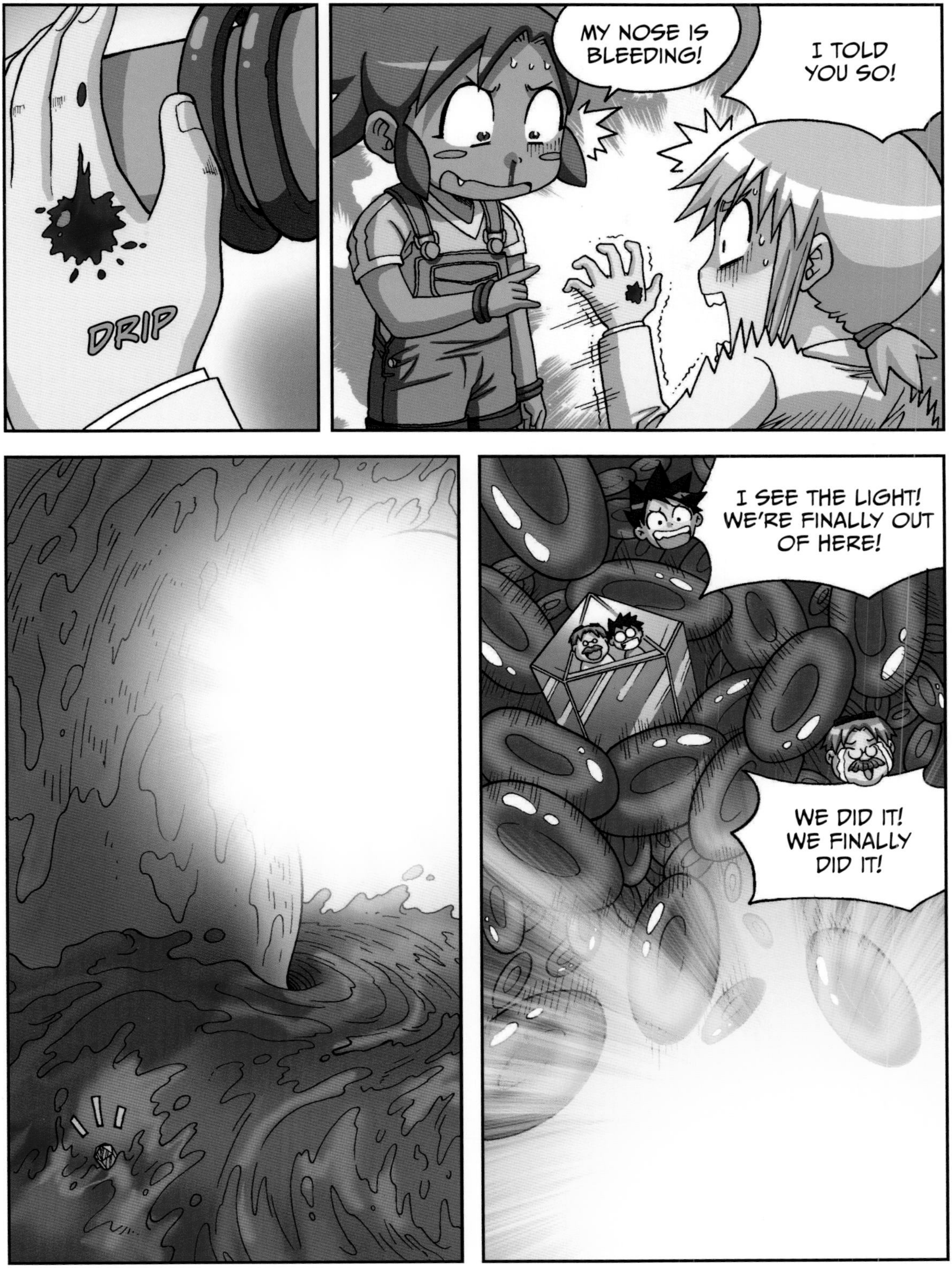
DRIP
MY NOSE IS BLEEDING!
I TOLD YOU SO!
I SEE THE LIGHT! WE'RE FINALLY OUT OF HERE!
WE DID IT! WE FINALLY DID IT!

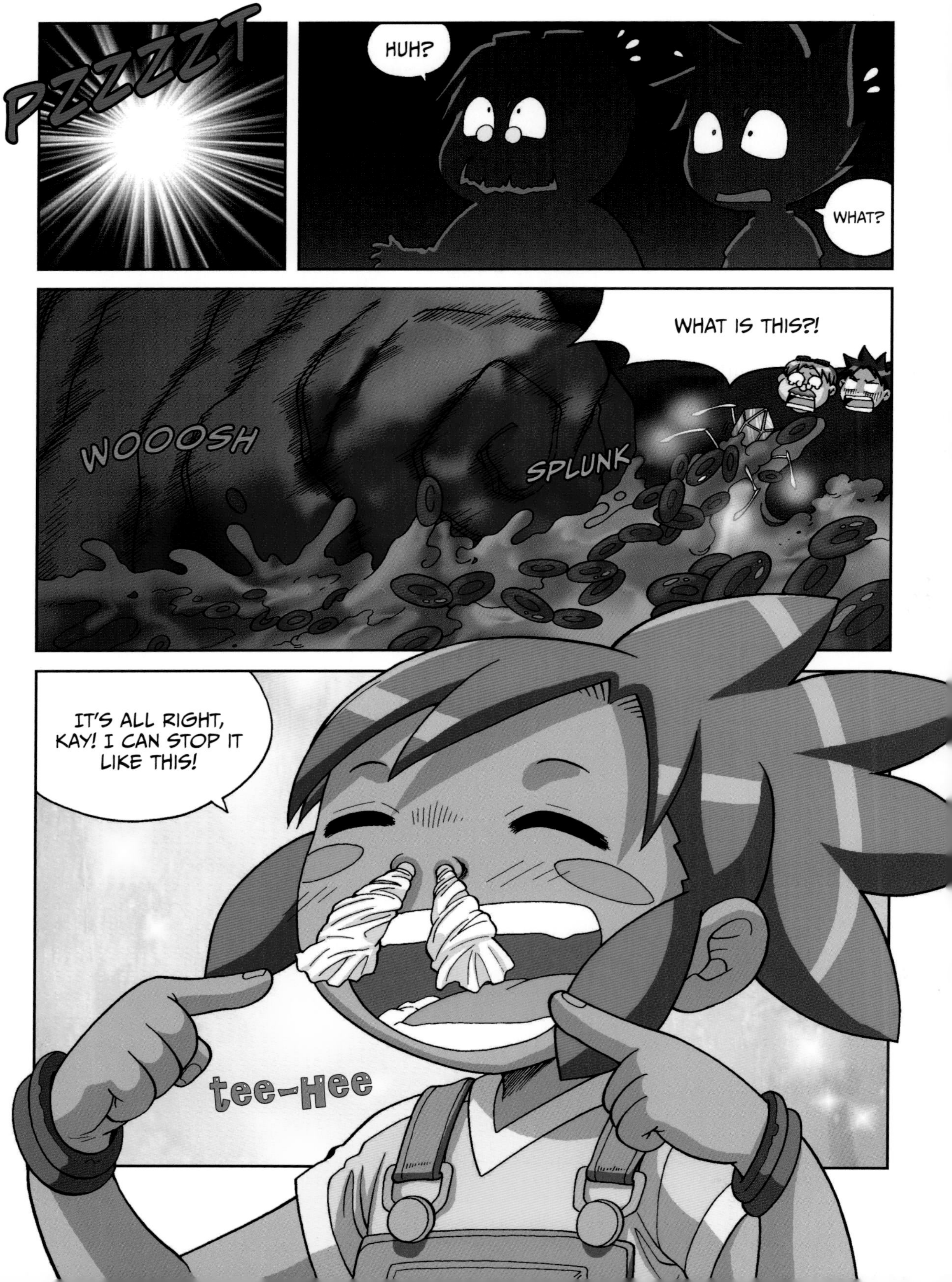
PZZZZT
HUH?
WHAT?
WHAT IS THIS?!
WOOOSH
SPLUNK
IT'S ALL RIGHT, KAY! I CAN STOP IT LIKE THIS!
tee-Hee

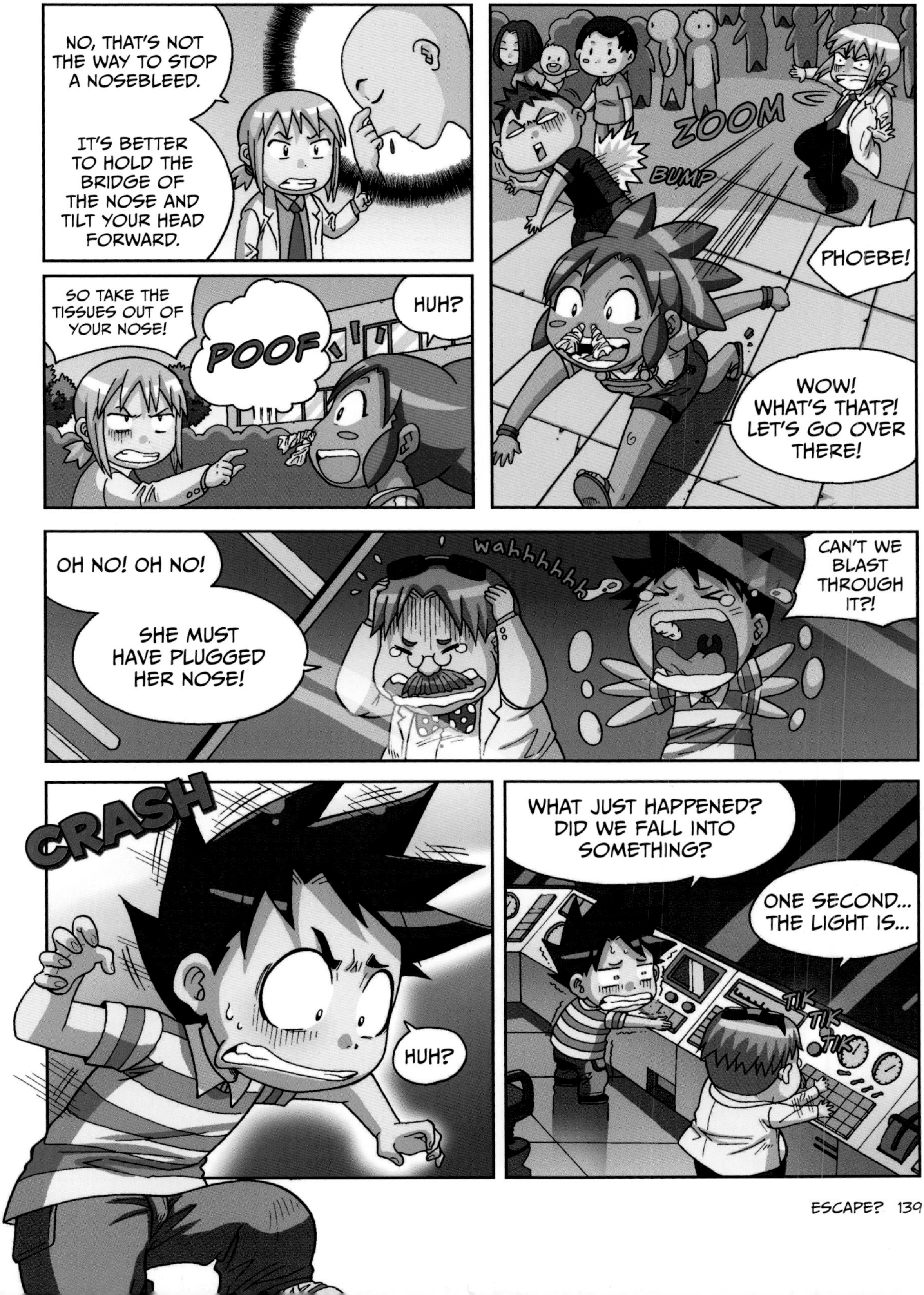
NO, THAT'S NOT THE WAY TO STOP A NOSEBLEED.
IT'S BETTER TO HOLD THE BRIDGE OF THE NOSE AND TILT YOUR HEAD FORWARD.
SO TAKE THE TISSUES OUT OF YOUR NOSE!
POOF
HUH?
ZOOM
BUMP
PHOEBE!
WOW! WHAT'S THAT?! LET'S GO OVER THERE!
OH NO! OH NO!
SHE MUST HAVE PLUGGED HER NOSE!
wahhhhhh
CAN'T WE BLAST THROUGH IT?!
CRASH
HUH?
WHAT JUST HAPPENED? DID WE FALL INTO SOMETHING?
ONE SECOND... THE LIGHT IS...
TIK TIK TIK

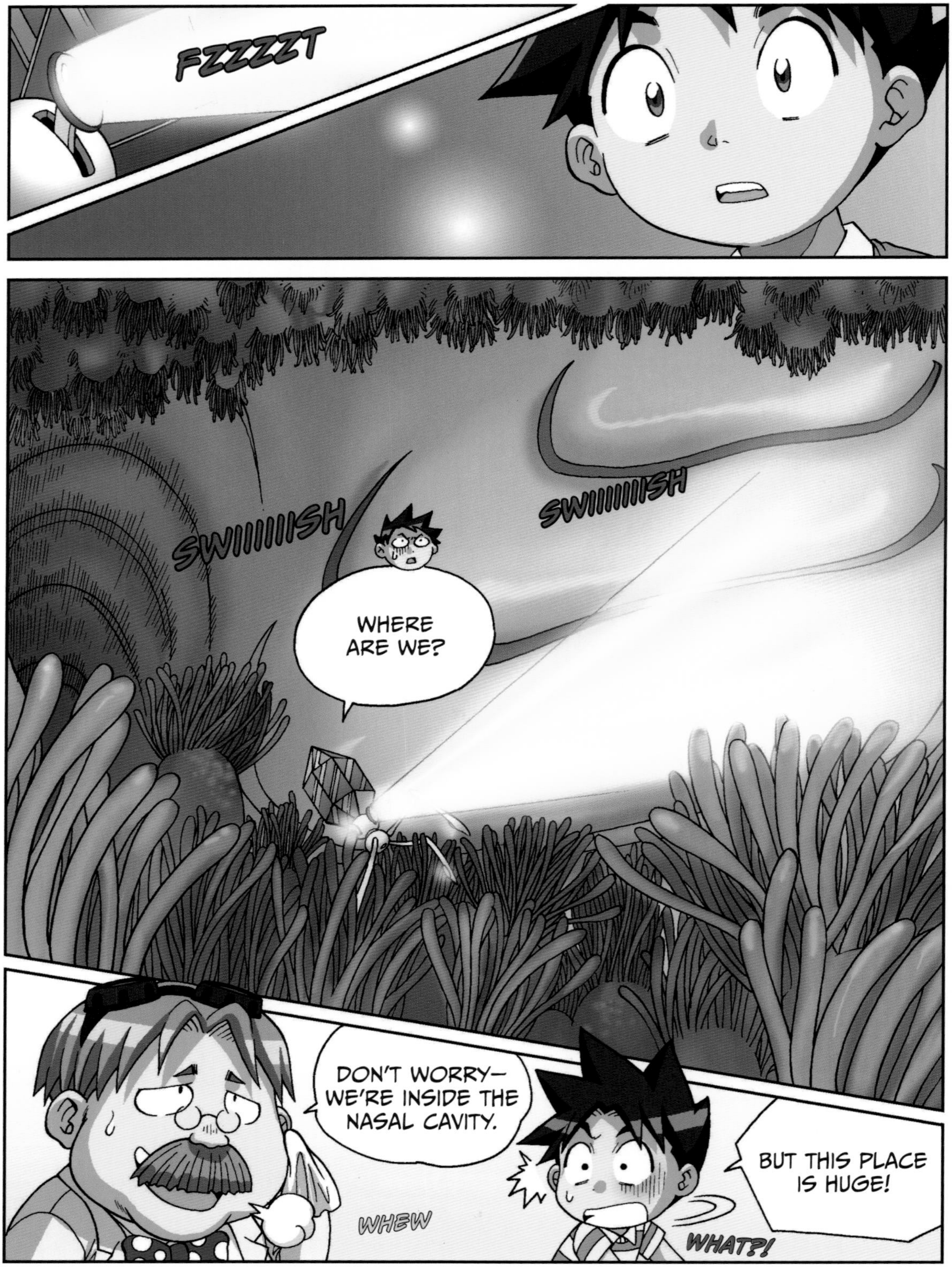
FZZZZT
SWIIIIIIISH
SWIIIIIIISH
WHERE ARE WE?
DON'T WORRY—WE'RE INSIDE THE NASAL CAVITY.
WHEW
BUT THIS PLACE IS HUGE!
WHAT?!

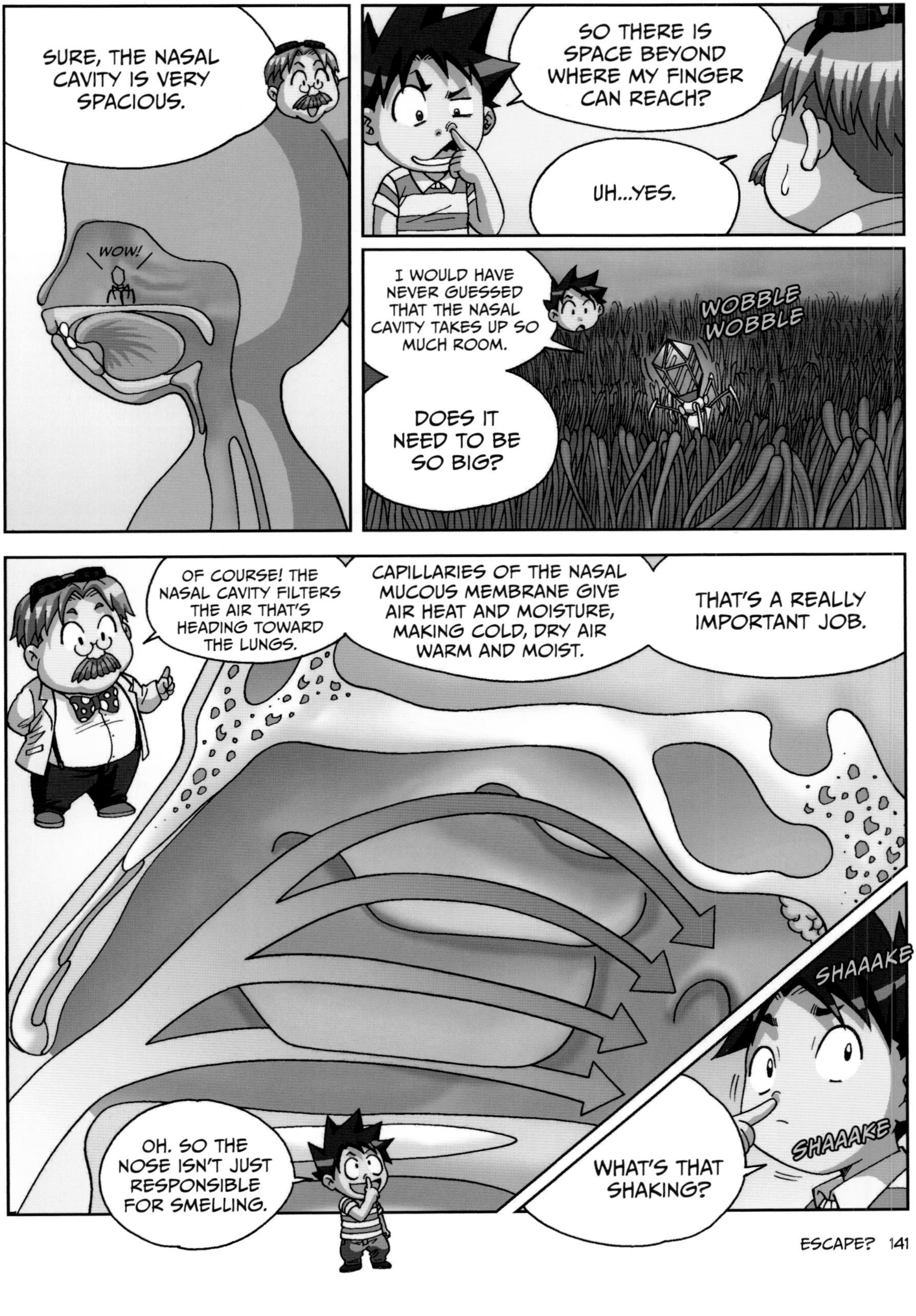
SURE, THE NASAL CAVITY IS VERY SPACIOUS.
WOW!
SO THERE IS SPACE BEYOND WHERE MY FINGER CAN REACH?
UH...YES.
I WOULD HAVE NEVER GUESSED THAT THE NASAL CAVITY TAKES UP SO MUCH ROOM.
WOBBLE WOBBLE
DOES IT NEED TO BE SO BIG?
OF COURSE! THE NASAL CAVITY FILTERS THE AIR THAT'S HEADING TOWARD THE LUNGS.
CAPILLARIES OF THE NASAL MUCOUS MEMBRANE GIVE AIR HEAT AND MOISTURE, MAKING COLD, DRY AIR WARM AND MOIST.
THAT'S A REALLY IMPORTANT JOB.
OH. SO THE NOSE ISN'T JUST RESPONSIBLE FOR SMELLING.
SHAAAKE
SHAAAKE
WHAT'S THAT SHAKING?

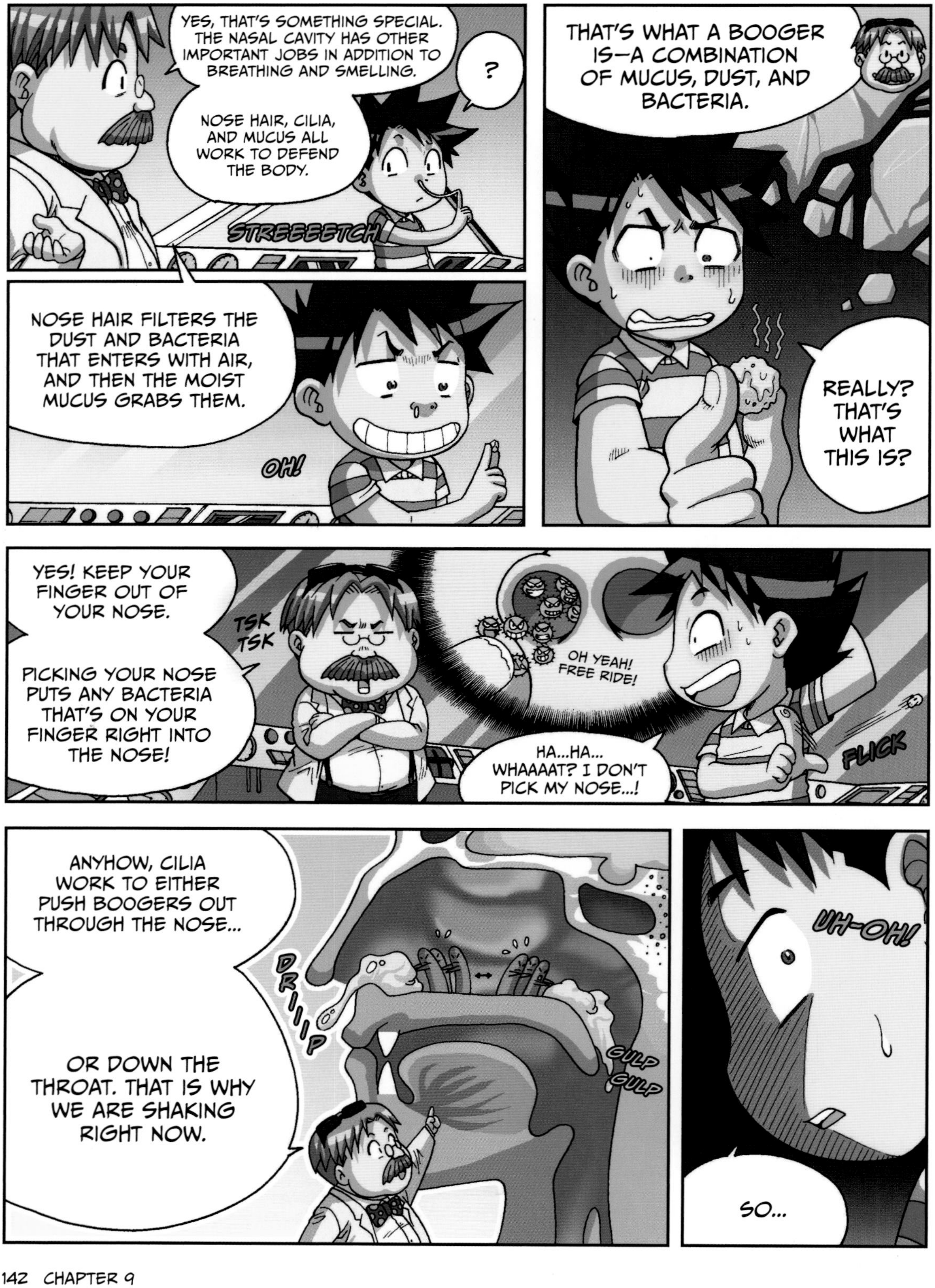
YES, THAT'S SOMETHING SPECIAL. THE NASAL CAVITY HAS OTHER IMPORTANT JOBS IN ADDITION TO BREATHING AND SMELLING.
NOSE HAIR, CILIA, AND MUCUS ALL WORK TO DEFEND THE BODY.
?
STREEEETCH
NOSE HAIR FILTERS THE DUST AND BACTERIA THAT ENTERS WITH AIR, AND THEN THE MOIST MUCUS GRABS THEM.
OH!
THAT'S WHAT A BOOGER IS—A COMBINATION OF MUCUS, DUST, AND BACTERIA.
REALLY? THAT'S WHAT THIS IS?
YES! KEEP YOUR FINGER OUT OF YOUR NOSE.
PICKING YOUR NOSE PUTS ANY BACTERIA THAT'S ON YOUR FINGER RIGHT INTO THE NOSE!
TSK TSK
OH YEAH! FREE RIDE!
HA...HA... WHAAAAT? I DON'T PICK MY NOSE...!
FLICK
ANYHOW, CILIA WORK TO EITHER PUSH BOOGERS OUT THROUGH THE NOSE...
OR DOWN THE THROAT. THAT IS WHY WE ARE SHAKING RIGHT NOW.
DRIIIIP
GULP GULP
UH-OH!
SO...

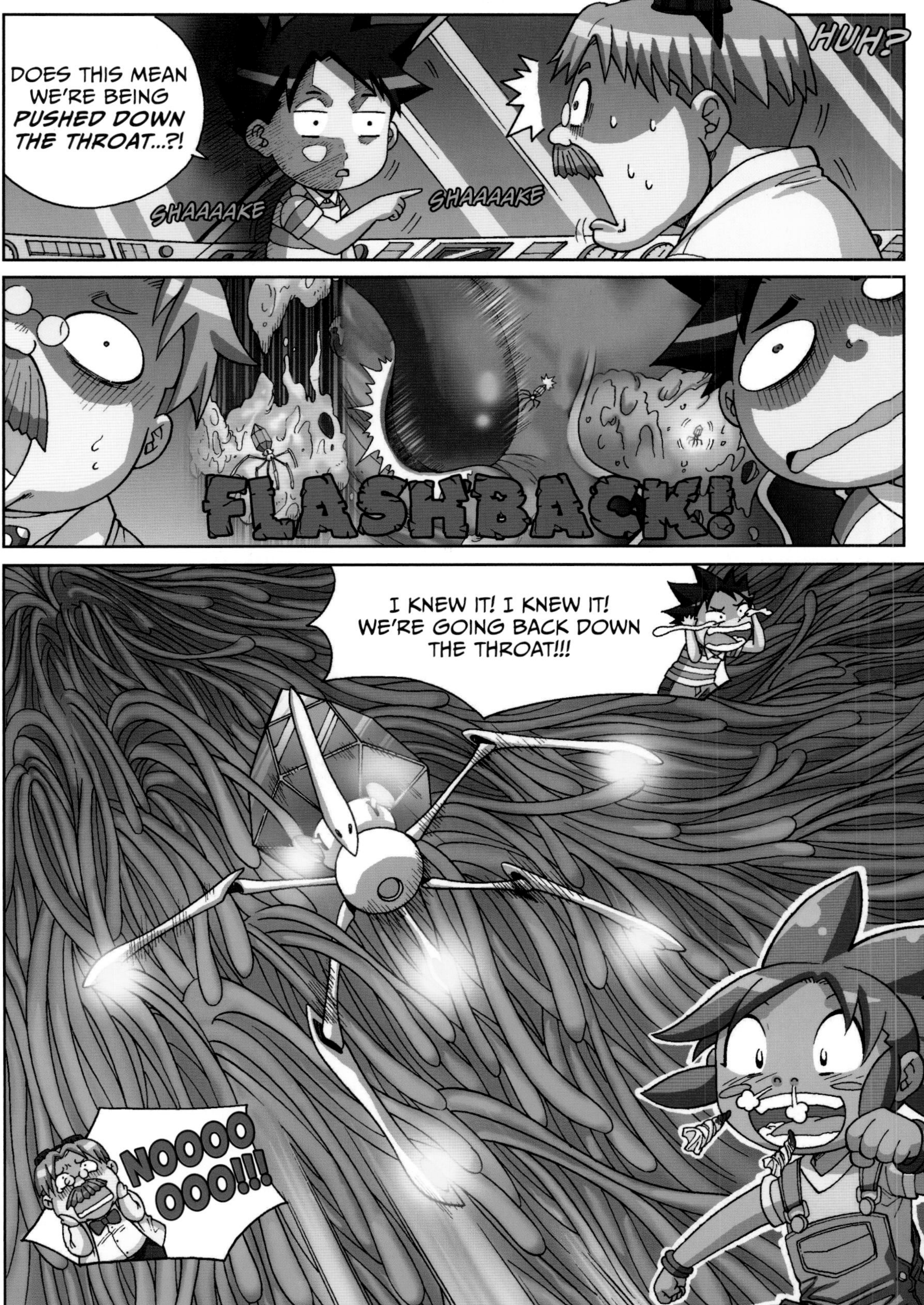
DOES THIS MEAN WE'RE BEING *PUSHED DOWN THE THROAT...?!*
SHAAAAKE
SHAAAAKE
HUH?
FLASHBACK!
I KNEW IT! I KNEW IT! WE'RE GOING BACK DOWN THE THROAT!!!
NOOOO OOO!!!

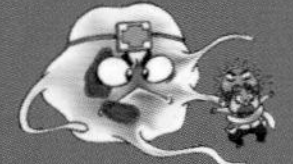

THE INCREDIBLE NOSE

The nose is part of the olfactory system, which is responsible for smelling odors. The nose also acts as an important part of the respiratory system. When you're studying the nose, you can think of it as being divided into the external nose (nasus externus) and the nasal cavity, and also into left and right sides by the nasal septum.

THE DOOR TO THE RESPIRATORY SYSTEM

Air that enters through the nose first passes the nasal turbinates, which consist of three layers: the inferior, middle, and superior turbinates. These structures, sometimes called *concha*, divide your nasal cavity into grooved passages. The inferior turbinates are the largest, and they control the flow of most of the air we inhale. They also moisten and filter this air. The middle turbinates protect the sinuses from direct contact with air. Lastly, the superior turbinates' main job is to protect the olfactory bulb, which is located on the underside of the brain. The paranasal sinuses, which resemble big empty caves around the nasal cavity, have many functions including moistening and warming inhaled air.

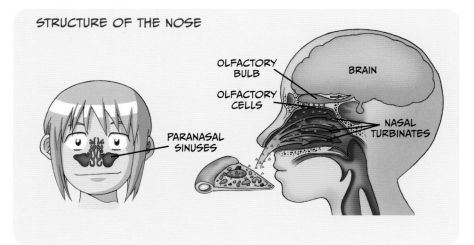

STRUCTURE OF THE NOSE

OLFACTORY BULB

OLFACTORY CELLS

PARANASAL SINUSES

BRAIN

NASAL TURBINATES

OOH, THAT SMELL

The olfactory membrane in the ceiling of the nose is responsible for smelling scents that enter the nose mixed with air. When the odor molecules from food stimulate the olfactory cells of the olfactory nerve, the brain senses the smell. The olfactory bulb in the brain processes this information. Smells have a strong link to memories because the olfactory bulb is so close to the structures in the brain linked to memory.

Smell is arguably the most sensitive of the five senses. We have about 5 million olfactory cells that we use to detect 3,000 to 10,000 different smells. Our brains learn to ignore certain smells after a while, which we can mistake for a weakened sense of smell.

© Yonhap News

A dog's sense of smell is about 45 times more sensitive than a human's, so they are often used to detect drugs and bombs and to search for missing people.

THE NOSE, VALIANT DEFENDER

The nose protects the body from airborne bacteria, viruses, and dust. Nose hair filters out big dust particles, and the nasal mucous membrane secretes mucus with antiviral components and sterilizing enzymes to catch smaller particles and bacteria. Boogers are made when dust and bacteria get caught in the mucus. The nasal mucous membrane becomes more active in response to an influenza virus or a cold virus, secreting a lot more mucus than usual in order to clean out any viruses, toxins, or dead cells. This is why you get a runny nose when you're sick. Having a runny nose is a sign that your body's immune system is functioning properly, and it will stop once the foreign nasal substances are cleared out.

DIFFERENT NOSES, DIFFERENT VOICES

The sound of your voice is affected by the shape of your vocal cords, but your nose also plays an important role. The sound created by the vocal cords' vibrations becomes louder when it passes through the nasal cavity and paranasal sinuses. Depending on the shape and thickness of these cavities, different people produce varied tones and timbres. Your voice becomes very nasal when you have a cold because the nasal cavity and paranasal sinuses become swollen and produce different types of vibrations. This is similar to how your voice changes when you pinch your nose shut.

WE HAVE TO GO BACK TO THE LAB RIGHT NOW!

WOW, YOUR VOICE IS RINGING VERY LOUDLY!

© Geheimnisträgerin

Just as a big drum's body can produce loud sounds, your voice can be loud because it vibrates inside the nasal cavity.

TRAPPED INSIDE THE EAR MAZE

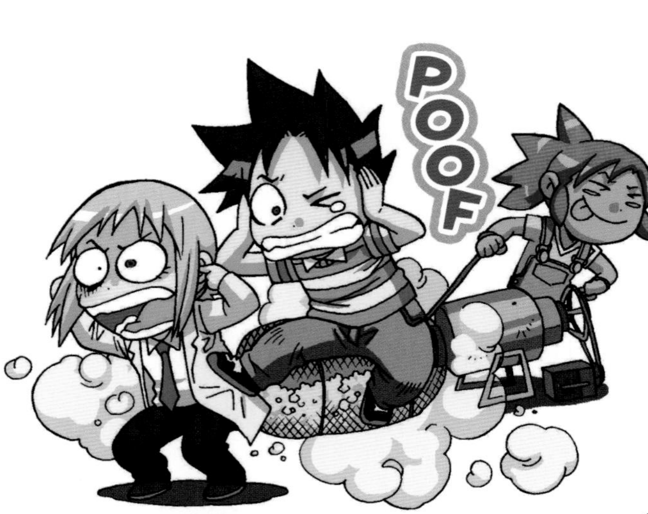
POOF

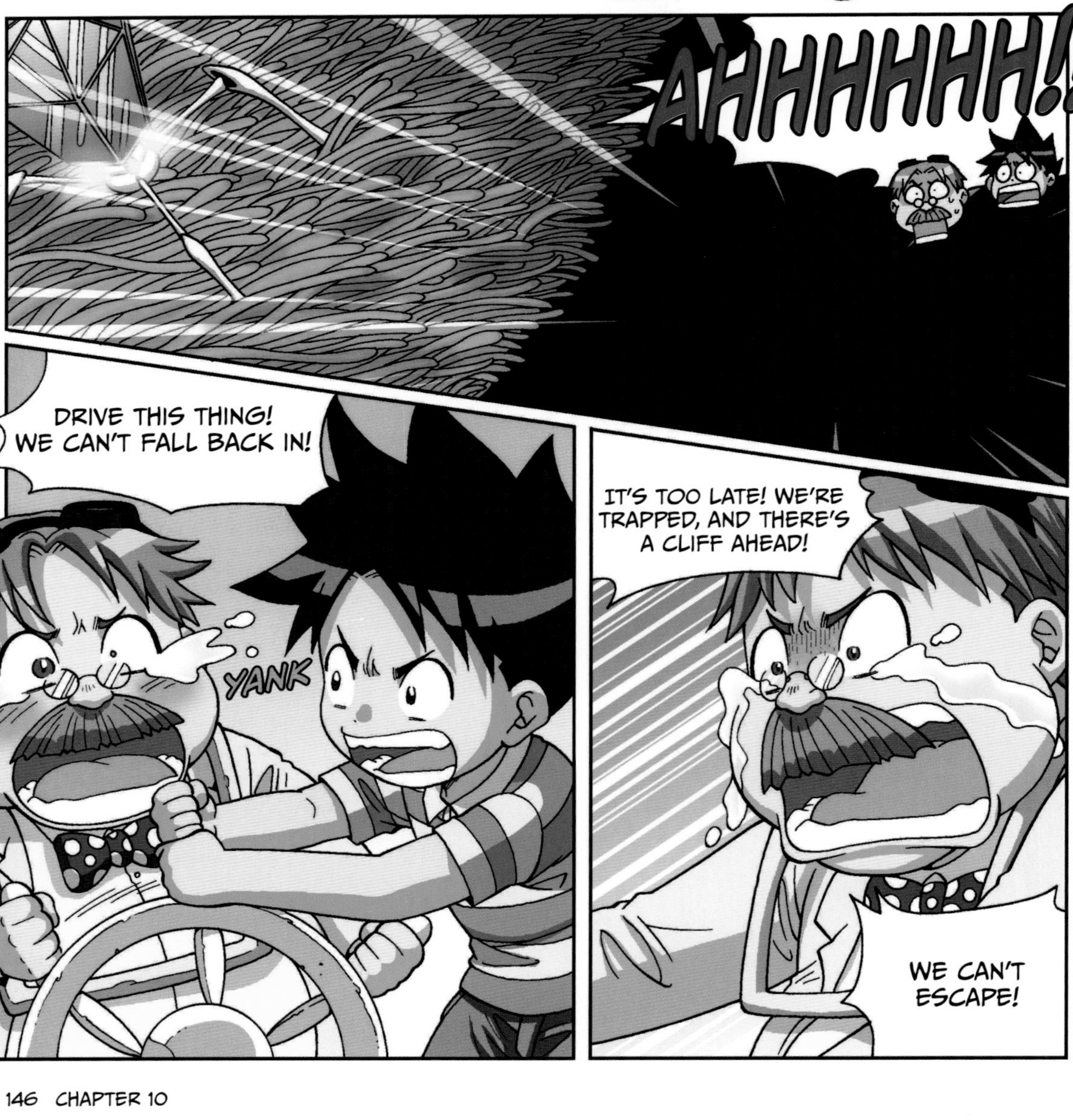
AHHHHHH!!
DRIVE THIS THING! WE CAN'T FALL BACK IN!
YANK
IT'S TOO LATE! WE'RE TRAPPED, AND THERE'S A CLIFF AHEAD!
WE CAN'T ESCAPE!

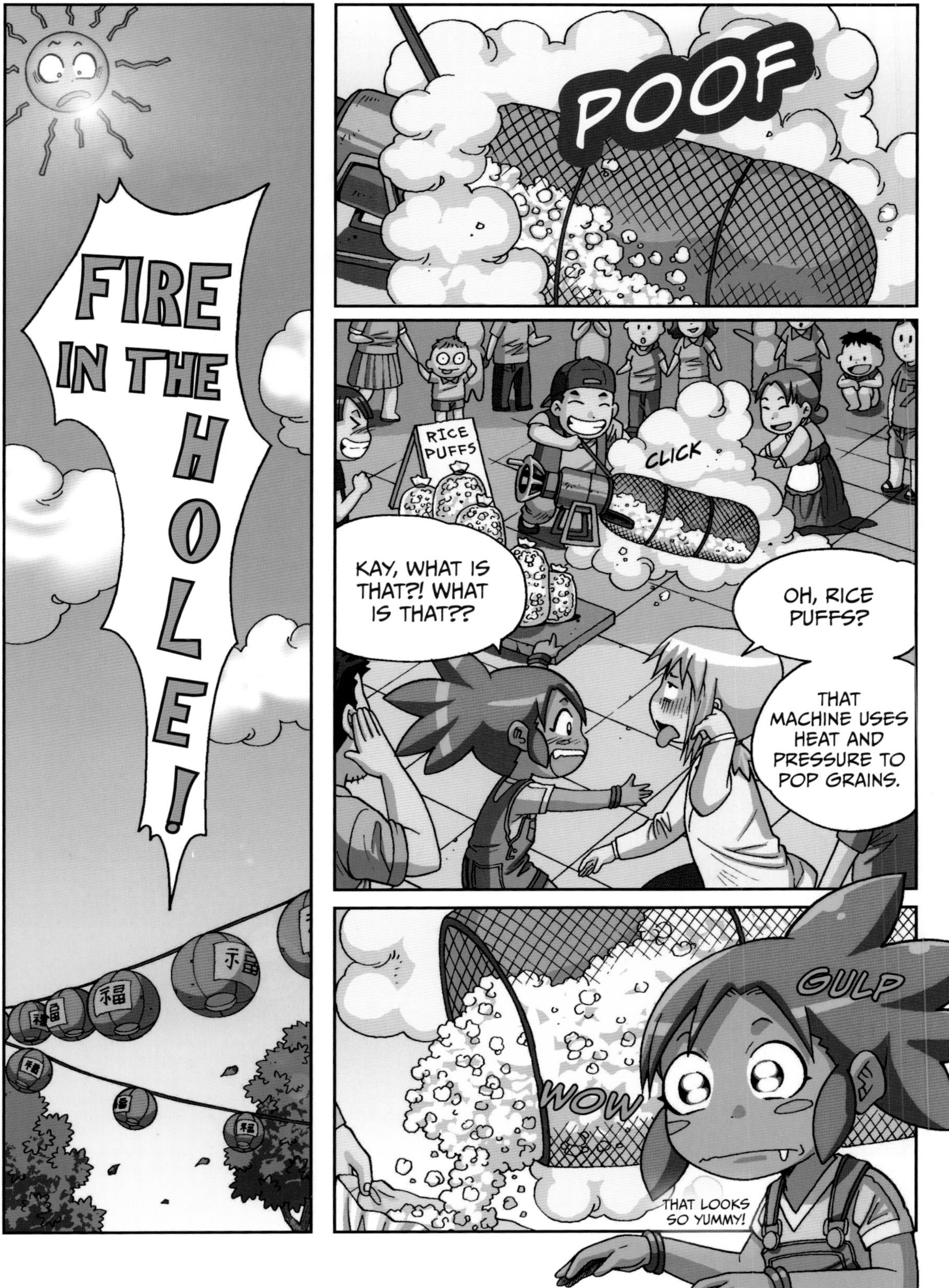
FIRE IN THE HOLE!
POOF
RICE PUFFS
CLICK
KAY, WHAT IS THAT?! WHAT IS THAT??
OH, RICE PUFFS?
THAT MACHINE USES HEAT AND PRESSURE TO POP GRAINS.
GULP
WOW
THAT LOOKS SO YUMMY!

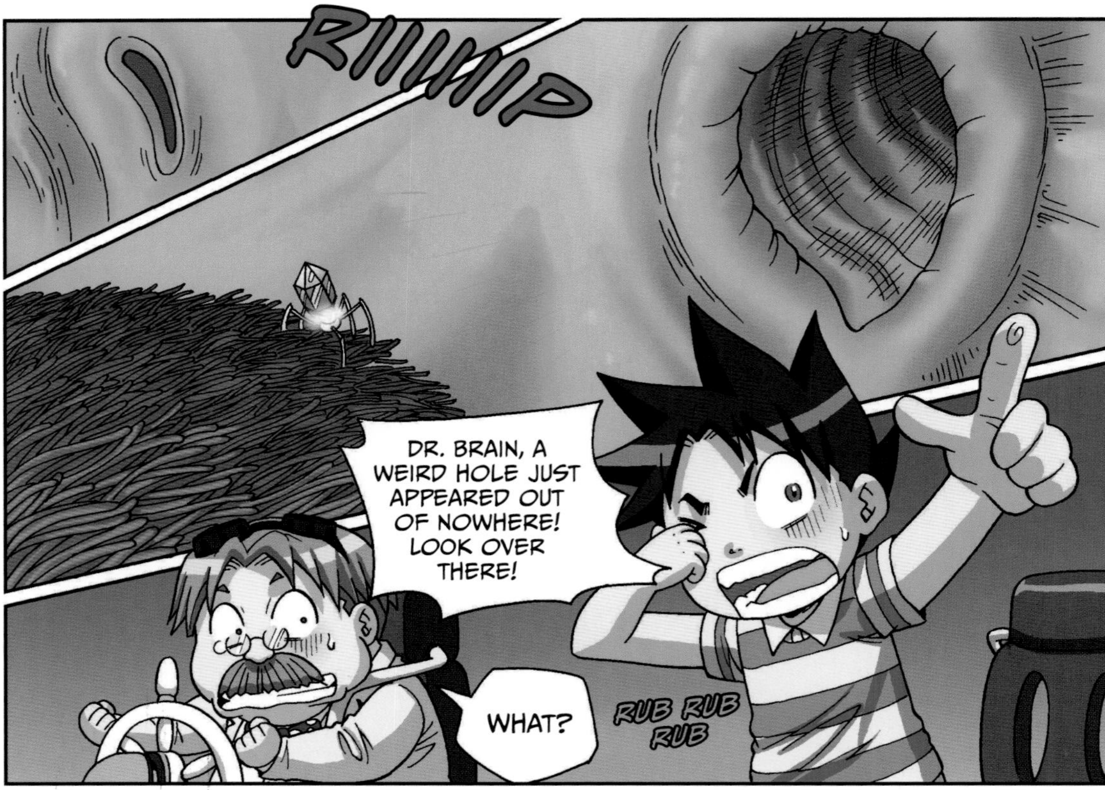
RIIIIIIP
DR. BRAIN, A WEIRD HOLE JUST APPEARED OUT OF NOWHERE! LOOK OVER THERE!
WHAT?
RUB RUB RUB

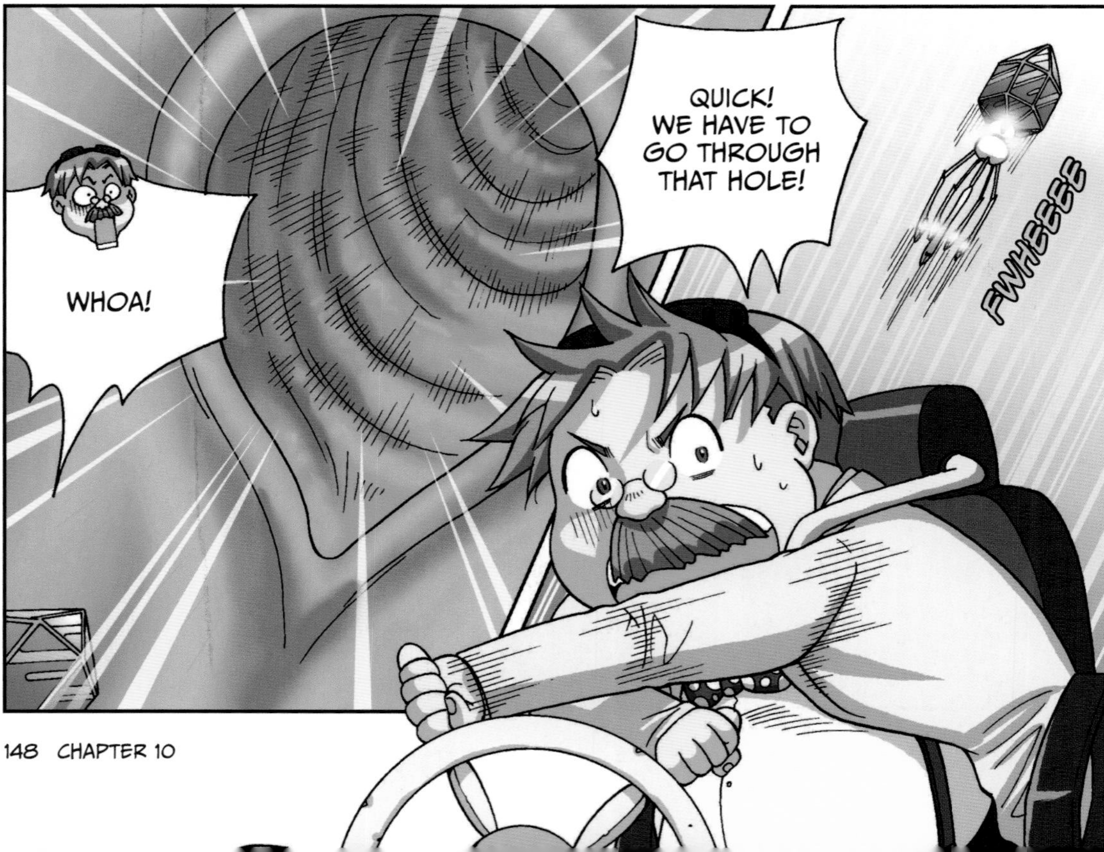
QUICK! WE HAVE TO GO THROUGH THAT HOLE!
WHOA!
FWHEEEE

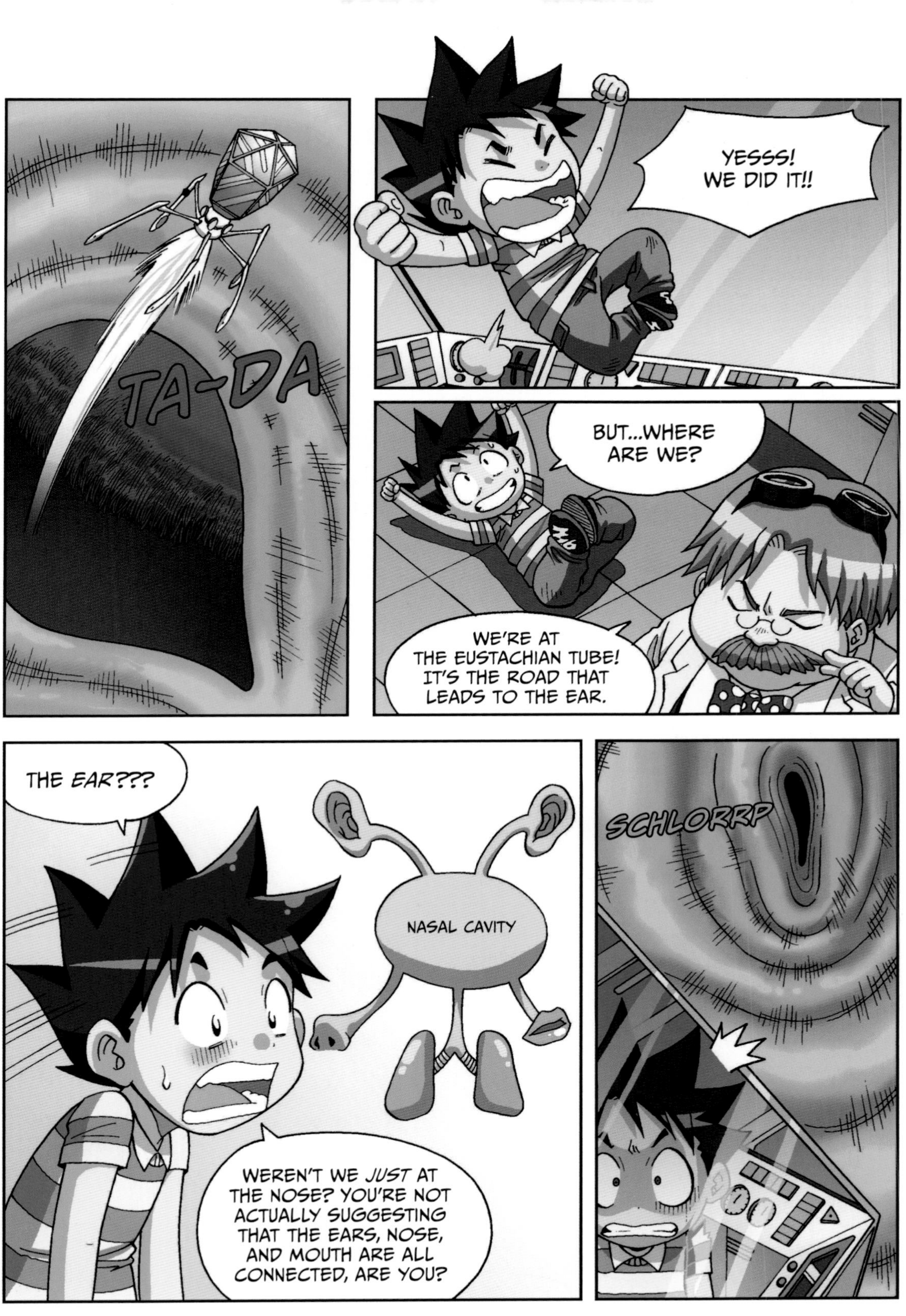
TA-DA
YESSS! WE DID IT!!
BUT...WHERE ARE WE?
WE'RE AT THE EUSTACHIAN TUBE! IT'S THE ROAD THAT LEADS TO THE EAR.
THE EAR???
NASAL CAVITY
WEREN'T WE JUST AT THE NOSE? YOU'RE NOT ACTUALLY SUGGESTING THAT THE EARS, NOSE, AND MOUTH ARE ALL CONNECTED, ARE YOU?
SCHLORRP

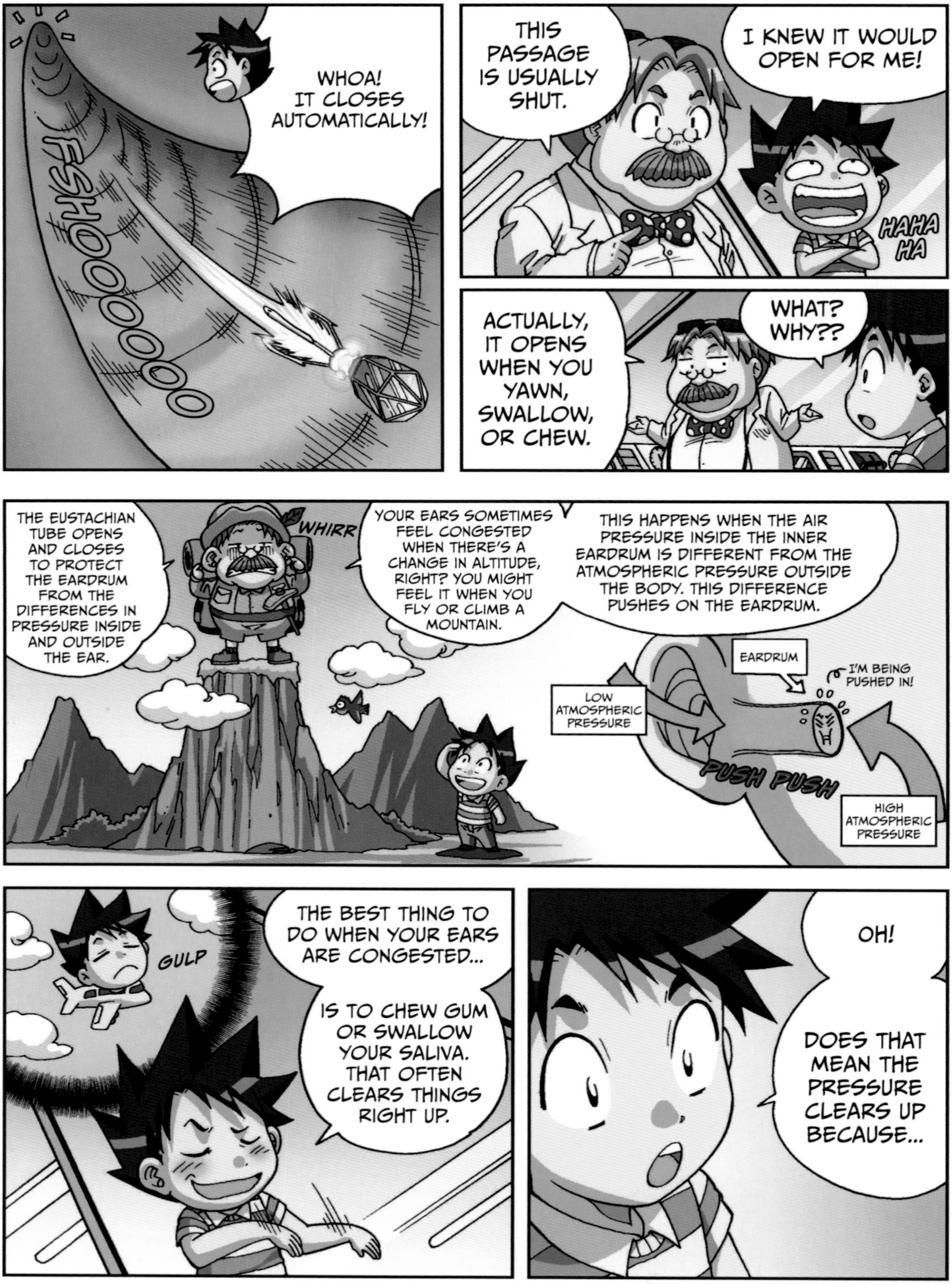
WHOA! IT CLOSES AUTOMATICALLY!
FSHOOOOOOOO
THIS PASSAGE IS USUALLY SHUT.
I KNEW IT WOULD OPEN FOR ME!
HAHA HA
ACTUALLY, IT OPENS WHEN YOU YAWN, SWALLOW, OR CHEW.
WHAT? WHY??
THE EUSTACHIAN TUBE OPENS AND CLOSES TO PROTECT THE EARDRUM FROM THE DIFFERENCES IN PRESSURE INSIDE AND OUTSIDE THE EAR.
WHIRR
YOUR EARS SOMETIMES FEEL CONGESTED WHEN THERE'S A CHANGE IN ALTITUDE, RIGHT? YOU MIGHT FEEL IT WHEN YOU FLY OR CLIMB A MOUNTAIN.
THIS HAPPENS WHEN THE AIR PRESSURE INSIDE THE INNER EARDRUM IS DIFFERENT FROM THE ATMOSPHERIC PRESSURE OUTSIDE THE BODY. THIS DIFFERENCE PUSHES ON THE EARDRUM.
EARDRUM
I'M BEING PUSHED IN!
LOW ATMOSPHERIC PRESSURE
PUSH PUSH
HIGH ATMOSPHERIC PRESSURE
GULP
THE BEST THING TO DO WHEN YOUR EARS ARE CONGESTED...
IS TO CHEW GUM OR SWALLOW YOUR SALIVA. THAT OFTEN CLEARS THINGS RIGHT UP.
OH!
DOES THAT MEAN THE PRESSURE CLEARS UP BECAUSE...

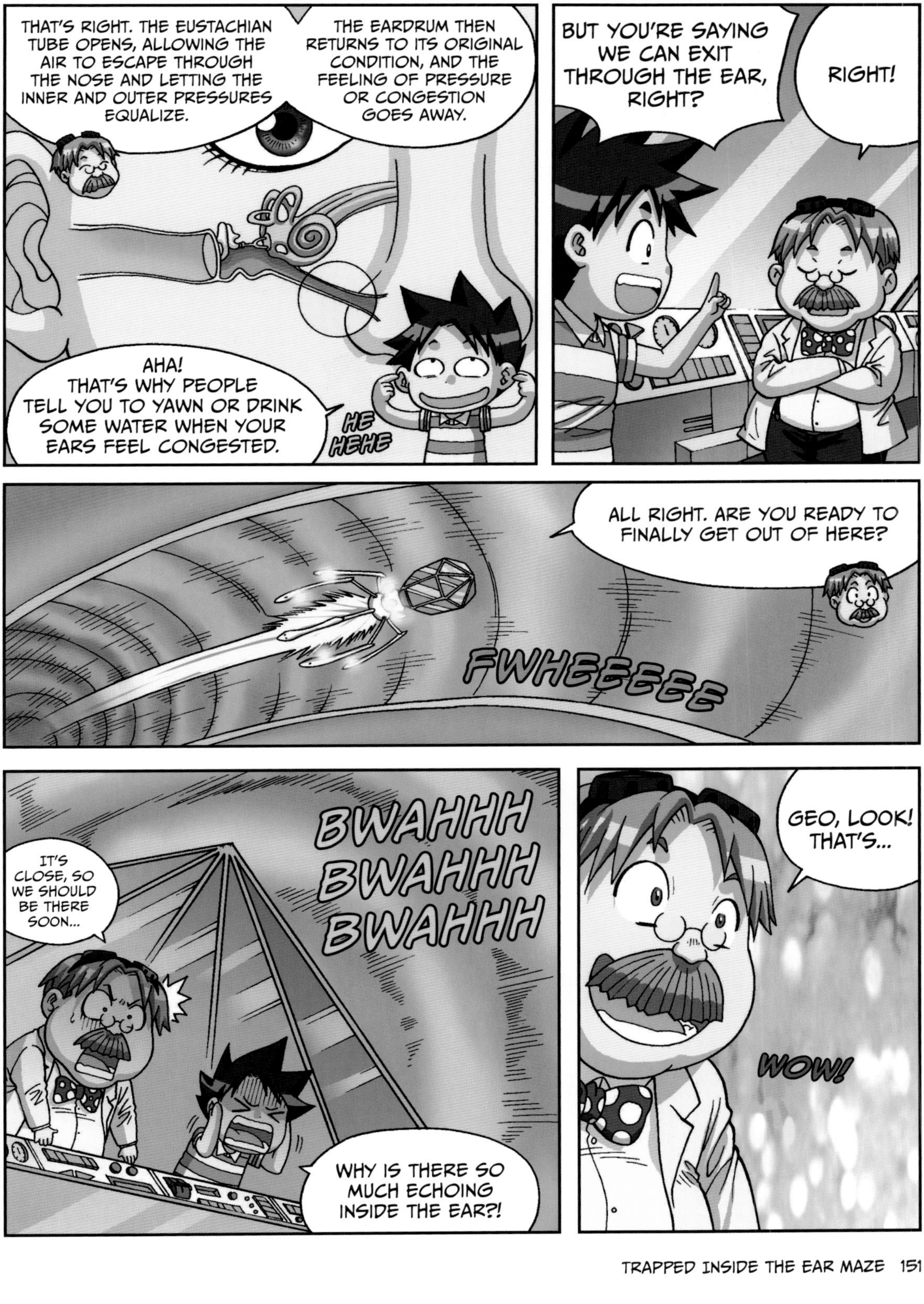
THAT'S RIGHT. THE EUSTACHIAN TUBE OPENS, ALLOWING THE AIR TO ESCAPE THROUGH THE NOSE AND LETTING THE INNER AND OUTER PRESSURES EQUALIZE.
THE EARDRUM THEN RETURNS TO ITS ORIGINAL CONDITION, AND THE FEELING OF PRESSURE OR CONGESTION GOES AWAY.
AHA! THAT'S WHY PEOPLE TELL YOU TO YAWN OR DRINK SOME WATER WHEN YOUR EARS FEEL CONGESTED.
HE HEHE
BUT YOU'RE SAYING WE CAN EXIT THROUGH THE EAR, RIGHT?
RIGHT!
ALL RIGHT. ARE YOU READY TO FINALLY GET OUT OF HERE?
FWHEEEEEE
BWAHHH BWAHHH BWAHHH
IT'S CLOSE, SO WE SHOULD BE THERE SOON...
WHY IS THERE SO MUCH ECHOING INSIDE THE EAR?!
GEO, LOOK! THAT'S...
WOW!

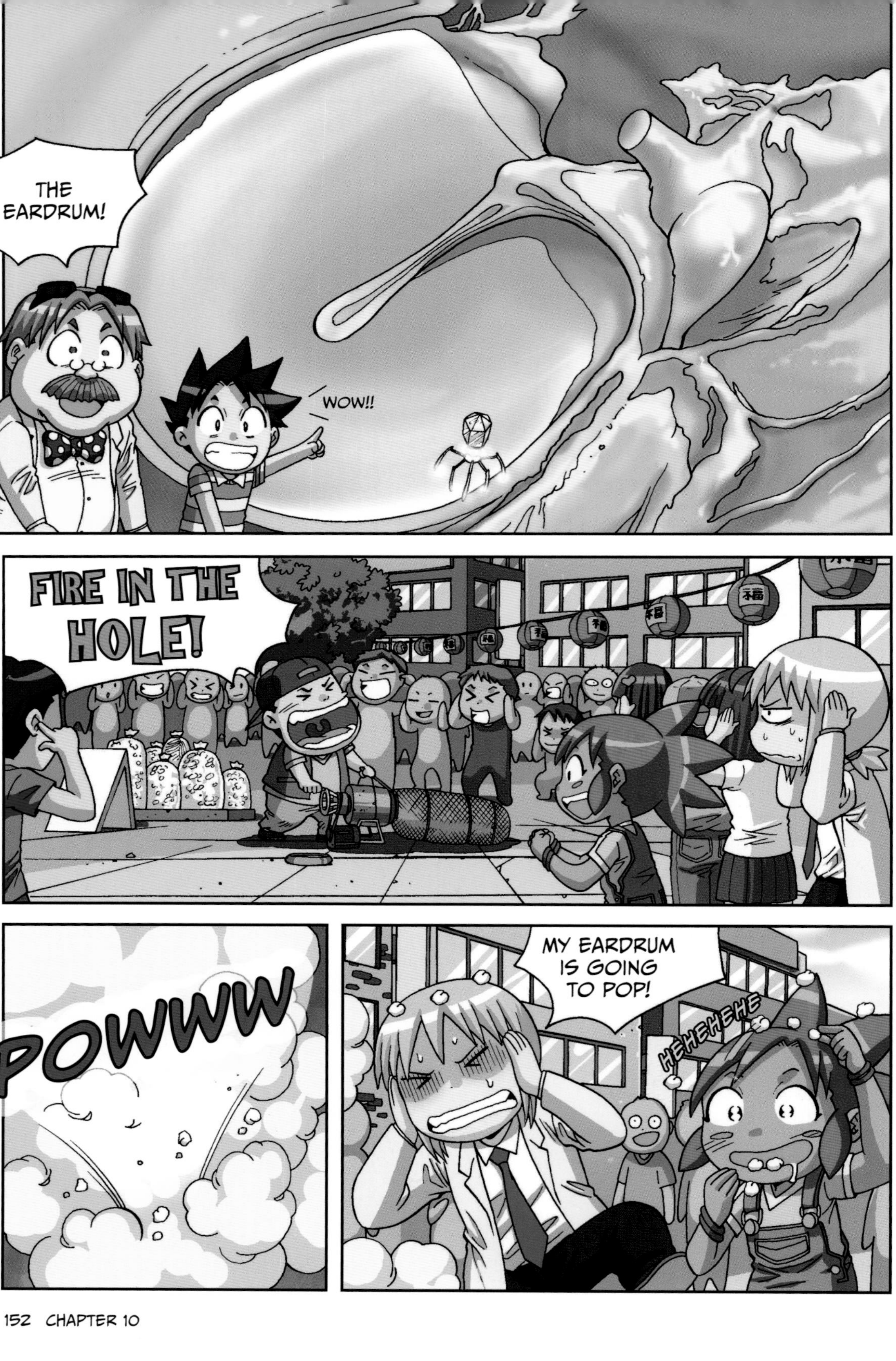
THE EARDRUM!
WOW!!
FIRE IN THE HOLE!
POWWW
MY EARDRUM IS GOING TO POP!
HEHEHEHE

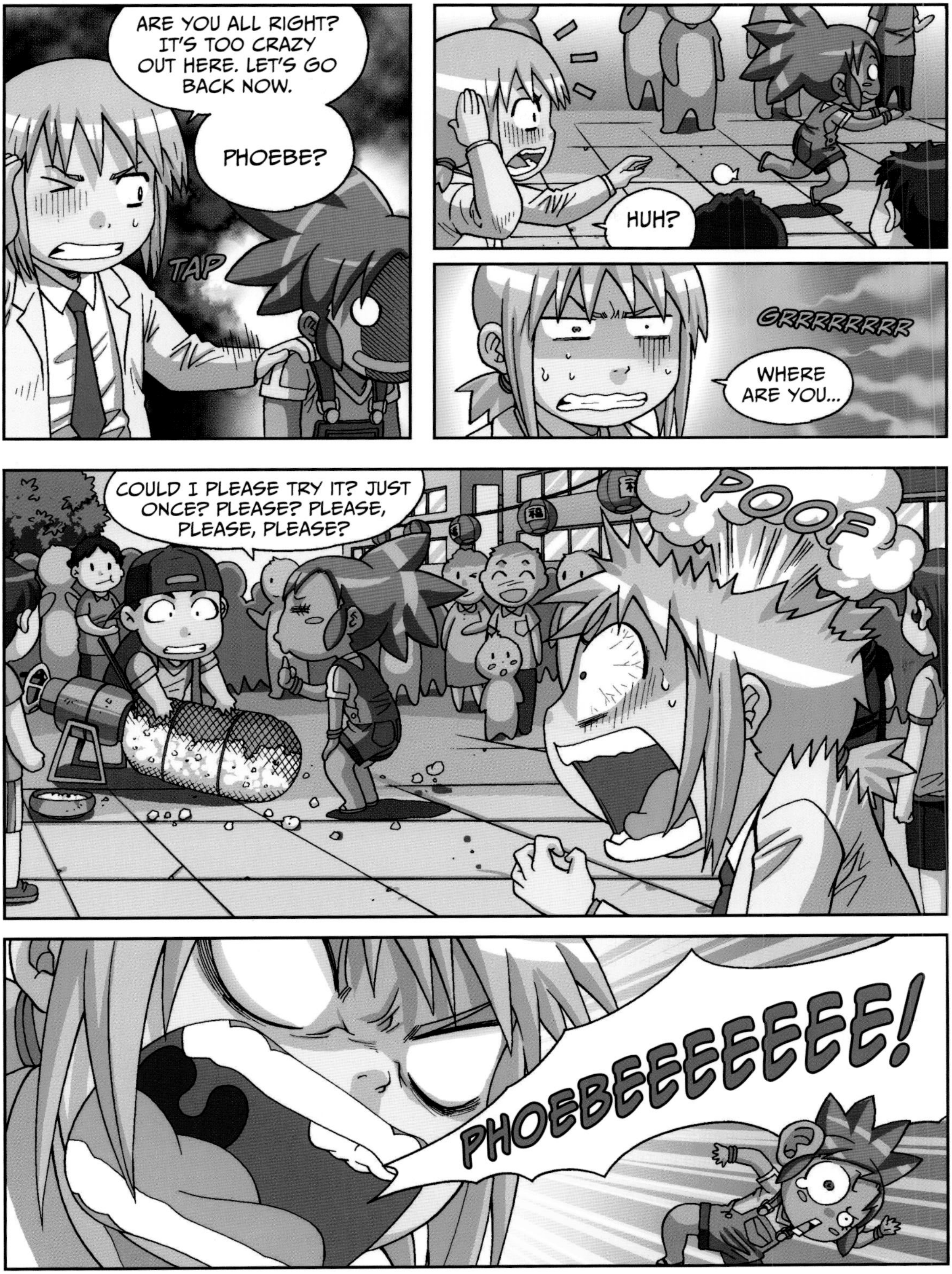
ARE YOU ALL RIGHT? IT'S TOO CRAZY OUT HERE. LET'S GO BACK NOW.
PHOEBE?
TAP
HUH?
GRRRRRRRR
WHERE ARE YOU...
COULD I PLEASE TRY IT? JUST ONCE? PLEASE? PLEASE, PLEASE, PLEASE?
POOF
PHOEBEEEEEEEE!

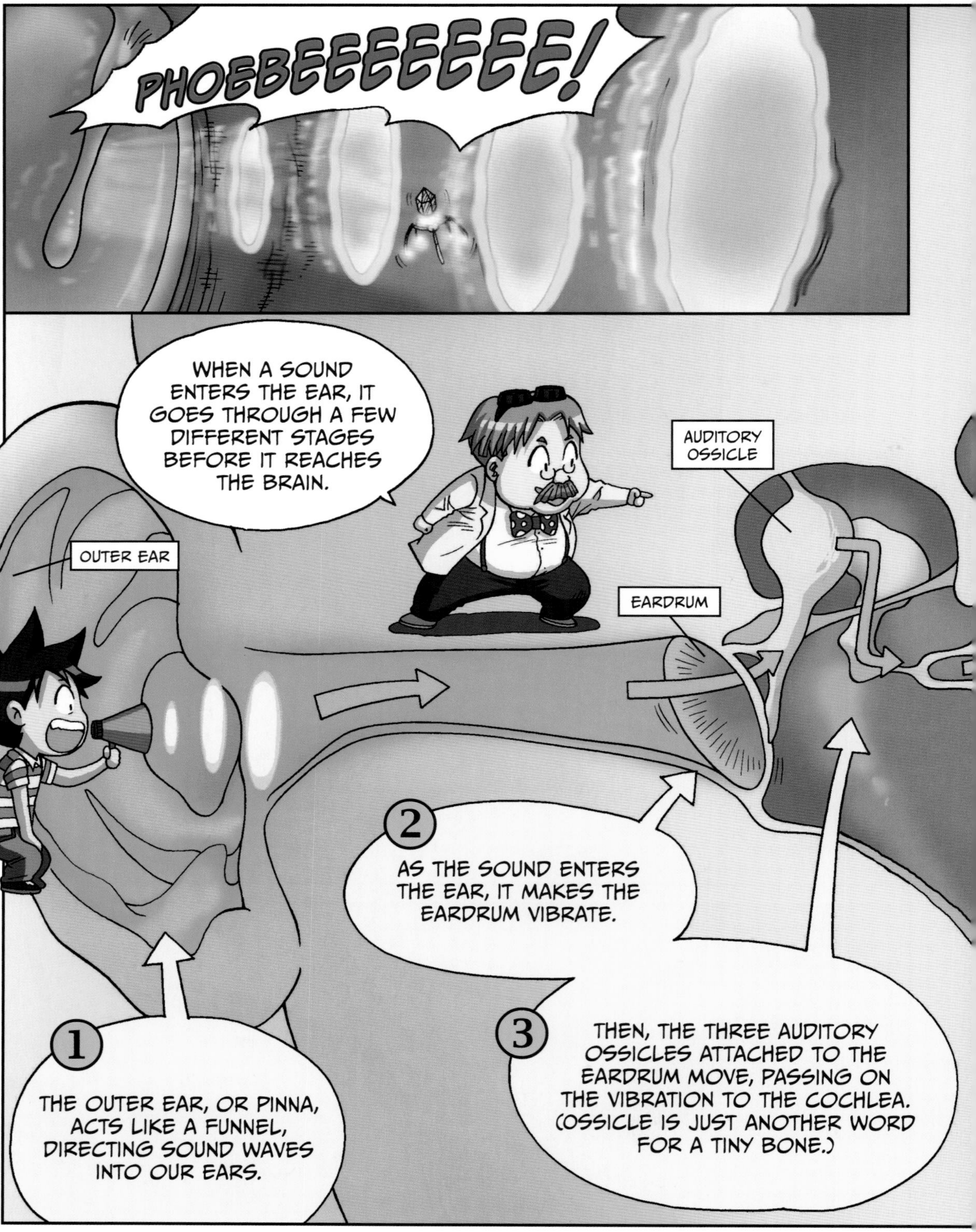
PHOEBEEEEEEEE!
WHEN A SOUND ENTERS THE EAR, IT GOES THROUGH A FEW DIFFERENT STAGES BEFORE IT REACHES THE BRAIN.
AUDITORY OSSICLE
OUTER EAR
EARDRUM
2 AS THE SOUND ENTERS THE EAR, IT MAKES THE EARDRUM VIBRATE.
1 THE OUTER EAR, OR PINNA, ACTS LIKE A FUNNEL, DIRECTING SOUND WAVES INTO OUR EARS.
3 THEN, THE THREE AUDITORY OSSICLES ATTACHED TO THE EARDRUM MOVE, PASSING ON THE VIBRATION TO THE COCHLEA. (OSSICLE IS JUST ANOTHER WORD FOR A TINY BONE.)

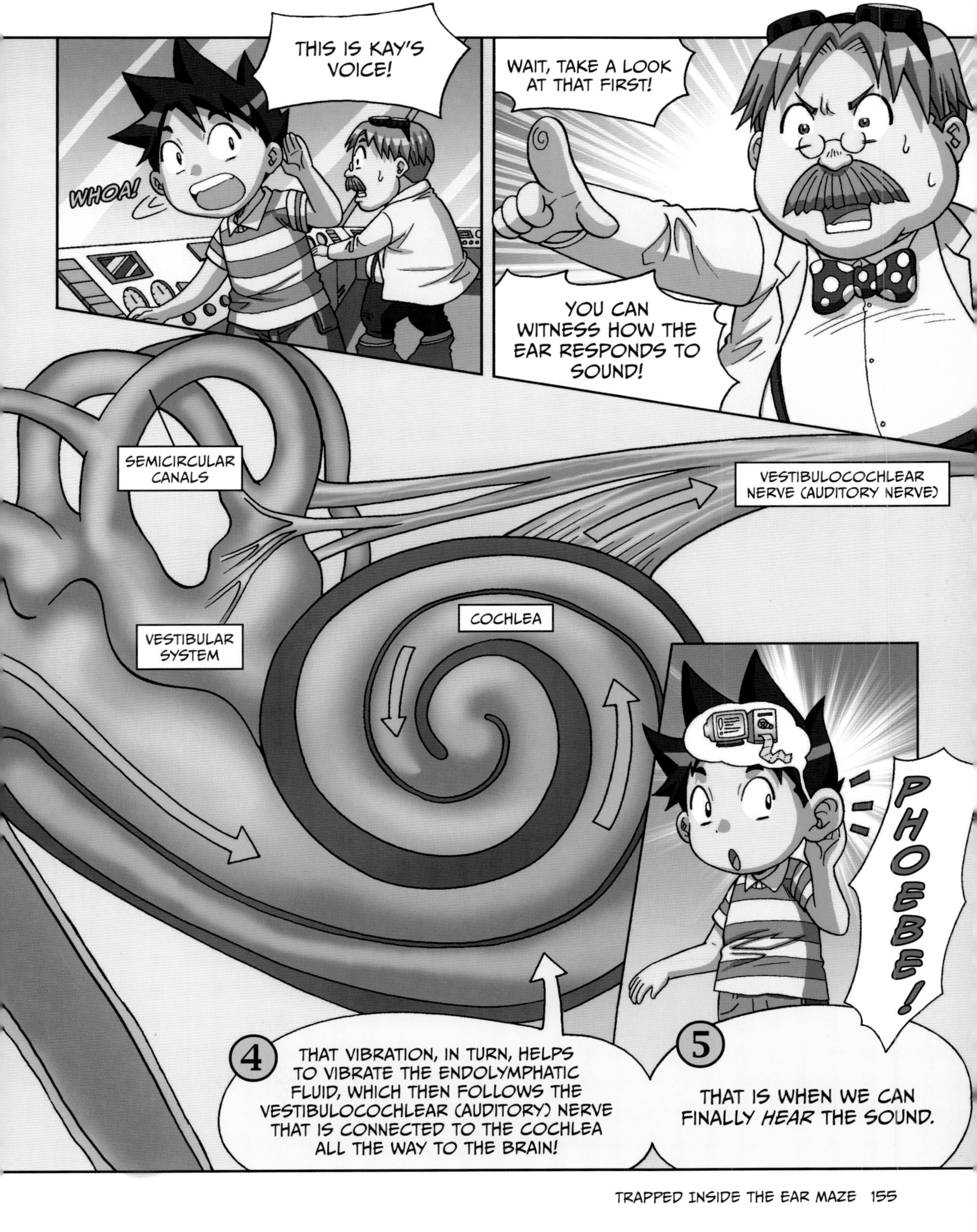
THIS IS KAY'S VOICE!
WHOA!
WAIT, TAKE A LOOK AT THAT FIRST!
YOU CAN WITNESS HOW THE EAR RESPONDS TO SOUND!
SEMICIRCULAR CANALS
VESTIBULOCOCHLEAR NERVE (AUDITORY NERVE)
COCHLEA
VESTIBULAR SYSTEM
PHOEBE!
4 THAT VIBRATION, IN TURN, HELPS TO VIBRATE THE ENDOLYMPHATIC FLUID, WHICH THEN FOLLOWS THE VESTIBULOCOCHLEAR (AUDITORY) NERVE THAT IS CONNECTED TO THE COCHLEA ALL THE WAY TO THE BRAIN!
5 THAT IS WHEN WE CAN FINALLY *HEAR* THE SOUND.

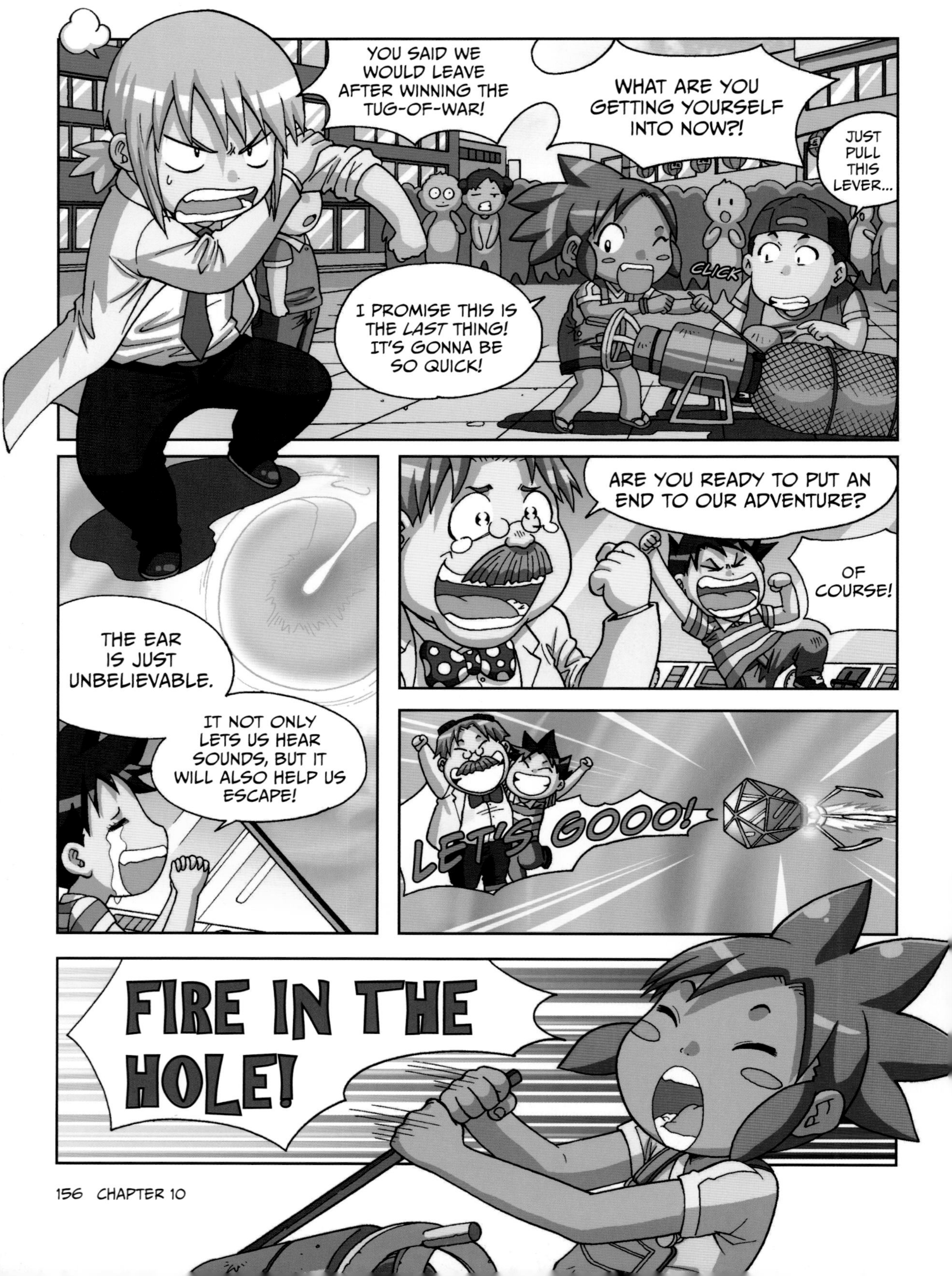
YOU SAID WE WOULD LEAVE AFTER WINNING THE TUG-OF-WAR!
WHAT ARE YOU GETTING YOURSELF INTO NOW?!
JUST PULL THIS LEVER...
CLICK
I PROMISE THIS IS THE *LAST* THING! IT'S GONNA BE SO QUICK!
THE EAR IS JUST UNBELIEVABLE.
IT NOT ONLY LETS US HEAR SOUNDS, BUT IT WILL ALSO HELP US ESCAPE!
ARE YOU READY TO PUT AN END TO OUR ADVENTURE?
OF COURSE!
LET'S GOOOO!
FIRE IN THE HOLE!

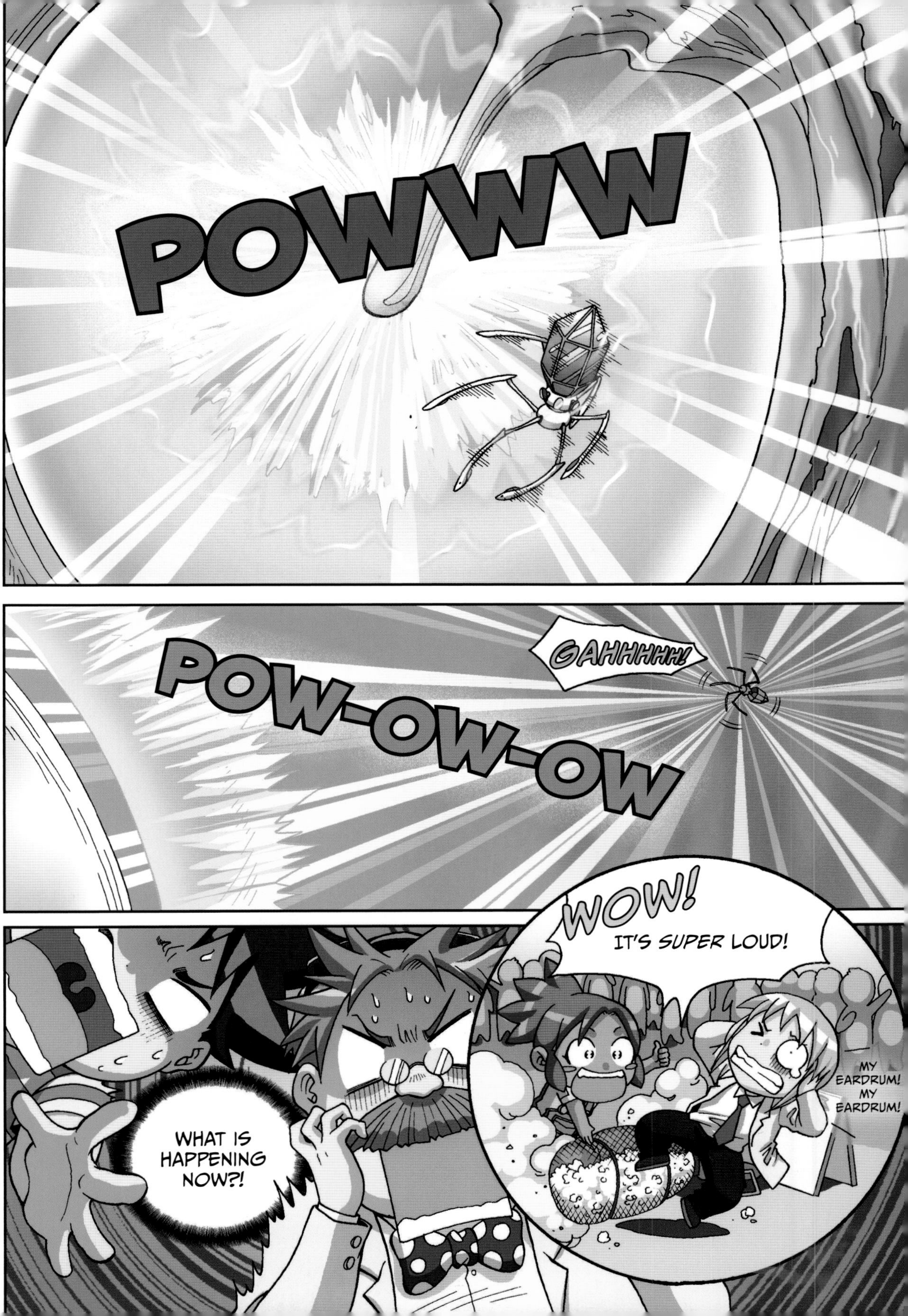
POWWW
POW-OW-OW
GAHHHHH!
WOW!
IT'S SUPER LOUD!
MY EARDRUM! MY EARDRUM!
WHAT IS HAPPENING NOW?!

YOUR AMAZING EARS

The ear has three parts: the external ear (also called the *pinna*), the middle ear (where the eardrum, or tympanum, is located), and the wonderfully complex inner ear. The external ear and middle ear help us hear sounds. The inner ear helps us maintain our balance (using the vestibular system), but it plays a role in hearing too, using the cochlea.

HOW WE HEAR STUFF

The sounds you hear are waves of compressed air. The pitch of a sound is measured using hertz, which refers to the number of vibrations that occur in one second. We can sense sounds in the range of about 20–20,000 hertz. A 20-hertz tone is a deep, chest-rumbling bass tone, while 20,000 hertz is a high-pitched tweet. Sound above 20,000 hertz is called *ultrasound*—we literally cannot hear these pitches. (Doctors use ultrasound waves to create sonograms, as well as for other imaging and medical purposes.)

When sound waves within our range of hearing pass the auditory ossicles (those three tiny bones) and arrive at the cochlea, the endolymphatic fluid inside the cochlea vibrates. This vibration stimulates the auditory cells, which then produce signals the brain recognizes as sound.

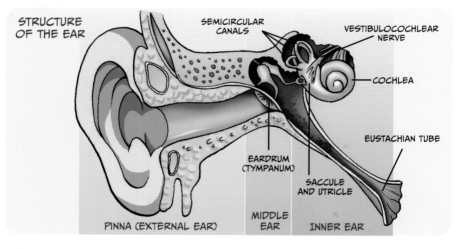

STRUCTURE OF THE EAR

SEMICIRCULAR CANALS

VESTIBULOCOCHLEAR NERVE

COCHLEA

EUSTACHIAN TUBE

EARDRUM (TYMPANUM)

SACCULE AND UTRICLE

PINNA (EXTERNAL EAR)

MIDDLE EAR

INNER EAR

MAINTAINING EQUILIBRIUM

Your vestibular system includes the three semicircular canals, the utricle, and the saccule. The semicircular canals inside the ear maintain your balance (or equilibrium) by sensing the rotation and tilt of the head. The ring-shaped semicircular tubes are positioned at roughly 90-degree angles to each other, allowing them to sense movement in any direction. The semicircular canals are filled with endolymphatic fluid and also contain motion sensors.

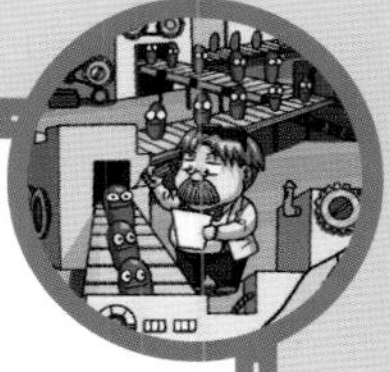

At the base of each canal, there's a bundle of cilia called *hair cells*. These aren't just regular old hair. When your head rotates, the endolymphatic fluid lags behind and bends the cilia, causing them to send signals to your brain. The semicircular canals in both ears must send their signals at the same time in order for you to maintain your balance. You can lose your balance after coming to a quick stop because the endolymphatic fluid within the semicircular canals keeps moving due to inertia—even after the body has stopped.

The vestibular system also contains two sacs, called the *utricle* and the *saccule*, that are important for keeping your balance. These sacs have hair cells too, and they are sensitive to gravity and acceleration. They're special because they have crystals in them called *otoliths* that stimulate the hair cells. The utricle detects horizontal movement (running forward and stopping) with a bed of hair cells lying horizontal on its floor. The saccule, on the other hand, detects vertical movement (going up and down) with a bed of hair cells vertical to its wall.

SEMICIRCULAR CANALS
SACCULE AND UTRICLE
VESTIBULAR SYSTEM
SEMICIRCULAR CANAL
ENDOLYMPHATIC FLUID
HAIR CELLS
TURNING LEFT
STATIONARY POSITION
TURNING RIGHT
SACCULE AND UTRICLE
OTOLITHS (EAR CRYSTALS)
OTOLITHIC MEMBRANE
HAIR CELLS
TILTING TO THE LEFT
BALANCED
TILTING TO THE RIGHT

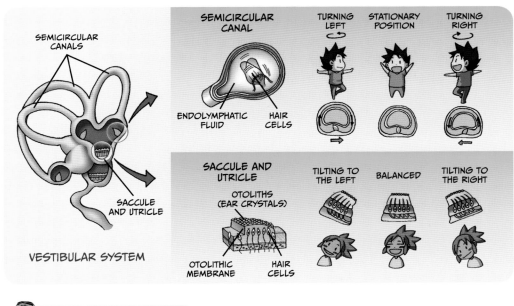

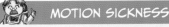

MOTION SICKNESS

The reason you might feel nauseated, or "motion sick," in a car or boat is because the information from your eyes and the balance-related information from your inner ear don't match. For example, if you're sitting inside a moving car and reading a book, your body appears stationary to your eyes. The vestibular system, on the other hand, sends a signal to the brain that you're moving. This is why looking out the window can help lessen your motion sickness; it settles the difference between the visual and balance-related information.

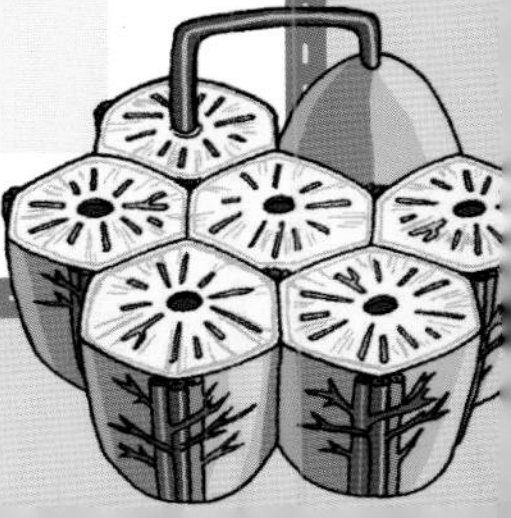

FINAL DECISION

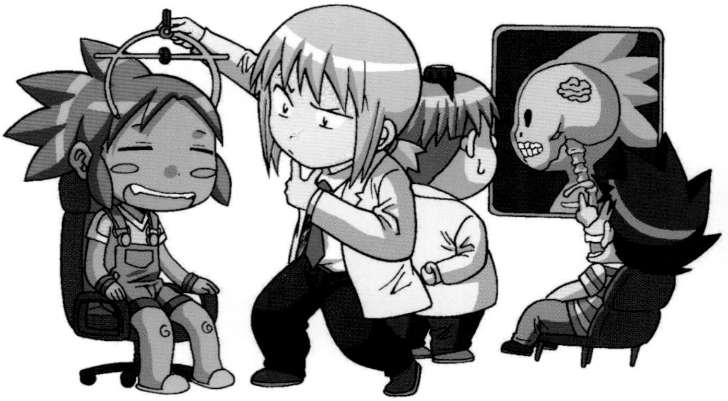

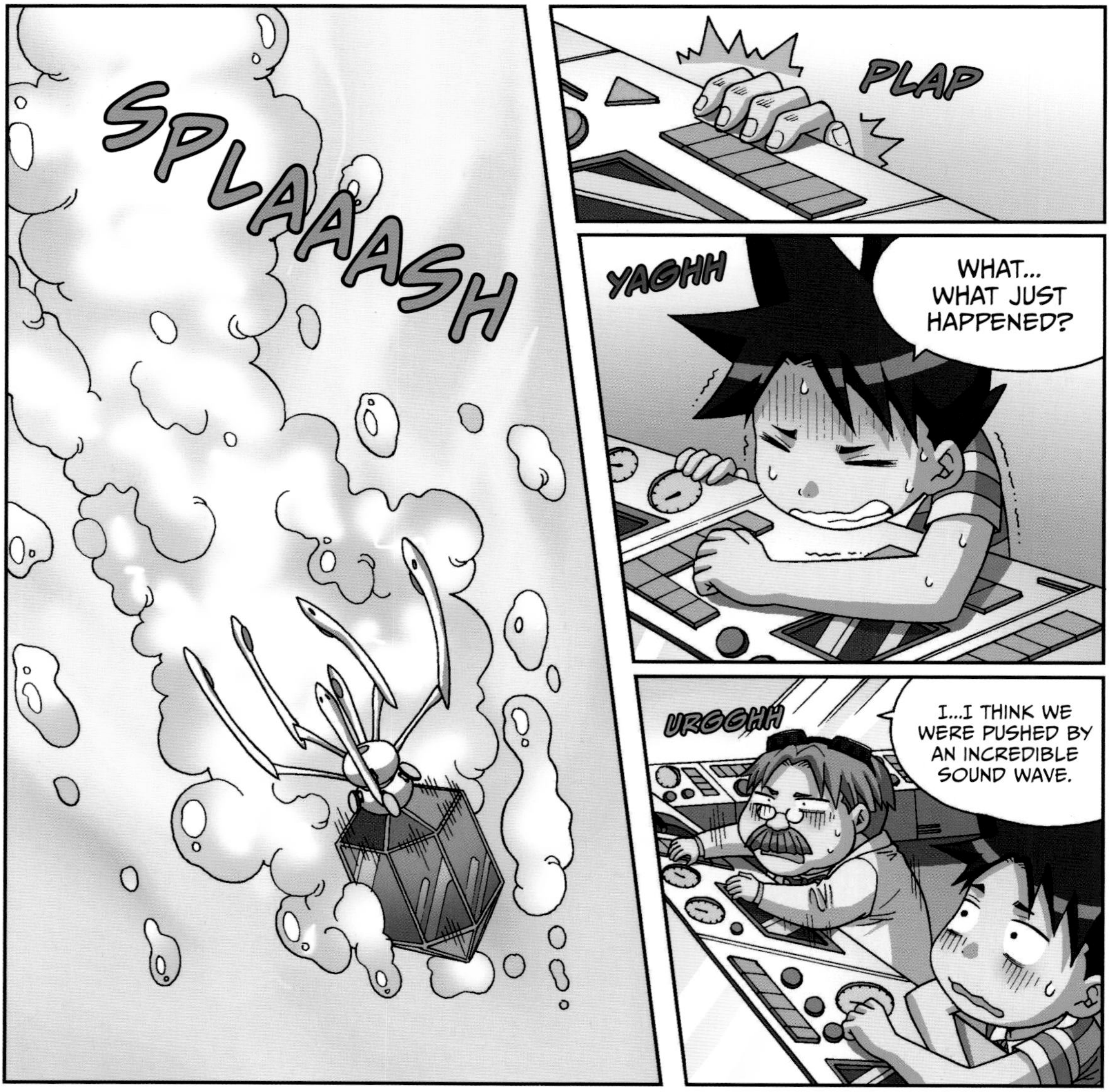

SPLAAASH
PLAP
YAGHH
WHAT... WHAT JUST HAPPENED?
URGGHH
I...I THINK WE WERE PUSHED BY AN INCREDIBLE SOUND WAVE.

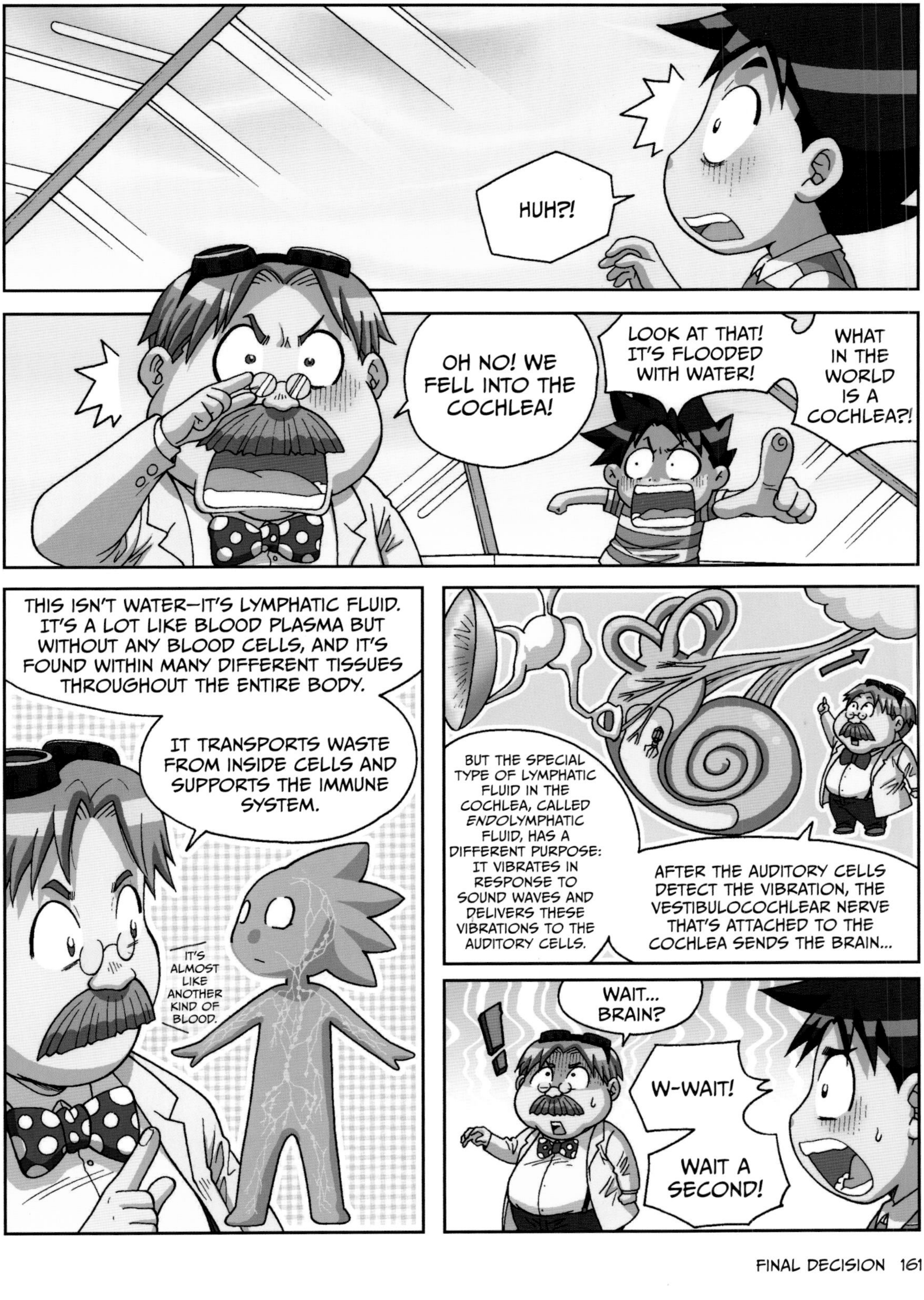
HUH?!
OH NO! WE FELL INTO THE COCHLEA!
LOOK AT THAT! IT'S FLOODED WITH WATER!
WHAT IN THE WORLD IS A COCHLEA?!
THIS ISN'T WATER—IT'S LYMPHATIC FLUID. IT'S A LOT LIKE BLOOD PLASMA BUT WITHOUT ANY BLOOD CELLS, AND IT'S FOUND WITHIN MANY DIFFERENT TISSUES THROUGHOUT THE ENTIRE BODY.
IT TRANSPORTS WASTE FROM INSIDE CELLS AND SUPPORTS THE IMMUNE SYSTEM.
IT'S ALMOST LIKE ANOTHER KIND OF BLOOD.
BUT THE SPECIAL TYPE OF LYMPHATIC FLUID IN THE COCHLEA, CALLED *ENDOLYMPHATIC FLUID*, HAS A DIFFERENT PURPOSE: IT VIBRATES IN RESPONSE TO SOUND WAVES AND DELIVERS THESE VIBRATIONS TO THE AUDITORY CELLS.
AFTER THE AUDITORY CELLS DETECT THE VIBRATION, THE VESTIBULOCOCHLEAR NERVE THAT'S ATTACHED TO THE COCHLEA SENDS THE BRAIN...
WAIT... BRAIN?
W-WAIT!
WAIT A SECOND!

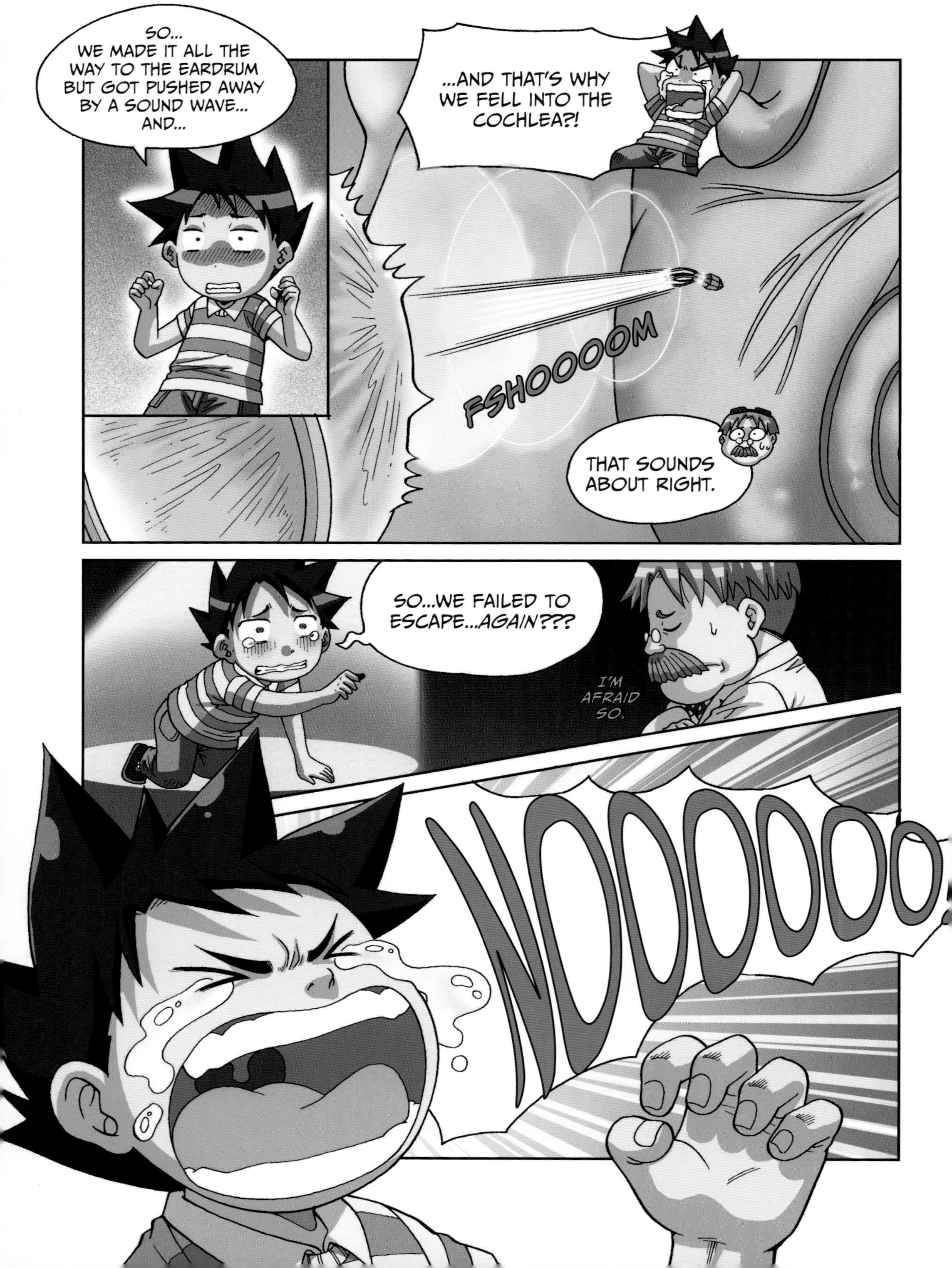
SO...
WE MADE IT ALL THE WAY TO THE EARDRUM BUT GOT PUSHED AWAY BY A SOUND WAVE... AND...
...AND THAT'S WHY WE FELL INTO THE COCHLEA?!
FSHOOOOOM
THAT SOUNDS ABOUT RIGHT.
SO...WE FAILED TO ESCAPE...*AGAIN*???
I'M AFRAID SO.
NOOOOOOO

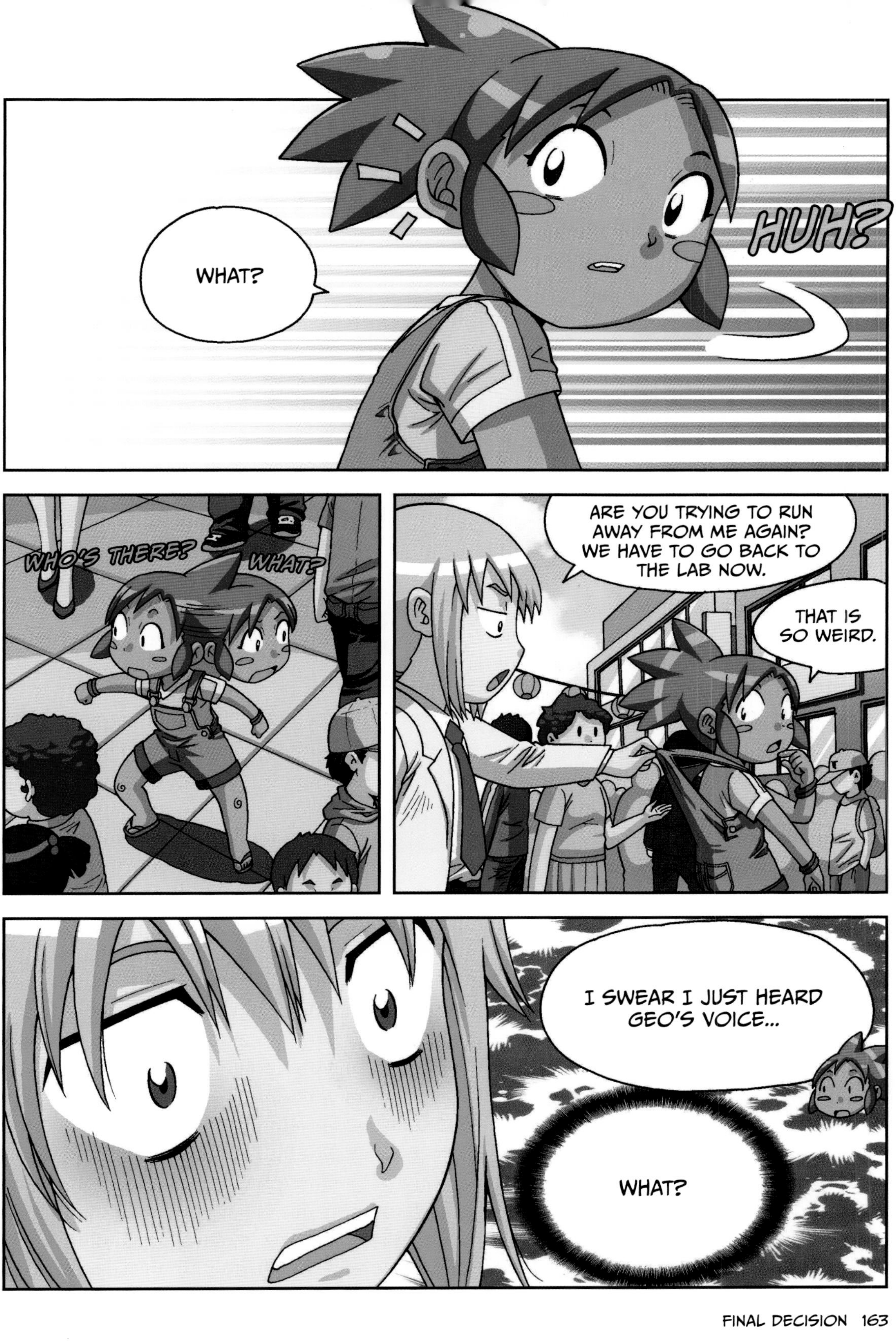
WHAT?
HUH?
WHO'S THERE?
WHAT?
ARE YOU TRYING TO RUN AWAY FROM ME AGAIN? WE HAVE TO GO BACK TO THE LAB NOW.
THAT IS SO WEIRD.
I SWEAR I JUST HEARD GEO'S VOICE...
WHAT?

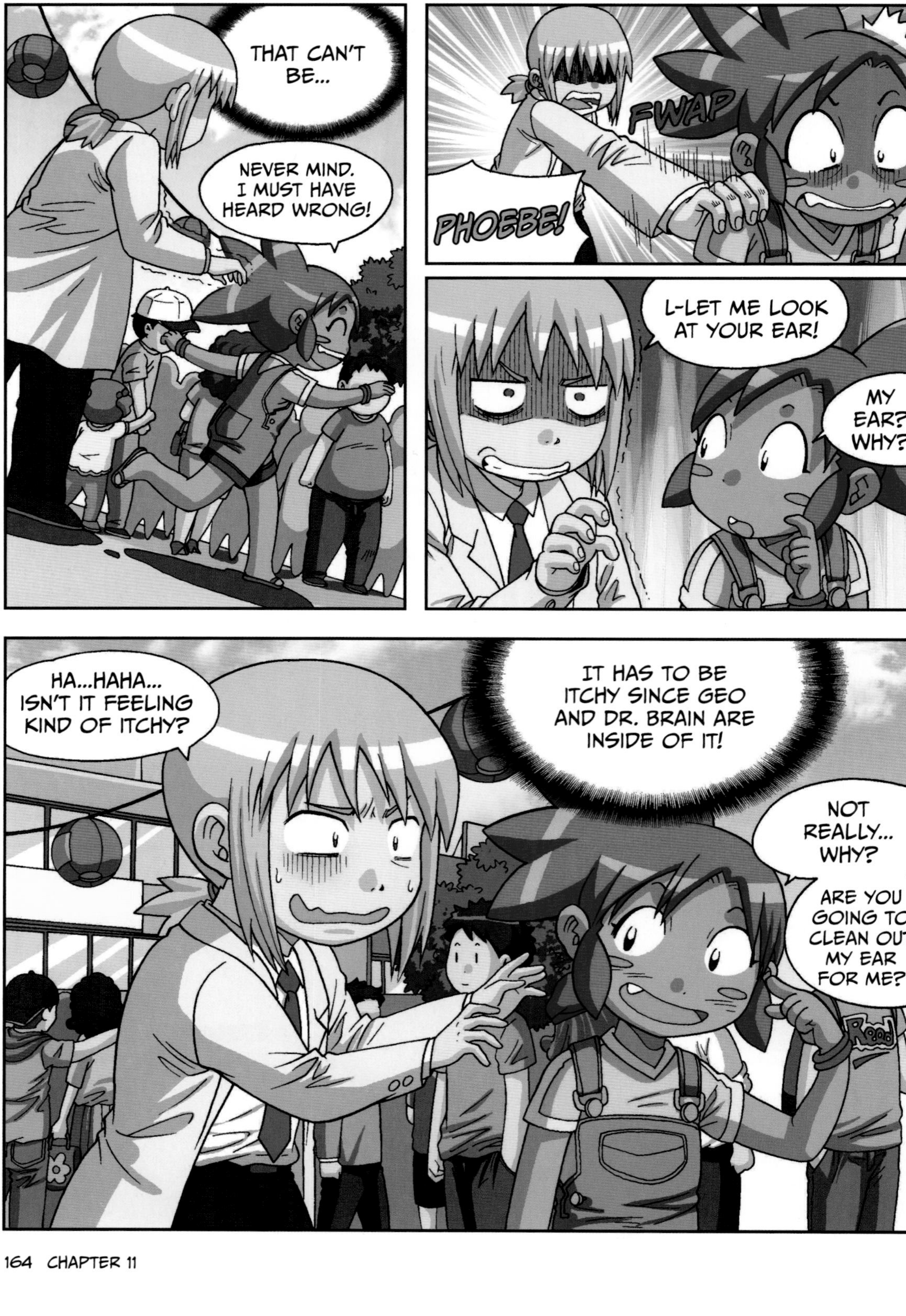
THAT CAN'T BE...
NEVER MIND. I MUST HAVE HEARD WRONG!
PHOEBE!
FWAP
L-LET ME LOOK AT YOUR EAR!
MY EAR? WHY?
HA...HAHA... ISN'T IT FEELING KIND OF ITCHY?
IT HAS TO BE ITCHY SINCE GEO AND DR. BRAIN ARE INSIDE OF IT!
NOT REALLY... WHY?
ARE YOU GOING TO CLEAN OUT MY EAR FOR ME?

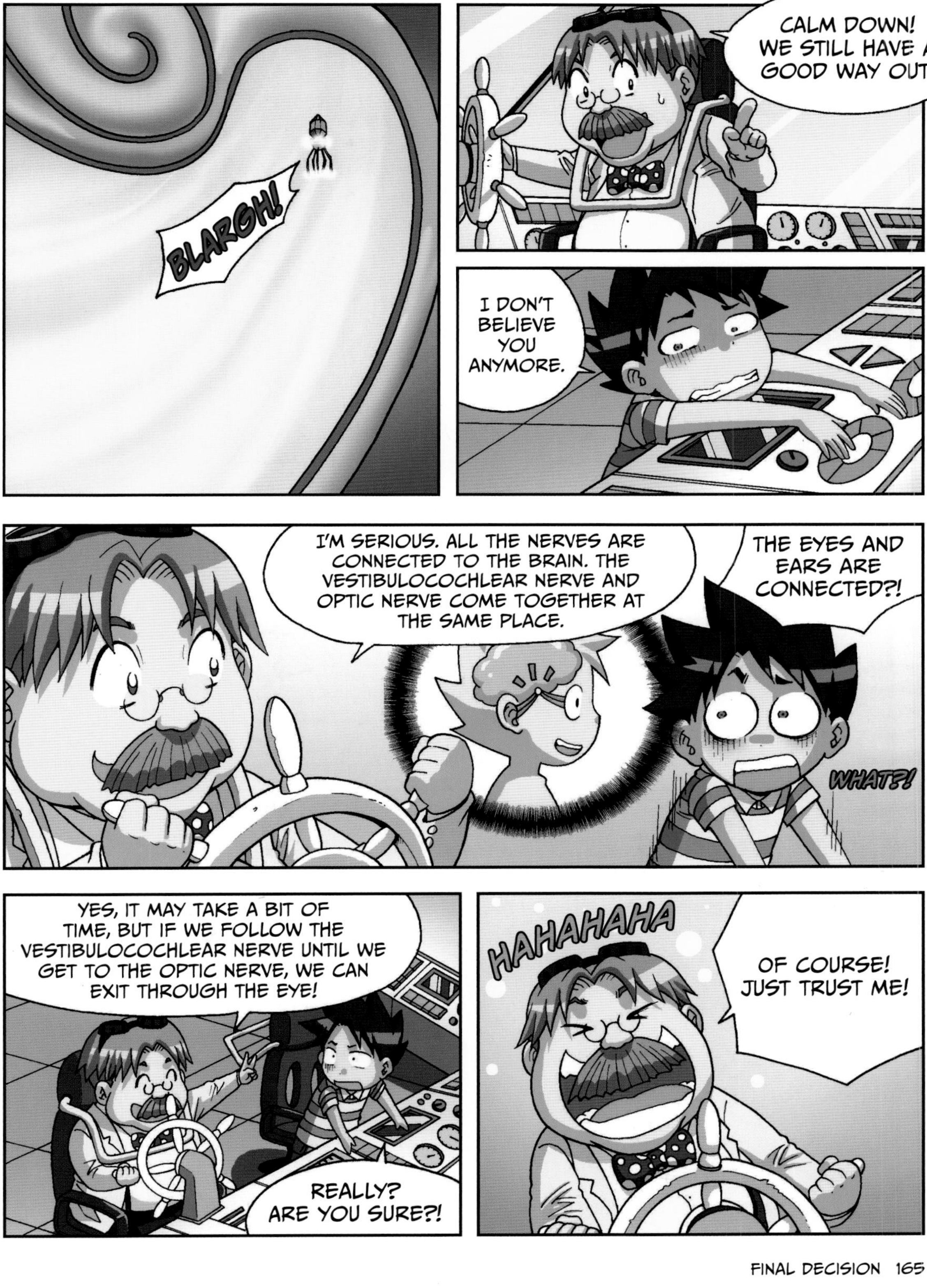
BLARGH!
CALM DOWN! WE STILL HAVE A GOOD WAY OUT.
I DON'T BELIEVE YOU ANYMORE.
I'M SERIOUS. ALL THE NERVES ARE CONNECTED TO THE BRAIN. THE VESTIBULOCOCHLEAR NERVE AND OPTIC NERVE COME TOGETHER AT THE SAME PLACE.
THE EYES AND EARS ARE CONNECTED?!
WHAT?!
YES, IT MAY TAKE A BIT OF TIME, BUT IF WE FOLLOW THE VESTIBULOCOCHLEAR NERVE UNTIL WE GET TO THE OPTIC NERVE, WE CAN EXIT THROUGH THE EYE!
REALLY? ARE YOU SURE?!
HAHAHAHA
OF COURSE! JUST TRUST ME!

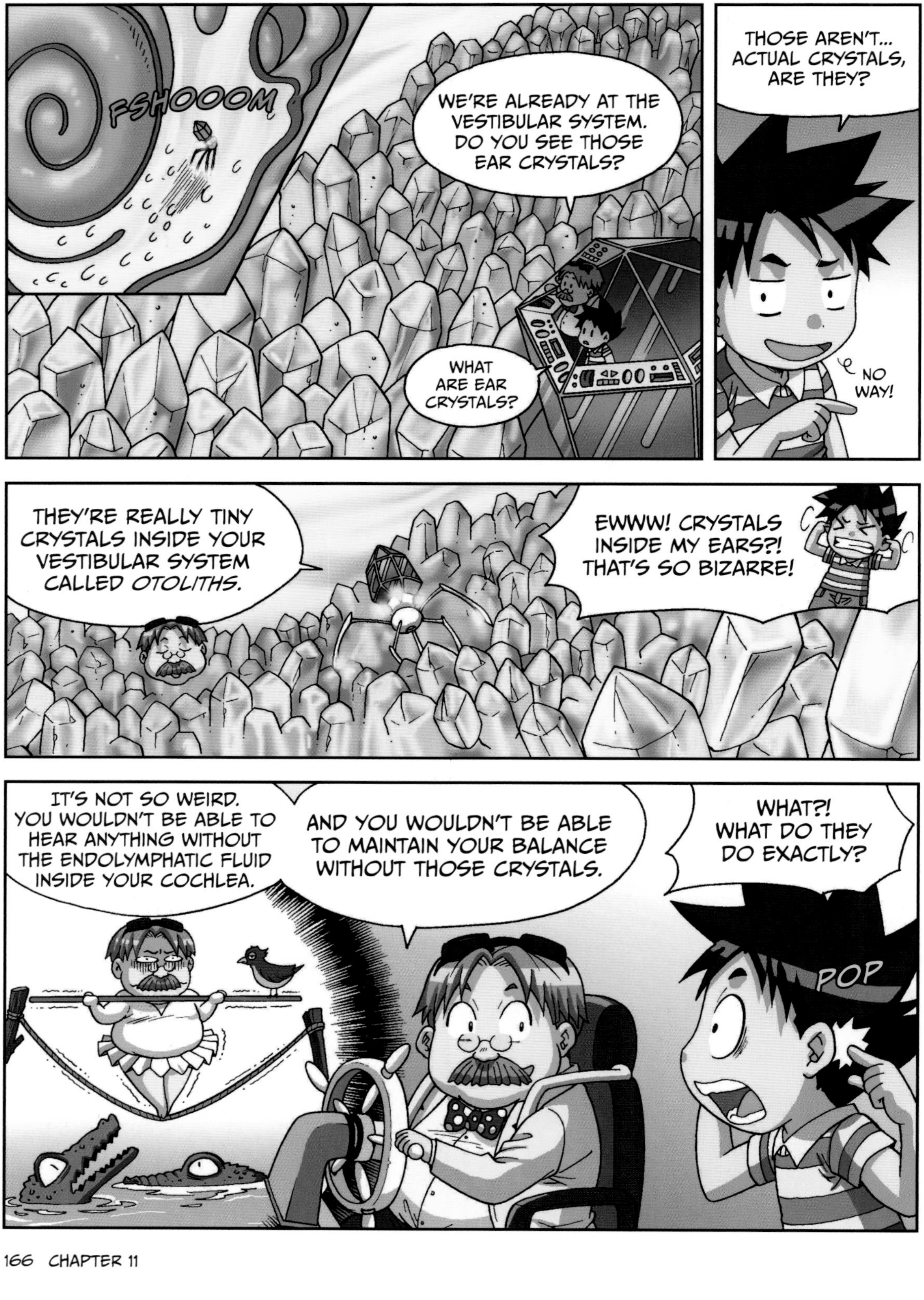
FSHOOOM
WE'RE ALREADY AT THE VESTIBULAR SYSTEM. DO YOU SEE THOSE EAR CRYSTALS?
WHAT ARE EAR CRYSTALS?
THOSE AREN'T... ACTUAL CRYSTALS, ARE THEY?
NO WAY!
THEY'RE REALLY TINY CRYSTALS INSIDE YOUR VESTIBULAR SYSTEM CALLED *OTOLITHS*.
EWWW! CRYSTALS INSIDE MY EARS?! THAT'S SO BIZARRE!
IT'S NOT SO WEIRD. YOU WOULDN'T BE ABLE TO HEAR ANYTHING WITHOUT THE ENDOLYMPHATIC FLUID INSIDE YOUR COCHLEA.
AND YOU WOULDN'T BE ABLE TO MAINTAIN YOUR BALANCE WITHOUT THOSE CRYSTALS.
WHAT?! WHAT DO THEY DO EXACTLY?
POP

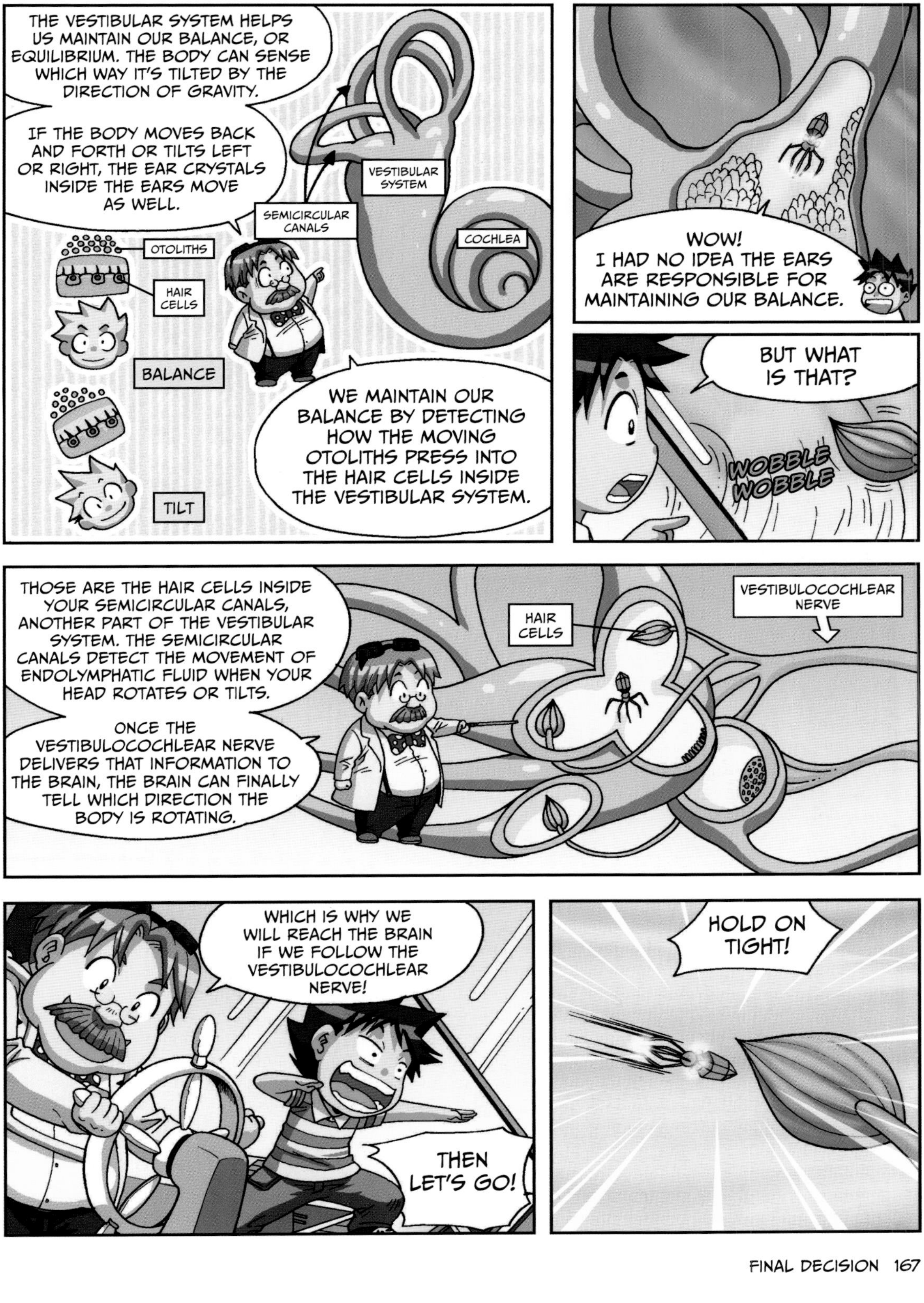

THE VESTIBULAR SYSTEM HELPS US MAINTAIN OUR BALANCE, OR EQUILIBRIUM. THE BODY CAN SENSE WHICH WAY IT'S TILTED BY THE DIRECTION OF GRAVITY.
IF THE BODY MOVES BACK AND FORTH OR TILTS LEFT OR RIGHT, THE EAR CRYSTALS INSIDE THE EARS MOVE AS WELL.
VESTIBULAR SYSTEM
SEMICIRCULAR CANALS
COCHLEA
OTOLITHS
HAIR CELLS
BALANCE
TILT
WE MAINTAIN OUR BALANCE BY DETECTING HOW THE MOVING OTOLITHS PRESS INTO THE HAIR CELLS INSIDE THE VESTIBULAR SYSTEM.
WOW! I HAD NO IDEA THE EARS ARE RESPONSIBLE FOR MAINTAINING OUR BALANCE.
BUT WHAT IS THAT?
WOBBLE WOBBLE
THOSE ARE THE HAIR CELLS INSIDE YOUR SEMICIRCULAR CANALS, ANOTHER PART OF THE VESTIBULAR SYSTEM. THE SEMICIRCULAR CANALS DETECT THE MOVEMENT OF ENDOLYMPHATIC FLUID WHEN YOUR HEAD ROTATES OR TILTS.
ONCE THE VESTIBULOCOCHLEAR NERVE DELIVERS THAT INFORMATION TO THE BRAIN, THE BRAIN CAN FINALLY TELL WHICH DIRECTION THE BODY IS ROTATING.
HAIR CELLS
VESTIBULOCOCHLEAR NERVE
WHICH IS WHY WE WILL REACH THE BRAIN IF WE FOLLOW THE VESTIBULOCOCHLEAR NERVE!
THEN LET'S GO!
HOLD ON TIGHT!

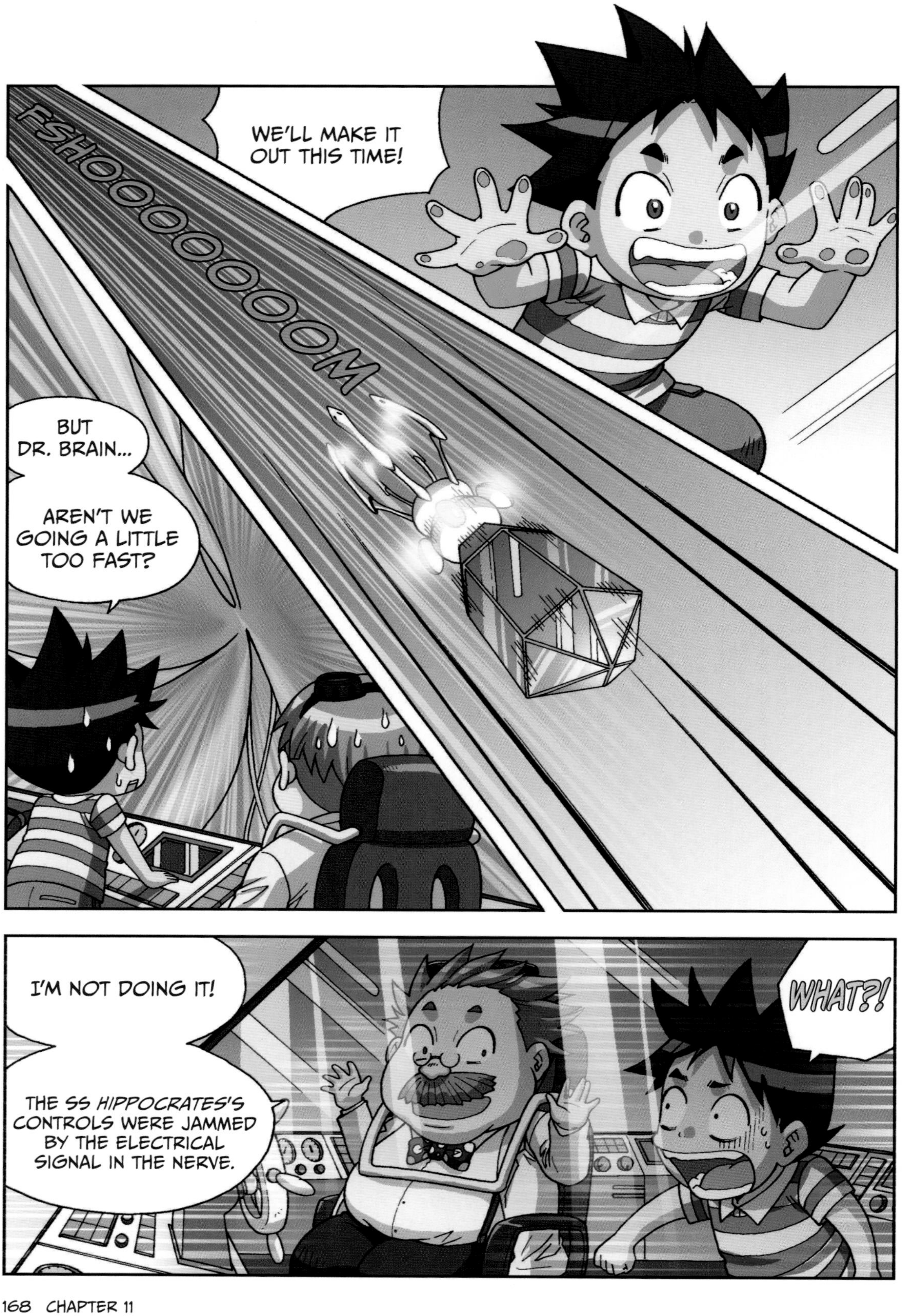
WE'LL MAKE IT OUT THIS TIME!
FSHOOOOOOOOM
BUT DR. BRAIN...
AREN'T WE GOING A LITTLE TOO FAST?
I'M NOT DOING IT!
THE SS *HIPPOCRATES*'S CONTROLS WERE JAMMED BY THE ELECTRICAL SIGNAL IN THE NERVE.
WHAT?!

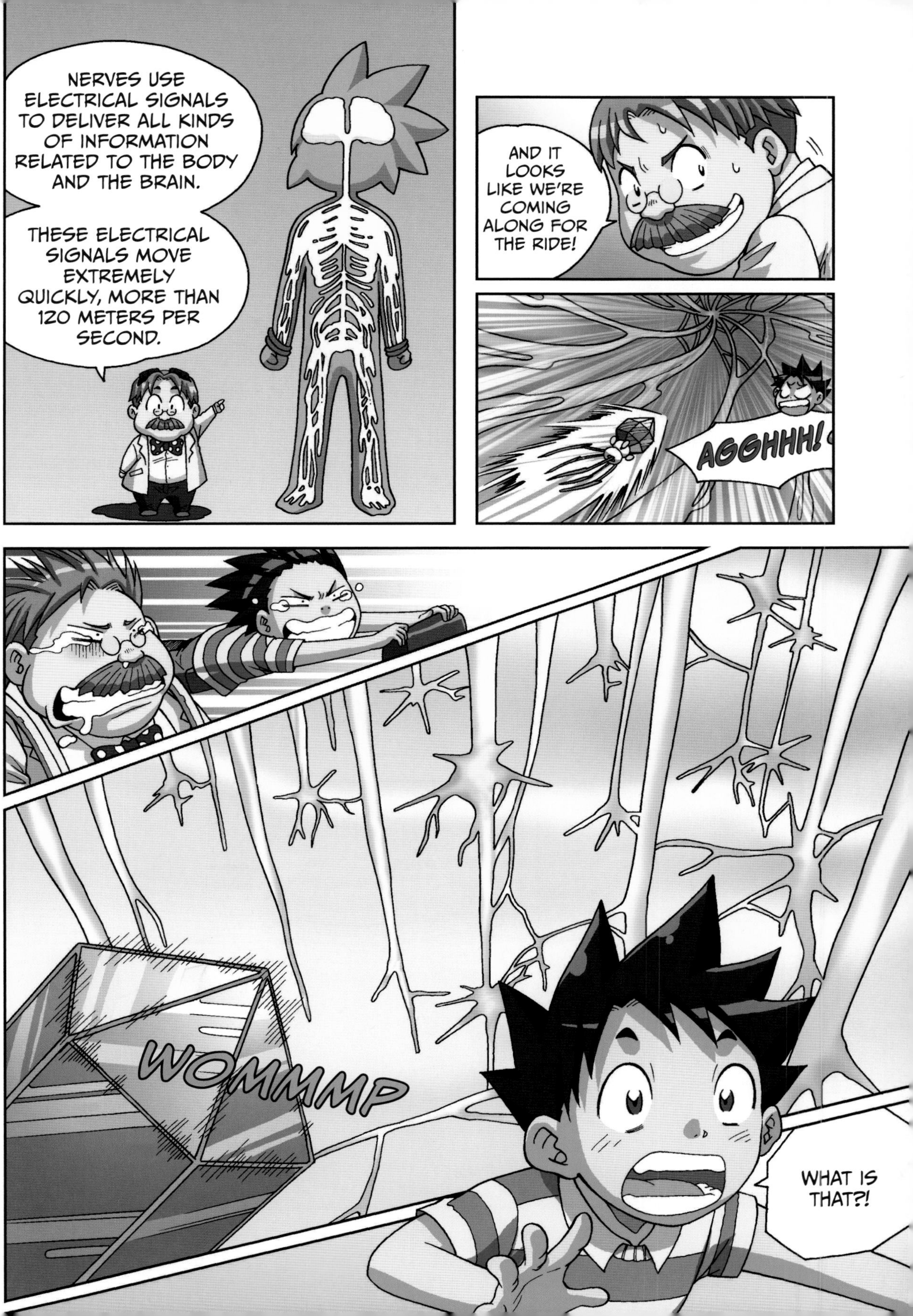
NERVES USE ELECTRICAL SIGNALS TO DELIVER ALL KINDS OF INFORMATION RELATED TO THE BODY AND THE BRAIN.
THESE ELECTRICAL SIGNALS MOVE EXTREMELY QUICKLY, MORE THAN 120 METERS PER SECOND.
AND IT LOOKS LIKE WE'RE COMING ALONG FOR THE RIDE!
AGGHHH!
WOMMMMP
WHAT IS THAT?!

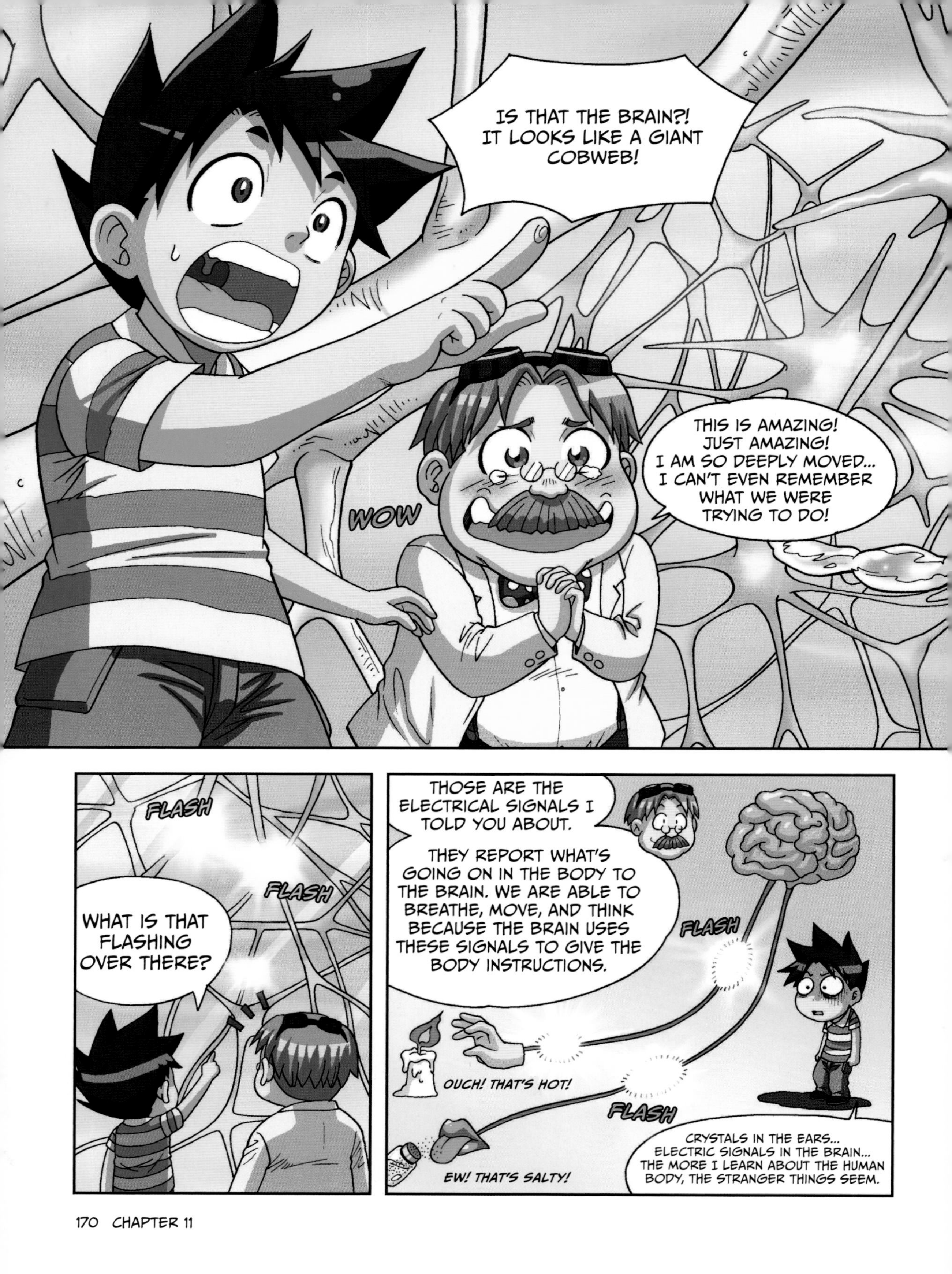
IS THAT THE BRAIN?! IT LOOKS LIKE A GIANT COBWEB!
WOW
THIS IS AMAZING! JUST AMAZING! I AM SO DEEPLY MOVED... I CAN'T EVEN REMEMBER WHAT WE WERE TRYING TO DO!
FLASH
FLASH
WHAT IS THAT FLASHING OVER THERE?
THOSE ARE THE ELECTRICAL SIGNALS I TOLD YOU ABOUT.
THEY REPORT WHAT'S GOING ON IN THE BODY TO THE BRAIN. WE ARE ABLE TO BREATHE, MOVE, AND THINK BECAUSE THE BRAIN USES THESE SIGNALS TO GIVE THE BODY INSTRUCTIONS.
FLASH
OUCH! THAT'S HOT!
FLASH
EW! THAT'S SALTY!
CRYSTALS IN THE EARS... ELECTRIC SIGNALS IN THE BRAIN... THE MORE I LEARN ABOUT THE HUMAN BODY, THE STRANGER THINGS SEEM.

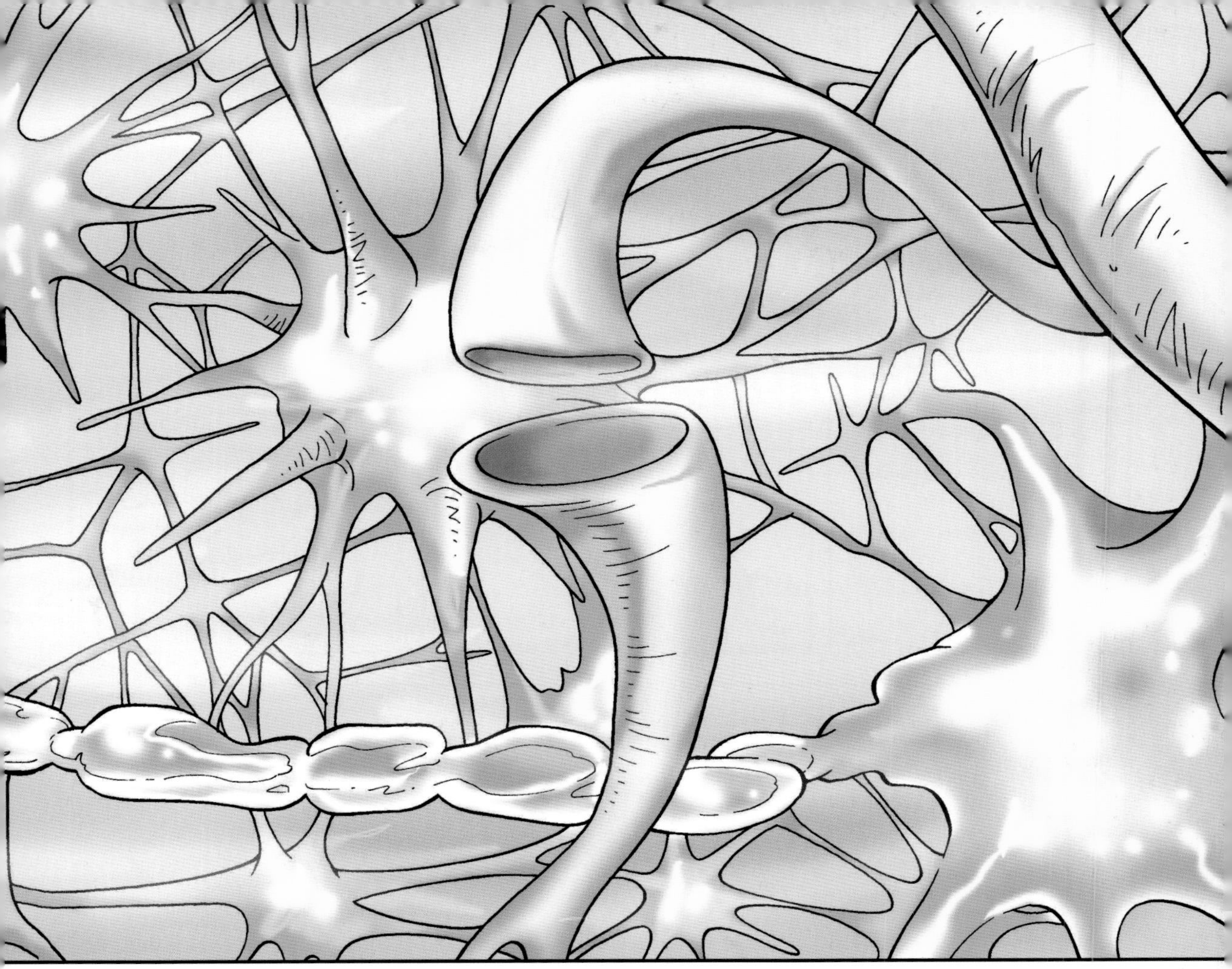

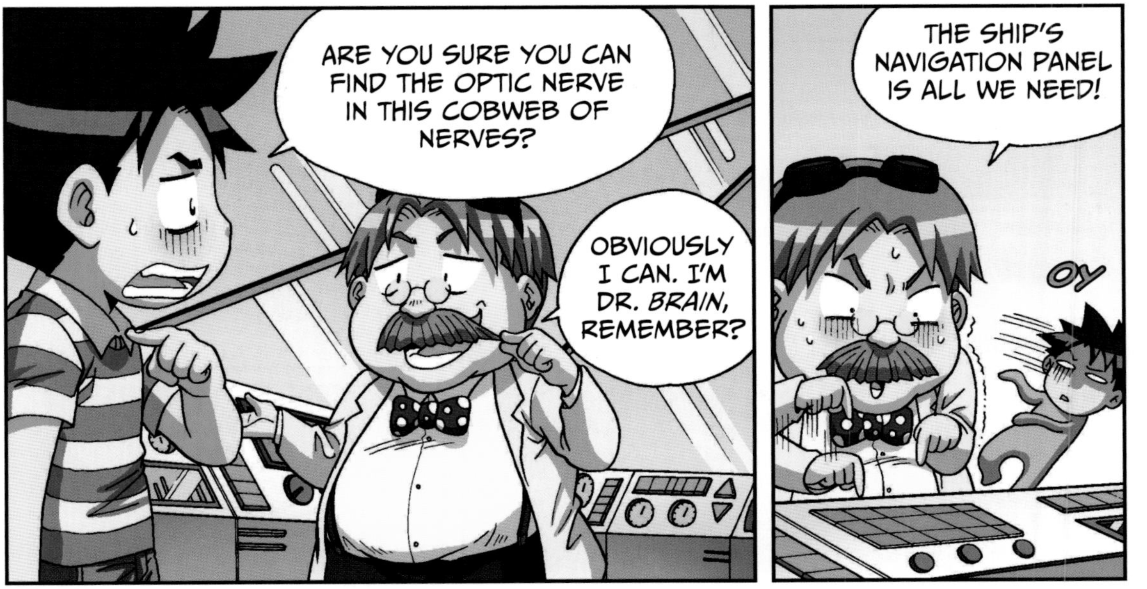

ARE YOU SURE YOU CAN FIND THE OPTIC NERVE IN THIS COBWEB OF NERVES?
OBVIOUSLY I CAN. I'M DR. *BRAIN*, REMEMBER?
THE SHIP'S NAVIGATION PANEL IS ALL WE NEED!
OY

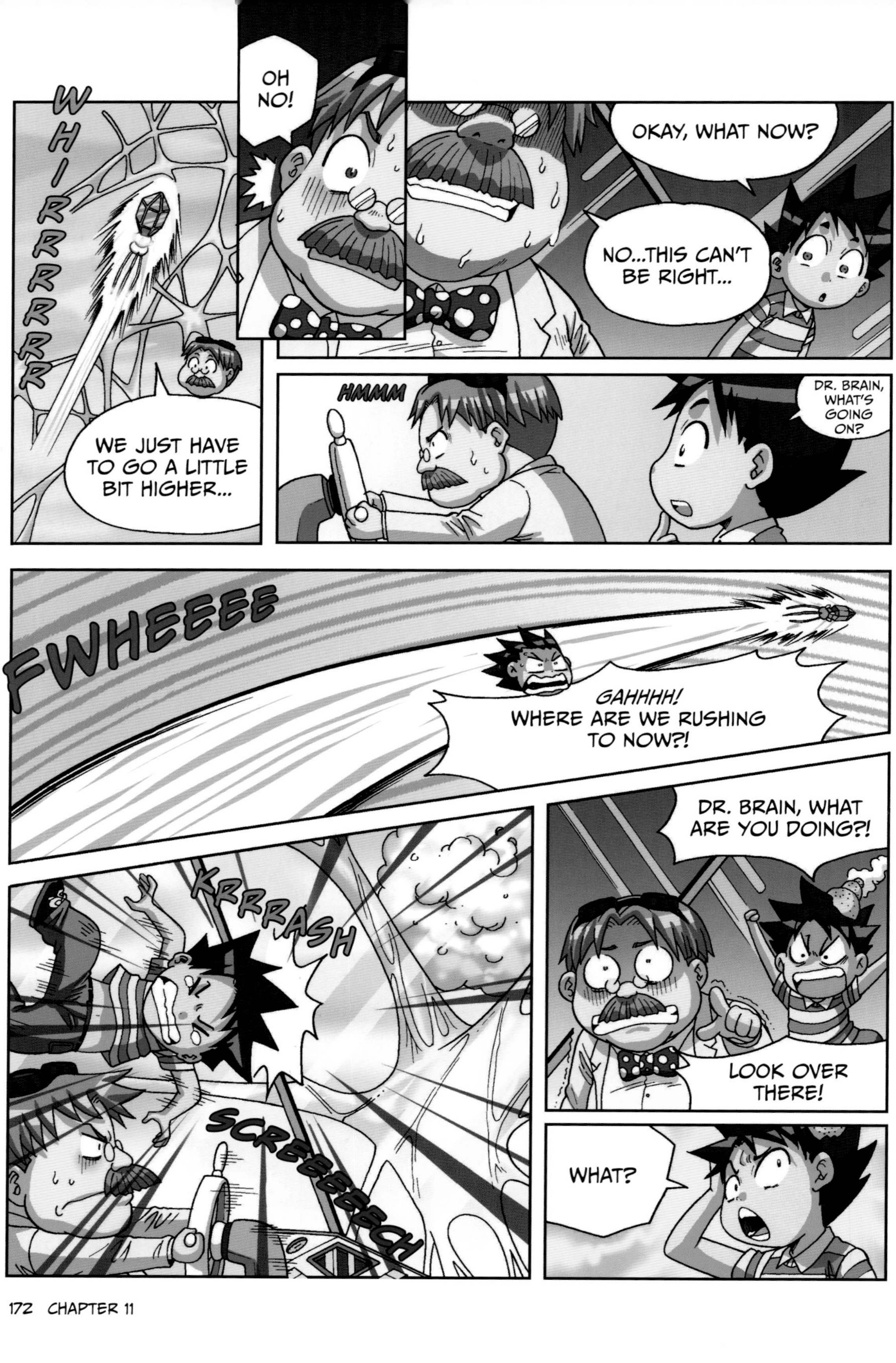
WHIRRRRRRR
OH NO!
OKAY, WHAT NOW?
NO...THIS CAN'T BE RIGHT...
WE JUST HAVE TO GO A LITTLE BIT HIGHER...
HMMM
DR. BRAIN, WHAT'S GOING ON?
FWHEEEEE
GAHHHH! WHERE ARE WE RUSHING TO NOW?!
KRRRRASH
SCREEEEEECH
DR. BRAIN, WHAT ARE YOU DOING?!
LOOK OVER THERE!
WHAT?

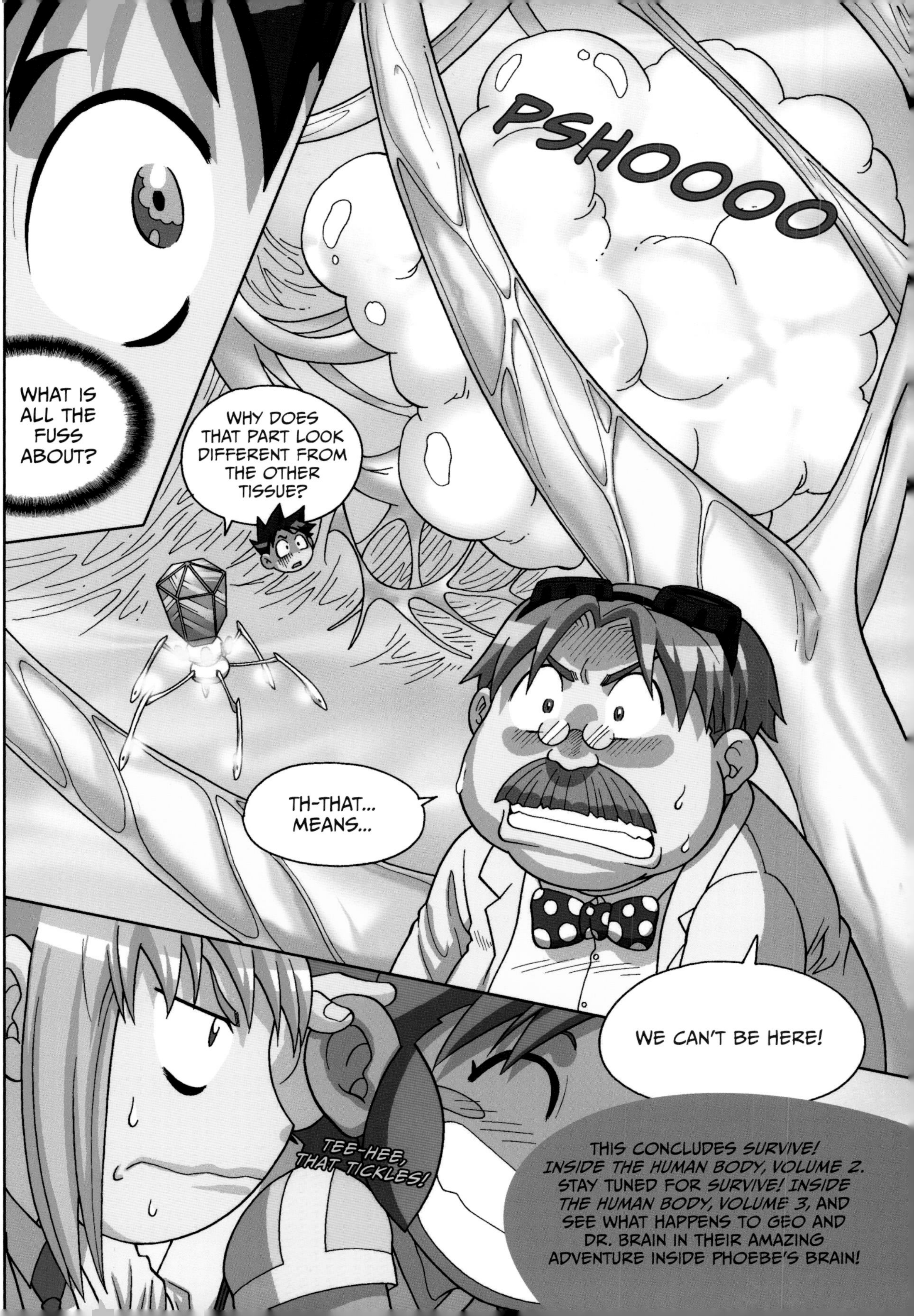
PSHOOOOO
WHAT IS ALL THE FUSS ABOUT?
WHY DOES THAT PART LOOK DIFFERENT FROM THE OTHER TISSUE?
TH-THAT... MEANS...
WE CAN'T BE HERE!
TEE-HEE, THAT TICKLES!
THIS CONCLUDES SURVIVE! INSIDE THE HUMAN BODY, VOLUME 2. STAY TUNED FOR SURVIVE! INSIDE THE HUMAN BODY, VOLUME 3, AND SEE WHAT HAPPENS TO GEO AND DR. BRAIN IN THEIR AMAZING ADVENTURE INSIDE PHOEBE'S BRAIN!

INDEX

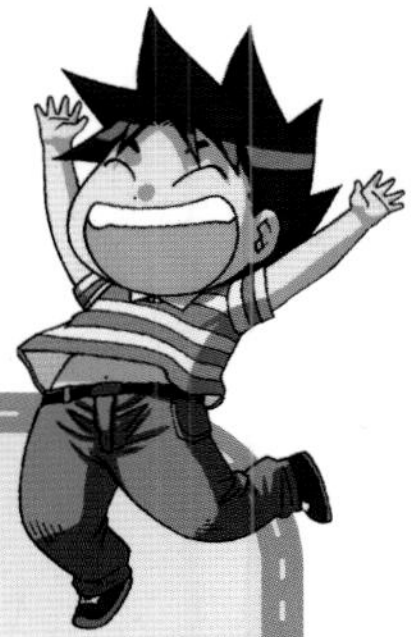

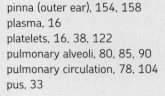

THE SURVIVE! SERIES

ABOUT THESE BOOKS

The *Survive!* series is a translation of a best-selling science comic book series from Mirae N Co., Ltd. of South Korea, with over 20 million copies sold worldwide. These books show kids real science in a fun and approachable way.

The editors at No Starch Press have checked and rewritten the translated text, and two medical doctors have reviewed the content for clarity and accuracy. The result is the book you hold in your hands.

We hope you enjoy *Survive!* Stay tuned for more of Geo's amazing adventures.

ABOUT THE AUTHOR

Gomdori co. is a group of authors, artists, and creative professionals who create fun and educational stories for kids. *Survive! Inside the Human Body* was written by Seok-young Song, an author who has worked on educational comics with Gomdori co. for over 12 years.

ABOUT THE ILLUSTRATOR

Hyun-dong Han studied manhwa (Korean comics) at Kongju National University. His debut series *New Tales of the Nine Tailed Fox* ran for six years, and he's well known for his work on *Ghost Tunes* and the *Survive!* series.